RE/PRESENTING CLASS

Essays in Postmodern Marxism

RE/PRESENTING CLASS

☐ *Essays in Postmodern Marxism*

Edited by

J.K. GIBSON-GRAHAM

STEPHEN RESNICK

RICHARD D. WOLFF

DUKE UNIVERSITY PRESS

Durham & London 2001

© 2001 Duke University Press
All rights reserved
Printed in the United States of America on acid-free paper ∞
Designed by C. H. Westmoreland
Typeset in Times Roman by Tseng Information Systems, Inc.
Library of Congress Cataloging-in-Publication Data appear on the
last printed page of this book.

CONTENTS

ACKNOWLEDGMENTS

□

As editors of this volume, we feel our greatest debt to our contributors. Their enthusiasm for the project, undampened by multiple rounds of comments and revisions, sustained our energies through the sometimes arduous process of assembling and editing the collection. We would like to thank them not only for their excellent work but also for their gracious tolerance of our meddlesome editorial style.

Certain resources were made available to this project without which it could not have been undertaken and completed. We are indebted to Monash University and the Small Grants Scheme of the Australian Research Council and to Linda Slakey, dean of the College of Natural Sciences and Mathematics at the University of Massachusetts Amherst, for funding the workshop at which the first drafts of all the papers were presented and discussed.

We are also indebted to the many individuals who helped the book take its final form. Three anonymous reviewers provided us with a set of insightful and useful comments on the first draft. Ken Byrne brought his usual good humor and excellent word processing skills to the time-consuming task of producing the manuscript. Sandra Davenport of the Department of Geography in the Research School of Pacific and Asian Studies at the Australian National University provided invaluable assistance with proofreading and produced the index. At the Duke University Press, our editor, Raphael Allen, has been wonderfully encouraging and perspicacious, helping us negotiate the practical and emotional pitfalls associated with bringing a manuscript to press. His faith in the project, and that of editor-in-chief Ken Wissoker, has buoyed our spirits immeasurably. We are indeed fortunate to have worked under their care. Thanks also to Justin Faerber at Duke for cheerfully shepherding the manuscript through the production process and to Jonathan Munk for copyediting.

Finally, we would like to express our deep gratitude to Jack Amariglio and the other members of the editorial board of Rethinking Marxism for their untiring support of this project, and also to the many members of the Association for Economic and Social Analysis (AESA) who have been engaged in the ongoing theoretical work from which this book has emerged. It is not often that a collective theoretical project develops in such a sustained and sustaining fashion. For several decades we have been inspired and energized by the work of AESA, and we deeply appreciate the intellectual creativity and generosity of its members.

The author and publishers wish to thank the following for permission to use portions of previously published copyright material: Portions of "Toward a Poststructural Political Economy" appeared in "Introduction: Class in a Poststructuralist Frame" by J.K. Gibson-Graham, Stephen A. Resnick, and Richard D. Wolff in *Class and its Others* edited by J.K. Gibson-Graham, S. Resnick, and R. Wolff, University of Minnesota Press (2000) 1–22. Portions of "Exploring a New Class Politics of the Enterprise" appeared in "Enterprise Discourse and Executive Talk: Stories that Destabilise the Company" by J.K. Gibson-Graham and Phillip O'Neill published in *Transactions of the Institute of British Geographers* 24:1 (March 1999) 11–22.

J.K. GIBSON-GRAHAM,

STEPHEN RESNICK,

AND RICHARD D. WOLFF

□

TOWARD A POSTSTRUCTURALIST

POLITICAL ECONOMY

Beginning (Again): Marxism as a Theory of Class

The essays in this volume undertake a multidirectional foray into what for political economy is relatively unexplored territory: Marxian class theory. For some this adventure may seem long overdue. As Bruce Norton powerfully argues, the political economic tradition has from the outset developed one strand of Marx's thought, *the theory of the capitalist totality,* at the expense of another, *the theory of class.* Though each of these has a prominent place in *Capital* and other writings of Marx, the former has become identified with Marxian political economy as it is now practiced, while the latter has been consigned to relative obscurity.[1] Attracted by the intellectual and political possibilities of class analysis—possibilities that seem unavailable within the dominant forms of Marxian thought—we are motivated to redress this imbalance of interest and attention.

The familiar object of Marxian political economy is the capitalist totality in its various incarnations: as capitalist "system" or mode of production; as the global capitalist economy; Fordist or post-Fordist model of development structuring a "capitalist" social formation; or simply and baldly as "capitalism." Centering on the process of capital accumulation, theories of the capitalist totality explore the related processes of economic growth, systemic regulation and crisis, transition and transformation, and long waves of capitalist development.[2] The capitalist enterprise is seen as the agent of capital accumulation (though this function is sometimes displaced onto the figure of "finance capital") and thus of systemic reproduction and expansion. The enterprise is also the locus of the exploitative class relation that makes possible the accumulation of capital. In this vision, class is functional to accumulation, a requisite but not theoretically interesting element of capitalist dynamics.

Traditional Marxian political economy strives to understand and trace the logic of accumulation as it unfolds in history. While references to capitalist "laws of motion" may now seem outmoded, the assumption that capital accumulation is the central dynamic of the economic totality is still widely accepted. This theoretical fixation has had consequential political effects. In the vicinity of capitalism's systemic embodiment and its naturalized tendencies toward expansion, anticapitalist political movements have tended to accept the necessity of accommodation. Since they are not poised—by virtue of an ultimate capitalist crisis—on the verge of socialist transition, they have seen themselves constrained to the "reformist" option of creating capitalism with a human (or perhaps a green) face. The progressive project of building an alternative, noncapitalist society is relegated to a revolutionary future, distant and discontinuous from the practical political terrain.

It is this disheartening political vision that has generated in us a desire for a different form of economic and social theory, one that offers a more complex present and a more open-ended future. Here we have turned once again to *Capital,* a work that may more easily be read for an analytics of class or a discourse of economic surplus than for a vision of systemic dynamics and dysfunction. Marx's analysis of capitalist class relations—those relations involved in producing, appropriating, and distributing surplus labor in value form—provides the basics of an accounting framework, a conceptual apparatus that can bring us to see the world in a different way.

Not only may we see through the lens of class theory the presence of exploitation (in both capitalist and noncapitalist forms) and trace its socially constitutive role; we may also sense the existence and possibility of nonexploitative economic relations. Not only do we recognize the role of surplus distributions in constituting and (re)producing specific social positions and formations, but also the real and present option of different distributions and the distinct social identities and practices they might foster or create.

The project of specifying the diverse class relations (and thus also class possibilities) that have existed and continue to exist opens up a world of economic variety where capitalism has been understood to reign. It also places an open-ended range of "revolutionary" political options on the ground of the present, where progressive politics has long encountered theoretical barriers to social and economic transformation. By offering a different approach to class theory, *Re/Presenting Class* (and other works in this emerging tradition) may potentially contribute to a changed configuration of class politics. Perhaps the politics of postponement, so familiar to those interested in class transformation, can be supplanted by a politics of opportunity and attainment.

Materialism in a Poststructuralist Vein

What has rendered accumulation theory intellectually and politically carceral is not the absence of class theory per se but rather the combined co-presences of epistemological realism, economic determinism, and teleological eventualism. These characteristics of classical and contemporary political economy—perhaps it no longer needs to be argued—present a set of abstract and arbitrary limits on what social analysis can say. To confine the potent and adventurous energies of theory within such narrow quarters now seems too obeisant to the authority of tradition, no matter how distinguished that tradition may be.

Indeed, the realism, determinism, and teleologism of Marxian theory (even in their attenuated recent forms) have come under sustained attack from a number of directions. Feminists protesting the obscuring and devaluing of unpaid household labor; unionists struggling for the recognition of state and service workers alongside those in private manufacturing; postdevelopment theorists criticizing the preeminence accorded industrial capitalism in the vision and enactment of "progress"; postcolonialists arguing against the peripheralization of the so-called Third World in and through Marxian theory, activists around gender, race, and sexuality rejecting the privileging of class actors and objectives—each of these is voicing suspicions of a prespecified hierarchy of determination and order of importance.

It is here that the countertraditional work of Althusser (among others) can be seen to resonate with the import of contemporary critiques. In the face of the economic reductionism of the dominant Marxian tradition, Althusser's work signals both the possibility and the political fruitfulness of another reading of Marx. Contributing his thought to debates within the French Communist party and in the philosophical context of an emerging poststructuralism, Althusser was motivated to read Marx not as an economic determinist but as a dialectician and a "materialist"—as one who refuses to ascribe priority and privilege to any social dimension, who honors the specificity of every site, practice, and conjuncture, who opposes the "reduction of the real to the concept." [3] Althusser termed his materialism "aleatory," referring to its disdain for necessity, its respect for contingency and particularity (Callari and Ruccio 1996, 26).[4]

Building on the Althusserian conception of the mutual implication of every social process in every other, Resnick and Wolff (1987) have adopted Althusser's term "overdetermination" (which Althusser himself borrowed from Freud) to signal the existence of a Marxian alternative to economic determinism. From the perspective of overdeterminist theory, the dialectic entails not only the co-implication of political, economic, natural, and cultural processes in every site or occurrence but also the resultant openness and incompleteness of identity/being. This recuperative vision of complex constitution and continual becoming is a necessarily radical one, required as part of a strategy to reopen Marxian theory to the complexities and possibilities that had been forgone through its preemptive closures.

Overdetermination can be understood as a provisional ontology that operates to contradict and destabilize the essentialist ontology of the dominant forms of Marxism (and indeed of the entire Western intellectual lineage). Standing against the essentialist presumption that "any apparent complexity—a person, a relationship, a historical occurrence, and so forth—can be analyzed to reveal a simplicity lying at its core" (Resnick and Wolff 1987, 2–3), it opposes the specification of a causal hierarchy in which some causes are necessarily dominant and others less consequential. Cultural, political, and natural forces cannot be presumed to be less historically formative than the economic, though different analyses may emphasize one or the other.

There is a second, epistemological reading of overdetermination which is as unsettling to the realist epistemology of traditional Marxism as is the ontological reading to its economic determinism. Just as no preordained hierarchy of causes exists to structure social explanation, so too is it impossible to establish a definitive hierarchy of interpretations. Interpretations are constituted within diverse and incommensurable discourses and perspectives. Texts and words are like everything else: complex, open to multiple readings, culturally and politically negotiable and transformable. We may create temporary discursive fixings, but these are always susceptible to destabilization by other formulations and interpretations. No ultimate arbiter exists to determine the "truth" of our understandings.

What might this mean for economic and social analysis, which has so long understood itself as attempting to produce adequate explanation? Clearly it suggests that any particular analysis will never find the ultimate causes of events, nor be able to definitively exclude the effectivity of any social or natural processes. In this context, the question about any relationship (between, say, economic development and heterosexuality) becomes not how important is one in the constitution of the other, but rather how do we wish to think of the complex interaction between these two complexities.

Marx's *Capital* can be read as a social analysis undertaken within an overdeterminist method. In its three volumes, Marx produced a detailed theoretical examination of the ways that capitalist class processes constitute and in turn are constituted by other social processes, generating an extensive knowledge of capitalist exploitation and surplus distribution. In the sense that class is the focal concept of the analysis, *Capital* can be said to be written from the "entry point" of class. In other words, the centrality of class is a feature of the particular analysis rather than a given of the social order.

Since it is not possible to establish "objective" validity outside the frame of a particular analytical regime or project, the question of the choice between different theories or entry points involves not which is more accurate or true, but the consequences of choosing one rather than another. Different questions will produce different answers, and those answers will make a difference. They will be socially constitutive, "performative" in shaping understanding and action. Thus it is a matter of (political) consequence rather than a matter of indifference what kinds of knowledge we produce and what effects we hope to produce with it.[5]

Given the difficulties and inconclusiveness of social theory and analysis undertaken from an overdeterminist perspective, one might be tempted to ask "why bother?" What does an overdeterminist and anti-realist approach have to offer, other than daunting complexity and uncertainty? Again the answer has to do with the project of opening what was formerly closed. Not only is overdetermination a method for widening the space of political effectivity in the process of social determination, a space that had shrunk or even disappeared in traditional political economy, it also foregrounds the openness of identities to political projects of resignification. In the absence of the closures of necessity/determinacy and of structurally ordained identity, there is room for the contingent efficacies of politics, including the politics of class.

Accounting for Class[6]

In *Capital* we encounter Marx's project of creating a knowledge of class society in its specifically capitalist form. The three volumes of *Capital* offer not only a critique of classical political economy, with its reductive conceptions of "human nature" and social dynamics, but also a positive theoretical intervention that might be called "accounting for class." Via the accounting of labor as *necessary* and *surplus,* the first volume of *Capital* made the process of (capitalist) exploitation intelligible. By mapping the distributions of surplus value to a variety of social destinations, the second and third volumes brought into visibility the socially constitutive role of capitalist class relations. Taken together, the three volumes offer the rudiments of a language of class.

While the notion of a surplus above and beyond what was necessary for reproduction had long figured in classical political economy, Marx was the first to produce a discourse of exploitation that hinged on the distinction between necessary and surplus labor. As he defined it, necessary labor "is the quantity of labor time necessary to produce the consumables customarily required by the producer to keep working," while surplus labor is "the extra time of labor the direct producer performs beyond the necessary labor" (Resnick and Wolff 1987, 115). In an exploitative relation this "unpaid" or "unremunerated" surplus labor (or its product) is appropriated by someone other than the producer.

The necessary/surplus labor distinction cannot be grounded in the ostensible reality of the body's "basic needs" for subsistence but must be seen as a particular way of fixing meaning. What is necessary and what is surplus is not predefined or given, in some humanist or cultural essentialist sense, but is established relationally at the moment of appropriation itself.[7] The boundary is an accounting device, inscribed on the body rather than emerging from within it, and the desire to move it can be seen to have motivated political struggles historically and to this day.

Marx used the distinction between necessary and surplus labor to identify what for him was the principal and as yet invisible violence of capitalism: the existence of a hidden flow of labor (taking the form of "surplus value") from the worker to the capitalist. Each worker in a capitalist enterprise produces in a day enough wealth to sustain her- or himself (for which she or he is compensated in the form of a wage) and also a surplus which is appropriated by the individual capitalist or by the board of directors of the capitalist firm. The exploitative process in which surplus labor is produced and appropriated is for Marx a *class* process, and the positions of producer and appropriator are *class* positions.

But the class positions identified by Marx are not limited to these two. The structure of *Capital* turns on a second distinction between what Resnick and Wolff have called the fundamental and subsumed class processes.[8] The former involves the moment of exploitation in which surplus labor is produced and appropriated in value form (explored in volume I), while the latter and no less important moment involves the distribution of appropriated surplus value to a range of recipients (explored in volumes 2 and 3). In the subsumed class process the surplus labor that has been "pumped out of [the] direct producers" and temporarily condensed in the hands of the capitalist can be seen to be dispersed in myriad directions—within the enterprise (into the accumulation of productive capital, or management salaries and benefits, or compensation for workers in marketing and sales) and out into the wider economy (for example, to financiers, merchants, landlords, advertising agents, governments, charitable organizations, organized crime, and others who provide conditions of existence of surplus value production).

Traditional class analyses generally focus on the class positions of surplus producer and appropriator while neglecting the flow of surplus labor from the appropriator (who is also the first distributor) to the receivers of surplus distributions. But these distributive flows can be seen as constituting a range of subsumed class positions. They can also be understood as connecting the moment of class exploitation to the ways that society is organized and enacted, highlighting the interdependencies within any economy. In class analyses that account for distributions of surplus labor and the class positions they entail, what emerges is a complex vision of the social ramifications of class.

Marx developed a third distinction, that between productive and unproductive labor, to distinguish those workers who are engaged in capitalist commodity production and productive of surplus value (and who are therefore involved in an exploitative class process) from those who are not (for instance, workers in advertising and marketing departments of commodity-producing firms, or workers in the financial sector, or workers like domestic servants who sell their labor power but are not involved in capitalist commodity production). The term "unproductive" refers to any labor that in Marx's particular accounting system was deemed not to be productive of surplus value. Unproductive laborers are paid out of surplus value if they are employed by capitalist firms engaged in commodity production (thus they are recipients of subsumed class payments) and receive a nonclass form of remuneration if they are otherwise employed.[9]

So far we have focused on three accounting conventions developed by Marx: the distinction between necessary and surplus labor; the distinction between fundamental and subsumed class processes; and the distinction between productive and unproductive labor. In *Capital,* each of these distinctions is elaborated with respect to capitalism. But while capitalism was Marx's principal object of investigation, he also employed the language of class to identify noncapitalist class processes that predated capitalism, have always coexisted with it, or indeed might succeed it. His theory of capitalism was formulated, for example, via a comparison with feudalism, with the difference between the two specified in terms of the ways that surplus labor was extracted and distributed within feudal as opposed to capitalist social arrangements. In addition, Marx identified a range of other forms of class process, including primitive communist, slave, ancient or independent, and communal or communist. What distinguishes each from the others is the way that surplus labor is produced, appropriated, and distributed (for example, feudal rent, as surplus value, under various types of force or agreement) and also the different ways in which they are socially embedded, constituted in each specific instance by an infinity of different "conditions of existence." In this simple typology of class forms we can discern the elements of a language of economic difference, and the possibility of complex class readings of internally differentiated social and economic formations. We also see the possibility of nonexploitative class relations. In the ancient or independent class form, for example, individuals appropriate their own surplus labor; in the communist or communal form, surplus labor is collectively produced and appropriated.

Like all systems of accounting, Marx's language of class highlights certain processes and obscures others, potentiates certain identities and suppresses others, and has the capacity to energize certain kinds of activities and actors while leaving others unmoved. As a movable boundary, the distinction between necessary and surplus labor has made exploitation a visible, tangible object of discourse and politics. The further division of appropriated wealth into various surplus distributions suggests its formative and proliferative potential and allows the tracing of some of the ways that exploitation participates in constituting other social practices. It also highlights surplus distribution as a potential object of political struggle. Finally, the open-ended list of different class processes suggests the scope for creative enactment of different (nonexploitative) economic futures.

The language of class does not merely enable explorations of the socially constitutive role of exploitation; in its proliferation of terms it opens up the economic field, offering a range of identity positions that could potentially be inhabited and providing a rudimentary typology of economic forms that might prompt imaginative extension and normative valencing. By accounting for class, Marx was, in the words of Ernesto Laclau, "widening the field of intelligibility in order to enlarge the scope of possibility." In this sense his work was a political intervention, not only into specific political contexts but into the very meaning of politics and the range of social possibilities that politics avails.

Re/Presenting Class: Analytical Projects and Social Possibilities

Anti-essentialist class theory opens up Marxian economic analysis to an enlarged conversation and the possibility of new engagements with non-Marxian analytical streams in the fields of organizational behavior, accounting, and economic anthropology and sociology. Parallel explorations into, for example, the constitutive nature of accounting frameworks (Miller 1998), principal-agent relations (Jensen and Meckling 1976), the embeddedness of economic organizations and behavior (Polanyi 1971; Swedberg and Granovetter 1992), corporate governance (Boden 1994), and the organization of markets (Fligstein 1996; Callon 1998) may enhance and potentially contribute to an understanding of class as an over-determined economic process. It is also possible to identify significant moments of overlap with the work of those who are interested in the many different forms of capitalist and noncapitalist economic practice that coexist today; for example, economic anthropologists interested in the intersections of community economies and market economies (Gudeman and Rivera 1990), or economic sociologists concerned with the prevalence of slavery in the contemporary global economy (Bales 1999).

Building on and contributing to these growing literatures on embedded, differentiated, and culturally constituted economic experience, the essays collected here coalesce around a shared interest in class analysis and disperse themselves among four principal topics or themes: (1) the capitalist enterprise; (2) the economic totality; (3) transition and development; and (4) class identity and politics. From this relatively concentrated theoretical and thematic base, they extend to a broad range of countries and time periods (including pre-Columbian North America, post-independence India, the former Soviet Union, the post–Civil War U.S. South, and Iran at the time of the revolution). In the rest of this introduction, we explore the four central themes as they are embodied in the essays, highlighting the political implications of thinking economy and society through the lens of anti-essentialist class theory.

The Capitalist Enterprise

As the site and agent of capital accumulation, the capitalist enterprise has had a prominent place in traditional accumulation theory. Defined as the expansion of the value of productive capital, accumulation as an activity involves the investment of appropriated surplus value in increased constant and/or variable capital, thereby allowing production to take place on an expanded scale. Familiar visions of systemic growth have their basis in capital accumulation by individual firms, which is seen as necessary for their survival but ultimately contradictory and crisis-generating for capitalism as a whole.

This vision of the firm, with its fixed roles as exploiter and expander (see Bruce Norton's essay), ascribes to it a central defining activity of capital accumulation. To fail to accumulate capital would be to violate its essential nature, to become other than itself; it is not possible within the bounds of accumulation theory. But when we step outside the confines of necessitarian theory and into the contingent field of overdetermination, investments in the accumulation of capital become understandable as one of many distributions of appropriated surplus value, no more central to the firm than any other (or, to say this somewhat differently, central to certain firms at certain conjunctures but not a generic imperative for every firm).

The following equation represents the net revenues (on the left) and corresponding expenditures of an enterprise in class terms (Resnick and Wolff 1987, 208–9):

$$SV + SCR + NCR = \sum SC + \sum X + \sum Y$$

Enterprise revenues include appropriated surplus value (SV); subsumed class revenues (SCR), for example, dividends paid on stock owned in commodity-producing firms; and nonclass revenues (NCR), for example, state subsidies and abatements. Each of these forms of revenue is associated with respective distributions on the right-hand side—$\sum SC, \sum X$, and $\sum Y$—that secure its conditions of existence.[10]

What becomes clear in this representation is that the firm does not require the positive appropriation of SV in order to have positive net revenues; thus, a distribution taking the form of investment in productive capital (i.e., capital accumulation) to secure the conditions of SV appropriation is not actually necessary for the firm's continued existence or growth. The equation decenters the firm from the fundamental class process of surplus value production and appropriation, which is only one possible source of revenue and one possible focus of expenditures. It also represents the enterprise as decentered from capital accumulation, which is one of a long list of distributions out of *sv* that may include, other than accumulation, payments of wages and salaries to managers and other unproductive employees, merchant fees, taxes, rent, interest, dividends to shareholders, advertising costs—indeed a virtually endless array of potential distributions.

As specified within the terms of the equation, every firm is configured differently, with varying kinds and amounts of fundamental, subsumed, and nonclass revenues, different distributions and different conditions of existence that they secure. Considered thus, the "theory of the firm" deviates from the generic narrative of firm behavior organized around a central imperative like profitability or capital accumulation, and may instead be viewed as a template for mapping the unique configuration of each firm's class and nonclass flows. In this volume Fred Curtis provides an example of a class analytic rendering of the capitalist enterprise, focusing on the liberal arts college in the United States. Making the argument that this institution, despite its usual nonprofit status, extracts surplus labor in value form, Curtis disaggregates its revenues and expenditures along the lines specified above, showing the way in which they serve (contradictorily) to reproduce the firm. For liberal arts colleges in the 1990s, the goal of capital accumulation and expansion of productive capacity is not a priority, and indeed disaccumulation is on the agenda for many as the pool of available students shrinks. Nevertheless, as competition among colleges has increased with the decline in student populations, many institutions find themselves attempting to increase absolute and relative surplus value by increasing faculty workloads and requiring that faculty apply their labor to tasks such as promotion and recruitment.

One of the by-products of a decentered representation of the firm and a theorization of the wide range of distributions of surplus (and other revenues) is that the scope of enterprise-centered class politics is potentially enlarged. This is the argument made in the essay by J. K. Gibson-Graham and Phillip O'Neill, who focus on BHP, the largest Australian multinational corporation. While the familiar rendering of the enterprise as focused on exploitation and accumulation gives us a corresponding class politics centered on capital and labor, the decentered firm of class theory offers surplus distribution as a field for a (class) politics of the enterprise. Enterprise politics can be seen as not simply encompassing struggles between capital and labor over the relative size of necessary and surplus labor, but as also potentially centering on the pool of appropriated surplus that is destined to be distributed to a wide variety of class publics and constituencies. If accumulation no longer has a prior and privileged claim on appropriated surplus, the unlimited and ever-changing set of surplus distributions is potentially subject to a range of claimants, whose claims may or may not be legitimated.

Environmentalists fighting for distributions to clean up hazardous wastes and restore degraded environments have most recently been successful in inserting their claims on surplus value distributions (see Vlachou, Gibson-Graham and O'Neill). Indeed, the environmental movement has been so successful that in many cases, including the case of BHP, certain environmentally sound technologies and practices, as well as more comprehensive environmental codes, of conduct have been adopted by firms. Such an internalization of external political forces, in which both the self-identity of the firm and its subsumed class distributions are reconfigured, reflects the overdetermination of the enterprise by its "constitutive outside." As one of the forces constituting the enterprise (and therefore implicated in its identity and form of existence), political projects asserting claims on enterprise distributions have the potential not only to create social changes but also transformations of the capitalist firm.

Reconceptualizing the Social and Economic "Totality"

Traditional Marxian economic theory constructs the capitalist economy as a self-regulating system or as a macroformation coextensive with the nation-state. This theoretical commitment functions to buttress the assumed dominance (and predominance) of capitalism with respect to other forms of economy. Complexities of uneven development and noncapitalist modes of production—if, indeed, they are seen to exist—are convened within and subordinated to a capitalist totality.

Perhaps this is the point where class theory will seem to diverge most noticeably from the tradition of accumulation theory. In many of the essays in this collection, the class character of a social formation is understood to be complex and diverse, and the different class processes (com-

munal, capitalist, ancient/independent, feudal, slave, or other) that comprise it are seen to be complexly interrelated rather than subsumed within
a unity. If the social formation is identified as capitalist, that identification signifies the presumed numerical predominance of capitalist class
relations rather than the coextensiveness of a systemic economy with a
given social space.

In unmooring the economy from a singular capitalist identity, Marxian
class analysis (as explicated in this volume) has certain affinities with the
project of feminist economists who argue that more than 50 percent of
all economic activity in both rich and poor countries is excluded from
national accounts (Beneria 1996; Ironmonger 1996). For these theorists,
calling an economy "capitalist" is an act of discursive violence, one that
obliterates from view the economic activity that engages more people for
more hours of the day over more years of their lives than any other. They
call for a recognition of a complex and differentiated economy, and of the
economic actors whose hidden practices of production are undervalued
or obscured.

But such theoretical attempts to move beyond economic monism face
an obstacle in the tendency to frame difference, once it is perceived, in
hierarchical terms. Representations of the relation of capitalism to noncapitalist forms of economy are usually structured by a binary hierarchy
of valuation that operates to demote and devalue the latter. Noncapitalist economic forms are seen as weaker, less capable of independence or
expansion. Thus, other modes of production are represented as giving
way to capitalism, or surviving only to the extent to which they support
capitalist reproduction; and so socialism must be enacted as a massive
eradication of capitalism if it is to protect itself from capitalist recursion.
It is against this background of devaluation and presumed weakness that
Dean Saitta's paper on pre-Columbian social dynamics argues for a perception of the "elasticity and durability of communal forms." Whereas
the Marxist archaeological literature on pre-Columbian cultures tends to
naturalize the dominance of exploitative class formations, and to represent communal forms as less robust and sustainable, Saitta makes a compelling argument for the long-term stability and viability of communal
forms of economic organization.

In the chapter on communisms in the Soviet Union, Stephen Resnick
and Richard Wolff represent a social formation that was dominated (in

a numerical sense) over the course of its history by state capitalist class processes but in which experiments in communal class processes took place. In each case, it was not the logic of capitalism or its natural expansiveness that terminated these experiments, but rather the political processes of the Soviet state.

The chapters by Anjan Chakrabarti and Stephen Cullenberg and by Gibson-Graham and David Ruccio likewise present a landscape of economic difference, depicting respectively the economy of India and the more abstract economy of postdevelopment theory as sites in which complex interactions between capitalist and noncapitalist class processes take place, with none accorded necessary dominance or an ordained place in an economic succession. The coexistence of diverse forms of class process intimates the possibility of creating nonexploitative class relations on the complex terrain of the present economy. To view the economic landscape less as dominated by capitalism than as discursively colonized by the rhetoric of capitalist dominance is to open up "realistic" present possibilities for class transition and transformation.

Transition and Development

In the context of Marxian political economy, transition has generally been understood as a unilinear process in which a relatively backward form of economy gives way to a more efficient or progressive form. Thus feudal economic forms and independent commodity production are seen to be superseded by capitalism, in a natural and predictable chain of succession (indeed, the former are often identified as "precapitalist modes of production"). Just as capitalism is presumed to be dominant over other forms of economy that may coexist within a social formation, so it is also the culmination of historical eventuation.

This teleological sequencing is called into question by a number of the essays in this volume, for which transition is neither unidirectional, total, nor preordained. Serap Kayatekin, for example, focuses on the widespread emergence of feudal class processes among practitioners of sharecropping in the postbellum U.S. South, which persisted into the second half of the twentieth century in a region, period, and sector that most historians have represented as wholly capitalist or at least disposed in that direction. Chakrabarti and Cullenberg make explicit the economic diversity that is implicit in Kayatekin's essay, mapping the coexistence of different class processes and practices in theory and on the empirical terrain of present-day India. In their work neoliberal economic policy is seen to have differential effects within an extremely varied economic landscape of multiple class structures, fostering class transitions in a number of directions rather than a consolidated unidirectional movement in a singular economy. What emerges is a vision of transition as multidimensional and open-ended rather than unitary and preordained.

When transition is conceptualized as a regular rather than infrequent occurrence, taking place on the level of the enterprise or establishment and not simply at the scale of the economy as a whole, a politics of transition becomes a viable project. Carole Biewener's chapter addresses the alternative finance sector, representing it as a productive location for fostering class transition. As a site of the socialization of wealth, this sector can play a generative role in the valorization of alternative class relations. In this sense it can be an engine of economic development of an unfamiliar sort.

The project of "taking back the economy" involves theorizing the economy not as an autonomous domain inhabited by logics and large actors but as a contingent and highly differentiated social space. This theorization displaces the singular vision of development as a process of modernization driven by capitalist industrialization—a vision that has drawn both support and criticism from Marxist quarters (for instance, in the essay by Gibson-Graham and Ruccio included here). Without a dominant directionality to social and economic change; without an agreed-on or externally imposed understanding of progress; without a belief in technical solutions to generic problems of efficiency and allocation, development becomes a project not of replication (of the experience of the West) but of exploration and invention, one that an interest in class might productively inform.

(Class) Identity and Politics

According to a familiar Marxian representation of class politics, society is structured by a principal antagonism (between capital and labor) and the social interests and political roles of class actors are given and known (see Norton's essay). In this modernist vision, subjectivity is centered on and by class, and interests and affiliations are structurally ordained. Capitalism is the overarching structure that governs political identity and constrains political possibility; in ordinary times it may allow space for class compromise and reformist politics or, at moments of crisis, for revolutionary projects of class transformation.

As a snapshot of a landscape of political agents and agendas, this brief representation has an outmoded feel. Whether it has been superseded by the advent of so-called postindustrialism and the consequent repositioning of the industrial working class (Joyce 1995, 3), or by sociological theories of the multiplicity and contradictoriness of class locations (Wright 1978), or by feminist and poststructuralist querying of fixed identity and centered subjectivity—for whatever reason, this modernist interpretation seems truncated, too sparsely populated, insufficiently animated or animating. Yet few alternative visions of class politics have emerged to take its place.

Some of the rigidities and immobilities in this familiar picture are associated with problems of "classification" that have historically been attached to class. When class is understood as a social *grouping* (rather than as the social *processes* of producing, appropriating, and distributing surplus labor), class analysis involves sorting individuals into mutually exclusive class categories, often a frustrating analytical project.

Compounding the difficulties of classification, we often find a composite conception of class, as jointly constituted by power (usually in the form of control over the labor process), property relations (ownership or nonownership of the means of production), and involvement in exploitation (as producer or appropriators of surplus labor).[11] If workers have control over the labor process—like, for example, the self-supervising academic workers Curtis writes of in this volume—but no ownership of the means of production, are they capitalists or members of the working class? Alternatively, should they be included in some intermediate and politically ambiguous class? What if they own the means of production but don't appropriate and distribute their own surplus labor, as in many employee-owned firms or like workers in state-owned firms in the former Soviet Union treated by Resnick and Wolff? The difficulty of placing particular individuals in class boxes has been met by the proliferation class categories and contradictory class locations (Wright 1978), or by privileging one aspect of an individual's experience over another to facilitate such classification.

When it comes to politics, the question of class identity has been less one of objective location in an economic structure (though that has been seen as a fundamental requirement of class belonging) and more an issue of subjective identification with a particular class collectivity. How a "class in itself" becomes a "class for itself," able to take on its historically ordained political responsibilities, is a perennial question for theorists of "class formation."

In conceptualizing class as the process of producing, appropriating, and distributing surplus labor, we have sidestepped some of the problems of classification associated with these other conceptions of class. In our understanding individuals may participate in a variety of different class processes and inhabit a number of different class positions, simultaneously and over time. A small business owner, for example, may appropriate her own surplus labor in an ancient/independent class process, while at the same time appropriating surplus value from her employees who work alongside her; and in the evening and on weekends she may produce surplus labor that is appropriated by her partner in a "feudal" domestic class process.[12] How this complex configuration of class positions interacts with her gender, race, and other identity positions in forming her self-concept(s) is a question to which there is no obvious, single, or permanent answer.

This fluid and uncentered understanding of identity is problematic for traditional Marxian conceptions of class politics, where politics is grounded in, and therefore dependent on, class interests and identifications. In the sense that it relies on a stable and central class identity, traditional class politics comprise a form of identity politics (though one seen to have implications for the identity of the entire social formation). If it is not possible to fix class identity as essential or unchanging, and if subjects are not united by presumed commonalities, what are the possibilities for a politics of class?

When class identity is unmoored from a capitalist totality, the productive contingencies of politics come to the fore. No longer destined simply to reform or transform capitalism, class politics becomes a field of openness and experimentation (including with noncapitalist economic forms).

Class identity becomes legible as a potential effect of politics, rather than merely its origin or ground. Commonality and community may be seen as produced, not simply expressed, through political mobilization. This vision enlarges the effectivity of politics, offering fewer closures and certainties and a greater range of challenges and possibilities.

It also suggests an active political role for theory, not (merely) in its traditional role of providing analyses for which politics will supply the actors and actions. Theory is involved in creating the terms in and through which subjects come to recognize themselves, to grasp their circumstances and imagine their futures. In the language of Althusser (1971), theory interpellates subjects—it hails them, calling them into being, provoking (self-)recognition, identification, and desire. As one constituent of class politics, class theory offers a range of subject positions that individuals may inhabit, constituting themselves as class subjects with particular political energies and possibilities. It is in this sense that theory is powerful and always political.

Many of the essays in this volume are motivated by this understanding, and by a desire to create a different discourse of economy as a condition of new political subjects and social possibilities. In several essays this concern is manifest as an explicitly normative intervention. The chapters by Vlachou on the environment and by Chakrabarti and Cullenberg on class transition in India are committed to developing an ethics as well as a language of class. Each of these essays can be read in its constitutive role, as creating a discourse of class that may generate new possibilities of identification and action, and as a normative project in which the author(s) sketch the contours or foreground the possibility of a more equitable and nonexploitative society.

Class politics is not simply a function of class identity, however. Satyananda Gabriel, in his chapter on the Iranian Revolution, offers a vision of class politics unaccompanied by the self-recognition of class subjects and yet clearly motivated by class. Gabriel's argument is that the turn to fundamentalism was a turn away from the shah's brand of international capitalism, and toward more traditional and indigenous class forms. Class struggles in this instance are engaged in by a wide variety of social actors and not simply those in particular class positions; they are, literally, struggles over class.

Gabriel's chapter offers a novel understanding of the Iranian Revolution, undertaken from an entry point that no other observer has adopted. His project is not to convince us that this is the only way, or even the right way, to analyze that revolution but to elicit things that cannot be seen through another lens. In this sense it is a partisan and political analysis, highlighting the dimension of class.

Conclusion

In this introductory essay we have sketched a few of the contours and emphases of a different Marxian political economy. Oriented away from the certainties, regularities, and centricities of accumulation theory (clearly outlined by Norton in the opening chapter of this book), animated by the openness and contingencies of class theory, this approach is recognizable as poststructuralist through the presence of certain characteristic predilections/orientations (see Amariglio 1997). Without wanting to prescribe and foreclose on a continuing project, we might include here:

(1) a view of subjects as constructed under particular social and discursive conditions rather than as individual representatives of a universal humanity, or as agents of an overarching structure;

(2) a wariness of essentialism—that is, the presumption that any category (e.g., the capitalist enterprise) represents social beings unified by a common characteristic (for example, rationality, profit-seeking, the centrality of capital accumulation)—and an associated interest in difference and differentiation within categories;

(3) a hostility toward economic determinism and a preference for complex and multidirectional conceptions of causation/constitution;

(4) a suspicion of totalizing frameworks and master narratives (including the "global capitalist economy" or the story of "development") that attempt to embrace or locate other aspects of social life;

(5) a vision of knowledges (or discourses) as implicated in and constitutive of power, and as an important medium through which other social processes are constructed.

Perhaps the most consequential point for us is the last. From a poststructuralist perspective, knowledge is plural, contradictory, and powerful rather than singular, cumulative, and neutral. It actively shapes "reality" rather than passively reflecting it. The production of new knowledges is a world-changing activity, one that repositions other knowledges and empowers new subjects, practices, policies, and institutions. It is for this reason that we are interested in producing a knowledge of class.

Notes

1 This does not mean it has been entirely neglected (see, for example, the works of Roemer [1982], Wright [1978, 1985, 1997], the collection edited by Nielsen and Ware [1997], all of which develop and extend Marxian theories of class).

2 In addition to the widely acknowledged work of the French regulation school (Aglietta 1979; Lipietz 1987) from which the Fordist and post-Fordist models of development are derived, we might include here the theory of social structures of accumulation (Gordon et al., 1982). For a critique of economic determinism in these ostensibly nonreductionist approaches, see Gibson-Graham (1996, chap. 7).

3 Laclau (1984, 43). In opposing the reduction of the real to the concept, Laclau is opposing *idealism* and simultaneously (re)defining *materialism* as antireductionism. This stands in sharp contrast to the more common understanding that materialism entails the privileging of economic (i.e., material) causes and constituents.

4 The Althusserian reading of Marx yields a radically different conceptualization of social constitution and causation, more sensitive to political possibility, cultural difference, and multiple determinations than is the economism of accumulation theory. In his discussion of the Russian Revolution, for example, Althusser makes the point that "the existing conditions" were its "conditions of existence" (1969, 208). All of these contributed in different and incommensurable ways to its existence/occurrence. To ask which was more important is analogous to asking whether the area of a rectangle is more dependent on its length or its width.

5 Critics of poststructuralism sometimes argue that the refusal to ground knowledge in "reality" (as its accurate reflection) means that for poststructuralist theorists "anything goes," perhaps forgetting that the absence of a particular criterion of knowledge does not necessarily entail the general absence of criteria. In addition, fears are sometimes expressed that the lack of epistemological groundedness and the resulting "uncertainty" of knowledge means that politics is impossible or at the very least impaired. From a poststructuralist perspective, however, certainty is not a possibility and discursive interventions shape politics in ways that are unpredictable but

nevertheless powerful. In the sense that discourses are constitutive of subjects and of possibilities of action, discourse can be said to be itself always a political project.

6   This section is slightly modified from J.K. Gibson-Graham et al. (2000).

7   Exploitation can thus be seen as one of the processes that presents the problem of economic necessity to the individual or other social unit.

8   Gibson-Graham (1996) calls these the *appropriative* and *distributive* class processes, respectively.

9   Marx adopted the terminology of *productive* and *unproductive* from Adam Smith, in a move that has caused considerable interpretive consternation among generations of readers. Rather than understanding the term "unproductive" to mean unproductive of surplus value, as Marx defined it, many have understood it as meaning socially unproductive and therefore expendable or making a less valuable social contribution than productive labor. Resnick and Wolff have had a similar experience with "fundamental" and "subsumed" class processes, borrowed from Marx's discussion of fundamental classes and from another source lost to memory at this time. While there was no intention to suggest the greater importance of the former over the latter, "subsumed" seems to carry almost unavoidable connotations of subordination.

10 Of course, the equality in this expression could just as possibly be an inequality.

11 Composite conceptions of class are often signaled by the summary term *relations of production*. We have chosen to define class simply in terms of exploitation (or the production and appropriation of surplus labor), separating out power and property so that we may theorize their complex and changing relations to class. Various conditions of ownership/nonownership and power over the labor process may accompany the process of exploitation. For extended discussions of these issues, see Wolff and Resnick (1986) and J.K. Gibson-Graham (1996, chap. 3)

12 See Fraad et al. (1994) for an explication of feudal servitude in contemporary households and associated debates about the historical and social range of the term *feudal*.

BRUCE NORTON

□

READING MARX FOR CLASS

The project that this volume promotes is in some respects a new one. Novelty is suggested, certainly, by ideas which surround and support it, drawing as many of them do on post-Althusserian Marxism and perspectives associated with poststructuralist and postmodern social thought. More to the point, such currents are invoked with a view toward establishing what for contemporary social theory would be a novel focus indeed: the multipartite, historically changing, and historically changeable workings of surplus labor performance and surplus labor distribution. Class.

Yet there is much about the effort that is not actually new. The ground for a class-analytic framework has long been prepared for settlement: As Stephen Resnick and Richard Wolff's *Knowledge and Class* demonstrates (1987, chap. 3), it was Marx who labored to clear these lands. Indeed, Resnick and Wolff's book offers a way to read *Capital* that connects its three volumes (along with related parts of *Theories of Surplus Value*) precisely as a sequential and sustained effort to theorize class processes in their capitalist forms. Whatever else it accomplishes, *Knowledge and Class* forcefully documents that for Marx this effort was of central concern.

Why then does the claim that one might elaborate a transformationally useful conception of class processes seem to be a new one? How is one to account for the hundred-year gap? Or, to put the question in the context in which the paper will place it: If Marx labored so insistently to forge a complex, multipositional class-theoretic framework for economic analysis, why has Marxian economics not hitherto taken the project as its own?

I contend below that an answer to the puzzle lies in the way in which the major traditions of Western Marxian economic theory developed during the century after Marx's death. The story ultimately concerns a destructive interaction between two distinct passions animating Marx's own writing: a struggle to identify, elaborate, and insist on the importance of complex, nonbinary concepts of class, on one hand, and an effort to position the capitalist mode of production as historically evanescent, a system whose internal contradictions necessarily develop so as to hasten its own end, on the other. My thesis is that whatever detente the two projects managed to maintain in *Capital* and *Theories of Surplus Value,* peace between them broke down after Marx's death. One, the effort to discern capitalism's destiny-determining inner contradictions, became the project of Western Marxian economics and spilled over to inform radical economics more generally. The other, the effort to conceive the historically changing dimensions of class exploitation—and envision associated transformational possibilities—found correspondingly less growing room.

The paper argues that the two phenomena are closely related. As one vision took hold and branched into the contending schools of Marxian accumulation and crisis theory, it developed in ways—prominently featuring a bipolar understanding of class and a related essentialist conception of the capitalist firm—that made the other project difficult to see or pursue. In effect, as Marx the deterministic economist entered the arenas of twentieth-century Western social thought, Marx the class theorist was pushed toward the exit, leaving behind for the most part only some hundreds of pages of seemingly arcane and unavoidably class-theoretic text with which to puzzle successive generations of *Capital* study group students. A Marxism that took as the sign of science its commitment to concepts of necessity, inner logic, and essential contradiction had as one effect an effacement of the class-theoretic possibilities Marx himself had sought to nourish. It was then only with the emergence of a Marxism self-consciously critical of such commitments (initially outside the conversations of "Marxian economics," perhaps most clearly in the work of Louis Althusser) that a class-theoretic project could take shape. That at least is the implication of the argument I develop below.

The Production of Bipolarity in Marxian Economic Theory

The Marx who has mattered most for accumulation and crisis theorists is the Marx who envisioned the capitalist mode of production as inherently in transit. Capitalism's transience is inherent because capitalism's existence is constituted by an internal dynamic, the contradiction between the forces of production and the social relations of production that structures all precommunist modes of production. The one-paragraph formulation in the preface Marx provided for *A Contribution to the Critique of Political Economy* in 1859 puts the general vision in classic form. As one section contends:

At a certain stage of development, the material productive forces of society come into conflict with the existing relations of production or—this merely expresses the same thing in legal terms—with the property relations within the framework of which they have operated hitherto. From forms of development of the productive forces these relations turn into their fetters. Then begins an era of social revolution. The changes in the economic foundation lead sooner or later to the transformation of the whole immense superstructure.

A few sentences later Marx provides a further dimension to these conclusions:

No social order is ever destroyed before all the productive forces for which it is sufficient have been developed, and new superior relations of production never replace older ones before the material conditions for their existence have matured within the framework of the old society.

For capitalism the implication is clear. While it serves to develop the forces of production for much of its life, after a certain point it both blocks their satisfactory further development and produces within itself conditions enabling a solution to the problem. After that point is reached, capitalism is both historically archaic and increasingly self-destructive.[1]

The vision has had lasting effects. The contending schools that fueled the revival of Western radical economics in the 1960s, falling rate of profit theory and the monopoly capital/stagnation framework, both understood themselves as identifying the workings of the essential contradiction that signals contemporary capitalism's ever-increasing dysfunctionality.[2] They framed their arguments accordingly. Both schools also read *Capital,* and not surprisingly what they found there were concepts and principles supportive of their efforts. As I argue below, these readings set the terms within which certain basic Marxian economic principles have been understood even by those (such as social structure of accumulation theorists and regulation theorists) who later sought and founded more "kismetic" approaches. For English-speaking Western Marxian economics, the past century was a short one. The mid-century work of Henryk Grossman, Paul Mattick, Paul Sweezy, Roman Rosdolsky, and Paul Baran in effect connected the assumptions of 1900 with the thinking of 1980. The connection has not been a kind one for those who would visualize class.

Socialism without a Complex Class Focus?

It has not been kind in two sorts of ways. On one hand the expectation that capitalism necessarily implodes has sapped Marxian economists' *interest* in pursuing class-analytic work. On the other hand the particular theoretical apparati theorists have developed to show why implosion (or at least crisis) is inevitable, as I shall argue, have sapped Marxian economists' *capacity* to freely explore class-analytic possibilities.

The first side of this dynamic merits at least brief recognition. In general terms, the more "scientific" Marxian socialism is (in Engels's sense), the less necessary or politically useful detailed class-analytic conceptions of capitalism and capitalist firms become.[3] If the advent of socialism involves first of all simply the development of capitalism, history plus political struggle should be sufficient to bring it about, entirely apart from efforts to think about such things as complicated and historically changing surplus distribution processes. The first strike that complex conceptualization of class processes has had against it is its irrelevance for the socialist project as traditionally understood.

Indeed, politically inspired efforts to change the way people think about the justice and desirability of market economic processes, whether class-theoretic or not, are, in the end, not of great interest to Marxists of this sort. All that ultimately matters is that first there are capitalists and workers and, second, that capitalist implosion is an absolutely inevitable tendency. Modes of thinking are subsidiary. On this issue Rosa Luxemburg, writing from a World War I prison to defend her underconsumptionist theory of capitalist crisis, spoke with memorable clarity:

According to Marx, the rebellion of the workers, the class struggle, is only the ideological reflection of the objective historical necessity of socialism, resulting from the objective impossibility of capitalism at a certain economic stage. Of course, that does not mean (it still seems necessary to point out those basics of Marxism to the "experts") that the historical process has to be, or even could be, exhausted to the very limit of this economic impossibility. Long before this, the objective tendency of capitalist development in this direction is sufficient to produce such a social and political sharpening of contradictions in society that they must terminate. But these social and political contradictions are essentially only a product of the economic indefensibility of capitalism. The situation continues to sharpen as this becomes increasingly obvious. (1972, 76)

The contradictions that produce socialism are "essentially only a product of the economic indefensibility of capitalism." *That,* not class, is what must be theorized.[4]

Luxemburg's words may sound extreme. For the founders of the two schools of thought that rose to prominence within Marxian economics in the 1960s they were right on target, however. Both Grossman and Sweezy invoke the two sentences that immediately follow the quoted passage to support their own interventions into Marxian economic theory—Grossman's launching of falling rate of profit theory and Sweezy's initial conception of chronic stagnation tendencies linked to capitalism's basic tendency toward underconsumption. As Luxemburg goes on (and Grossman and Sweezy both approvingly quote):

If we assume, with the "experts," the economic infinity of capitalist accumulation, then the vital foundation on which socialism rests will disappear. We then take refuge in the mist of pre-Marxist systems and schools which attempted to deduce socialism solely on the basis of the injustice and evils of today's world and the revolutionary determination of the working classes. (Luxemburg 1972, 76; cf. Grossman 1992, 71; Sweezy 1942, 207 [Sweezy's translation])[5]

The sentences, reverberating through the decades, nicely counterpose a concern to theorize injustice (of the sort that might indeed help stimulate an interest in class analysis per se) and Marxism, the science of history, the special province of the Marxian economist. How does one read *Capital*? One guideline is clear: Only utopians, wandering myopically in the aforementioned mist, highlight injustice without demonstrating historical necessity. In the world of Luxemburg, Grossman, and the Sweezy of 1942, to read Marx's work as Resnick and Wolff suggest, as constructive of a framework capable of comprehending class processes in capitalist economies — and placing exploitation in capitalist economies clearly on the agenda of human affairs — would be to construe Marx himself as having conspicuously failed to grasp the basic concepts of historical materialism. Concepts of class are important in traditional schools of Marxian economics. Their role, however, is not to provide an understanding of exploitation and its alternatives so as to promote transformational possibility, but rather to ensure the certainty of progressively deepening capitalist distress.

Capitalists and Workers: Classical Marxism

The sort of concepts of class that proved serviceable in such an effort were simple and clear-cut. The binary vision originally presented in the *Communist Manifesto* works best of all. The concepts worked out in volumes two and three of *Capital,* in contrast, encumber rather than assist any simple script. The latter envision many important avenues — from rent and interest to such things as merchants' profits and the salaries of supervisory managers — through which claims on surplus value can be registered, and therefore denote many important "class positions," in Resnick and Wolff's term, some of which are likely to grow simply as the complexity of capitalist production and distribution processes increases. Hence they open up toward logically indeterminate possibilities. A certain number of such surplus value distributions had to be recognized by Marxian theorists, if only because Marx devotes large sections of *Capital* to conceptualizing them. They did not however have to be construed as important.

Apart from the *Communist Manifesto,* nowhere were the multiple cuts of surplus value repressed quite so declaredly as in the classical Marx-

ism associated with the Social Democratic Party of Germany. As prominently propagated by Engels and Karl Kautsky in the 1880s and 1890s,
classical Marxism inscribed as Marxism's fundamental insight the conclusion that capitalist development progressively spins out only two great
increasingly antagonistic classes.

Jonathan Diskin has recently emphasized a source of classical Marxism's confidence in this scenario. In *Socialism: Utopian and Scientific*
Engels understands both class polarization and ever-deepening crisis as
expressions of the essential contradiction that structures capitalist development, namely, the "incompatibility of socialized production with capi-
talistic [or private] appropriation" (Engels, 1978, quoted in Diskin 1996,
286). Capitalism entails strictly private appropriation of surplus value,
but foments within itself the growth of socialized production, first of all
in the labor processes promoted by capitalist firms (and later through car-
tels, trusts, joint stock companies, increasing recourse to state regulation
of competition, and so on). Thus workers, who "*represent and embody in
their being* the principle of social labor and production" necessarily find
and act out ever-increasing conflict with the privately appropriating bourgeoisie (Diskin 1996, 289; emphasis in original). Also necessarily, the
proletariat, representing the social side of the contradiction that capitalism inherently promotes, grows ever larger. The bipolar class categories
classical Marxism bequeathed to its successors expressed a contradiction antecedent to themselves — the dynamic that, as was thought, drives
capitalist development to its destination in socialism.

The essential contradiction classical Marxism identified at the heart
of capitalism was a particular one, but its effects on the possibilities for
class analysis illustrate the general point with which this section began.
If Marxian economics sets as its task the delineation of the contradiction
that spells capitalism's doom, class concepts must find their role within
that effort, and in the end there are only two important roles to be found.
In classical Marxism capitalism set the old (privately appropriating bourgeoisie)[6] against the new (socially organized workers). Later traditions,
such as falling rate of profit theories, pose the dying system's victims
(usually workers very generally defined) against its defenders. In either
case, what necessitates and ushers in socialism is a primordial conflict
within capitalism's inner workings, and primordial conflicts by definition pit one side against another. If "classes" are groups of people acting

out a conflict thought to express a totality's essential contradiction, two is a charm. Three, however, is a crowd.[7] A rich and complex variety of historically changing class positions would be an unwelcome specter indeed.

Capitalists and Workers: Crisis Theories

Responding to Eduard Bernstein's skepticism in the relatively stable Germany of the late nineteenth century, Karl Kautsky downplayed the importance of capitalist crisis to the coming of socialism. While indeed inevitable, he argued, crises aren't necessary to socialism's birth: Even without crisis capitalism throws an ever-increasing number of socialized and impoverished workers into direct conflict with a smaller and smaller number of capitalist beneficiaries.[8] This normal, noncrisis pattern of development is what most sharpens capitalism's bipolar social contradictions to hasten the system's demise (Howard and King 1989, 82; cf. Sweezy 1942, 194).

With time Marxian economists' emphases changed. Worker incomes sometimes grew, and job classifications proliferated; stable periods of capitalist development might or might not inevitably sharpen social contradictions. In any case, between the world wars and again in the 1970s, crises recurred, and crisis theory became an increasingly prominent component of Marxian economic analysis. As Marxian economists of various schools maintained, capitalist development entails tendencies toward an ever-deepening crisis (whether acute or chronic in nature, or actual or delayed in expression).

Freed, perhaps, from overt ties to classical Marxism's binary vision of capitalism's essential contradiction, were class concepts now afforded more room for development? Their fate depended in part on the analytical makeup of the particular crisis theory traditions which came to prominence. As it happened, one position (falling rate of profit theory) was bipolar in foundation, and its logic implied that there was no particular need to elaborate beyond a bipolar view; the logic of the other position (underconsumption/stagnation theory) meant that there was a positive need *not* to.

The underconsumptionist case is perhaps the more dramatic. It has also been more influential than is sometimes recognized. Underconsumptionist interpretations of Marxian crisis theory were favored by Engels (Howard and King 1989, 11), continually pushed by Kautsky, revised by Luxemburg in the first decades of the twentieth century, and successfully promoted by Sweezy (1942), Paul Baran, and others associated with *Monthly Review* from the 1950s on.

In all its variants, underconsumptionist argumentation has drastically constrained the conceptualization of class, for it has required that Marxian theory posit, first of all, that there are only two.[9] If capitalist economies encounter fundamental and necessarily increasing problems of demand as their development progresses, it is because workers are restricted in their consuming power and capitalists, for reasons that vary across frameworks, are unable to take up the slack. Since wages (as is traditionally assumed) are spent, demand problems turn particularly on the allocation of surplus value. Here, if a traditional argument is to hold, the crucial point is that the entire question be conceived as in the first instance simply a matter of "the capitalists' " behavior. All surplus value belongs to the capitalist; the decision whether to spend on consumption or save and/or spend on investment is "his." Hence the dynamics of aggregate demand turn first of all on that decision.

Kautsky, whose commitment to a bipolar conception of class has already been noted, first situated the shortfall of capitalist consumption by contending that the concentration of capital shifted surplus value from small capitalists (with relatively large consumption spending habits in relation to their incomes) to big capitalists (who spend a smaller fraction of their income).[10] By 1902 (and again in 1910–11) he had pointed simply to competitive constraints on the consumption spending possibilities of the rich, which tended to hold the growth of capitalist consumption behind the growth of the output of consumption goods (Howard and King 1989, 83, 101). The thinking seems abstract and schematic, but it is basic Marxian principle as underconsumptionists have seen it, and it turns entirely on the idea that the distribution of surplus value is a matter for "the capitalist" to determine. Forty years later Sweezy began his own construction of "the fundamental contradiction of capitalist society from which all other contradictions are ultimately derived" (1942, 172) simply by putting Kautsky's conception of the capitalist in more precise terms.[11]

Thus the poignant postwar moment in which Baran and Sweezy constructed the " 'elementary logic' of the system" in the United States via a model in which only two systemically "normal" kinds of spending are funded by surplus—capitalist consumption (defined as consumption out of dividend earnings) and investment—is understandable. *Monopoly Capital* kept faith with precedent. It continued the only approach possible if Marxian underconsumptionist theory were to be sustained. In that approach, sanctioned by classical Marxism and long outliving it, capitalists and workers are the only normal or fundamental agents of capitalist economies; hence the two classically recognized functions of the capitalist—to accumulate and to consume—are the only "normal" spending out of surplus income. If one of these forms of spending is systematically hampered—and *Monopoly Capital* styled giant enterprises as unwilling to increase dividend distributions sufficiently to match profit accruals during boom periods, so that capitalist consumption tended to lag behind profit earnings—a fundamental tendency toward stagnation might be claimed.

When establishing capitalism's basic tendencies, or "normal" functioning, underconsumption analysis theorizes by excluding.[12] What it excludes are the various class positions funded by cuts of surplus value. In Resnick and Wolff's terms, it expels from capitalism's basic makeup the "subsumed class process," the flows Marx begins to take up in volumes two and three of *Capital* through which surplus value is distributed to many kinds of claimants. Insofar as such flows form a section of the puzzle that is not expendable if a constructively useful class analysis is to come to life, a class-repressive reading of Marx was thus the more or less inevitable by-product of Sweezy's and Baran's efforts to promote an underconsumptionist strain of Marxian crisis theory in the United States in the decades after World War II.

Falling rate of profit theorists, in contrast, had little positive reason to exclude analysis of the various cuts of surplus value. But given the dimensions of their argument, neither did they have reason to take them up in any systematic way. A deep commitment to a bipolar conception of capitalist functioning is inscribed in the framework from its inception, through its quasi-Hegelian construction of the nature and theoretical role of the "social relations of production" (or, following Rosdolsky [1977], the concept of "capital in general"). Where classical Marxism's productive relations were a sort of antithesis of sociality, representing the private, greedy, anarchic, and archaic elements of capitalism which its own unintended production of interdependence chafes against, falling rate of profit theorists' productive relations consist of an active and directly class-defined antagonism: *capitalists,* who incessantly struggle for more surplus value, confront *workers,* the source of capitalists' needed sustenance, who are limited in number, time, and capacity to increase their output of that sustenance.[13] Hence falling rate of profit theory is an intensely class-focused tradition. It centers exclusively on *one* class relation, however, the "relation of capital to living labour, i.e. . . . its striving for the appropriation of surplus value" (Rosdolsky 1977, 249). Since the tradition sees the latter as the source of a logic of all capitalist development, whatever more complex class analysis falling rate of profit theorists might elaborate has to find a place within that vision.[14]

As it happened the vision's bipolarity was only reinforced by the argument's structure. In the longer term, the heterogeneous claims on surplus value cannot matter, except as countertendencies of strictly limited countervailing potential. From Grossman to Mattick and Shaikh, falling rate of profit theorists have long insisted that their framework leaves no room for the state to offer effective amelioration for capitalism's crisis tendencies, since in the end the state can do nothing to offset a fundamental tendency toward shortfall of surplus value (see, for example, Yaffe 1973, 225–28; Shaikh 1983, 142). Distributions of surplus value, however much they might reduce enterprise profit rates, occupy an analogous position. Their burden might be reduced to ameliorate an immediate crisis, perhaps, but in the longer term such reduction offers no solution to the problem posed by capitalism's fundamental contradiction. The system's fate is determined by the aggregate trend, given that that trend is inevitably downward.[15]

Moreover, in basic outline falling rate of profit theorists already *knew* where surplus value went; their entire analysis pointed to the dominance of a privileged destination, namely, reinvestment in physical capital stock. The latter dominates all possible alternatives because (as, most often following Rosdolsky [1977], falling rate of profit theorists read the first volume of *Capital*) mechanization is the unique resolution/intensification of "capital in general"'s contradiction; it is the only means by which surplus value production can be increased on an ongoing basis despite the limited and sometimes unyielding nature of the exploitable labor force. As Anwar Shaikh concludes,

> The tendency towards substitution of machinery for living labour, . . . is according to Marx an absolutely necessary outcome of the capitalist-controlled labour process. . . . (A)utomation is both intrinsic to capitalism and is its dominant form of technical change. It is the technological expression of the social relations of production under capitalism. (Shaikh 1978, 238)

Here capital not only relentlessly "seeks" to appropriate all possible surplus value; capital seeks to return surplus value to the production process in the form of physical capital stock as well.[16] In this sense the class question Resnick and Wolff pose under the heading "subsumed class process" ("How does surplus value get distributed?") is not really poseable as a question in this tradition. Its most, and in some contexts only, important dimension is thought perfectly well understood at an abstract level of analysis. It is a matter of basic logic — the self-destroying logic of capital.

Class and Implosion in Marxian Economic Theory

In the *Theory of Capitalist Development* (1942) Sweezy presented Marxian economic theory's crucial difference from revisionist interpretations as its adherence to the principle that "crisis-producing forces tend to become ever more severe in the course of capitalist development," so that the expectation that the productive relations necessarily fetter the productive forces is sustained (215). For Sweezy this expectation is Marx's "unambiguous and consistently maintained" position; to be truly Marxian a crisis theory must conform to it (190).

Roman Rosdolsky's reading of *Capital*'s production, *The Making of Marx's Capital* (1977), draws the same line. For Rosdolsky the tendency of the rate of profit to fall is the logically necessary implication of Marx's concept of capital. That has been the consistent theme of falling rate of profit advocates from Grossman and Mattick to Rosdolsky, Yaffe, and Shaikh. Shaikh's lucid entry on "Economic Crises" in the *Dictionary of Marxist Thought,* indeed, is organized around the idea; it construes commitment to the necessity of crisis (and the necessity that crises deepen in severity over time) as what crucially distinguishes Marx and truly Marx-congruent economic theory from such contemporary crisis-"possibility" analyses as underconsumption and wage-squeeze theories (Shaikh 1983, 139).

Despite Shaikh's distinctions,[17] we have argued that although classical Marxism, falling rate of profit theory, and underconsumptionist/stagnation analysis differ wildly in specifics, they in fact share a general structure: They all build an analysis demonstrating the necessary end of the capitalist system on a bipolar class foundation. More precisely, they build this necessity on a concept of the inner nature of capital; the latter, in each case, entails only two classes, capitalists and workers. The search for necessity has wed Marxian economics to a concept of "capital" that entails a reductive conception of class.

Crisis Theory's Capitalist

That a claim of absolute historical necessity requires anchorage in a two-sided, or contradictory, abstract concept is clear; nowhere else will such a claim find footing sure enough to resist all challenge. Marxian economists have found bedrock in concepts of two-sided capital. Classical Marxism had capital as the source of both private appropriation and its mortal enemy, ever-spreading social interdependence.[18] Falling rate of profit theorists' capital seeks more surplus value so relentlessly that it must turn to an aid (mechanization), which eventually undermines profitability itself.[19] The monopoly capital variant of underconsumption theory deploys a third variation: it conceives capital as the locus of an essential urge to grow, among whose implications is the eventual production of concentrated market structure, and with that a barrier to its own inner drive's continued expression.

If these conceptions of capital's fate-determining duality have engraved class bipolarity into Marxian economic theory, they have also left a peculiar mark on the meaning of the two poles, capitalist and worker. The positions themselves are straightforward. The capitalist role is always twofold: capitalists exploit (appropriate surplus value) and expand (reinvest). Workers, in turn, produce the surplus value which capitalists appropriate. We have seen that something of a shift in theoretical positioning occurs in the move from classical Marxism to later frameworks. In outline, active agency moves ever more clearly toward capitalists, and in a particular way: the capitalist's role as expander, or reinvestor, of surplus value in physical capital stock, becomes the capitalist's most emphasized feature, and the key issue in economic theory generally. Workers continue to be exploited and capitalists continue to exploit[20]; otherwise there would be no surplus value. The system's fate hinges more or less entirely, however, on certain hypotheses about the other component of the capitalist position, the expander, or capital accumulator, role. Thus falling rate of profit theorists' task is to demonstrate that "mechanization"'s claim on appropriated surplus value is so relentless and so dominates alternative claims that a rising organic composition of capital and falling profit rate must result. Monopoly capital/stagnation theorists must show that firms' drive to expand, innate to units of capital, is so rigid that it leads giant firms to continue to save robustly even after market concentration has blocked their investment spending possibilities, leading to the chronic tendency toward aggregate demand shortfall which is monopoly capitalism's new "law of motion."[21] In both frameworks an *origin* must be built up in order that a *telos* might be conceived, and that origin is the accumulation-seeking (or surplus-value seeking/accumulation-forcing) unit of capital. It is the reification of the capitalist-as-expander role that ensures the system as a whole can *not* expand indefinitely. It is the unconditioned necessity with which firms seek expansion that produces the absolute certainty that expansion must eventually slow. Hence the concepts of "class" that have secured post-classical Marxian economists' arguments have turned above all on theses about a process—the reinvestment of surplus value—that is not, strictly speaking, a class process at all.[22] When Marxian economists have read *Capital* for class it is in good part *this* sort of conception of class they have found, a conception of the exigencies of the capitalist class position insofar as it involves and requires reinvestment of surplus value.

Mapping Marx's Work

If we seek to understand how it is that Marxian economists have not seen Marx himself as a theorist of class in more than bipolar and instrumental terms, a significant part of an answer is simple in outline: Their attention has not been directed to the right pages. A class-analytic approach to *Capital* focuses on the ways in which volumes two and three extend, change, and above all disaggregate the analysis begun in volume one. Volume one concerns the production of surplus value; as concerns class it takes up the two class positions involved, capitalist and worker. As Resnick and Wolff have stressed, parts of volumes two and three (in volume three, especially sections that *follow* the better-known analysis of the tendency of the rate of profit to fall in part three) then introduce positions funded by distributions of surplus value to agents other than industrial capitalists—prominently including merchants, moneylenders, and landlords, but also moneydealers (dealers in foreign currencies), supervisory managers of joint-stock companies, and owners of industrial enterprises (shareholders) (Resnick and Wolff 198, 124–32). By both building on and extending some of Marx's suggestions, Resnick and Wolff suggest other "subsumed class positions" that a class analysis might also encompass. As they have it, in volumes two and three Marx also develops a class analysis of the two aggregated concepts introduced in volume one—capitalist and worker. He distinguishes, for example, between productive and unproductive workers, and between a variety of types of capitalists, as well as between capitalists and certain subsumed class positions (as receivers of surplus value) sometimes conflated with the capitalist position per se (1987, chap. 3).

The point for our purposes is that, facing *Capital,* a complex class analysis develops for a reader focused on the interplay of volume one and later volumes. The later volumes make distinctions and draw lines not drawn when capitalist exploitation is first conceptualized. A class-analytic approach is achieved in part by respecting and looking for distinctions that volume one itself conscientiously represses.

How might Marxian economists have read Marx without stressing the transformational implications of the multipositional conception of surplus value production and distribution he elaborates? Another facet of an answer presents itself. Approach the surplus-distribution and other class-theoretic analyses in volumes two and three of *Capital* as if the basic principles of Marxian economic analysis are already fixed, having been fully established in volume one (or volume one plus part three of volume three). In that case one is not, in these pages, plumbing new dimensions of a radically different way of thinking about economic processes. One is just filling in details.[23]

Relocating the Firm/Rereading Volume One

Thus far the analysis has been limited in breadth in that it has largely concerned three formative but aged, or perhaps aging, Marxian accumulation theory traditions. Our scope can be broadened. The authors of these frameworks have taught the English-speaking world much of what it knows about how to read Marx to find Marxian economic principle. From Ernest Mandel and Paul Sweezy to Roman Rosdolsky and David Harvey, recent contributors to the traditional schools we have considered figure prominently in the ranks of Marx's most erudite and persuasive economically oriented interpreters. Their teaching far overflows the boundaries of the traditions they originally labored to promote and extend. If many Marxian and radical economic theorists now advocate alternative approaches, and clearly reject certain of the traditional frameworks' contentions, as I argue, they also hold fast to certain more general understandings and expectations that are also in part the legacy of these frameworks.

One such general understanding concerns the nature of the capitalist firm. The crossroads considered in the previous section concerned two incompatible ways to link the three volumes of *Capital,* one finding the lineaments of necessity in volume one, one refusing any such endeavor. We might have put the matter more concretely as a question of two incompatible ways to theorize and position the capitalist firm, for the differing ways to read *Capital* involve and lead to two different conceptions of the unit of capital.

We have seen the firm theorized by traditional accumulation and crisis theory traditions. Whether approached as the innately expansion-seeking unit of capital (Steindl, Baran, and Sweezy) or the incarnation of the social relations of production (understood by Rosdolsky et al. as the struggle by capital to extract ever-more surplus value from labor), the firm is the bearer of necessity in these frameworks. Its incessant urge to expand ensures that eventually expansion will no longer flourish. The firm is thus the origin of economic dynamics and the protagonist of the overall plot; it is capitalism and the end of capitalism all in one.

More recently emergent frameworks, like social structures of accumulation and regulation theories, admittedly stray from the template in important ways. In particular they abandon the claim that the end is known; gone is the idea that after "a certain stage of development" the relations of production must restrict the productive forces' continued growth, as is, for the most part, commitment to the conceptualization of an essential internal contradiction that makes this idea possible. Yet if the traditional *telos* is cut loose, the *origin* developed to produce the *telos* remains.[24] What is a capitalist firm? For social structures of accumulation theorists and regulationists of various kinds, the answer is self-evident. To the extent that it is capitalist a firm is an entity that seeks to exploit and expand as fully and rapidly as conditions (which *do* vary) permit. The firm of Marxian economics remains what it has been for many decades: the incarnation of the bipolar capitalist class position that traditional crisis theories elaborated and enshrined.[25]

To take an interest in complex, nonbinary class analysis one must be willing to abandon this fixed point. If it is multipositional in class dimensions, the capitalist firm a class-theoretic analysis envisions must be the site of a complex of surplus value distribution processes (as well as production processes).[26] It is not then just an exploiter and expander. Nor, in any case, is its "inner nature" or basic constitution knowable in a meaningful way at an abstract level of theory. If the firm is to be conceived as a complexity freed of its duty to anchor a teleological argument, it might be posed as an open, rather than given, complexity — a site continually transformed both by "internal" forces, such as historically changing technological patterns and administrative models, and by more general processes shaping the society within which it exists.

Put differently, class-theoretic analysis would move the firm from the role of fixed point and origin of economic dynamics to a position as the object of inquiry. If the intent is to transform a complexity in certain of its dimensions, that complexity should focus theoretical work. Hence the firm might be positioned as something of a mystery: an entity whose dimensions and constraints are revealed only as the product of a reduction-averse labor of theoretical elaboration, and, in any case, only provisionally. From the perspective of Marxian economic theory, the call for class is in part a call to dislodge the firm from the burden of theoretical anchorage, thereby freeing the theory to admit that the firm is not, in fact, already entirely known to it.

Such a firm's surplus-value distribution patterns might be expected to *change* historically. As J.K. Gibson-Graham (1996, chap. 8) has vividly stressed, they might also be changeable. For someone seeking to understand firm-transformational possibilities, in this view, respect for complexity and surprise is a better starting point than reduction. It is a better starting point, more particularly, if theory is to be of use in constructing enterprises that appropriate and distribute surplus differently.

Firm and Capitalist in Volume One

A final question. Would such a theoretical repositioning effectively amount to rejecting Marx? Marx's firm, after all, *is* well known—as an exploiter and expander. Its position within the theory is also firmly established—as the starting point and foundation, not the semi-mysterious object of inquiry. No?

Not necessarily. To reposition the firm as suggested is to read *Capital* critically and differently, but to keep reading it. Reading *Capital this* differently might seem impossible; in effect we begin with a frontal attack on central tenets of the traditional crisis-theoretic approach to Marxian economic principles, march sideways, and work from there. As I contend below, however, once freed from the crisis theory gaze, Marx's own words at certain points greatly assist the effort. Resnick and Wolff have already demonstrated as much in their class-theoretic readings of sections of volumes two and three and related work in *Theories of Surplus Value* and the *Grundrisse* (1987, 109–63). In what follows I seek to show that similar reinterpretation beckons the class-theoretic reader even in volume one. In the very passages of volume one where he is said to enunciate the basics of his theory, indeed, Marx, approached with fresh eyes, does not seem to argue in a way consistent with the principles he is said to announce there; moreover the principles themselves do not seem to be stated, in these pages at least, in the way we have come to believe.

The passages crisis theorists have most often turned to are found in section seven of volume one, where Marx first introduces the subject of "The Process of Accumulation of Capital." Most often they refer more particularly to chapter twenty-four ("The Transformation of Surplus-Value into Capital"), section three ("Division of Surplus-Value into Capital and Revenue: The Abstinence Theory"). The most memorably vivid single passage is perhaps also the most often cited:

Accumulate, accumulate! That is Moses and the prophets! "Industry furnishes the material which saving accumulates." Therefore save, save, i.e., reconvert the greatest possible portion of surplus-value or surplus product into capital! Accumulation for the sake of accumulation, production for the sake of production; . . . (Marx 1976, 742)

Here would seem to be a most concise and powerful statement of the principle Marxian crisis theories have been built on: that in capitalist economies firms accumulate "for accumulation's sake," that is, as the result of their (or capitalism's) basic nature, and hence as an abstractly fixed imperative. The passage is presented in that light by important works in several traditions. Baran and Sweezy, for example, introduce their analysis of postwar U.S. capitalism by surveying the contemporary giant firm and concluding:

Over the portals of the magnificent office building of today, as on the wall of the modest counting house of a century or two ago, it would be equally appropriate to find engraved the motto: "Accumulate! Accumulate! That is Moses and the Prophets." (1966, 44)

The sentences also figure prominently in the presentation of falling rate of profit theory, most notably the variation introduced by Ben Fine and Laurence Harris, who begin their chapter on crisis theory with the words "For Marx accumulation is the essence of capitalism: 'Accumulate, accumulate: that is Moses and the prophets' " (1979, 76). The same phrase is featured in various encyclopedic entries on the basics of Marxian economics of the past several decades (for example, Fine 1983, 3–4; Mandel 1990, 25). David Harvey's influential *The Limits to Capital* (which understands crisis theory along lines closely related to Fine and Harris [1979]) also brought the passage to center stage, presenting its last sentence fragment ("Accumulation for the sake of accumulation, production for the sake of production") as for Marx "the rule that governs the behavior of all capitalists" and the key to the understanding of capitalist crisis (Harvey 1982, 29; cf. 157, 192). And when David Gordon introduced a new kind of Marxian long-wave framework, social structures of accumulation theory, in 1978, he began by turning to this same section (Gordon 1978, 27; cf. Alcaly 1978, 17).[27]

But when read in the context of the argument within which it occurs (section three of chapter twenty-four) the passage turns out to be far more complex—and far less foundational—than it has been depicted. Indeed as I submit Marx's argument here is in an important sense the reverse of its traditional interpretation. It does not contend that accumulation is an incessant and invariant force, a destination for surplus value that simply overpowers alternative possible destinations; it contends precisely that accumulation's claim as a fraction of surplus value *changes* as conditions change over time. The quote itself refers not to capitalism's essential nature but to the historical conditions of its infancy, now quite outdated, as Marx argues. And, in a complication which Marxian economists have dealt with simply by excising the offending sentences from their quotations, Marx presents the stirring words not as his own, but as the viewpoint of classical theory.

I do not mean to suggest that there is no basis for the traditional interpretation. An equally familiar passage that precedes the quote by several pages (and accompanies the quote in various contemporary authors' works) does suggest a basis for it if read in a particular way. We might start there. The section considers the division of surplus value between the capitalist's consumption spending and accumulation. Insofar as the capitalist is a personification of capital, Marx begins, he consumes very little and accumulates as much as possible. "As capital personified," "as a personification of capital," or "insofar . . . as his actions are a mere function of capital," as he variously puts it, a capitalist is indeed fully devoted to accumulation (1976, 739). "Capital," in this usage, *is* evidently the dual drive Marxian economists have discerned—to exploit and expand. The section expands on the need to accumulate at some length, arguing both that "except as capital personified, the capitalist has no historical value, and no right to . . . historical existence" and the quite different assertion that Marxian economists have embraced, namely, that "in so far as he is capital personified, his motivating force is not the acquisition and enjoyment of use-values, but the acquisition and augmentation of exchange-values." In the midst of this discussion Marx writes well-known sentences, quoted in entirety in Harvey (1982, 29) (and nearly so in Sweezy [1942, 80–81], Alcaly [1978, 17], and Gordon [1978, 27][28]) in which his basic insight into capitalism's inner workings is said to be revealed:

Only as a personification of capital is the capitalist respectable. As such, he shares with the miser an absolute drive towards self-enrichment. But what appears in the miser as the mania of an individual is in the capitalist the effect of a social mechanism in which he is merely a cog. Moreover, the development of capitalist production makes it necessary constantly to increase the amount of capital laid out in a given industrial undertaking, and competition subordinates every individual capitalist to the immanent laws of capitalist production, as external and coercive laws. It compels him to keep extending his capital, so as to preserve it, and he can only extend it by means of progressive accumulation. (739)

Alcaly, Harvey, and Gordon all immediately follow this quote with the commandment to accumulate (from Marx 1976, 742) that we have already encountered.

These pages are quoted so frequently in part simply because they are compelling statements of the necessity to accumulate if "the capitalist" is to continue to be a capitalist. Between the coercive laws of competition, scale requirements, and the capitalist's own incentives insofar as he seeks to be influential and "respectable" or in any case behaves "as a personification of capital," the reinvestment option might clearly lay claim to every dollar of accrued surplus value it can command.

But what is it that makes these words into a statement of general Marxian theoretical principle? Surely neither the laws of competition nor a posited invariance to the scale implications of technological change (long since rendered suspect at best), would in themselves support the conclusion that "accumulation for accumulation's sake" is "the rule that governs the behaviour of all capitalists" (Harvey 1982, 29). Accumulation for the sake of continuing to be a capitalist is not quite the same thing, since many other allocations must equally well be made to accomplish that effect. To reach the stronger conclusion Marxian economists have had to shoulder a further burden. They have had to read this passage as if Marx here contends that "the capitalist" does indeed, as a general rule, act "as capital personified." For Marx, in that case, the division of surplus value *is* shaped by an animating spirit or "motivating force": the "absolute drive towards self-enrichment," or the "acquisition and augmentation of exchange-values" — the drive to accumulate — we have already encountered.

We can see how prepared crisis theorists would be to read the passage in this way. The frameworks we considered above labored long and hard to argue that the capitalist class position entails two simple functions, exploiting and expanding, and because the latter is an expression of the innate nature of capitalism, it occurs in an abstractly determinate way. Here would seem to be Marx succinctly expressing precisely this view. Insofar as the capitalist acts as "capital personified," he accumulates as the result of an "absolute drive."

The problem with the interpretation is that the section of *Capital* that contains these passages (section 3 of chapter 24) turns out to be devoted to constructing the capitalist in quite opposite terms. The careful and carefully repeated wording in the quote above — "in so far as he is capital personified," "as capital personified," "as a personification of capital," and so on, is not gratuitous.[29] As Marx is about to contend, sometimes capitalists do *not* act "as capital personified." Indeed, as he soon suggests, the only time they ever did was in industrial capitalism's infancy! As the text continues:

In so far, therefore, as his actions are a mere function of capital — endowed as capital is, in his person, with consciousness and a will — his own private consumption counts as a robbery committed against the accumulation of his capital, just as, in double-entry bookkeeping, the private expenditure of the capitalist is placed on the debit side of his account against his capital. Accumulation is the conquest of the world of social wealth. It is the extension of the area of exploited human material and, at the same time, the extension of the direct and indirect sway of the capitalist.

But original sin is at work everywhere. With the development of the capitalist mode of production, with the growth of accumulation and wealth, the capitalist ceases to be merely the incarnation of capital. He begins to feel a human warmth towards his own Adam, and his education gradually enables him to smile at his former enthusiasm for asceticism, as an old-fashioned miser's prejudice. While the capitalist of the classical type brands individual consumption as a sin against his function, as "abstinence" from accumulating, the modernized capitalist is capable of viewing accumulation as "renunciation" of pleasure. "Two souls, alas, do dwell within his breast; the one is ever parting from the other." (Marx 1976, 739–41; quotation is from Goethe's *Faust*)

Our capitalist, it seems, no longer enjoys the purity afforded one who seeks one goal only. No longer a personification, he is something of a divided subject. Nor is the transition from the "incarnation of capital" to this "modernized capitalist" only a matter of subjectivity. The paragraph that follows traces a series of changes in the capitalist's needs and behaviors as they affect surplus value allocation over time:

At the historical dawn of the capitalist mode of production—and every capitalist upstart has to go through this historical stage individually—avarice, and the drive for self-enrichment, are the passions which are entirely predominant. But the progress of capitalist production not only creates a world of delights; it lays open, in the form of speculation and the credit system, a thousand sources of sudden enrichment. When a certain stage of development has been reached, a conventional degree of prodigality, which is also an exhibition of wealth, and consequently a source of credit, becomes a business necessity to the "unfortunate" capitalist. Luxury enters into capital's expenses of representation. (1976, 741)

This "capitalist"—still a lone individual, and still considered at a high level of abstraction, but now at least "modernized"—is already here a multidestinational allocator of surplus value, for if additional consumption spending is needed in the face of the "world of delights," it is also needed for the business necessities, the "expenses of representation," posed by a world of speculative opportunities and unreliably informed credit sources. Following only accumulation itself, the latter expense is perhaps the first subsumed class payment Marx delineates in the three volumes of *Capital*.[30]

The self-consciously abstract level at which all of part seven of *Capital* is written only adds to the point. Although crisis theorists do not generally stress or even note them, a class-theoretic reading of volume one would heed Marx's own warnings on this score. The "two souls" which dwell in the capitalist's breast are not the whole story, for surplus value is not simply divided between capitalist consumption spending and an accumulation fund. In order to even take up the question of accumulation, and accumulation's possible effects on capitalist production (the sole focus of volume one), Marx has temporarily had to repress all the other claims. He tells us so in introducing part seven as a whole:

The capitalist who produces surplus-value, i.e., who extracts unpaid labour directly from the workers and fixes it in commodities, is admittedly the first appropriator of this surplus-value, but he is by no means its ultimate proprietor. He has to share it afterwards with capitalists who fulfil other functions in social production taken as a whole, with the owner of the land, and with yet other people. Surplus-value is therefore split up into various parts. Its fragments fall to various categories of person, and take on various mutually independent forms, such as profit, interest, gains made through trade, ground rent, etc. We shall be able to deal with these modified forms of surplus-value only in Volume 3.

In addition to abstracting from circulation (or demand) considerations in the discussion of accumulation in volume one, then, as Marx tells us, we here abstract from the complexity of surplus value distribution as a whole. As he puts it in the following paragraph:

We treat the capitalist producer as the owner of the entire surplus-value, or, perhaps better, as the representative of all those who will share the booty with him. We shall therefore begin by considering accumulation from an abstract point of view, i.e. simply as one aspect of the immediate process of production. (Marx 1976, 709–10)

As a result, when considering its determination (though not its effects on production) volume one of *Capital* posits accumulation much like Adam Smith did: as a question of the individual capitalists' temptation to consume and thereby veer from his social duty and socially respectable role as accumulator (Smith 1937, 314–32). Those issues are politically and economically important, and the ways in which theorists have construed them of great interest; Marx jumps into the discussion with delight. As a basis for an understanding of either class *or* accumulation dynamics in contemporary capitalist economies, however, the discussion in volume one will not in itself get one very far. As Marx warned, much remains to be elaborated. From a class-theoretic point of view, at least, the question of just *who* "the capitalist" is, and *how* the capitalist's distribution of surplus value is determined, changes as one moves from volume one to volumes two and three and beyond.

What has happened in all this to "accumulation for accumulation's

sake"? Whatever the level of abstraction, Marx's eleventh commandment appears now at best as but a description of one moment within a
historically changing dynamic. He presents the slogan, after all, only after
depicting the change in contemporary capitalist consumption behaviors
we have just seen, and after a further paragraph in which he repeats and
underlines the point by reviewing in some detail the findings of an empirical work by "Dr. Aikin" published in 1795. The latter divides Manchester manufacturers' consumption spending habits into four historical
periods, finding "great progress" toward "expense and luxury" already
by the last thirty years of the eighteenth century (Marx 1976, 741–42).

On this historical note, and at precisely this point, Marx launches the
ode to former days and a former theory. Quoted more fully it reads differently than the excerpted version one usually encounters:

What would the good Dr Aikin say if he could rise from the grave and see
the Manchester of today?

Accumulate, accumulate! That is Moses and the prophets! "Industry furnishes the material which saving accumulates." Therefore save, save, i.e. reconvert the greatest possible portion of surplus-value or surplus product into
capital! Accumulation for the sake of accumulation, production for the sake
of production: this was the formula in which classical economics expressed
the historical mission of the bourgeoisie in the period of its domination. Not
for one instant did it deceive itself over the nature of wealth's birth-pangs.
But what use is it to lament a historical necessity? If, in the eyes of classical
economics, the proletarian is merely a machine for the production of surplus-
value, the capitalist too is merely a machine for the transformation of this
surplus-value into surplus capital. Classical economics takes the historical
function of the capitalist in grim earnest. In order to conjure away the awful
conflict between the desire for enjoyment and the drive for self-enrichment,
Malthus, around the beginning of the 1820s, advocated a division of labour
which assigned the business of accumulating to the capitalist actually engaged
in production, and the business of spending to the other sharers in surplus-
value, the landed aristocracy, the place-men, the beneficed clergy and so on.
It is of the highest importance, he says, "to keep separate the passion for expenditure and the passion for accumulation." The capitalists, who had long
since turned themselves into good livers and men of the world, complained
loudly at this. (Marx, 1976, 742–43)

The earnest and comical "effort to conjure away the awful conflict be-tween the desire for enjoyment and the drive for self-enrichment" is Mal-thus's in the 1820s. Marx chuckles at it. Why then do these words also conjure up a spirit of twentieth-century Marxian accumulation theory? I suggest that crisis theorists have not been able to share in Marx's laugh-ter at classical theory's dilemmas because their own approach parallels classical theory's too closely. They are unable to see Marx's own analy-sis of the accumulation/consumption decision as qualitatively different from Adam Smith's humanist reasoning, wherein accumulation was as-sured predominance over consumption because man's desire for better-ment ultimately ensures that result (Smith 1937, 325–6; cf. Norton 1995). For them, Marx simply shifts accumulation's abstractly fixed determi-nants from human to systemic nature; the urge to accumulate remains. Thus they have no use for the divided subject Marx announces: " 'Two souls, alas, do dwell within his breast; the one is ever parting from the other.' " No thanks! Like Smith's or Ricardo's, the crisis theorists' capi-talist is always and necessarily "capital personified" in the sense Marx delineates here. Crisis theorists *also* conjure away "awful" conflicts in the capitalist's surplus-value distribution decision. Unlike Marx's, their capitalists are univocal; they feel no conflict or contradiction when it comes to the subsumed class process (or the distribution of surplus value). They simply seek to accumulate.[31]

Holding fast to the very views Marx mocks, crisis theorists have been understandably unable to include the references to classical theory in these pages. If Marx laughs at classical theory's struggles (as well as expressing respect, perhaps, for the seriousness with which they saw accumulation as the early industrial capitalists' necessary historical role), how can that laughter be understood? Crisis theorists have dealt with the problem simply by deleting from their quotations the paragraphs that precede "Accumulate, accumulate!" and the sentences that immedi-ately follow "Accumulation for the sake of accumulation; production for the sake of production." Indeed, they have had to delete portions of the very sentences that they have presented as embodying the basic in-sights of Marxian economic analysis. The quotation immediately follow-ing "Accumulate, accumulate!" —from Adam Smith—is not generally noted. The phrase "this was the formula in which classical economics expressed the historical mission of the bourgeoisie in the period of its domination" is nearly always eliminated, leaving the first half of the sentence ("Accumulation for the sake of accumulation, production for the sake of production") looking quite misleadingly like Marx's own view.[32] Needless to say, the entire latter half of the passage quoted above figures not at all.

The history of Marxian economists' interpretations and invocations of these passages is a dramatic one. Crisis theorists of a variety of traditions have had a use in mind for these pages, and they have not let analytical detail or textual awkwardness—or even Marx's laughter—get in the way. That Marx might have been trying to describe historical change, rather than foundational constancy, in the capitalist's distributions of surplus value, has not been a possibility they have read here. That Marx was not simply embracing classical theory's understanding of the capitalist's behavior they also could not see. Had they been able to see and read these things, the closure they have sought to establish in volume one would not be establishable, the firm they have found in volume one would not be there, and the purposes and protocols of Marxian economic theory might have become the object of a far richer debate—a debate in which the class-theoretic possibilities Marx's work inspires might eventually indeed be freed from the teleological conceptual commitments that have thus far so largely entangled them.

Notes

1 Cullenberg (1994, chap. 2) provides a powerful analysis of teleological thought and the "Hegelian totality" in Marxian economic thought, starting from this passage in Marx.

2 Paul Baran and Paul Sweezy, leading monopoly capital authors, are perhaps less visibly associated with the forces/relations framework than falling rate of profit theorists since they don't utilize the terms explicitly until near the end of *Monopoly Capital*. In its final chapter, the book does frame its argument in terms of a contradiction between the forces and relations of production, which Baran and Sweezy also put more particularly as "the ever sharpening conflict between the rapidly advancing rationalization of the actual processes of production and the undiminished *elementality* of the system as a whole" (1966, 338; cf. 341; emphasis in original).

3 For provocative discussions of this relationship see for example Ruccio (1992), Callari and Ruccio (1996), Diskin (1996).

4 Compare Ernest Mandel's statement in his introduction to the Vintage edition of volume one of *Capital:* "In *Capital* Marx's fundamental aim was to lay bare the laws of motion which govern the origins, the rise, the development, the decline and the disappearance of a given social form of economic organization: the capitalist mode of production" (Marx 1977, 12).

5 Grossman adds to Luxemburg's words his own vividly economic determinist criticism of her opponent, Otto Bauer:

> From (Bauer's) position it followed that capitalism would be destroyed not through any objective limits on the growth of accumulation but by the political struggle of the working class. The masses would be drawn to socialism only through painstaking, day-to-day educational work. Socialism can only be the product of their conscious will.
>
> Tugan-Baranovsky showed some time back that a conception of this sort means giving up the materialist conception of history. . . . He pointed out that if we hope for the downfall of capitalism purely in terms of the political struggle of the masses trained in socialism, then "the centre of gravity of the entire argument is shifted from economics to consciousness." (Grossman 1992, 70–71)

6 In Engels's thinking the bourgeoisie actually represents both old and new. The capitalists' actions represent both sides of the contradiction: they seek to hold on to private appropriation but, by their moves to control competition and stabilize markets, promote increasingly socialized institutions. See Diskin (1996, 290–91).

7 Hilferding (1981, originally published in 1910), is no exception, insofar as he treated finance capital as a class-unifying force, "the highest stage of the concentration of economic and political power in the hands of the capitalist oligarchy" (1981, 360; quoted in Howard and King 1989, 99).

8 Admittedly, Kautsky's 1899 emphasis on the centrality of noncrisis forces in the making of socialism should be seen as in good part a temporary tactical move. In *The Class Struggle* (1892) he had written that "irresistible economic forces lead with the certainty of doom to the shipwreck of capitalist production" (quoted in Howard and King 1989, 71). In 1901–2 he returned to an aggressive crisis theory stance, berating revisionism on grounds that "the conception of a melioration of class antagonisms is incompatible with our theory of crises. If the latter is correct the capitalist mode of production is headed for a period of continuous depression" (quoted in Sweezy 1942, 199).

9 The precise requirement is that only two classes matter in determining capitalism's inner workings or basic tendencies. As Sweezy put it in 1942, after

establishing the tendency toward underconsumption and before introducing "third persons" with claims on surplus value for purposes of more concrete analysis: "The basic structure of capitalist society presupposes only
two classes: capitalists and workers. Since all others are in principle dis-
pensable, we have so far abstracted from them in our analysis of value and
accumulation" (226–27).

10 Kautsky, *The Class Struggle*, 1892, summarized in Howard and King 1989,
70.

11 The argument is deductive and it starts from concepts of the inner nature
of the capitalist: capitalists don't spend sufficiently on consumption goods
because their nature as capitalists requires them to direct their surplus value
first of all to accumulation. In Sweezy's words:

Now the basic fact of capitalism, on which the behavior of the system ultimately
depends, is the drive of capitalists to get rich. Satisfying this desire requires two
steps: (1) making as much profit as possible, and (2) accumulating as large a part
of it as possible. The first involves steadily improving the methods of production, chiefly by using more and more machines and materials per workers; the
second involves accumulating larger and larger proportions of a growing profit
total. Translating this into the terminology of the previous paragraph we get
the following: that accumulation rises as a proportion of surplus value and that
investment rises as a proportion of accumulation. All the while consumption
is rising because capitalists increase their own consumption and lay out a part
of their accumulation in increased wages. But, and this is the significant point,
since the increment of capitalists' consumption is a diminishing proportion of
total surplus value, and since the increment of wages is a diminishing proportion of total accumulation, it follows that the rate of growth of consumption (i.e.
the ratio of increment of consumption to total consumption) declines relative to
the rate of growth of means of production (i.e. the ratio of investment to total
means of production). In other words, the *ratio of the rate of growth of consumption to the rate of growth of means of production declines.* This is a result
which flows logically from the characteristic pattern of capitalists' behavior.
(1942, 181–82; emphasis in original)

12 Underconsumptionists like Baran and Sweezy bring other cuts of surplus
value back into the analysis—indeed to a prominent if entirely circum-
scribed position as "countertendencies"—but only after they have already
established the basic system's inner tendency toward demand shortfall and
stagnation.

13 In David Yaffe's rendition: "The concept of capital is a contradictory one.

On the one side we have capital as 'value in process,' as value attempting to expand itself without limit, and on the other side we have the working population, the limited basis of that expansion" (1973, 195).

14 Cf. Fine and Harris (1979): "the determining contradiction in capitalism is the antagonism of the two great classes" (36). Or: "It is the struggle of capital-in-general with labour-in-general which is at the root of capitalism's reproduction and the limits to it" (ibid.).

15 The classic treatment is Grossman (1992, 149–54). Much like Sweezy (see n. 10 above), Grossman writes that "this group of third persons which was initially excluded from the analysis of pure capitalism has to be reintroduced at a later stage" (153). When Grossman "reintroduces" them he concludes that "because the services of third persons are of a non-material character, they contribute nothing to the accumulation of capital. However their consumption reduces the accumulation fund. . . . If the number of these third persons were cut down, the breakdown of capitalism could be postponed. But there are several limits to any such process, in the sense that it would entail a cut in the standard of living of the wealthier classes." At a well-known point in the *Grundrisse* Marx also positions such things as ground rent and taxes as costs whose reduction might stave off falling profit tendencies. See Rosdolsky (1977, 379–80), Marx (1973, 751).

16 Falling rate of profit theorists therefore tend to meld the search for surplus value and the reinvestment of surplus value into one seamless whole, from which vantage point a complex class analysis is difficult to envision. As Paul Mattick put it, "The increase of productivity, of surplus-value, and of the accumulation of capital are all one and the same process. They all imply that capital invested in the means of production grows faster than that invested in labor power" (1969, 58). From another angle: "The tendency of the rate of profit to fall is a theoretical conclusion derived by applying the labor theory of value to the capital formation process" (ibid., 63). See also Norton (1992, 157–62).

17 Leaving aside the question of Marx, Shaikh's placement of monopoly capital/stagnation theory in the possibility camp is ironic. Sweezy's views on necessity we just saw. Josef Steindl (1976), the work in the tradition which most influenced Marxian economists, set out to build a conception of capitalist history founded precisely on the principle that capitalist growth is a self-determining process whose most important dimensions follow a necessary trajectory. For examples see Steindl (1976, 191).

18 Thus while workers represent the social, in the end it is also capital that actively foments growing sociality through efforts to control competition, use of the state, and so on. See Diskin (1996, 290–91).

19 In this vein DeMartino (1993) probes Marxian conceptions of necessity as they shape long-wave theories.

20 We might briefly note in all this the passing of the worker as creator. The positive agency classical Marxism ascribed to workers, as fomentors of an antagonism that would only grow in depth and shift in balance as time passed, smashing through one system by creating the basis for another, is no longer central to Marxian economists' arguments. Capitalism still dies, but now from distress and dysfunction more or less entirely produced by the capitalists' own behavior, not from its gestation of a new kind of worker. While falling rate of profit theorists (most notably Ernest Mandel) hold on to strong conceptions of workers as opposers of capitalist logic, the more positive dimension the older framework had turned on is largely lost (most dramatically in Baran and Sweezy's *Monopoly Capital*).

21 Criticizing this theoretical project is the focus of Norton (1995).

22 Reinvestment of surplus value takes place in the realm of circulation; capitalists purchase commodities for use in further production processes. See Marx (1976, 709; 725).

23 Baran and Sweezy may seem to be an exception insofar as they do position various kinds of "unproductive" cuts of surplus value as important parts of the postwar U.S. economy. They don't, however, see these flows as class issues; they see them as signs that the forces of production can no longer expand once the accumulation process has undermined the social relations of production by creating oligopoly (so that surplus value that should go to accumulation flows instead to "wasteful"—i.e., nonaccumulation— outlets). In short, in an argument that first appears in Sweezy (1942, 274– 86), they position them as a *memento mori* for the capitalist system. Thus Baran and Sweezy perform what from a class-theoretic point of view is a remarkable inversion. Having suggested that Marx doesn't treat the various nonaccumulation cuts of surplus value as systematically as he should have (he "treated these as secondary factors and excluded them from his basic theoretical schema" [1966, n. 10]), they present their work as rectifying that failure. They approach the task however by conceiving the cuts of surplus value in question as *expressions* of an already existing contradiction—that between the relations of production and the forces of production they construct using an analysis that conceives of only the two class positions theorized in volume one, capitalist and worker! The effect is to position concepts of class as thoroughly instrumental players in a drama that is really about an unfolding totality conceived in class terms that are at best bipolar. Nor do Baran and Sweezy hesitate to take the final step, concluding that in the world of monopoly capitalism even productive workers are so

much in the minority, so undermined by the wasteful and irrational system, and so bought off by capitalism's charms that they no longer merit attention as potential agents of constructive change (ibid., 363). Here the movement by which concepts of a self-destructive totality override class reaches bitter fruition.

24 See Graham (1992) and Ruccio (1989) for criticism of the "accumulation-ism" retained by these frameworks.

25 Bowles, Gordon, and Weisskopf's version of social structures of accumulation theory is so committed to this foundation that they speak of periods of more or less rapid "accumulation" purely on the basis of higher or lower average rates of profit. Investment spending, they argue, simply tracks profit rates, so that as profit goes "accumulation" goes as well (Bowles, Gordon, and Weisskopf 1986). The assumption that investment spending simply tracks profit rates is common to many theorists in the "wage squeeze" crisis theory tradition that developed from the late 1970s on. See Bhaskar and Glyn (1995) for empirical investigation (and mild criticism) of the assumption. Their study concludes in part that "our results do not show that enhanced profitability is always a necessary, let alone a sufficient condition for increased investment" (p. 192).

26 For pathbreaking work both on this and the more general issue of the "centeredness" of the firm, see Resnick and Wolff (1987, chap. 4), Amariglio and Ruccio (1994), Cullenberg (1994, chap. 4), and Gibson-Graham (1996, esp. chap. 8). The latter provides a stimulating and radical rethinking of the firm as a site of surplus value distribution as well as a review of recent work related to the firm's decentering.

27 Some of these usages are also analyzed in an earlier working paper (Norton 1994) that the present summary draws on.

28 Notably, the latter three all leave out the first sentence, and the following "as such," beginning their quotes with the more general statement, "The capitalist 'shares with the miser'."

29 Resnick and Wolff place great stress on the importance of understanding and/or interpreting Marx's shorthand use of "personification" of class positions (1987, 110, 161–63). The current example is a case in point.

30 For a theory of accumulation as a subsumed class payment, see Resnick and Wolff (1987, 184–91; cf. 129).

31 David Harvey's interpretation of this passage is an example. After surveying Marx's discussion of the " 'Faustian conflict between the passion for accumulation and the desire for enjoyment,' " Harvey unilaterally resolves the tension Marx himself reveled in, simply declaring, with classical theory,

that "the passion for accumulation drives out the desire for enjoyment" (Harvey 1982, 28).

Sweezy (1942) is less dismissive. He surveys both what he sees as Marx's delineation of the drive to accumulate and the capitalists' growing need to consume in these pages, and concludes that "while the drive to accumulate remains primary, it does not exclude a parallel, and even in part derivative, desire to expand consumption" (1942, 81). Sweezy is not afraid to embrace the latter; under no circumstances will he conceive that it threatens the integrity of the former, however.

32 David Gordon (1978), for example, motivates his outline of social structures of accumulation theory by quoting *Capital* as follows:

In capitalist economies, as Marx noted in a famous passage, the capitalist ". . . shares with the miser the passion for wealth as wealth."

But that which in the miser is a mere idiosyncrasy, is, in the capitalist, the effect of the social mechanism, of which he is but one of the wheels . . . It compels him to keep constantly extending his capital, in order to preserve it, but extend it he cannot, except by means of progressive accumulation. Accumulate, accumulate! That is Moses and the prophets! Accumulation for accumulation's sake, production for production's sake . . . (Gordon 1978, 27; ellipses in original).

This passage joins *without* ellipses three sentences from the passage on page 739 with three sentences from page 742, with all intervening context, satire, and reference to classical theory, historical periods, and capitalists acting "as capitalists" omitted. A wide variety of crisis theorists quote these passages similarly. Baran and Sweezy are a partial exception. The latter *do* note that Marx himself originally used the "accumulate, accumulate!" passage to describe "the historical dawn of capitalist production" (1966, 42–44). They do not, however, admit that it was classical theory's description, not Marx's, and that Marx laughs loudly at the notion that this phrase adequately describes contemporary capitalist consumption behavior.

J.K. GIBSON-GRAHAM

AND PHILLIP O'NEILL

□

EXPLORING A NEW CLASS POLITICS

OF THE ENTERPRISE[1]

In this essay, we attempt to produce a decentered and desolidified representation of the enterprise, one that does not accord with any particular logic or story line. We see this disrupted and disruptive representation as opening up political options that are invisible in the vicinity of a coherent and ultimately predictable firm. The goal is to create an imaginative space within which a different and expanded (class) politics of the enterprise might emerge, and especially to enable new claims on the social wealth that flows through the corporation.[2]

Using the class-analytic insights developed by Resnick and Wolff (1987), particularly their analysis of the enterprise as a site of distributive flows (164–230), we focus on displacing what we have called the "monopoly capitalist" representation of the firm. In this popular left representation, the quintessential capitalist enterprise is a giant manufacturing concern with power in factor and product markets and driven by the imperative of capital accumulation (Norton 1995). The firm's principal distributions of surplus value are to capitalist consumption and, more important, the accumulation of productive capital. Given the inevitable necessity of the latter, any politics of distribution focused on the firm (whether initiated by the workers, the state, or other agents) must encounter a prior and necessary claim on surplus value. This claim tends to displace competing claims and, with them, the possibility of imagining alternative distributions.

Our discussion centers on the recent experience of the steel division of Broken Hill Proprietary (BHP), Australia's largest industrial corporation. An expansion-oriented multidivisional and multinational firm, BHP is readily understandable as a "monopoly capitalist" enterprise enacting the imperative of capital accumulation on a global scale. Class politics at BHP follow the contours of a familiar story, complete with standard characters and plot: well-compensated unionized male steelworkers (labor aristocrats or primary segment workers, depending on your perspective) achieve high wages and good working conditions through controlling access to employment, and fall on hard times when the enterprise begins to pursue more profitable investments in other industries and locations.

Our goal is to undermine this quite coherent and predictable representation by decentering the story of the firm from capital accumulation and simultaneously decentering the vision of enterprise and class politics from the capital–labor relation. Each of these moves opens up an array of alternative political possibilities, but at the moment those possibilities are hidden in the penumbra of the unthought and untried. To bring one example to light, we briefly explore a recent successful environmental and community claim against BHP, noting the way that the struggle has involved changes in identity and practice for the corporation. What was inimical to BHP—apparently counter to its nature and well-being—has become incorporated as part of its official identity and program. And what began as a "nonclass" struggle over environmental degradation and community livelihoods has become retrospectively intelligible as a "class" struggle over surplus distributions. This example evokes what has been called the "politics of becoming" (Connolly 1997), in which identity is produced and transformed by the political struggle itself.

The field of political possibility seems very wide (if uncharted and full of pitfalls) when enterprise politics is not subordinated to a central dynamic such as capital accumulation or enterprise reproduction; the field of class politics can be very inclusive if it is not entirely given over to a focus on relations of exploitation. In this era of large capitalist enterprises, we are interested in multiplying the constituencies and publics that feel entitled to interact with corporate practices, and that desire to establish their rights and legitimate their claims to a share of the social wealth that flows through the enterprise.

BHP: Exemplar of the Monopoly Capitalist Enterprise

Broken Hill Proprietary Limited (BHP) has assets of about U.S. $20 billion and is Australia's largest and, arguably, most internationalized corporation, with operations and offices in 59 countries employing more than 65,000 people. BHP commenced operations in 1885 as a silver, lead, and zinc producer and exporter at the famous Broken Hill mine in the desert regions of western New South Wales. Using profits generated from this lode, the company switched to the mining of iron ore and coal and the production of iron and steel during World War I. By 1935 BHP had become a monopoly steel producer in Australia, the world's most protected economy, with integrated steelworks located at Newcastle to the north of Sydney and Port Kembla to the south. In the period between 1950 and 1970 the corporation diversified into iron ore and manganese mining for export, oil production, and investment in offshore steel fabrication. And in the period from 1970 to the present the company has become a truly global minerals and energy conglomerate through the acquisition of corporations such as the U.S. Utah International Inc. (1984) (which included the enormous Escondida copper deposit in Chile), the U.S. Energy Reserves Group (1985), the international oil conglomerate Pacific Resources Inc. (1989), Hamilton Oil Corporation (1991), and Magma Copper Inc. (1995). In 1997, BHP was divided into four main international business groups: BHP Copper, BHP Minerals, BHP Petroleum, and BHP Steel. That year BHP ranked 266th on the *Fortune* Global 500 list of the world's largest industrial companies, and in 1996 it managed an annual cash flow of over U.S. $15 billion, 40 percent of which was generated outside Australia.

Not surprisingly, the historical narrative of BHP's growth and geographical spread has played an active role in stories about Australia's economic development. Just as the Newcastle steelworks built in 1915 by BHP was often referred to by BHP managers as the "mother plant" because of its dual role as the reliable supplier of feedstock for a national network of rolling mills and as the nursery for future company technicians and managers, so BHP appears in economic histories as the strong "parent" to a national economy based on the large-scale extraction and processing of raw materials.

Viewed from the left "the Company" [3] is often positioned as the master subject of a story that displays many of the elements of the "monopoly capitalism" tale: domestic market dominance achieved via protection and other forms of state collusion, use of a segmented workforce that enhanced the potential for labor exploitation, environmental devastation in both the extractive and the manufacturing operations, and the destruction of indigenous cultures. According to the narrative conventions of this story, these elements are positioned and interrelated by a singular driving purpose: that of capital accumulation (Norton 1995).

The accumulative capabilities of BHP have long been accorded grudging respect, especially, of course, by those who possess what have been seen as "gilt-edged" shares in the corporation. But even on the left, where one encounters a more critical attitude to the "Big Australian," an unwillingness to question the accumulative growth imperative of the company amounts to a form of respect for its "elementary logic" (Norton 1995, 743). Hence, in the political economic (left-oriented) literature on Australia's restructuring during the 1970s and 1980s, BHP is portrayed as a continually evolving structure that in each incarnation reproduced the core exploitative class relation between capital and labor under reshaped conditions of competition, emerging from each restructuring process newly equipped to engage in successful capital accumulation (Donaldson 1981; Donaldson and Donaldson 1983; Fagan 1984, 1986; Larcombe 1983).

Despite its potential for crisis, the dynamic of capital accumulation is ultimately a teleology (of expanded reproduction) for the monopoly firm. In a sense, then, the distributive story of the enterprise is already told: Surplus value is appropriated and distributed principally to investments in productive capital. The opportunities we are interested in considering in this chapter are those that might attach to a conception of the enterprise that is more complex, contingent, and open. If the field of surplus distribution were not simply ceded to investments in capital accumulation, what alternative distributions might become imaginable and susceptible to enactment?

A Restructuring Story

In 1981 Robert Chenery was appointed assistant general manager of BHP's Newcastle steelworks, under General Manager Jack Risby. Chenery had joined the company in 1962 as a trainee metallurgist in Port Kembla and had risen quickly through the ranks into management with a reputation as an ambitious, project-oriented achiever. In December 1995 Katherine Gibson and Phillip O'Neill interviewed Risby at his home and Chenery at the University of Newcastle. This story is drawn from the interviews.

When Risby took over management of the Newcastle steelworks in 1980 he took over a dodgy concern. The profitability of Australian steelmaking was declining rapidly — production technologies had been allowed to stagnate; returns to organized labor were very high by world standards; and downstream demand in the protected Australian economy had markedly declined.

Soon after Risby and Chenery came to Newcastle, a reorganized approach to financial and organizational management led the BHP Treasury to dictate that the steel manufacturing division had to be rationalized. Treasury suggested a switching of investment funds from domestic steel plants to sites offshore, consolidation of steel production at the Port Kembla plant, and the overall redirection of funds to non–steel-producing divisions of the corporation. In 1982 it was signaled that as part of this strategic plan the Newcastle steelworks was to close down.

Chenery had been at Newcastle steelworks for three months when closure was threatened. Having just moved into a challenging job and not relishing this derailment of his career, he reacted to the mandate from Treasury by stepping up efforts to restore the plant to profitability. Together with a young cost analyst he devised a plan to cut the workforce by 50 percent, though neither of them had any idea whether it was technically feasible to run the plant under those conditions. Over the objections of Risby, who wanted more modest layoffs, he pushed ahead with his restructuring plan.

Within a relatively short period of time, the Newcastle steelworks was operating in the black. Chenery was exultant:

Melbourne, at that stage, had to change their minds and say "Well, we'd better not close Newcastle after all, I mean this thing's profitable!" Now the net result of all that was we saved it! Suddenly they are approving a blast furnace reline and I think it was about a $26 million development which actually modernised one of our little blast furnaces.

BHP Treasury in Melbourne was temporarily convinced of the viability of the Newcastle plant and the unions and community met the news with relief, despite the loss of over 5,000 jobs.

Chenery and Risby had effectively participated in a class compromise with the steelworkers to "keep the jobs" — for some of the local men, at least.[4] When the Australian Labor Party came to power federally in 1983 under the leadership of the ex-president of the Australian Council of Trade Unions, Bob Hawke, this sort of class compromise was written into the National Steel Industry Plan, a tripartite agreement between BHP, the unions, and the federal government. The plan enabled BHP to restructure its steel operations by reinvesting in new steelmaking technologies at the Port Kembla plant; undertaking monopoly-protected investments in new, smaller-scale mills in greenfield sites; and reorganizing labor relations at its other steel sites, including Newcastle and Whyalla (O'Neill 1997).[5]

Viewed through the lens of class politics, this story has a familiar ring. When times are good the principal goal of unions and workers is to maintain jobs and improve conditions of employment (with an emphasis on compensation). When times are hard, as they were in this case, attention shifts to conditions of retrenchment and the concessions that will be wrested from the workers who remain. In either case, the focus of political struggle and intervention is on the capital–labor relation and the conditions under which capitalist employment/exploitation will be sustained.

The story of the thwarted closure of the Newcastle steelworks is a narrative of reproduction, coauthored and jointly enacted by steel industry managers, unionists, and representatives of the interventionist state. Each actor's role is clearly scripted within the reproductive agenda that has increasingly constrained and confined class politics (and especially union politics) during the twentieth century, placing the value of reproducing the steel industry, and the position of productive laborers within it, almost above and beyond question. As we can see from this and many similar examples, class politics embodies its own teleology of reproduction, one that is encoded in the master script that shapes the contested course of political struggle.

Class and the Enterprise: An Alternative Conceptualization

In the popular monopoly capitalist representation of the enterprise, the contours of class interest and antagonism are starkly apparent. While this story centers the corporation itself on profit maximization and capital accumulation, these processes are enabled only by the exploitation of workers and the extraction of surplus value from which accumulation proceeds. At the core of the capitalist enterprise, then, is seen to be an exploitative class relation, and at the core of class politics—understood in these terms—are struggles over the existence and extent of exploitation. These struggles are shadowed by the understanding that the survival of the enterprise is predicated on capital accumulation, so that interruption or reduction of that process will ultimately be deleterious to worker interests (largely defined as continued employment).

But the vision of the enterprise as a coherent and rational entity, governed by a central imperative of expansion and self-actualization, is difficult to sustain in the face of stories like that of BHP's steel restructuring experience. Chenery's successful efforts to keep the Newcastle plant open in defiance of head office intentions testify to the existence and effectivity of competing agendas within the corporation, and to the remarkable power of minority voices to prevail over the concerted and ostensibly dominant voice of the head office. As Chenery himself acknowledged, his heroic role in saving the plant flew in the face of corporate rationality, suggesting that no central logic governed the movements of BHP:

Melbourne were going to close it. And it would be better for BHP to have less steelworks. No doubt about it. Why have two?

Emerging from this story, and from Chenery's account of his continuing conflicts with top managers in Melbourne, is a portrait of the firm as a fluid and contested site of personal agendas, whims, ambitions, rivalries, conflicts, and compromises that often set the direction of the entire corporation. This story offers a complicated vision of competing and contradictory corporate orientations and goals—Chenery, for example, was a domestically based, production-oriented steel man who expressed horror and amusement at some of BHP's hugely unsuccessful speculative investments in minerals and oil overseas—and it allows us to glimpse a variety of irrationalities, contingencies, failed or aborted initiatives, reversals of direction, and incommensurable knowledges (and ignorances) at the enterprise level. One might safely say, on the basis of our conversations with Risby and Chenery, that BHP manifests a marked inability to constitute itself as the rational calculating subject of popular enterprise lore.[6]

It seems that, like others, we are beginning to discern on the horizon of enterprise discourse the surfacing of another vision of the firm—as an entity that is not so unitary, intentional, or given to self-actualization.[7] But unlike the representation of the enterprise, the understanding of class politics—and the range of actions and alliances it enables—is still relatively narrow and closed. We are therefore interested in using Resnick and Wolff's antiessentialist class analysis to open up possibilities for an elaborated and diverse (class) politics around and within the corporation.

At the most basic level of their analysis, Resnick and Wolff proliferate the possibilities for enterprise-oriented class politics by defining class as a process with two moments: (1) an exploitative moment in which surplus labor is produced by and appropriated from productive laborers; and (2) a distributive moment in which appropriated surplus labor is distributed to a wide variety of social destinations. Each of these moments incorporates a number of class positions: those of the producers and appropriators (or first receivers) in the exploitative moment, and those of the distributor and the receivers of surplus labor in the distributive moment. Class politics—the politics centered on or affecting class processes—may be focused on distributions of appropriated surplus labor as well as on the form and extent of its appropriation, and it may involve a wide range of class subjects (including individuals or collectivities inhabiting the distributive class positions), not simply laborers and appropriators. This vision effectively decenters the conception of capitalist class politics from the capital–labor relation, opening up the possibility of a range of possible class-related interventions in the vicinity of the enterprise.

A second aspect of Resnick and Wolff's approach that is useful to us is related to the first: their vision of the enterprise as an overdetermined site of distribution/dispersion as well as appropriation/condensation. In the context of this vision, not only is the entirety of appropriated wealth distributed to a variety of destinations both within and without the firm, but no one destination has preordained priority over the others. This places capital accumulation in a new light. While distributions of surplus intended to increase productive capital may be the highest priority for a particular firm at a particular moment, their priority cannot be presumed.

Finally, Resnick and Wolff's representation of the enterprise includes a third aspect that effectively decenters the enterprise from class (though their terminology affirms the centrality of class to their larger analytical project). Their accounting of flows through the enterprise traces both class and nonclass flows. The latter include all those revenues and expenditures that arise from nonclass relationships and transactions: buying and selling property, for example, or receiving government subsidies. The specification of nonclass flows suggests that there will be a range of nonclass subject positions (inhabited by individuals and collectivities that are related to the firm via participation in nonclass transactions and other forms of nonclass interaction) in the vicinity of the corporation. In our discussion of enterprise politics, we would hope to broaden the scope of possibility by considering the role of these nonclass subject positions and their potential affiliation to class struggles and outcomes in the environment of the firm.

Accounting for Class

Any enterprise accounting attempts to represent a fluid and ever-changing entity in terms of static categories that are ultimately arbitrarily applied. In constructing the normal company accounts required by tax offices, shareholders, and stock exchanges the myriad of different transactions, stocks, and flows that constitute a company are arranged into an established accounting order that has evolved its structure over centuries of business practice (Hopwood and Miller 1994; Poovey 1998). An antiessentialist class analysis of the enterprise introduces a new way of arranging these flows into an account that highlights class and nonclass payments. Just as with "established" corporate accounts, the categories we employ are discursive artifacts that attempt to impose an order on somewhat chaotic and hard-to-define transactions.

The rationale for producing an alternative accounting framework is that it suggests many more opportunities for intervention and distributional struggles than those specified by the monopoly capital story and other centered representations. Analytically, our attention is directed to the multiple transactions and flows that constitute the class and nonclass payments taking place within an enterprise and between the enterprise and its larger social context. This encourages us to recognize a number of class and nonclass economic subjects that are rendered invisible within a simple monopoly capital conception of enterprise and class politics.

The first step in using an antiessentialist analysis of the enterprise is to recognize and distinguish between the different forms of revenue and expenditure that flow through an industrial capitalist enterprise such as BHP. The following expression is one representation of these flows. On the left-hand side are all the inflows and on the right-hand side are all the outflows:

$$SV + DCR + NCR = \sum DCP + \sum X + \sum Y$$

In this expression *SV* represents the surplus value appropriated by the board of directors of the enterprise from the productive workforce in the capitalist exploitative class process. In the case of BHP this would include surplus value extracted from productive steelworkers, coal miners, metalliferous miners, oil riggers, metal fabricators, geologists, metallurgists, surveyors, and others. Here *DCR* stands for distributive class revenues flowing into BHP as distributions of surplus value from other firms. It (*DCR*) would include monopoly rents from domestic industrial consumers of BHP products bought at protected prices, dividends paid to BHP from equity investments such as those in Fosters Brewing, franchise payments from companies that utilize BHP brand names including Supracote and Colorbond, and so on. All the nonclass revenues earned by the enterprise are represented by *NCR*. In BHP's case these revenues are comprised of a host of flows, including dividends received from stock held in non–commodity-producing enterprises, value harvested from short-term investments in financial markets and through buying and selling businesses, transfer payments from the state via industry plans, windfall gains from redevelopment of industrial and mining lands for real estate projects, and the sale of monopolized commodities (at prices exceeding values) to end-use consumers.

On the other side of the expression, $\sum DCP$ refers to all the distributive class payments that enable the production process (and the production of sv) to proceed. In the case of BHP these payments include interest payments to banks and financial institutions; payments to advertisers and public relations officers; payments of wage premiums to selected workers; wages paid to those employees not involved in productive labor, such as typists, clerks, and accountants; executive packages to managers; taxes to the state and federal governments; rent and royalty payments where applicable for access to land and resources; and so on. In the history of BHP many of the payments that conventionally would have flowed to the Australian government (especially royalty, rent, and tax payments) have been minimized "in the national interest." One example was the accelerated depreciation allowances available to BHP under the National Steel Industry Plan for new investments in steel plant and equipment. $\sum x$ refers to all the payments that are made to other capitalists to enable the derivation of the DCR flows, and $\sum y$ represents all the payments made to enable the generation of NCR flows. In the case of BHP these payments would include: the cost of debt used to finance the holding company structures set up to stave off a hostile takeover bid in the mid-1980s; policing the use of brand names by other businesses; the costs involved in maintaining monopoly access to resources in other countries (e.g., payments to the state and state officials) and to domestic consumers of iron and steel products (e.g., lobbying costs); payments made during the 1990s to protect the company's portfolio involving ongoing asset purchases; and the maintenance of sustainable debt-to-equity ratios and appropriate cash-flow management. Clearly, it would be difficult to actually distinguish $\sum x$ and $\sum y$ within an enterprise.

This method of accounting alerts us, first of all, to the contingent role that the exploitative capitalist class process plays in enterprise performance, highlighting the fact that for many enterprises surplus value extracted from the productive work force is but one of a multitude of income-generating processes. This serves to deflate the confident corporate representation of labor as the source of all (financial and other) troubles. It also suggests the narrowness of focusing (class) interventions only on the capital–labor relation and the generation of surplus value.[8]

Second, the analysis foregrounds the distributive class payments made by the enterprise as well as the many other payments that circulate within and outside it. The enterprise thus becomes visible as a dissipative body, no more bent on collection/consolidation than on distribution/dispersion (Gibson-Graham 1996, chap. 8). Our point is that all of these transactions and flows can be the object of an invigorated (class) politics of distribution.

Third, the disaggregation of payments into these three categories of flow makes it clear that distributions intended to expand productive capital (i.e., for capital accumulation) are but one among many payments made by the corporation. For purposes of revenue generation, portfolio or real estate investment may be a much more successful strategy than direct investment in productive capital. In addition, payments to lawyers, court settlements, writeoffs of bad investments, advertising and public relations, rent and royalty payments, and so on loom large on the right-hand side of the equation. Clearly corporate expenditures are not solely or even primarily directed toward capital accumulation. This suggests that new distributive claims could be inserted among this welter of claims without defying the "logic" of the corporation.

Fourth, the examination of nonclass revenues and payments implies the existence of a wide range of potential constituencies or "publics" who could be seen as having legitimate distributive or other claims on the corporation. When the government of Papua New Guinea (PNG) grants sole access to resources via a long-term mining lease, and the corporation obtains monopoly rents as a result, the PNG population (through its representatives) is effectively guaranteeing nonclass revenues for the corporation. The people of Australia are similarly implicated in the government's provision of monopoly access to domestic markets for BHP steel. Each of these national populations is thus a stakeholder in BHP and could potentially be mobilized as a constituency with a distributive claim. The accounting of nonclass as well as class flows allows us to identify some of the nonclass constituencies who might come to see themselves (and come to be perceived) as having a legitimate claim on enterprise distributions.

Finally, the accounting framework allows us to sketch the contours of a multidimensional field of interaction whose outcome at any one point in time is the enterprise. Conceived as a nexus of flows whose patterns and direction are constantly changing, the firm becomes difficult to visualize as a unified subject or as a solid and self-reproducing structure. Lacking a stable identity/form, its ability to be cast in a standard and predictable narrative is undermined (O'Neill and Gibson-Graham 1999). Moreover the simultaneity of the accounting framework conspires against the temporality and teleology of traditional enterprise stories. In relaxing the narrative imperatives for a single directionality of change, for an ordered sequence of causes and effects, for a central and linear story, the enterprise accounting widens the field of eventuation and intervention.

Class Politics as It Was and Could Be

At the time that closure was threatened in 1982 the Newcastle steelworkers were successfully negotiating another pay increase. As members of the Federated Ironworkers of Australia, these steelworkers had long enjoyed a relatively powerful bargaining position with respect to management that had enabled them to win high award wages and overaward payments. This bargaining position was shored up by barriers to entry into the steel labor market and by the availability of economic rents produced within the steel sector by monopoly market conditions.[9] From a class-analytic perspective, these conditions helped the union win a wage that reflected not only a payment in exchange for productive labor power (w^1) but also a payment to ensure access to labor (w^2), which was a distributed payment out of capital's appropriated surplus fund (Resnick and Wolff 1987, 151–4). It is one of the charters of strong unions that can exert control over entry in an advantaged economic sector to maximize this w^2 payment. And in Australia's industrial history, unions in heavy and resource-based industries have traditionally been very successful in this area of industrial relations. In 1982 wage bargaining between steelworkers and management had once again focused on the size and nature of w^2.

That same year, Melbourne broached the closure, Chenery initiated his rescue operation, and workforce numbers began their decline. And here the poverty and truncation of labor's traditional agenda becomes poignantly apparent. In the face of plant closure and mass layoffs it is often assumed that the best working-class outcome is to fight to save the plant and maintain employment at a diminished level. Access to a wage (which includes a w^1 and perhaps a slightly smaller w^2 payment) is maintained for a reduced number of workers, often in exchange for more oppressive labor practices and increased exploitation. But access to a wage is also exchanged for the imaginative possibilities that must go undiscovered when a familiar strategy is pursued. In this case, some white male steelworkers were allowed to keep their jobs, which meant for them a reduced and precarious version of business as usual. For their laid-off counterparts, and for the Newcastle community at large, this settlement failed to open up any new economic, social, or environmental possibilities.[10]

As we argued above, the traditional union strategy focusing primarily on wages and working conditions, pursued here under conditions of restructuring, is basically a strategy of reproduction. Yet in Newcastle the steel industry was not to be reproduced, or at least not in the form on which several generations of fathers and sons had relied. Changes in steelmaking technology, shifting corporate strategies and priorities, and a variety of other forces had made the closure of the Newcastle steelworks virtually inevitable, despite the heroic efforts of managers and unions to postpone it.[11] Under these circumstances the community and future workers are, arguably, ill-served by a strategy that is intent only on reproducing (or temporarily prolonging) the historical conditions of employment. But what other options are available? What would it mean to pursue a strategy of nonreproduction?

It is at this point that we would like to begin to speculate about the possibilities of a different kind of class politics centered on the enterprise. Workers may or may not view themselves as generating the surplus value that corporations allocate to their own agendas and obligations. Yet it is clear that the social wealth collected at the enterprise level — whether or not it is understood to be derived from exploitation — is a massive and potent force. Those persons and activities to which it is distributed are supported and sustained, whereas social destinations that do not receive flows of surplus value may languish unresourced. In this sense the corporation can be seen as the center of an outpouring of potentiating flows, as the wealth momentarily captured at the enterprise site spreads out to nourish an array of economic and noneconomic activities and institutions.

If workers in a position to bargain considered the potential distributions of their surplus labor and sought to influence the direction of those flows—that is, if they inhabited an imaginative world not governed by the narrative conventions of the monopoly capital story, a world in which innovative distributive claims were possible—they might direct their political energies to novel and nonreproductive ends. Instead of trying collectively to increase individual distributions of w^2 or to maximize individual retrenchment payments, they might secure distributions toward the collective future of their families and communities, preparing for the time when steelmaking no longer provides the means of life. Here we might imagine a corporate-endowed fund set up to develop collective or community-based enterprises, or environmentally sensitive ones, or ones where gender and racial equality are the stated objective.[12]

Joining with others in the local community, workers might engender class and nonclass claims for different forms of "economic development" not necessarily harnessed to reproducing the past or to the imperatives of capitalist industrialization. In the process they might come to value other dimensions of their complex subjectivities, and to inhabit more fully and positively their identities as individuals with needs and desires for a healthy environment, a range of gender roles, a vital and diverse community, and a different future. Opening up to and developing these other aspects of themselves might enhance the possibility of links with those who are not so class- or worker-identified (for example, women, environmentalists, community members, children). But unfortunately the contours of traditional class politics militate against these hopeful possibilities. The reproductive strategy of traditional unionism tends to narrow and consolidate worker subjectivity (rather than amplifying it in the manner just suggested), erecting a barrier to a new politics of enterprise that is just as powerful as the reproductive strategy itself, and just as inappropriate to the current situation.

In terms of the case study of the threatened closure of the Newcastle steel plant discussed here, our speculations regarding possible options and potential subjectivities comes, perhaps, too late. Had an alternative conception of a post–steel-based Newcastle region been in circulation during the early 1980s, the outcome of the restructuring period may have been very different. When there were over 11,000 workers to be compensated by a closure, the scale of the claim that might have been made on

BHP by the workforce and community would have been much larger than at present. Today the closure of the steel plant directly affects only some 3,200 workers and, while the severance package and retraining support being offered these workers has set a new best-practice benchmark on the national industrial scene,[13] opportunities for more collectivized payments to the community have not eventuated. The transformative vision of a hybrid economy in Newcastle will have to wait, perhaps to be realized by another generation.[14]

Coda: Politics of Becoming/Becoming of Politics

A recent successful action against BHP may serve to suggest the potential for a viable enterprise (and class) politics of distribution. In an unprecedented move, an Australian law firm filed suit in 1994 in the state of Victoria (where the head office of BHP is located) and in the PNG courts on behalf of 30,000 PNG landholders living downstream of the Ok Tedi copper and gold mine. These landholders' livelihood has been severely damaged by mining operations, especially by mine runoff following the 1984 collapse of a tailings dam in the course of construction (Low and Gleeson 1998, 207). The court action was the culmination of years of struggle on the part of the indigenous villagers, PNG activists, international activists, and environmentalists.[15] During 1995 demonstrators in Australia disrupted shareholders meetings and took every opportunity to publicize the potentially irreversible damage done to the environment and future livelihood of the villagers in the Ok Tedi region by BHP's mining activities. While BHP attempted to document the value of "development" for the people of Ok Tedi by means of a concerted advertising campaign, the outraged demonstrators and villagers gained a discursive validity and moral force that clearly influenced the outcome. After much legal maneuvering, BHP settled out of court in June 1996, agreeing to pay A$110 million as a compensation package to villagers downstream of the mine, an additional $40 million to downstream villages most affected by the effluent, and approximately $500 million to dredge the river to relieve flooding and build an alternative tailings from disposal system that prevents mine tailings entering the river (Low and Gleeson 1998, 208).[16] The total payment exacted from the company was not insignificant.

One of the interesting aspects of the Ok Tedi story is the way in which the responsibilities of the enterprise are being redefined to include communities and future generations affected by the environmental consequences of past and present mining activity—even in territories outside the traditional jurisdiction of a court (Lee 1997). Another way of saying this is that the Ok Tedi struggle forced a new accounting framework onto "the Company," one that includes distributive payments for environmental and social costs that the corporation traditionally left underfunded. In the context of BHP's new explorations in Dominica, this new accounting framework seems to be at least nominally in place. Company spokesperson Jerry Ellis says that BHP has opened a dialogue with the native (Carib) people in the region of a proposed copper mine. Ellis acknowledges that at Ok Tedi "we got some things wrong . . . we don't want to do it again." In Dominica, if the mine goes ahead, "we will pay more attention [to environmental and indigenous rights issues] than most companies, not the reverse" (Horstman 1996). Perhaps another indication that the claims and rights of external groups such as indigenous communities are beginning to be internalized by BHP is the recent initiation of a formal Guide to Business Conduct.[17] This corporate initiative may potentially herald a new accounting regime in which distributions to secure both worker and community rights and preserve the environment become parts of the regular cost calculus of the corporation.

This speculative example provides a glimpse of what William Connolly calls "a politics of becoming" (1997). Such a politics does not entail the realization of aims and goals by identities that are already defined, but the constitution of new identities through the process of political struggle. For Connolly, the politics of becoming arise in those difficult cases of interdependence when the suffering of some is directly related to the well-being, security, or wholeness of others. When those others respond to the sufferers' initiatives "even while they disturb their own sense of identity" (p. 7), they come into a new relation to constituencies that have previously been perceived as a threat. This mutability in the face of insistent claims shifts "the cultural constellation of identity/difference" (p. 6).

Translating Connolly's vision of interpersonal and interconstituency politics onto the terrain of enterprise politics, we may understand the case of Ok Tedi as initiating a shift in the identity of BHP. In the course of

the history of the Ok Tedi mine, BHP has moved along a trajectory, starting from a position of extraordinary insensitivity to the environment and
the subsistence needs of the indigenous people of PNG.[18] Forced to respond with a huge monetary settlement to the demands of native peoples
and environmentalists, the corporation seems to have begun to internalize, however reluctantly and minimally, some of the values and priorities
of its antagonists. This new "identity," codified in the form of an ethics
policy, may be called on by constituencies both within and outside the
corporation, competing with and sometimes winning out against the residual identity of social and environmental despoiler.[19]

From the perspective of our class analysis, the chain of events surrounding Ok Tedi exemplifies not only the politics of becoming but also
the becoming of politics, as new political subjects emerge and assert their
claims to corporate distributions. To the extent that their success helps
secure future distributions of surplus value to indigenous peoples in the
vicinity of other BHP mines, the Ok Tedi villagers have created a new
class position in the distributive class configuration of BHP. But they have
also been involved in creating new conditions of capitalist exploitation
in mining operations, in the sense that the company can no longer pursue such operations without attending to social and environmental consequences. To the extent that environmental quality and continued production are no longer opposed to each other, miners need not necessarily
see themselves in opposition to environmentalists or indigenous peoples;
these constituencies' claims on distributed shares of surplus have been
internalized and regularized by the corporation, and indeed have become
a condition of continued operation rather than a threat. The environmental aspect of worker subjectivity—the part of themselves that needs and
enjoys the natural environment and mourns its destruction—is thus no
longer so starkly in conflict with the part of themselves that works for a
living, and this less divided relation to self may sometimes translate into
a less hostile or ambivalent relation to those who struggle for environmental quality and indigenous rights.

But there is another point to be made about class politics here, a more
abstract and perhaps more difficult one. And that has to do with the
nonclass distributions and the nonclass subject positions they constitute
in the distributive environment of the corporation. Certainly it is not

straightforward to classify the payment to the Ok Tedi villagers unambiguously as a distribution out of surplus value intended to secure the conditions of capitalist exploitation. It could just as easily be seen as a payment that was wrested from the corporation to guarantee its continued ability to attract other kinds of revenues, such as monopoly rents, or even to maintain the legitimacy of its claims to any and all revenues, not merely surplus value. What this implies is that drawing a clear boundary between distributive class and nonclass positions may be difficult to accomplish; under some lights the Ok Tedi villagers could be seen as distributive class subjects receiving a payment out of surplus value, whereas from other perspectives they may not.

Without making too much of this point, we wish to highlight a possible implication for class (and not simply enterprise) politics. Just as expenditures in our (or any) accounting framework may be difficult to categorize, so may class positions and identities. Yet if the blurring of boundaries between class and nonclass payments is understood to mean that these are implicated in each other (even to the extent that they may be impossible to distinguish) and co-implicated in the constitution of the firm, a lesson for class politics may emerge. Politics is fragmented, and political subjects are unable to form connections across issues and other boundaries in part because those political subjects do not recognize their co-implication (Mouffe 1995). But the class accounting schematically laid out above provides a useful template on which to trace the various revenue flows that BHP has secured over the course of its existence and to identify the various class and nonclass constituencies that have made those flows possible. Within the frame of our revenue and expenditure expression all these constituencies can be seen as implicated in the corporation's development and co-implicated in each other.

BHP attained its current size and wealth not only by extracting surplus value from its labor force but through its monopoly access to national resources and markets over a period of some 112 years of operation. This monopoly access was granted by the Australian people through their proxy, the state. In the latest incarnation of this revenue source, the Steel Industry Plan offered BHP increased domestic market protection, accelerated depreciation arrangements, and bounty payments to domestic steel users (O'Neill 1997). This represented a major redistribution of resources from the Australian people to "the Company," which would be considered nonclass revenues in the terms of our class accounting.

Clearly the Australian people as a collectivity are not exploited by the corporation, yet alongside steelworkers and other BHP workers they have contributed munificently to the revenue side of our expression and to the growth and successful development of BHP. In our view this is not only grounds for a distributive claim on BHP by Australian citizens but a basis for an alliance between those citizens and BHP workers. If these two overlapping constituencies could collaboratively formulate and enforce their demands on the corporation, the lesson of Ok Tedi suggests that they might be able to capture a sizable distribution of corporate wealth. What form this might take and what purposes it might serve remain to be imagined. Following our own proclivities and preoccupations, we can imagine the establishment of a fund to experiment with alternative (noncapitalist?) development initiatives on a national or regional scale.

This fantasized coming together of class and nonclass constituencies blurs the distinction between inside and outside with respect to the corporation. In fact, it could be seen as a politics of the constitutive outside, in which those ostensibly outside the corporation recognize their implication in its existence and translate that recognition into a distributive claim. It also disrupts the binary hierarchy of value that has historically ordered the relation of class-identified subjects to other constituencies (and indeed tends to order all political projects with respect to their others). Finally, it represents the potential opening of class subjects to their constitutive interdependence with nonclass identities, embodying a recognition that what enables one's own position is someone else's and that one's own constitutive outside is a potential source of solidarity, power, and imaginative enlargement. In the process of pursuing a politics animated by this more inclusive class subjectivity, "class" may lose its privileged ability to name the politics that emerges, but it gains a broader field of play.

Conclusion

In this chapter we have brought together three political arenas and concerns—enterprise politics, class politics, and the politics of distribution

—in an attempt to create a space for new political initiatives. In its existing form each of these sorts of politics seems truncated and stymied, imaginatively constrained by narratives of reproduction and centered forms of subjectivity. The corporate object of most enterprise politics is seen as a rational, intentional unity embarked on a path of expanded reproduction; its configuration of surplus distributions is dominated by capital accumulation. Class politics is likewise oriented toward reproduction—of the exploitative class relation and of a subjectivity centered on work and employment.

The reproductionism and centering that we discern in both enterprise representations and class politics have, we believe, a dampening effect on the politics of distribution. If corporations must prioritize and maximize investments in productive capital in order to survive, where is the space for other distributive claims? To open up such a space we use the accounting framework of Resnick and Wolff to portray the corporation as a decentered nexus of flows, in which no one revenue or expenditure has clear priority over the others. This theoretical approach also enables us to rethink the enterprise as involving a complex configuration of class and nonclass processes, revenues, expenditures, and subjects, and thus to begin to enliven some of the possibilities for a wide-ranging, enterprise-focused (class) politics of distribution that are lurking in the shadowy realm of the imaginable but as yet unimagined.

What our analysis makes visible to us is the co-implication of exploitative and distributive class and nonclass subject positions in the fate of the enterprise, and the corresponding co-implication of these subject positions in each other. This mutual dependence and constitutivity suggests that very diverse subjects could come together in a common project (for, indeed, they have already come together in the project of generating and sustaining the enterprise, and of producing, at least partially, themselves and each other). The terrain and range of class politics would be greatly enlarged if we could open up the field of distribution and if class subjects were to come alive to their interdependence with the nonclass.

Notes

We would like to thank Richard Wolff and Stephen Resnick for their helpful comments on a draft of this chapter.

1 Some portions of this essay have been previously published in O'Neill and Gibson-Graham (1999).

2 This paper is part of a series of attempts (Gibson-Graham 1996, chap. 8; O'Neill and Gibson-Graham 1999) to "disorganize" and "loosen up" the representation of the firm, to make the corporation that emerges in our political imaginations appear more susceptible and vulnerable to (internally and externally generated) programs and desires. Our interest is in disrupting the image of the firm as a rational calculating subject that clearly defines, and successfully pursues, its best interests. We are aided in this project by a growing multidisciplinary literature on the enterprise, which we explore in the other papers in the series, that attempts to provide a less coherent vision of corporate behavior than has historically been available in mainstream economics or radical political economy. In this essay we draw primarily on the disruptive class analysis of the enterprise in Resnick and Wolff (1987) to pursue our disorganizing agenda.

3 This is the familiar term used by many of those associated with BHP. The significance of the nickname is found in the way that BHP becomes a metonym for all companies, its seemingly monolithic power standing in, in Australia at least, for the symbolic power invested in capitalist (as opposed to any other kind of) enterprises.

4 Risby reflected that this compromise entailed close and continual negotiations:

> In the 1980s we had to be very close to the unions in Newcastle and it was a matter of being *very close*. To understand our position we virtually had to train their [the unions'] senior people into understanding balance sheets. It was a continual conference with the unions—to try and get them to understand why it [the cuts] was all necessary. You know, the long term future of their members was the most important thing. What really helped me was that I had worked with a lot of the fellows. I had worked on steelmaking and all the rest of it. And I understood them [the workers], probably better than all the rest of them [managers]. Perhaps when a lot of the people could see that change was coming pretty rapidly they thought that, you know, "we think we trust him," "he wouldn't do it if it wasn't necessary" . . . I could walk around the plant [in the 1980s] and still see men I'd worked with [in the 1940s]. Even union officials who I'd worked with in the past . . . that helped me enormously.

5 Partly through Chenery's efforts to keep the Newcastle plant open, it retained a place in this plan but suffered a major decline in status, being reduced to supplying "vanilla"-grade steel products to a stagnant domestic market.

6 See O'Neill and Gibson-Graham (1999) for an extended discussion of the interviews and the understanding of the corporation they enable. The term "rational calculating subject" is a version of Thompson's "universal calculating subject," a prevalent representation that constitutes the firm as a unity (e.g., management) rather than as a "heterogeneous, dispersed, non-unitary and fractured entity of social agency" (1986, 176–7). It should be noted that this conception of the firm as a centered, rational, and optimizing entity was in fact initially developed within neoclassical economics.

7 These alternative visions of the firm have mostly been developed within economic sociology, organization, and management studies. See, for example, Granovetter (1973), Boden (1994), and Hopwood and Miller (1994).

8 The continual placing of the word *class* in parentheses when we refer to enterprise politics is intended to convey the tentativeness of our characterization of a new (distributional) politics of enterprise, and to acknowledge that many of the interventions we might suggest or imagine may not appear to their protagonists to be class interventions, despite their visibility to us as initiatives that impinge on class processes in important ways. We are reluctant to engage in the colonizing practice of naming as we explore this (for us) uncharted terrain.

9 Most notably the steelworkers at Newcastle were more resistant to the entry of women into their labor market in contrast to the situation at Port Kembla (where the steelworkers are largely members of the more progressive Amalgamated Metal Workers Union). Here women were recruited in a highly controversial equal opportunity exercise in the 1980s.

10 Given the association of steel with a dominant "macho" masculinity, a principal basis of gender identity is also lost to those who are laid off, with no encouragement to rework it and no means to replace it. In the British film *The Full Monty,* retrenched steelworkers are portrayed as similarly deprived of their gender identity. As one of them comments to others at the job center where they are looking for work, "A few years and men won't exist— we'll be extinct, obsolete, dinosaurs, yesterday's news."

11 Admittedly the actions of Chenery did keep the plant open for what became another fifteen years, but during this time an exhaustion strategy was put into place that made the plant into a cash cow for other more privileged activities elsewhere in the company and world (O'Neill 1997).

12 At this point in our speculations the reader might become concerned that we have lost sight of the constraint that distributions are conceptualized as securing the conditions of existence of the revenues on the other side of the equation. Thus any new demand on distributive payments (for non-

reproductive purposes) potentially produces a revenue crisis for the firm. We are not so unrealistic as to imagine that unlimited demands for payments can be accommodated by the corporation. But we are willing to err on the side of optimism about the potential for increased payments to progressive ends. As a BHP public relations manager commented to us recently, corporate managers are scared of communities—they can handle the most politically sophisticated unionist, but when it comes to an enraged grandmother concerned about jobs and environmental pollution, they quake at the knees. His comment suggests that the opportunities for inserting alternative claims on enterprise distributions may be much greater in certain situations than is generally understood. As we have been arguing, the enterprise is a fluid entity that is always reshaping the way in which it produces and allocates social wealth. While established conditions of existence for enterprise reproduction may be threatened by new distributional claims and payments, these may be the means by which a new set of conditions becomes the norm.

13 The Pathways Project was initiated in 1998 to help BHP employees in Newcastle make the transition to new forms of employment. Retrenched workers receive generous severance packages, including access to retraining opportunities at company expense. These have included courses in aviation and massage as well as assistance in new business formation.

14 For an account of development agencies' responses to the closure of the Newcastle steelworks, see O'Neill and Green (2000).

15 In 1994 the German partner in the mining venture withdrew under the intense criticism of German activists (Low and Gleeson 1998, 208).

16 For a more detailed account of the complex story of legal maneuvering, see Gordon (1995), Lee (1997), and Low and Gleeson (1998).

17 For an account of the development of this guide, see Malam (1998).

18 Former BHP scientist Michael Abramski testified that BHP monitored levels of cyanide and copper in the river at a point 100 kilometers downstream of the mine, whereas in Australia "it is customary to meet criteria for maximum pollutant levels within metres of the effluent input into the river" (Background Briefing, Australian Broadcasting Corporation, May 28, 1995). This effectively meant that 100 kilometers of the river was sacrificed to the mine. In addition, the levels of acceptable pollutants were approximately ten times the acceptable levels in Australia and other wealthy countries.

19 This scenario is not farfetched, given the experience of many firms in industries experiencing environmental regulation. According to a former ex-

ecutive in the electronics industry, initially firms will tend to greet regulation with half-hearted compliance or even resistance, yet within a decade or less many find that environmental compliance has become a major center of both cost-cutting and technological innovation (James Hamm, personal communication with the authors, Dec. 1999).

FRED CURTIS

□

IVY-COVERED EXPLOITATION

Class, Education, and the Liberal Arts College

Colleges and universities are educational institutions; business enterprises are economic; and power resides in government. These forms of reductionism are as common as they are uncomfortable. Anyone who has spent any time teaching at the college or university level has experienced power relationships and the rhetoric of competition and economic constraints as well as "education." This chapter challenges such reductionist thinking by understanding the liberal arts college as a complex social site comprised, in part, of knowledge practices, disciplines, and forms of power (à la Foucault) and the production, extraction, and distribution of surplus labor (i.e., class processes). In particular, class is not understood as the province of the industrial capitalist enterprise; nor is academia seen as opposed to a classless "ivory tower." In this way, the paper contributes to the growing antiessentialist literature that opens class analysis to various sites within society, including households, the state, labor unions, and nonprofit organizations, among others.

In extending Marxian theory to the liberal arts college, this paper argues that professors can be exploited there—producing more than they receive in value. By making visible the class structure of a college in this way, I highlight the remarkable similarity between the productive labor of a college professor and that of a worker on a factory assembly line or behind the counter of a fast-food establishment: All are productive of surplus value. In that sense, they occupy a similar class position in society, despite their otherwise very different positions of power, status, working conditions, and income.

Education and Class

Education is a special human activity. It is a site of intellectual nurturing and it is also a way to get up and out, to improve one's life in both material and nonmaterial ways. As an educational institution, the liberal arts college is often viewed as an "ivory tower," an institution essentially different from the capitalist profit-seeking economy.[1] Capitalism is seen as affecting the college via *external* pressures on curriculum and teaching and by the employment of college graduates.[2] But this is not the whole story. Rather, the liberal arts college can itself be seen as partly constituted by capitalist class relations, and these *internal* class relations of the college create contradictions for the special educational purpose of the college.

In general, then, this chapter rethinks the traditional depiction of the liberal arts college as an essentially educational institution with nonprofit, tax-exempt status.[3] In reconceptualizing the major revenue and expenditure flows of the college in class-analytical terms, the paper presents a new way of thinking about this institution including the multiple, interactive class and nonclass roles that faculty members play. In particular, it also allows us to understand how the teaching, curricular, tenure, and budgetary processes common to faculty work life are complexly related to class and to struggles over class.

By showing that educational or academic processes are joined together with the production, extraction, and distribution of surplus value within the liberal arts college, this chapter suggests ways in which such capitalist exploitation may itself undermine "the liberal arts education." It analyzes how disciplinary boundaries, tenure, the administrative structure of the college, and its nontuition sources of income may both support the extraction of surplus value from faculty members and, at the same time, contradict the curriculum and pedagogy of the liberal arts college. From this point of view, the educational dimension of the "academic" institution of the liberal arts college is complexly and contradictorily related to the class-exploitative dimension of the college.

Class Analysis of the Liberal Arts College

The liberal arts college is a capitalist enterprise and faculty members are academic proletarians producing surplus value that is appropriated and distributed by trustee-capitalists. This is neither a familiar nor a comfortable view. A more common view is that the liberal arts college is a nonprofit, tax-exempt academic institution, essentially different from the for-profit capitalist enterprise. This is both a structural judgment (the college is a nonprofit institution) and a subjective assessment by faculty members, administrators, and students (that the essence of the college is academic and that professors are scholars/educators and not workers). I have come, however, to see the liberal arts college as both a nonprofit educational institution *and* a capitalist enterprise, whose two "sides" both reinforce and contradict one another.

The Academic Commodity

It is difficult for faculty members to see ourselves as academic proletarians producing commodities for sale, though perhaps today it is less difficult than it used to be. While we prepare and teach classes, develop new courses, work with students, and conduct our scholarly research, we also participate in faculty meetings and read reports where a common theme is our financial situation, competition from other liberal arts colleges and state universities, and ways in which faculty can help the college compete more effectively. We compete — as a capitalist enterprise — with other liberal arts colleges (and public and private universities) to sell our particular commodity. But what is it that we are competing to sell? What is the commodity produced by the college?

The liberal arts college produces and sells a specific educational commodity, the academic course, usually as part of a full-time package of courses.[4] The exchange-value of this commodity is tuition. The use-value of the course may include the specific knowledge gained, entertainment, credits toward fulfilling major or general graduation requirements and hence the bachelor's degree, and any usefulness the course might have in obtaining employment and future success in self- or paid employment.[5] Indeed, the sales effort by the public relations and admissions offices focuses on the special experience (use-value) of a specific liberal arts college, its curriculum, special programs, faculty, success of its graduates, prestige, and so on versus competitor schools. But the actual commodity being sold by the college and purchased by students, on their admission, is the package of courses.

To say that students purchase the course commodity from the college and that faculty members produce this commodity is to delineate only one aspect of the relationship between students and faculty members and of the complex work life of faculty members. Teaching produces not only a commodity but also new understandings, emotional responses, changed (power) relations, and so on. Faculty members befriend, advise, counsel, and learn from students as well as instruct them.[6] All of these aspects may—and in a liberal arts college, often are—part of "teaching," as essential to it as the production of the academic commodity.

Faculty-workers:
The Production and Extraction of Surplus Value

One of the aspects of teaching at a liberal arts college is the class dimension.[7] Faculty members who teach courses produce, inter alia, both commodities (courses) and surplus value. They produce commodities whose value is greater than the salary of the faculty plus the portion of the academic means of production used to produce them. Faculty members are paid a wage (salary) for their labor-power; the means of academic production are purchased as commodities; and the product made with them, the course, is sold as a commodity to students. The college is thus partly constituted by a capitalist production process. Faculty members produce both value and surplus value.

This point can be illustrated with a numerical example (summarized in table 1).[8] Assume that the tuition at a liberal arts college is $19,000 per year and that, on average, students take eight four-credit courses per year (the number needed to graduate in four years) for a per-course full-time tuition of $2,375 (roughly $600 per credit). Further assume that each course has an average enrollment of fifteen students for a per-course revenue of $35,625. If half of this amount goes to pay for the means of academic production (electricity, computers, library materials, lab sup-

Table I

A. Tuition	$19,000
B. Per-Course Full-time Tuition (assumes 8 courses taken per year)	$2,375
C. Number of Students per course, average	15
D. Per Course Tuition Revenue (B × C)	$35,625
E. Assume Means of Production (= constant capital) − ½ value revenue, D	$17,812.50
F. Value Added by Productive Laborers, per course (D − E)	$17,812.50
G. Average Teaching Load per Faculty Member per Year	5
H. Value of Labor per Faculty Member per Year (F × G)	$89,062.50
I. Value of Constant Capital per 5 Courses (E × G)	$89,062.50
J. Total Value of Courses Taught per Faculty Member per Year (H + I = G × D)	$178,125
K. Average Annual Faculty Salary	$50,000
L. Average Annual Faculty Benefits (25% of Salary)	$12,500
M. Average Annual Faculty Compensation (Variable Capital Needed to Produce 5 Courses = K + L)	$62,500
N. Surplus Value (Value of Labor Performed less Variable Capital) (H − M)	$26,562.50
O. Rate of Surplus Value (N/M)	42.5%
P. Rate of Profit (N/{I + M})	17.5%

plies, and so forth), the remaining $17,812.50 per course is the value added by faculty members as they teach the course.[9] Assume that the average teaching load is five four-credit courses per year, so that the annual value of labor performed per faculty member is $89,062.50.

If the average faculty salary is $50,000, with an additional 25 percent in benefits, the average compensation is $62,500 per year. This leaves $26,562.50 in surplus value, equivalent to a profit rate of 17.5 percent or a rate of surplus value of 42.5 percent.[10] The amount of surplus value would be larger if: (1) faculty taught more courses per year; (2) there were more students per course on average; (3) faculty were paid less or had lower benefits, or (4) less of the academic means of production were funded out of tuition income. The first two of these possibilities constitute an increase in the work load (number of hours per week involving in preparing and teaching courses) or an increase in absolute surplus value.[11] The latter two constitute an increase in relative surplus value.

An objection to this example is that the "profit" (or "net income") calculated above leaves out many of the costs of operating a liberal arts college, including secretaries, administrators, and admissions staff, among others. They have been omitted in showing the extraction of surplus value just as General Motors' secretaries, marketing staff, and executives are omitted in calculating that amount of surplus value produced by auto workers while making cars and trucks. The wages and salaries of such nonfaculty employees are not part of variable capital (the productive labor payroll) necessary to the production of courses. The labor of support staff, administrators, and so on, while not directly productive of academic courses, is a necessary support to them. Their "unproductive" labor is paid out of surplus value, not out of capital.

The following equations describe the revenue and expenditure flows of the liberal arts college in class terms:

(1) Y_{fc} = gross tuition income = $c + v + s$

where Y_{fc} = the capitalist fundamental class income received as tuition dollars for the sale of the academic commodity;

c = constant capital = the value of the academic means of production funded out of tuition dollars;

v = variable capital = the salary and benefits of the faculty members who teach/produce courses;

s = surplus value;

$v + s$ = the value added by faculty members as they teach courses.

(2) $E_k = c + v$ = expenditure out of gross tuition income to maintain the constant and variable capital of the college at an unchanged level.

(3) Y_s = "net" capitalist fundamental class income

= $Y_{fc} - E_k = s$ [= net tuition income].[12]

(4) $Y_s = E_{sc}$

where E_{sc} = the distribution (expenditure) of the surplus value income to support various offices and functions of the college that are necessary to keep it functioning as both a capitalist enterprise and an educational institution.

Trustees and the Distribution of Surplus Value

If surplus value is being produced by faculty members, who is extracting the surplus and how is it being distributed? The surplus-extracting capitalists of the private liberal arts college are the members of the Board of Trustees. The trustees are the collective legal owners of the liberal arts college; they are empowered to hire, fire, and give tenure to faculty. By virtue of their complex position, they both extract surplus value from academic commodity-producing workers and distribute it, partly within the college.

Trustees set policy that determines how this surplus-value income is distributed. Typically, it is expended to reproduce the college as both an academic institution and a capitalist enterprise, including the appointment of administrators to carry out the day-to-day management of the college. Hence part of the surplus value is expended to support the admissions, business, financial aid, and public relations offices, all of which act to ensure that the academic commodity is sold and the extracted surplus value is actually realized in the form of money income (tuition revenue). Another part of the surplus value goes to support the offices of academic administration, including the provost, academic deans, registrar, and department chairs.[13] Among other functions, these offices enhance the extraction of surplus value by maintaining faculty productivity, e.g., via administering course evaluations and the tenure process (discussed below) and negotiating faculty compensation. They may also develop curricula and new programs to keep the college's "product" competitive. Further, part of the surplus value is distributed to secretaries, laboratory assistants, library staff, and others whose work directly supports faculty teaching. Finally, part of the surplus value is, in effect, distributed to students in the form of tuition discounts or "unfunded financial aid."

The materials and equipment costs and the salaries needed to keep the nonteaching offices operating are paid out of the surplus value extracted from faculty productive laborers. This does not imply that the work done by "nonteaching" laborers is unnecessary to the survival of the college as both an educational institution and a capitalist enterprise. The "nonteaching" operations of the liberal arts college are functions similar to the marketing, sales, finance, supervision, collective bargaining, product development, and support staff activities of industrial capitalist firms. They are critical to the survival of the firm, but they are not productive of surplus value.

While private liberal arts colleges distribute surplus value in some ways analogously to industrial capitalist firms, there are two major differences between them. First, as nonprofit, tax-exempt institutions, private liberal arts colleges do not distribute surplus value to the state in the form of taxes. Colleges do not pay income, profits, capital gains, or sales taxes, although they do pay payroll and Social Security taxes (the latter often being counted as part of faculty and staff "benefits").[14] Second, in order to maintain its "tax-exempt" status, the college must maintain its "nonprofit" status by adhering to the so-called nondistribution constraint. The college may not distribute its surplus value to trustees or administrators (i.e., as in the form of dividends, profit shares, or bonuses) (Weisbrod 1988, 11–12). College trustees may not receive personal financial benefits due to their class position of capitalist within the college,[15] yet they still extract and distribute the surplus value.

Donations, Grants, and Capital Gains—Nontuition Income

The "capitalist college" also differs from the industrial capitalist firm in terms of the former's particular noncommodity sources of income. The typical private liberal arts college is said to be only partially (60–70 percent) "tuition driven." Only a portion of its total income comes from the production and sale of the academic commodity by the college. The rest comes in the form of interest and dividend payments, donations, grants, and the like.[16] These income sources are critical for the financial survival of the college.

Nontuition revenues may be divided into two categories: (1) surplus value distributed to the college by capitalists; and (2) all other sources of income, or subsumed class and nonclass income, respectively.[17] College subsumed class income comes from two major sources. First, it is received in the form of dividends on shares of stock held in capitalist corporations and interest on corporate bonds (i.e., part of the college's "endowment income"). Second, it is received as donations from individuals, most notably capitalists who extract surplus value from productive laborers outside the college (e.g., in industrial firms). This latter distribution of subsumed class income to the college takes the form of monetary donations from trustees, alumni/alumnae, or other benefactors who occupy the class position of industrial capitalist. Thus, the income equation of the college is expanded to:

(5) $Y = Y_{fc} + Y_{sc}$

where Y_{sc} = surplus value extracted by industrial capitalists and distributed to the college as subsumed class income.

All the other noncommodity sources of income are "nonclass": They are neither surplus value directly extracted within the college (Y_s) nor surplus value directly distributed *to* it by capitalists from outside the college (Y_{sc}). Such nonclass income includes donations from anyone other than capitalists, grants from the state or foundations, and capital gains on the sale of stock or other assets (another portion of "endowment income"). Thus, the college's income equation is expanded once again to:

(6) $Y = Y_{fc} + Y_{sc} + Y_{nc}$

  where Y_{nc} = nonclass income to the college.

To receive donations or grants, the college generally must maintain its nonprofit, tax-exempt status, which allows donors to write gifts off against their income taxes. The college must also balance its books and present the image of the kind of educational institution of interest to particular donors. Hence, educational decisions may be affected by the need to secure such incomes.[18]

Once received, such subsumed and nonclass revenues (i.e., nontuition income) are spent so as to reproduce the college as: (1) an educational institution; (2) a capitalist enterprise; and (3) a recipient of subsumed and nonclass incomes. These are not discrete expenditures or separate categories for three different purposes. Rather, the same expenditure may fulfill all three "functions."

For example, when an industrial capitalist or philanthropic foundation donates $20 million for the construction of an academic building (Y_{sc} or Y_{nc}, respectively), that money is spent partly on construction of the building and partly on the overhead of the university. With its classrooms, scientific, computer and/or language laboratories and equipment, and faculty offices, the academic building becomes part of the academic means of production and thus supports the educational function of the college. At the same time, the fact that this portion of the academic means of production is funded out of subsumed class or nonclass income rather than tuition income (Y_{fc}) means that less tuition income goes toward constant capital. This increases the amount of surplus value realized out of the sale of the academic commodity.

In this sense, the particular expenditure of Y_{sc} or Y_{nc} may create conditions under which Y_s is greater than it would otherwise be due to the lower E_k requirements. The additional surplus value thus realized may be distributed within the college to support the development or the alumni affairs office ("overhead costs") that secured the donation of the building in the first place or for other purposes. The expenditure equation of the college can now be written as follows:

(7) $E = E_k + E_{sc} + E_{nc}$

  where E = total expenditures of the college;

E_k = expenditures to replace constant and variable
capital;

E_{sc} = expenditures made out of extracted surplus value to
reproduce the capitalist fundamental class process
of the college and hence the Y_s income stream;

E_{nc} = expenditures made out of Y_{sc} and Y_{nc} (nontuition)
income to reproduce the Y_{sc} and Y_{nc} income streams
to the college.

In addition to purchasing the "big ticket" academic means of production, some of the nontuition dollars are spent (E_{nc}) to support various administrative offices on campus, in particular the alumni/alumnae relations, development, and president's offices. These offices work to secure future streams of such subsumed and nonclass income. Some of this income is also expended in fees to portfolio managers and in making new investments in stocks, bonds, and real estate. Finally, a portion of this money may be spent on new programs or new faculty positions (e.g., endowed chairs).[19]

Seen from this class perspective, tuition need not cover all the "costs of academic production" for surplus value to be produced by faculty and other productive laborers. Thus, a positive rate of exploitation may exist simultaneously with a claimed accounting loss (tuition revenue less than costs) by the college. Further, the legal nonprofit status of the college signifies nothing a priori about the class relations of the academic institution. Nonprofit status may be a prerequisite for subsumed and nonclass income, however, particularly when such status makes donations tax-exempt. All such nontuition income, as illustrated above, may be essential for the survival and prosperity of the college both as an educational institution and as a capitalist enterprise in a competitive academic marketplace.

Contradictions in the Liberal Arts College: Class and Education

Having laid out this class analysis of the liberal arts college, the rest of this chapter shows how it can be used to illuminate the work life of faculty members and contradictions between class and education. These examples are intended as illustrations; much more can and should be said about each of them. The aspects of faculty life explored here are tenure, the disciplinary structure of the college, the budget process, and nonacademic work performed by faculty members.

The Labor Process and Tenure

One way that the liberal arts college looks least like the industrial capitalist enterprise is in the labor process where faculty members teach courses/produce commodities. Faculty members control their work lives. They determine the curriculum, teaching assignments, course preparation and content, and the allocation of time between teaching and other work. These common perceptions highlight the autonomy of faculty members and hence their differences from productive industrial workers. While such autonomy is real, it is also limited and contested. It is the object of complex struggles, including class struggles, within the college.

One of the key requirements for the extraction of surplus value is that there exist political processes that secure the highest possible production of surplus value by workers. Where workers have specialized knowledge of the requisite concrete labor needed to produce the particular commodity (i.e., where the work takes place on a craft basis), such political processes of supervision may be limited in their effects. This is the case in liberal arts colleges where teaching is done by individual faculty members in specific disciplines and subfields and courses are not aimed at a mass audience (unlike some public universities). Further, courses are not standardized either across or within disciplines and fields, both as a result of the academic freedom and vision of faculty members and the need of the college to differentiate its curriculum (commodity offerings) from those of its competitors. Finally, in most liberal arts colleges, the faculty is understood to have control over the curriculum (the faculty "owns" the curriculum). This situation gives faculty the potential to resist efforts to increase the extraction of surplus value, especially once tenure has been achieved.

In class terms, tenure (appointment to the permanent faculty of the college) limits the extraction of surplus value by trustee-capitalists; this is one of the major reasons that it is continually under attack.[20] Tenured faculty members cannot be (easily) fired, and they usually receive the highest faculty salaries. This limits the ability of the administration to reduce faculty salaries, and hence increase the extraction of surplus value, either through collective bargaining or by replacing tenured faculty with lower paid junior or adjunct faculty. Further, tenured faculty are relatively immune from pressures (couched in terms of job security) to increase their "productivity." On the other hand, during the tenure process, junior faculty members may have less autonomy and control and be subject to high "productivity" pressures.

The tenure process is the evaluation (over a period of up to six years) of junior faculty members to determine whether they will be awarded a permanent position. It involves the tenured members of the candidate's department, faculty at other schools as outside evaluators, the department chair, the academic dean, the college tenure and promotions committee, the provost, the president, and, ultimately, the trustees of the college; only the latter are actually empowered to grant tenure. To earn tenure, junior faculty members must demonstrate proficiency or excellence in teaching, scholarship, and professional service, and also integrity and service to the college.

The tenure process may work to limit class struggles over surplus value by junior faculty members. Strong arguments by tenure candidates in favor of higher salaries and against increases in teaching load (or other work; see below) may lead to a negative tenure vote, particularly as one's case moves upward through the academic hierarchy. It may also lead junior faculty members to avoid joining faculty unions or opposing the administration (or senior members of their own departments) in faculty meetings or other arenas. Thus, the tenure process has a potentially negative effect on faculty class struggles over wages, work load, and working conditions. Overall, then, tenure has contradictory effects on class struggles.

It may also have negative impact on education in several ways. First, it may lead junior faculty members to teach only what is approved by senior faculty members and the administration. This may limit innovation, heterodoxy, and interdisciplinary work (which may not "count" toward tenure). Second, faculty may be loath to take risks in developing new courses or pedagogies that may result in poor student or peer reviews of their classroom performance. Third, tenure considerations may lead junior faculty members to spend less time on teaching altogether, as they perceive—often correctly—that good teaching performance matters less than research output (publications).[21] Finally, the job security of tenure may result in less work of poorer academic quality by some faculty members.

Such negative educational impacts of the tenure process are not automatic, however. Tenure is also understood as the guarantor of academic freedom and thus supports critical approaches, innovation, and heterodoxy. Further, overt use of administrators' or trustees' power to fire or deny tenure to junior faculty members due to their participation in class struggles may well stir up other faculty members, including those with tenure, who regard such interference as a violation of academic freedom. Of course, such trustee or administrator power is not usually expressed nakedly but rather is cloaked in academic or meritocratic rationale. Much depends on the social relations of faculty members and institutional "ethos" of the particular college, including past tenure and class struggles.

The Departmental Structure of the College

The tenure process is connected to another aspect of the college that has impact on both class and educational struggles: the division of the faculty and the curriculum into academic departments. Faculty members are hired into specific departments by academics with training in particular disciplines (e.g., economists hire economists into economics departments).[22] Senior faculty members in their department and scholars in the same discipline at other universities (outside reviewers) are the first and second levels determining the tenure-worthiness of junior faculty members.

This departmental structure reinforces what Herman Daly and John Cobb have called "disciplinolatry":

The most important relations of the members of a department with persons outside it are not with members of other departments within the university, but with other practitioners of the same discipline in other universities. The primary loyalty of university professors is likely to be to the guilds and the promotion of their discipline rather than to their particular university or to their students. . . . The discipline becomes their god. We call this "disciplino-latry." (Daly and Cobb 1994, 33–34)

Disciplinolatry in this sense weakens faculty members in class struggles over the appropriation and distribution of surplus value by reinforcing faculty identification as economists, chemists, philosophers, and so on. That is, it may reduce the class solidarity of faculty members within a given college.

Disciplinolatry is weaker (though certainly not absent) in liberal arts colleges than in the universities mentioned by Daly and Cobb; the ethos of the liberal arts and fairly common instances of interdisciplinary pro-grams, research, and teaching undermine it in many liberal arts colleges. Yet at the same time that the ethos of the liberal arts may be less favorable to disciplinolatry, the tenure process (as noted) and the departmentaliza-tion of the college budget process (see below) reinforce it.[23]

Disciplinolatry has negative educational and ideological effects. It is antiholistic and reductionist; it inhibits or prevents students from under-standing the connections among the theories and objects of analysis of the different disciplines; and it devalues critical perspectives. As Daly and Cobb put it:

Concentrated attention is paid to socializing students into the discipline and to preparing leaders for the future through graduate programs.

Once socialized into the guild, relations with other members of the guild are far more comfortable and satisfying than those with outsiders. There is a wide range of common assumptions that express themselves also in shared values. In this way the external threat to these assumptions and values is mini-mized. The result is, of course, what has come to be assumed within the disci-pline appears self-evident and in no need of critical analysis. New genera-tions build on the work of earlier ones without asking whether these earlier achievements are truly relevant to the new situation. (1994, 34)

These effects of disciplinolatry concurrently tend to inhibit faculty class struggles, limit education to more reductionist and less interdisciplinary work, and socialize students into academic guilds that accept the abstrac-tions of the guild as reality, to paraphrase Daly and Cobb (1994, 34). In so doing, such disciplinolatry, embedded in the institutions and class struggles of higher education, may obscure class understandings and critiques, both in the industrial world and in academia.

The Budget Process

Typically trustees and, through the power delegated to them, administrators, determine the parameters of expenditure of college revenues. One such parameter is the budget allocation for the academic or "instructional" program. Given this parameter and the constraints of tenure, contracts for junior faculty, and across-the-board raises (i.e., academic payroll rigidities), faculty then struggle among themselves for additional "discretionary" monies for merit increases, new programs, equipment, as well as for replacement or additional faculty members. Most of this "fighting over crumbs" (as one of my colleagues puts it) takes place on an interdepartmental basis, that is, it reinforces disciplinary or departmental boundaries. Such interdepartmental struggles over additional resources may encourage tenured faculty members to maintain their own teaching load at high levels, as deans and provosts reward high department teaching and service work loads. This pits department against department in ways that may: (1) increase the production of surplus value; (2) further reinforce disciplinolatry; and (3) inhibit faculty from successfully fighting against the budget parameters (i.e., by engaging more fully and successfully in class struggles over the extraction and appropriation of surplus value). Thus the tenure process, the division of the college into academic departments, and the budget process have complex effects on both the production and extraction of surplus value and also on education.

Faculty Time and Nonacademic Work

In addition to teaching courses, faculty members at liberal arts colleges are also involved in academic administration (e.g., serving on curriculum committees). They are frequently asked to engage in "unpaid," nonacademic, non–commodity-producing work.

College faculty members frequently sit on committees, direct programs, or chair academic departments. Such forms of academic administration are frequently uncompensated, whether by additional pay or by reductions in teaching responsibilities. It is unpaid, nonclass labor with significant effects on the college. First, it frequently results in the effective operation of the academic programs of the college. Second, it may leave the impression with faculty members that they have some significant power in the college and that faculty and administrators have the same, similar, or complementary goals. This may reduce faculty opposition to administration moves that have the effect of increasing the extraction of surplus value,[24] especially if deans and other administrative officials are faculty members on "temporary" appointment to the administration.[25]

Faculty members do not just perform academic work (teaching, research, and academic administration); they also perform other, nonacademic tasks. If, due to the particular labor process of teaching and tenure, the college administration is limited in its ability to extract greater amounts of surplus value from faculty members, assigning nonacademic work to faculty members may resolve certain fiscal contradictions by reducing some internal distributions of surplus value. For example, having faculty members do all their own typing and clerical work reduces E_{sc} distributions of extracted surplus value to faculty secretaries, thereby leaving more funds for other purposes (e.g., to support the staff of the dean).[26]

Further, faculty may be asked to participate in various admissions, alumni affairs, or development activities as part of the college's struggle to compete—for both students and nontuition income.[27] Faculty may be more effective than nonfaculty staff in some of these activities, especially admissions and alumni relations functions involving personal contacts.

The use of faculty time in such nonacademic pursuits may have two financial benefits for the college. On the one hand, it may reduce certain E_{sc} expenditures; the work is done for no additional pay by faculty rather than by paid nonacademic staff. This relieves some financial tension even without increasing extracted surplus value. On the other hand, such use of faculty time may also increase sales of the academic commodity (help fill the freshman class) and increase alumni donations and other nontuition income (elements of both Y_{sc} and Y_{nc}).

In addition, involvement of faculty in such activities both presupposes and reinforces an ethos of doing what is "good for the college" (versus what is good for faculty members), partly by reinforcing faculty contact with past and future students. It may also contribute to faculty awareness of the competition faced by the college and of its financial problems. This may, ultimately, make it more difficult for some faculty members to struggle for higher wages or reduced work loads given their perception of a financial crisis or at least of strict financial constraints.

Many faculty members see the struggle for higher wages as a student–faculty conflict rather than as class struggle between faculty-workers and trustee-capitalists. Given the power relations of the budget process, they are not necessarily wrong: Higher salaries may indeed become higher tuition or less money to fund academic programs. In such a case, the class struggle within the college between faculty-proletarians and the trustee employers of academic labor-power is displaced onto the student purchasers of the academic commodity. Such displacement also inhibits pressure for increased wages due to faculty concerns about competition with other schools, the high cost to students of their education, and faculty desire to broaden the (class) base of the student body.

Faculty performance of unpaid nonacademic labor may have negative impacts on academic activities, both teaching and research. Faculty members in liberal arts colleges are engaged in a variety of nonacademic tasks virtually on a daily basis. This limits their ability to engage in research, keep current in their field, or spend more time in teaching their courses and working with students in groups or individually.

Less time spent in preparing classes and in meeting with students may worsen the (real or perceived) quality of the education students gain by taking courses and working with faculty members. Liberal arts colleges provide small class environments and ready access to faculty members as part of what is purchased by tuition. Reducing access to faculty members or reducing time faculty members have for keeping current in their discipline or preparing classes hurts the educational process. Given the often rigid deadlines and heavy demands of administrative and nonacademic work and the priority placed on research and publication (especially for junior faculty), the loser may often be teaching. The alternative is to increase the combined academic plus nonacademic work load for faculty members, a choice many faculty members do make given their commitment to both students (teaching) and research.

If the nonacademic work of faculty members reduces academic quality sufficiently, it will become more difficult to sell product (fill the incoming class).[28] Less time spent on scholarly activity may have the same effect on product (educational) quality. In addition, less scholarship may ultimately give the administration more control over the labor process and the extraction of surplus labor in two ways. On the one hand, the less research faculty members do, the more they may come to depend on textbooks and the more their courses may be standardized, thus reducing their craft control over the labor process and making them more vulnerable to pressures to increase their teaching work load. On the other hand, less research leading to fewer publications in prominent journals reduces both individual and overall faculty bargaining power. Faculty become more easily replaceable and have fewer good alternatives regarding employment, either in or out of academia. Thus nonacademic work performed by faculty members "for the benefit of the college" has complex and contradictory effects on both education and class struggles.

Conclusion

This chapter has presented a class analysis of the liberal arts college. In addition to all its other aspects, the college is constituted by the production, extraction, and distribution of surplus value. It is also comprised by the receipt of subsumed class and nonclass incomes. The analytical framework developed here can be used to examine the work life of faculty members—teaching as a labor process, tenure, academic departments, budget fights, and so on—and to show how many of the activities of faculty work life are complexly constituted by class and nonclass elements, thus providing a different way of understanding the issues and struggles of the liberal arts college.

But where does this leave us? Having developed this class analysis very consciously and now understanding the pressures and tensions of my job in a new, class-analytical way, I may still make choices as a faculty member that result in increased productive or unproductive labor by faculty members (i.e., by myself and my colleagues). I may vote or otherwise support my own increased exploitation. Faculty members have class as their essence no more than does the college; we may make choices that work against our "class interests" and in favor of students or education, despite partaking in a self-conscious class analysis.

Nevertheless, the class analysis of this paper gives us new ways to think about the possibilities for both class and educational struggles in our work lives as faculty members. The analysis shows that the class goals of faculty-workers are not necessarily antithetical to the needs of education and students, such an opposition when it occurs being a complex result of the structure and relationships of a specific college. It opens the possibility of linking class and educational struggles, e.g., uniting faculty and students in budgetary struggles. Such struggles would aim at reforming the capitalist college without changing its class structure.

The analysis also raises the possibility of colleges where educational processes are not combined with capitalist processes of the production and extraction of surplus value—colleges where, for example, surplus labor is appropriated and distributed collectively by the faculty performers of that surplus labor. Faculty would no longer be excluded from decisions about how, to whom, and for what (educational or noneducational) purposes to distribute the surplus labor they produce. Faculty would be the trustees and might hire administrators to carry out their policies.

In such a communal college the requirements of surplus value extraction that reinforce disciplinolatry and limit heterodox and critical work might be eroded and power relations among faculty members and between faculty and students might be transformed. Thus the transition to a communal organization might work to enhance the educational mission of a college. These possibilities—opened up by the class analysis of this paper—need further thought and elaboration.

The paper has begun the task of examining the liberal arts college in terms of the production and extraction of surplus. A next step might be to consider how public (state-supported) and private universities differ from the liberal arts college in these class terms.[29]

Finally, nonprofit status, tax exemption, worker autonomy and control, professionalism, and other such "nonclass" characteristics may lead many to conclude that a given institution (e.g., a private liberal arts college or a not-for-profit hospital) is not a site where surplus value is produced and extracted. This chapter has shown that such characteristics may not only obscure class relations; they may also be conditions of existence for the reproduction of the capitalist extraction of surplus value in these institutions. In addition, however, the analysis has also shown that such "nonclass" characteristics may create the possibilities for professional workers to limit and resist the extraction of surplus value more than in overtly "for-profit" firms (despite lack of protection by labor laws). This recognition has importance for the Marxian analysis of higher education and other "nonprofit" institutions (such as some hospitals) and for the issues of the privatization of public enterprises and the commercialization of private not-for-profit charitable enterprises.

Notes

I want to thank the following colleagues and students for their helpful comments on various drafts of this chapter: Masato Aoki, John Bleakney, Ron Caplan, Harriet Fraad, Dorene Isenberg, Josh Karan, Bill Olson, Steve Resnick, David Ruccio, Bernie Smith, Karen Thomas, Rona Weiss, and Rick Wolff.

1 This paper concerns the private liberal arts college and not other institutions of postsecondary education. The conclusions drawn here are not necessarily applicable to private or public universities, with their graduate programs, focus on research, and different income streams. Drew University, where I teach, is comprised of an undergraduate liberal arts college, a graduate school, and a theological school. This paper draws only on my experience with the undergraduate college.

2 See Aoki (1992) and Bowles and Gintis (1976).

3 The liberal arts college is defined here as an undergraduate institution whose curriculum and students are concentrated overwhelmingly in liberal arts disciplines, as opposed to professional studies (e.g., business). This definition is taken from Breneman (1994, 3). Faculty members' academic work is concentrated on teaching undergraduates, although faculty are also engaged in scholarly activities and administrative duties.

4 The college also sells nonacademic commodities, including housing, meals, textbooks, supplies, T-shirts, toiletries, and snacks. Here, the college is acting as a merchant (Wolff and Resnick 1987, 197–200). The sale of such nonacademic commodities has sometimes put the liberal arts college in competition and conflict with stores in the local community. These issues are not discussed here given the focus on the academic aspect of the college.

5 Students do not purchase education, which is a complex social activity that may require courses (and interactions with faculty members) as one of its conditions of existence (see Aoki 1992.) Further, students do not purchase a college degree with their tuition dollars. Not all students matriculate or

complete their degree requirements, even after they have paid tuition and taken courses. Students can and do fail.

6 On these nonclass dimensions of teaching, see bell hooks (1994).

7 Class is also present in terms of the curriculum of class, the class background of faculty and students, and the relations of the college to the industrial capitalist economy (e.g., in preparing its future workforce). These aspects of class in higher education have received attention elsewhere (Aoki 1992; Bowles and Gintis 1996; Nisinoff et al. 1992; and Ryan and Sackrey 1984). Little or no attention, however, has been paid to the liberal arts college as a site of surplus value production and extraction.

8 This example is loosely based on data from several liberal arts colleges.

9 Other, large elements of the means of academic production (such as classroom buildings) are funded out of nontuition sources of income (discussed below) and hence not purchased out of capital.

10 With a 1996–97 tuition of \$19,872 for full-time students, an average faculty salary of \$57,200 and benefits equal to 30 percent of salary, and an average (in the spring 1996 semester) of sixteen students per course, Drew faculty members will produce \$25,000 of surplus value per faculty member in the academic year 1996–97. This is equivalent to a rate of surplus value of 33.6 percent and a rate of profit of 14.4 percent. I want to thank Dorene Isenberg, Mike McKitish, Dick Rhone, and Horace Tate for the relevant data.

11 In this context, attempts to increase faculty "productivity" are seen as often involving a lengthening of the amount of work time, either due to teaching more courses or spending more time per course due to larger enrollments.

12 This is a different concept of "net tuition income" than that discussed by Breneman (1994). For him, net tuition income is gross tuition income less unfunded student aid. In Marxian terms, Breneman's concept of net tuition income reduces capitalist fundamental class income (Y_{fc}) by the amount of one of the distributions (E_{sc}) made out of surplus value (Y_s). His concept obscures the class incomes and expenditures that a Marxian analysis highlights.

13 Department chairs typically teach a reduced number of courses for unchanged or increased salary. Financial support for their administrative activities is funded out of E_{sc}. In this case, chairs are both producers of surplus value and recipients of subsumed class income. If, however, department chairs teach the same load of courses as other faculty members and receive no extra compensation or reduction in teaching load, then no such subsumed class expenditures are made.

14 I am indebted to Mike McKitish on this point.

15 They receive nonfinancial benefits, however, including considerable social recognition and status.

16 I am omitting the income from room and board, and so on; see n. 4.

17 For further definition of the terms "fundamental," "subsumed," and "nonclass," see the editors' introduction to this volume.

18 In this case donors (or administrators seeking such donations) may attempt to change college curriculum, control faculty hiring, or otherwise intervene in the operation of the college as a condition for such donations. Such interventions may be seen as threats to academic freedom and resisted strongly by faculty members.

19 Thus the expansion of academic means of production and growth of the productive labor force (e.g., expansion of the teaching faculty) — or the accumulation of "academic capital" — may be funded out of subsumed and nonclass income rather than out of surplus value.

20 For example, see Magner (1996).

21 That research counts more than teaching in the tenure process—even in liberal arts colleges that value teaching—is a result of disciplinolatry, discussed below. The devaluation of teaching versus research is also the result of the faculty labor market, which unsuccessful tenure candidates reenter. As Winston puts it, "the local, ephemeral, personal, real-time nature of good teaching—versus the durable, portable atemporality of good research—reduces the value of teaching in the faculty market" (1994, 11).

Tenure considerations may also lead to faculty members concentrating on mainstream research topics that are more likely to be published in the major journals in their fields rather than critical, heterodox, or innovative work that either may not be published or may be published in less prestigious and thus "less tenure-worthy" journals.

22 Of course, only the Board of Trustees has the ultimate power to hire faculty or anyone else, power that in this instance they delegate to departmental and administrative managers.

23 See Saltzman and Curtis (1994, 129–31) for an example of how disciplinolatry had contradictory effects on our interdisciplinary course on homelessness.

24 Faculty members on budget or other administrative committees may be able to convince their colleagues that they should support this or that program ahead of salary increases "for the good of the college" more effectively than the dean, provost, or president could.

25 The problematic aspects of this faculty role became starkly visible when the Yeshiva (University) decision denied National Labor Relations Act recog-

nition to a faculty union due to the administrative role of faculty members. This decision has prevented unionization and limited collective bargaining at liberal arts colleges; see Levy (1987).

26　On this point, Rick Wolff writes, "I have been struck by how subtle are the ways in which top managers of most capitalist industrial enterprises can allocate to themselves all sorts of surplus allocations that they 'are not supposed to.' In the case of private colleges, consider the plush offices, expense accounts, travel allowances, and dozens of other 'perks' that amount to surplus allocations. These are the 'special funds' and 'discretionary funds' so beloved of top college administrators (and often deeply resented by everyone else on the campus who rightly suspect them)" (personal communication, 1996). Such "special funds" can also by used to reward faculty support for administrators' priorities.

27　Untenured faculty may face special pressures to engage in such work as "service to the college," frequently an important criteria for tenure, though such work is not limited to untenured faculty. In recent years, tenured faculty members at Drew have, inter alia, participated in special weekend admissions events, written to or called prospective students, attended alumni functions, contributed articles to alumni newsletters, and worked to develop a new academic program, part of the (trustee) impetus for which was to get Wall Street executives more (financially) involved with Drew.

28　As students get less time with faculty members and as liberal arts college courses become less differentiated due to nonacademic demands, students may become less willing to pay the high tuition of private liberal arts colleges and more willing to attend cheaper public universities.

29　In this context, several graduate students at the University of Massachusetts have raised the issue of their relationship to faculty members in their academic departments, with whom they share a common class position as surplus-producing workers but have different nonclass positions with regard to the levels of their pay (teaching assistant stipend versus faculty salary), status, power relations, and degrees. I am indebted to Steve Resnick and Rick Wolff for raising this issue with me.

ANDRIANA VLACHOU

□

NATURE AND CLASS

A Marxian Value Analysis

Environmentalism has thus far failed to take hold as a mass movement in the Western countries where it has nonetheless emerged as a political force. One major reason for this failure is the widespread alienation of workers from environmentalists. The "jobs versus environment" dilemma so often encountered in ecological debates summarizes the seemingly intractable conflict between the interests of these two social groups.

In this paper, I suggest that an overdeterminist class analysis of the nature–society relationship can perhaps form the basis for closer collaboration or even coalition between these otherwise separated constituencies. Such a class analysis stresses the complex interdependencies among natural and social processes, rather than constructing a nature–society opposition that puts workers and environmentalists at odds (Harvey 1993).

Different class structures contribute to different kinds of production, competition, technical change, population movements and growth, and so on; all of these affect the natural environment in which these activities occur. Different class structures influence the people caught up in them to form different attitudes toward nature and one another, and these attitudes likewise affect the natural environment. Whatever happens to the natural environment is constituted, in part, by the particular class processes that exist and interact in that environment. Hence it follows that individuals concerned with explaining and/or intervening in the transformations of the natural environment may want to understand and address class structures.

Natural processes also play distinctive roles in shaping the kinds of class processes that exist in a society, how they interact, and how they evolve. If natural resources are depleted or changed through some natural process, class processes based on them may collapse or relocate to other social formations; in some circumstances, the tensions and contradictions within a class structure may explode under the added burden of depleted resources. Any alteration in natural processes will participate in altering class processes. Indeed, it is ultimately impossible to separate the social impacts of natural changes from the social impacts of class changes. It follows that the social movements concerned to challenge and transform existing class structures must be alert to changing natural processes and their effects on the class configurations they target in their activities.

If natural processes are seen to depend in part on class processes and vice versa, an argument emerges for an alliance of sorts between social movements focused on these different domains. What might further strengthen that argument would be the recognition that class processes are themselves part of any individual's environment, impacting his or her life alongside natural processes. Exploitation, like pollution, damages, injures, and kills. If the devotees of movements to transform class relationships and those of movements to transform human relationships to nature could come to share each other's goals, the resulting alliance would likely be a stronger social force than either could produce on its own. Moreover, it could be an alliance of theoretical depth and moral principle as well as political expediency. To take one step in the direction of such an alliance—by paying some systematic theoretical attention to the interdependence of class and nature—is the goal of this chapter.

In the next section I attempt to theorize the relationship between nature and capitalist society in terms of the Marxian theory of value and surplus value. In the third section I discuss the role of class and other economic conflicts in shaping policies to secure natural conditions and resources in modern capitalist societies, while in the fourth section I explore the impacts of these sorts of policies on capitalism, presenting concrete examples. In the last section, I offer some conclusions and implications of the analysis for realizing an ecosocialist project to change capitalist social formations.

Nature and the Theory of Value

Some Marxists appear to believe that Marxian economics has had or can have limited analytical insights to offer environmentalism. Among them, Leff (1992, 1993, 1995) writes from an overdeterminist standpoint, and thus his position is very challenging for Marxists of an overdeterminist persuasion.[1] I believe, however, that it is possible to show that Marx's theories of value and surplus value can be used to account for the degradation of natural conditions and resources, a task to which I now turn.

In Marxian theory, nature is a source of wealth, a source of use values, but can create neither value nor surplus value. The source of value is labor. Natural resources and conditions, however, overdetermine the production of value and surplus value, as well as their distribution. Moreover, natural resources and conditions may be either "free goods" or commodities (i.e., they may command a price). For the latter to be the case, several conditions must be present. Critically important among them is whether socially necessary labor time has been expended for their provision and/or a monopoly position has been established over them by (capitalist or other types of) landed property. The air we breathe, for example, that sustains our very existence is not a commodity because neither has socially necessary labor time been expended for its provision, nor has a monopoly position of private property been established over it.

Natural resources (land, minerals, water, and so forth) affect the production of value in specific ways. Natural resources are sustained by natural processes and conditions that are not reproducible through (capitalist) production proper. These supporting natural processes and conditions participate in the determination of the socially necessary labor time for the production of natural resources and other types of commodities by affecting *labor productivity*.[2] When capitals use more (less) favorable natural resource bases in terms of quality and location, they increase (decrease) labor productivity in this production sphere. Moreover, if the use by capitals of less favorable natural bases is generalized so that they become the average, normal conditions of capitalist production, the value of the commodities produced is increased as fewer use values are produced in the same labor time.

Natural resource bases also affect the production, realization, and distribution of surplus value. Natural resource commodities constitute elements of constant capital and they also are, or provide, use values that sustain human life, and for this reason may be significant elements of variable capital. The generalized use of qualitatively superior natural bases increases labor productivity and reduces the value of the means of subsistence of labor power. Assuming that the length of the working day and the real wage remain unchanged, this leads to an increase in the surplus value produced. On the other hand, the generalized use of less favorable natural bases is expected to have the opposite effects on the value of labor power. In particular, an increase in the value of labor power that leads, *ceteris paribus,* to a decrease in surplus value may affect both the accumulation process and other subsumed class processes necessary to secure the conditions of existence of the capitalist extraction process, instigating various fundamental and subsumed class conflicts.

The generalized use of less favorable natural bases also increases the value of certain elements of constant capital (e.g., raw materials) and the value of commodities produced with them. This leads, other things being equal, to an increase in the organic composition of capital and to a decrease in the profit rate. Various conflicts can then arise over the extraction and distribution of surplus value to deal with the decrease in the profit rate. International trade could also be initiated or intensified to secure natural resources of better quality and of lower price to counteract the increases in the values of constant and variable capital and the fall in the profit rate. Alternatively economic and social crises may arise out of the tensions and struggles created by the reduced availability or quality of natural resources. In the case of such crises, fundamental and subsumed class processes may not be able to continue in their habitual ways; they may be interrupted and reorganized in drastically different ways, including the way nature is appropriated.

Individual capitals can also appropriate more surplus value than they produce in the realization process if they utilize qualitatively better-than-average natural resources and conditions. To illustrate this point, let us assume that we have capitalist class-production processes and that land and other natural resource stocks are owned only by capitalists. Suppose also that a given demand for commodities requires the utilization of natural resource bases of different qualities to produce the necessary quantities. Under these conditions, the market price of natural resource commodities is determined by the price of production of commodities produced under the least favorable natural conditions. Individual capitals producing under the least favorable conditions should cover the cost of production and enjoy the average rate of profit economy-wide; otherwise they would leave the sector. Capitals producing under more favorable natural conditions will have a higher labor productivity and thus a smaller unit cost. Selling their products at a market price regulated by the price of production of commodities produced under the least favorable conditions, they earn an excess profit. As Marx indicated, "the natural force is not the source of surplus profit but only its natural basis, because this natural basis permits an exceptional increase in the productiveness of labor" (Marx 1967, vol. 3, 647). The surplus profit is what Marx called *differential* rent. It is well known, for example, to the students of the oil market that the oil multinationals that gained control over the low-cost crude oil of the Middle East have been enjoying large differential rents for years.

Differential rents based on the different qualities of natural resource bases cannot be eliminated in the same ways that surplus profit tends to be eliminated in industry. In industry, surplus profit is secured when individual capitals have higher-than-average productivity in a sector. Competition among capitals within that sector, however, leads to diffusing the most efficient technologies and organizations of production and tends to generalize the higher productivity and reduce or eliminate surplus profit. In the case of natural resource commodities, it is not possible to generalize the higher productivity of labor by diffusing the most efficient technique since higher productivity is based on natural processes and conditions. In a dynamic setting, however, as we will see later, technical, economic, and other social processes come together with natural processes and conditions, affecting labor productivity and its natural "limits" and thus overdetermining the labor time socially necessary for commodity production.

Let us now assume that land and other natural resource endowments are owned by landlords. In this case, as Marx indicated, "landed property is based on the monopoly by certain persons over definite portions of the globe, as exclusive spheres of their private will to the exclusion of all others" (Marx 1967, vol. 3, 615). "The possession of (a) natural force constitutes a monopoly in the hands of its owner; it is a condition for an increase in the productiveness of the invested capital that cannot be established by the production of capital itself" (Marx 1967, vol. 3, 645). It should be noted that the state, as well as individuals, groups, or enterprises, can occupy the position of landlord. A law could be enacted, for example, stipulating that certain natural resources and conditions are held in "common property" by all the citizens in a nation and that control over access to them belongs to the state.

Access to monopolized land or its natural forces is essential for certain surplus extraction processes to be initiated or continued, and the capitalist must pay a portion of appropriated surplus value to the landlord to gain access to natural resources and conditions. This payment must be made even by capitals producing under the least favorable conditions. This payment is the *absolute* ground rent and is added to the price of production of natural resource commodities produced under the least favorable conditions to set the market price of these commodities. Actually, absolute rent is a monopoly payment and leads to the formation of a monopoly price in the sphere of natural resource production. Absolute ground rent paid to the state occupying the position of landlord often takes the form of a tax or the price of a permit giving access to natural resources and conditions.

Competition between capitalists and landlords (a struggle over a subsumed class payment) determines the size of the absolute rent. It should be noted that if the natural resource stocks that sustain a natural resource commodity are known to exist in large quantities, then the competition among landlords to offer accessibility to the natural resource base can reduce or even eliminate absolute rent. On the other hand, competition among capitalists to get access to the most favorable natural resources and conditions enables landlords to appropriate, as ground rent, a portion of or the entire surplus profit. Capitalists will remain in the sector as long as they enjoy the normal or average profit.

The quest for differential rent and its distribution has played a significant role in shaping the oil market on a world scale. The control over the low-cost Middle Eastern oil was an important factor in building and securing worldwide the monopoly position and excess profits of the seven biggest oil multinationals.[3] As a consequence, in the 1960s and early 1970s the "independents" (i.e., smaller oil companies) waged a fierce struggle against the majors to secure access to low-cost oil reserves, offering higher royalties to oil field owners. The importance of this struggle in explaining the turmoil in the oil market during the 1970s has been appreciated by many analysts of the industry (Penrose 1976; Vernon 1976; Wilkins 1976).

Expanded reproduction of capitalism intensifies the use of natural resources and conditions. Under given technical and social conditions, capitalist expansion may surpass the regenerative or the carrying capacity of nature, resulting in depletion of natural resources and destruction of the assimilative capacities of the environment. Capitals then come up against "natural limits" as they face a "scarcity" of natural resources; pollution also restricts the availability of environmental conditions of a certain quality. These tendencies may lead, in turn, to higher values and prices of natural resources and other commodities, increasing capitals' production and realization costs. These higher costs affect the production and distribution of surplus value (including the profitability of capitals) and may affect the value of commodities. In particular, in their search for cheap raw materials and wage goods, individual capitals first use high-quality or easily accessible natural resource bases. As capitalist development depletes the natural resources of higher quality, labor productivity decreases. As I have argued before, in this case and under given technical and social conditions, if the decreased productivity of labor becomes generalized, the value and the price of natural resource commodities increase. In addition, as the value of wage goods increases, the surplus value produced is decreased. If the social demand for natural resource commodities is stable or increasing, differential and absolute rent may also increase.

Increases in prices and rents may be bounded from above, however, by a "backstop technology" or by demand, given some degree of elasticity. In the case of exhaustible energy resources, for example, the price of a renewable energy source may set a limit to their increasing prices. Technical innovation leading to resource-saving or to substitution of depleting resources with renewable ones; exploration and discovery of new resource deposits; changes in demand; new cultural values reevaluating nature — all of these shape the availability and the use of natural resources bases. In this sense, "exhaustibility" is overdetermined and relativized (Vlachou 1994, 23–124). Such changes are, on the one hand, induced by the increased costs, rents, and prices of natural resources and other commodities that are caused by historically and socially produced "exhaustibility" and the tensions it creates. On the other hand, although they affect "scarcity," such change may come forth from different quarters of capitalist society.

Environmental conditions do not enter the market as separate, individual commodities, so it is not obvious how to theorize them and their deterioration in terms of value theory. Environmental conditions (and certain plentiful natural resources) have often been treated by capitals as use values sustained by nature, to which they all have free access. It has not been easy for individual landlords or capitalists to bring them under their exclusive control; however, the degradation of environmental conditions reduces the labor productivity of some or all capitals. Acid rain, for example, causes damages to buildings, materials, and final products of industrial firms (and households). As long as environmental degradation reduces only the labor productivity of a limited number of industrial capitals suffering from pollution, without affecting the average conditions of production of the suffering sector, it affects only the distribution of surplus value but not the determination of value in that sector. On the other hand, if environmental degradation becomes generalized so that a polluted environment constitutes the average conditions of production in the sector, then the reduced productivity of labor becomes the normal condition, resulting in an increase in the value of the commodities whose production is affected by pollution.

Similar arguments can be developed with respect to the effect of pollution on the reproduction of labor power. A generalized decrease in labor productivity may result, for example, from the effects of widespread pollution on the physical condition of workers. In this case, the value of labor power is expected to increase as workers need additional commodities to preserve their physical condition. Assuming that the length of the work day remains unchanged, the surplus value produced decreases. This, in turn, may result in various tensions over the production and distribution of surplus value.

It should also be noted that pollution deteriorates the natural conditions and processes involved in agriculture, forests, and fisheries. In this case, we can conceptualize the effects of pollution on natural systems as creating less favorable natural resource bases and apply the theorization developed earlier in this section.

Under certain conditions, some of which will be discussed later, it may become necessary for a number of capitalists to secure the natural conditions of production by incurring environmental expenditures. As polluters, they may use pollution abatement processes; as victims they may undertake "defensive" activities (utilizing water- or air-cleansing devices and so forth). In these cases, they may employ concrete labor-time to mitigate pollution or its effects; they may produce "environmentally friendly commodities" or use "defensive" devices that are produced as commodities.

The environmentally friendly commodities (EFCS) may coexist in the market with commodities that satisfy exactly the same human needs but pollute the environment. For example, cars equipped with catalytic converters, which control hydrocarbon and carbon monoxide emissions and can be supplied with unleaded gasoline, may coexist with cars that lack such converters. The environmentally nonfriendly commodities (ENFCS) may cost less than the similar EFCS. Then the crucial question is, as Sandler (1994, 51) puts it, whether, and under what conditions, the concrete labor and constant capital required to make commodities environmentally friendly are productive or unproductive expenditures. If, for example, we consider them productive, they are then elements of constant or variable capital and they determine the value of the commodity and the surplus value produced. If, on the other hand, we consider them unproductive expenditures, they are paid for out of the surplus value extracted and affect its distribution among alternative uses (including accumulation) that secure conditions of existence of the capitalist class process, and as such they do not enter into the determination of value directly.

In the context of value theory, I think that environmental expenditures determine the value of the relevant commodity only when the reduced pollution regime and the associated environmental expenditures constitute the normal, average conditions of production in the industry. In this case, environmental expenditures are elements of constant and variable capital and as such affect the production of surplus value directly. If, for example, it is required by law that every car has to have a catalytic converter, the related expenditures are elements of constant and variable capital. For the reduced pollution regime to become a constituent element of the normal conditions of production, however, economic, natural, cultural, and political processes have to interact to make environmentally friendly commodities a desideratum of production, that is, to make environmental quality an attribute of commodities produced.

Environmental quality as an attribute of produced commodities is socially and historically shaped. In particular, changes in natural conditions and resources are shaped by class and nonclass struggles that are fought at all the levels of society while their outcomes are often mediated by the state. Among the nonclass struggles, we can distinguish the ongoing effort to produce a cultural reappraisal of nature as a source of "aesthetic and life-sustaining services," including the revival of traditional, religious, or mystical respect for nature. Gismondi and Richardson (1994) and Szasz (1991) emphasize the importance of social struggles in shaping environmental policies. In an important article, the former examine the ideological and social struggles that took place in a public hearing over the building of the world's largest single-line bleached kraft pulp mill along the Athabasca River in Alberta, Canada, which would be responsible for releasing highly toxic pollution. Interestingly, the authors claim that these battles "are not confrontations lost or won simply on the battlefield of meanings and values. The acts by subordinate groups of questioning convention, subverting dominant discourses, and asserting counterdiscourses, are highly political. They occur in the midst of complex sociological and historical processes" (1994, 236–37). Szasz (1991) discusses the struggles that took place between 1976 and 1988 over hazardous waste regulation in the United States. He describes how the "do not intervene in production" limit for regulation was upheld in 1976, and documents the erosion of this limit in subsequent years (1991, 19). He attributes this erosion to the complex and varied political impacts of the broad-based hazardous waste movement that developed in the United States after 1980. Additional cases of economic struggles shaping environmental regulation are presented in the next section.

The Shaping of Policies Toward Nature

Class conflict is an important determinant of social change. The discussion of the relationship between nature and capitalism in terms of value and surplus value theory in the previous section has revealed many instances that could give rise to class and other social struggles over the appropriation of natural resources and conditions.

The degradation of nature produced by capitalism threatens its natural conditions of existence. Capitalists may not find water, land, minerals, clean air, and other natural resources and conditions in the requisite quantities, qualities, and prices in which they need them at a certain point in time. Thus pollution and the exhaustion of natural resources jeopardizes the capitalist class process itself. This threat, however, prompts changes in capitalist behavior toward securing these very important natural resources and conditions. These changes are shaped, as mentioned earlier, by struggles undertaken at the economic, political, and cultural levels of the society. Such changes can produce new ways of appropriating nature by capitalism and can in turn further affect the production and distribution of surplus value. They may also influence the average conditions of production and thus the value of commodities. The state as a site in society, which is in interaction with the other sites in society, may undertake various processes to secure new ways of appropriating nature. State policies in a capitalist social formation are shaped by, among other things, the fundamental struggle between labor and capital, by the struggles between capitalists and other surplus labor–extracting classes, and by the struggles between fundamental and subsumed classes over the appropriation of nature. Assuming for discursive purposes that in a capitalist society there exist only capitalist fundamental and subsumed class processes, I shall concentrate in this section on the struggles fought at the economic level over the appropriation of nature.

Individual capitalists who experience increases in costs due to pollution may struggle against capitalists who cause that pollution. In many cases of environmental regulation, we find capitalists suffering from pollution to have successfully struggled against polluters in an effort to make them "internalize" environmental costs. Polluting capitalists are not usually willing to control their emissions on an individual basis. They argue that pollution abatement will increase their costs and deteriorate their competitive position, increasing their risk of being driven out of business.[4] In addition, capitalists who use depleting natural resources as inputs in their production processes and experience increasing costs struggle against other capitalists and consumers, attempting to pass cost increases on to them and keep their profit rates intact. They may also turn against landlords to reduce the rents paid to them and/or against workers to reduce wages.[5]

Workers in capitalist firms and other people also struggle to protect their conditions of life and standards of living, which are threatened by ecological destruction. Pollution has significant negative effects on human health, causing morbidity and increased mortality. This, in turn, results in increased medical costs, absence from work, declines in productivity, and even premature death. Certain wage goods may also become more expensive. In an effort to protect themselves or especially their children from pollution, people may move to relatively unpolluted areas and pay higher rents, resulting in reductions in their real wages. If oil, gas, and electricity prices are increasing, heating, cooking, lighting, and so forth become expensive, resulting again in real wage reductions. Capitalist employers may experience the consequences that ecological degradation has on working people. Workers may ask their employers for wage increases to meet their increased costs due to environmental degradation. Alternatively, people may organize in local movements to protect their conditions of life against polluters.

The state might be called on by different capitals and/or by working people to mediate access to nature. The state then becomes the site of a variety of struggles. In recent years, the European Union (EU) has become for its member countries a quasi-state site of struggles over nature. Environmental regulation by the state has historically been the product of economic and other social struggles within and outside the state. As a result of these different struggles, the state takes on a subsumed class position resembling that of landlord, having control over the access to natural resources and conditions held in "common property" and regulating their use in various ways. This position of the state creates a conflict between it and polluting capitalists over the use of natural resources and conditions and over the payment of rent.

Different state policies toward nature have different effects on individual capitals or groups of capitals (e.g., polluting capitals versus those suffering from pollution) and on subsumed classes and workers. The state, being subsumed to capitals suffering from pollution and also being responsible to working people, establishes policies to reduce pollution. At the same time, the state is subsumed to polluting capitalists and, from this perspective, environmental policies should not jeopardize their existence. Environmental policies may try to "create" incentives that will induce polluting capitalists to reduce pollution to the optimal or desirable social level with the lowest possible costs to them. State-established incentives may induce polluting capitalists to choose among alternative options to reduce pollution (abatement technology, substitution of polluting production technology with a less polluting one, use of less polluting fuels, recycling, and so forth) in a cost-effective manner. The state may also try to establish an enforcement policy (monitoring procedures and fines for violations) that is efficient and effective. In these ways, the goal of attaining higher environmental quality is met while absorbing as little social labor as possible, leaving the rest for the production of surplus value and for securing other important conditions of the existence of polluting capitalists. If environmental policy is not localized but applies to the majority of capitals in a sector, then pollution control expenditures are productive; that is, they determine both surplus value and the value of the commodities produced in this sector. Thus, generalized state regulation aiming at a reduced pollution regime helps establish new regulating conditions of production in the polluting sectors. The reduced pollution regime involves the use of constant and variable capital and further affects both fundamental and subsumed class processes, being manifest in the creation and distribution of surplus value.

Environmental policies, theorized as the outcome of struggles fought within and outside the state, may take the concrete form of direct administrative controls, taxes on emissions, subsidies based on controlled pollution or on abatement technology, marketable emissions permits, and allocation of private property rights. In addition, public projects may be undertaken by the government for preventing further environmental destruction or for restoring environmental quality, for providing environmental education, for enhancing knowledge and developing technology relating to environmental protection, and so forth. Since environmental policies have a different effect on individual fundamental and subsumed class processes, certain classes (or portions of them) may resist or support certain types of policies during the process of establishing them. One important way to assess environmental policies is to reveal these confrontations and their outcomes.

From the perspectives of polluting capitalists and state administrators, and on the basis of economic efficiency, *taxes and marketable permits* appear to have an advantage over other instruments. Emission taxes and marketable permits are, in principle, preferable to polluting capitals since they are more conducive to the market mechanism and imply less state interference in their day-to-day affairs. The polluting firms choose the level of pollution reduction to minimize the total costs of dealing with pollution. They are expected to control pollution up to the level where pollution control costs are less than the tax or the permit fee that alternatively would be paid for uncontrolled emissions. The competitive position of the firms tends to be protected, at least in a static world, since all polluting firms incur taxes (permit costs) or abatement costs, or both. In a dynamic setting, taxes and permits allow greater cost savings for capitals than the direct controls in the face of less costly and more effective abatement technologies; for that matter they encourage the development of more effective and cheaper pollution-control technologies.[6] Significantly, Porter and van der Linde (1995, 120–21) maintain that, from a dynamic point of view, properly designed environmental policies can trigger innovations that lower *total costs of a product* or improve its quality and thus increase global competitiveness. A decrease in total costs of production, *ceteris paribus,* leads to an increased surplus value realized for innovating capitals, while an increase in the competitiveness of these capitals leads to increasing profitability in the future. Environmental regulation thus affects the distribution and the extraction of surplus value.

Moreover, the state might also prefer taxes and auctioned permits since they bring in revenues. Taxes and prices of permits are actually rent payments to the state for letting polluting firms have access to the carrying capacity of environment. There is often a tense struggle between state administrators and polluting firms over the determination of pollution reduction levels that would affect the level of unit taxes and the prices of permits.

On the other hand, there seem to be some differences between taxes and permits in terms of their impact on different segments of polluting capitals and on the state. The permit system might be preferable to both large-scale polluters and regulators. Polluters might prefer it because they may economize on compliance costs, especially if the initial distribution of permits is free of charge. On the other hand, a number of polluting capitals, especially the small ones, may strive against the permit system. Search costs, market imperfections, and strategic behavior may lead to very high abatement costs for them. From the perspective of the environmental authority, the permit system allows it to have direct control over the quantity of pollution; that is, it increases the certainty of the state's environmental effectiveness. It also saves the environmental authority information costs in performing its landlord role, because it does not require the state to have knowledge of the abatement cost, while the exchange of permits leads to efficient allocation of pollution abatement.

Direct administrative controls are usually considered to be costly and to discourage innovation since they often focus on pollution control technologies rather than outcomes, and they do not employ well-defined phase-in periods tied to industry investment cycles. In addition, uniform emissions standards for all polluters across different industries, often imposed by regulatory programs, do not allow firms to take advantage of abatement cost differentials across polluting industries.[7] As Baumol and Oates (1979, 241) have observed, however, business owners and managers evince a determined and sometimes bitter opposition to fiscal methods of environmental control. One reason for this is that enforcement of direct controls allows a certain amount of leeway; the polluter may be able to negotiate with the regulatory agency or take its case to the courts where it may find an easy escape, as the low fines charged for violations of prohibition indicate. A second reason, mentioned by the same authors, has been provided by James Buchanan and Gordon Tullock who argue that, while emissions taxes will normally cause some reduction in profits, direct controls may even increase the profitability of certain capitals. If direct controls effectively limit output and the entry of new firms into polluting industries, environmental measures may succeed in restricting production. The result is, in effect, a legal cartel which, by enforcing scarcity, increases both prices and profits (ibid., 241–42). This argument exemplifies how environmental policy can create another vehicle and arena for capitalist competition. Generalizing this point, certain capitals may even lobby for environmental policy of any kind whether in an effort to promote their sales at the expense of their competitors, to regain their position, or to secure a monopoly position in a polluting industry, especially if, as heavy polluters, they were forced to use an abatement technology.[8]

Regarding *subsidies,* although polluting capitals that are required to reduce their damage to the environment will naturally turn to the state for financial support, they may find other capitalists and working people suffering from pollution in opposition to this option. The latter have strong arguments against polluting capitalists because not only have polluters profited at their expense but they also ask them to finance their pollution abatement. Equity in the state's treatment of economic units is important for capitalist legitimization. Consequently, it is not surprising that the Organization for Economic Cooperation and Development (OECD 1989, 27) and the EU (see, for example, Marin 1990, 381) have adopted the "Polluter Pays Principle" as a general rule guiding environmental policy.

In addition, unit subsidies for reductions in emissions may increase the profits of a polluting enterprise that would be unprofitable under a tax, thus keeping it in business, and may also increase entry, resulting in an overall increase in emissions (Baumol and Oates 1988, chap. 14). Thus marginal polluting capitals may strive for subsidies, while pollution victims and perhaps their competitors will tend to struggle against them. Polluting firms that would be unprofitable under tax may also find their employees on their side on this issue. Such alignments may after all give rise to a subsidy program. The EU, for example, has introduced emission reduction subsidies in several cases of pollution control.

Similar policies may be established to secure the availability of natural resources for capitalist production. First, as the higher quality or easily accessible resources are worked first, followed by the lower quality and less accessible ones, the value of natural resource commodities will increase. The costs for capitals using natural resource commodities will tend to rise, creating incentives for capitalist firms to use substitutes, to develop resource-saving technologies, recycle old scrap, and so forth. This tendency may be reinforced by state policies. In the case of very critical energy resources, for example, the state may assist the long-term transition to renewable energy sources by financing research and development projects and subsidizing the market penetration of these resources; however, the pace of this adjustment and the intensity of policies are heavily influenced by the energy companies that have strong international monopoly positions.

In the case of open-access resources like fisheries, state policies that seek to avoid overuse and extinction take the form of direct controls (limiting fishing time and fishing areas, prohibiting the use of certain types of fishing boats and nets, and so on) and of economic instruments (taxes and transferable fishing quotas). Direct controls have proven not to be cost-effective; quotas, on the other hand, not only are considered more efficient but can also increase the income of fishermen if the government initially allocates them free of charge.[9]

In summary, we can conclude that state regulation to secure natural conditions and resources is overdetermined by class and other economic struggles. Significantly, state regulation (in any form) may apply to the majority of capitals in an industry. In this case, to comply with environmental regulation, capitalists use constant and variable capital. As I have mentioned above, these expenditures then participate in the production of surplus value and also determine the value of relevant commodities. The generalized state policies toward nature shape new regulating conditions of production for capitalism so that protecting the environment becomes a new source of surplus value. Thus environmental policies affect the capitalist class process and, for that matter, the appropriation of nature in capitalist economies.

The shaping of a new environmental regime is, however, full of contradictions. Natural conditions and resources are one among many sets of conditions that capitalism has to secure for its existence. All kinds of possible conflicts can arise in the effort to secure as many of them as possible. In particular, as we have seen, capitalists struggle against each other and against state regulators over the nature of environmental regulation. In addition, labor and ecological movements are fighting for quality of life and may thus constitute a threat to capitalism's existence. Policies toward nature are affected by all these social processes and tensions. Indeed, they are constituted by them, and as such they are contradictory and their outcomes uncertain. Gismondi and Richardson (1994, 237) recognized that the environmental review process undermined the power of state and capital, even if only temporarily (the bleached kraft pulp mill began operating in 1993). Szasz (1991) by contrast presents a "happy end" to his story of struggles over the reduction of hazardous waste at the point of generation. By 1987 a considerable number of companies were claiming that waste reduction efforts were good business.[10] In both cases, however, the final outcome has been conducive to capitalism.

The Impact of Environmental Policies on Capitalism

Although the aforementioned struggles and resulting policies to secure natural resources and conditions may tend to foster the emergence of disruptive discourses and subjectivities, they may not after all challenge existing capitalist class structures with their many undesired results. Indeed a great number of concrete examples indicate that these struggles and policies are conducive to capitalism. They tend to create a market for pollution abatement equipment and conservationist technologies, for environmental specialists, and for environmentally friendly commodities. New industries are developing to meet the demands of "green markets." Economic and other nonclass changes are instigated in other spheres of social life in response to a developing ecologically sensitive culture. Special television programs on environmental issues, ecology sections in newspapers, journals and scientific books on ecology, novels and movies communicating a new ecological ethic, and so forth may be concomitant with a developing green capitalism.

Let us examine a few examples of the ways by which capitalism copes with ecological problems. Capitalism, for one, has not been harmed in its dealing with the ozone (O_3) depletion problem. Ozone depletion is a global problem and its solution requires international cooperation. In 1988, twenty-four nations signed the Montreal Protocol by which they agreed to reduce the principal gases (CFCs and halons) responsible for the problem to 50 percent of 1986 levels by mid-1998. Since the problem grew worse sooner than expected, a new agreement was signed by fifty-nine countries in 1990 to eliminate the seriously implicated gases by the end of the century. To convince the less developed countries to adopt more expensive but less dangerous substitutes, a special fund of $240 million was established by the agreement. To implement this agreement, countries have initiated various policies. The United States, for example, has used a transferable permit system to achieve the targeted reductions, combined with taxes on producers or importers of ozone-depleting substances. The permit system in this case was found to be more efficient than direct controls and fixed taxes. Since allowances for CFCs and halons were allocated to the seven major domestic producers of these chemicals, in their case taxes were considered necessary to restrict windfall profits caused by supply restrictions in the face of inelastic demand for CFC and halon allowances (Tietenberg 1992, 435–38). We can conclude that even in the case of a global environmental problem like ozone depletion, effective solutions have been reached via international agreements, and in this process capitalism has not really been challenged. Of course, it has had to adjust to more expensive, ozone-nondepleting alternatives that may cause difficulties for capitals in securing their other conditions of existence.

Similarly, recycling is becoming an increasingly profitable business operation. Recycling reduces both environmental damage and the natural resource exhaustibility problem. The rising costs of waste disposal, the increasing prices of virgin raw materials, and state incentives (for example, tax credits and exemptions) have made recycling attractive in many capitalist countries. In Japan, for example, about 40 percent of solid waste is recycled, including about 50 percent of paper, 55 percent of glass bottles, and 66 percent of food and beverage cans. In Tokyo, enterprising firms tour neighborhoods, collecting paper waste and rags in exchange for new bathroom and facial tissue (Tietenberg 1992, 190). Thus, although there are many problems and the pace may not be rapid enough, there is clear evidence that a recycling market is on the rise, reducing both pollution and depletion.

Another recent and interesting development in the EU is the Community eco-label award scheme (regulation E.E./880/92). This scheme is intended to "promote the design, production, marketing and use of products which have a reduced environmental impact during their entire life cycle" and "provide consumers with better information on the environmental impact of products." The award scheme is based on voluntary application of the competent body or any interested organization or individual and involves the payment of a fee by the applicant. The award of the eco-label confers rights to a logo that can be used in advertising the product. This scheme clearly establishes a new and desired quality aspect of commodities that is expected to greatly affect the realization and production of environmentally friendly capitalist commodities. It will certainly affect the competitive position of different capitals and, in general, enhance green capitalism.

The case of pollution control in Greece is a typical example of the struggles fought by less competitive capitals outside or within the state, or with the help of the state at the international level, to secure natural resources and conditions, and at the same time survive the competition of more productive international capitals. The big cities of Greece today face very serious environmental problems, most of which are found in the Greater Athens Area (GAA). According to 1991 Census data, 3.5 million of the Greek population of 10.2 million live in Athens. Almost 40 percent of Greek manufacturing was concentrated in the GAA in 1986. Industrial activity contributed 19 percent of smoke, 100 percent of particulate, 72 percent of SO_2, 28 percent of NO_x and 32 percent of HC emitted in the GAA.

A number of policies have been established to cope with urban environmental problems in Greece. These policies are currently shaped by a fierce resistance on the part of firms, especially the less competitive ones, since increases in their costs due to environmental regulation jeopardize their position in relation to European (and non-European) competitors.[11] It also should be noted that a number of environmental policies were first established by the EU and subsequently the Greek government has had to harmonize Greek law with the EU's legal system, no matter how painful this might be for certain capitals and other classes. Within this framework, the Greek state sometimes uses delay as a form of struggle against EU policies to meet the demands of different domestic classes and movements.

Environmental policies toward industrial firms in Greece mainly consist of direct controls. The use of economic incentives for reducing pollution from the industrial sector has been both limited and not as effective as expected (Pelekasi and Skourtos 1992, 110–11). Legal limits on the amount of pollutant an individual source is allowed to emit (i.e., emission standards) have been established for a number of air, water, and land industrial pollutants. Even today, however, monitoring industrial pollution emissions in a systematic way takes place only in the two largest cities of Greece, Athens and Thessaloniki. Compliance with the emission standards is ensured by periodic inspections and by sanctions established against violators. These sanctions can be avoided and also may not be severe enough. Also, firms have to acquire a permit to establish a new industrial plant or to restructure an old one. For this, they have to submit an environmental impact assessment for activities that are expected to have environmentally harmful effects. Because the GAA was considered highly polluted, no permit was granted in the GAA for establishing new plants or expanding old ones for several years, following Presidential Decree 84/1984. In 1987 (and thereafter), however, under great pressure from capitalists, the government has allowed the establishment of new plants and the expansion of old plants (along with some restructuring) in the GAA, by stretching the law (Kallia-Antoniou et al. 1989, 51–69).

Despite the contradictions and the painful adjustment process, environmental policies toward industry have resulted in considerable reductions in air pollution in Greece. According to the Ministry for the Environment, Physical Planning, and Public Works (1995, 327), the five-year plan (1986–1990) for reducing air pollution in the GAA achieved the following reductions: 50 percent in smoke, 79 percent in particulate, 46 percent in SO_2, 24 percent in NO_x, 100 percent in CO, and 30% in HC. Nevertheless, the problem of industrial pollution is still serious in the GAA and there is a constant public demand for the state to forbid the establishment of new plants in the area. In addition, the compliance of firms with emissions standards is not very satisfactory. In general, however, capitalism in Greece does not seem incapable of dealing with environmental problems. It seems to be greening painfully rather than collapsing under ecological tensions.

From the preceding discussion, we may conclude that the "natural constraints" on capitalism seem capable of propelling another round of capitalist change and growth. This should not come as a surprise, since capitalism has always changed and expanded through the many contradictions and tensions it creates (O'Connor 1993, 36). It is in this sense that I have maintained elsewhere (Vlachou 1993a, 1994) that there is no a priori tendency for capitalism to produce environmental crises; green capitalism might be a viable option.

Green capitalism itself, however, will not be free from contradictions and tensions. Securing the natural conditions of capitalism's existence may be in conflict, at least in the short and medium terms, with providing other conditions of existence. It may also cause new tensions, including unemployment. Labor, environmental, and other social movements may challenge capitalism on the grounds of its many undesirable effects. On the other hand, capitals are also in constant change with the aim to meet these challenges. At the same time, capitals also struggle one against the other over the appropriation of nature. The possibility of social change and revolution has always been grounded in the many contradictions and undesirable effects of capitalism and the struggles waged over them. It is thus conceivable that socialism (and not green capitalism) could be the outcome of such a contradictory and overdetermined interaction.

In my opinion, it is from the standpoint of this open-endness that eco-socialists should firmly present the option of socialism and work for it. Socialism is understood here as involving a transition from the prevalence of a capitalist form to that of a collective form of production, appropriation, and distribution of surplus labor, defined as communism or communalism.[12] There have been and still are many debates over the economic, political, and cultural conditions of the existence of communism. These debates indicate, on the one hand, the difficulties of establishing a blueprint for socialism. On the other hand, however, they show the many possibilities that exist and should be explored by social movements in discursive and democratic projects of social transformation (see Dryzek 1992).

Conclusion

Class aspects are important determinants of ecological problems and of policies to solve them. At the same time, ecological problems affect the production and/or the distribution of surplus value and also the determination of the value and prices of commodities, and thus they can instigate class and nonclass conflicts over the appropriation of nature. I have argued in this paper that natural resource depletion and the degradation of the environment first enter into the determination of the value of commodities by affecting labor productivity. In addition, concrete labor may be used to mitigate ecological problems and to produce environmentally friendly commodities. If this occurs and furthermore the clean environment regime becomes the regulating condition of production in a sector, then the labor (in its abstract form) used for environmental protection becomes part of the socially necessary labor time to produce the relevant commodities. For this to happen, various economic, political, and cultural processes must combine to bring the new environmental regime into existence and generalize it.

Changes in values and in surplus value realized propel and also register capitalist efforts to cope with ecological problems. They give "incentives" to capitalists and they are also the outcome of capitalists' "adjustments." Thus the degradation of nature and the ways capitalism deals with it can be insightfully conceptualized using the Marxian concepts of value and surplus value.

Environmental policies are the outcome of various social struggles over the appropriation of nature. Among them, struggles related to the production and distribution of surplus labor play an important role. Moreover, the available evidence seems to indicate that green capitalism is on the rise, propelling another round of capitalist change and growth; however, since green capitalism is shaped by intracapitalist struggles and by the challenges of social movements, including the ecological movement, it is full of tensions and contradictions. This suggests that there may be openings for introducing the possibility of socialism into ongoing and emerging debates and struggles.

Despite their differences, there is a lot of common ground in the aspirations of environmentalists and socialists, suggesting that alliances could be built between them. If they approach each other with respect and sincerity, they may be able to reach an understanding that capitalist exploitation cannot be part of any ecological project. Environmentalists can no longer downplay the fact that they live in a social system in which capitalist profit and surplus appropriation penetrate deep into every aspect of life. By joining forces with socialists, they can be more effective in promoting a sustainable relationship between society and nature (including human nature). Moreover, overdeterminist Marxists, who argue that every social process is shaped by the influences of all the other social and natural processes, are well situated to join hands with ecologists working for economic egalitarianism, democracy, ecological and cultural diversity, quality of life, and so forth. They might argue that a different organization of social labor—specifically, a collective organization of the production and appropriation of surplus (social) labor—could contribute to creating a sustainable relationship between nature and society.

However, in building a coalition between environmentalists and socialists, the issue of *political efficacy* emerges in view of their many differences. Political efficacy seems to require integrating differences into a workable strategy, able to challenge capitalism. From this perspective, I concur with J. O'Connor (1988, 33–38) and E. Leff (1993, 63–66) that postmarxism (despite its several significant, in my opinion, epistemological contributions) and social anarchocommunalism have failed to present a strategy capable of challenging contemporary capitalism. For a start, I think that Marx's concept of social labor can still provide a unifying element to build a politically effective coalition for social change. Social labor, an aspect of socialized human nature, is a common human experience, in the sense that it has always sustained societies and thus individual human lives. In addition, social labor is decided by and performed within (class) societies, and thus it is, in a broad sense, under the control of society. Social labor also mediates the interaction of nature and society. As a result, a strategy to create a sustainable relationship between nature and society could be based on the organization of social labor, different from that currently existing in capitalist societies. Overdeterminist socialists argue for a collective organization of production and appropriation of surplus (social) labor.

Roemer (1994, 130) observes that history at this point may not be on the side of (any kind of) socialism. At the same time, he asks socialists to be patient and to "understand how brief a moment is seventy years in human history, to remember how continuous has been the struggle of mankind against inequality and injustice, and to realize how enduring are those problems that engendered the socialist idea almost two centuries ago." From this perspective, socialism of some unknown sort can still be a possibility.

Collective forms of appropriating both nature and surplus labor may preserve and promote the values of collectivity; they may also foster respect for the environment that enables the production and enjoyment of social wealth. On the basis of these understandings, and with a vision of the interdependence of social forms and natural processes, environmentalists and socialists may work together to create communal economic relations and new relations to nature. Perhaps some of the insights put forward in this paper will contribute to such a project.

Notes

I wish to thank the editors, James O'Connor, Anwar Shaikh, Basilis Droucopoulos, Dimitris Milonakis, and Thanassis Aliferis for helpful comments on an earlier version of this chapter.

1 Specifically, according to Leff (1993, 52), "the question of the environment challenges the theoretical status of the concept of social labor and the concept of value." "Marx's theory of production is incapable of putting a value on natural and cultural resources" (ibid., 48). "The failure to put a value on natural resources means that ecological imbalances, the decline in soil

fertility, and the depletion of non-renewable resources are not reflected in the value of capital and in the price formation of natural use values, while accumulation and reappraisal of capital is reflected in the destruction of resources that capital does not take into account" (ibid., 51). "The environmental crisis," continues Leff, "thus marks the explanatory limits of a theory in which natural use values are valued only insofar as they incorporate labor time or internalize the 'scarcity' of natural resources through the market" (ibid., 52).

2 Elements of theorizing the appropriation of nature in terms of the Marxian theory of value and surplus value can be found in Vlachou (1983), Massarrat (1980), Harvey (1982), and Leff (1995).

3 I have estimated elsewhere (Vlachou 1983, 293) that in 1972, 84 percent of the crude oil reserves owned by the seven biggest multinationals outside the United States and the former "socialist" countries were concentrated in the Middle East.

4 The current debate within the European Union and at the international forums over CO_2 emissions reduction policies to deal with the global warming problem vividly exemplifies this point. The business side insists that no policy should be inaugurated if it is not applied to (at least) all industrialized countries.

5 For a more detailed analysis of the class struggles waged around energy resources, see Vlachou (1983).

6 It is interesting to note that the U.S. Environmental Protection Agency has initiated an Emissions Trading Program in recent years to provide more flexibility in meeting air quality goals and also to promote cost-efficiency. In Europe, on the other hand, to achieve similar goals many have introduced emission charges.

7 Tietenberg (1985, chap. 3), for example, provides a survey of empirical (neo-classical) studies that find the costs of environmental policies under direct administrative controls to be significantly higher than their least-cost levels.

8 The argument advanced and documented by Porter and van der Linde (1995) in their attempt to end the "arm wrestling match" between polluting firms and the state over environmental regulation is that environmental improvement allows firms to better their positions in international markets.

9 When the state assumes control over open-access resources, it may actually dispossess traditional noncapitalist users like fishermen—who may be involved in an ancient or communal class process—of the resource through regulation that gives greater access to capitalist firms. In this case, we often observe fishermen waging a fierce struggle against regulation that favors capitalist fishing (St. Martin 1998).

10 Szasz (1991, 42) observes that "the history of hazardous waste regulation suggests a transitional form of environmental politics that makes progress by simultaneously using and abusing the democratic aspects of the State, a strategy that, for want of a better term, we may provisionally label 'policy Luddism.' " He also notes (ibid., 43) that "the asymptotic approximation of pollution prevention, achieved through a truly popular and democratic grassroots mobilization that pits people against capital and state regulations, provides the empowering experience of collective action, and radicalizes participants."

11 Environmental regulation may even drive small-scale and less profitable enterprises that already face economic difficulties out of business. These problems have been exacerbated in recent years by the continuing austerity programs and tight monetary policies implemented to meet the criteria of the Maastricht Agreement for the Economic and Monetary Integration of the European Union.

12 Conceptualizations of socialism and communism from an overdeterminist Marxist standpoint can be found in Resnick and Wolff (1988), Vlachou (1993b, 1994), Ruccio (1992), and Cullenberg (1992).

CAROLE BIEWENER

□

THE PROMISE OF FINANCE

Banks and Community Development

Radicals have often looked to financial institutions in general and banks in particular as sites for furthering progressive social change. Indeed, credit schemes have been a feature of many progressive community development initiatives ranging from the Grameen Bank in Bangladesh to the 1977 Community Reinvestment Act in the United States and the French *Parti Socialiste*'s initial plan to "socialize" credit in the early 1980s. In these initiatives, however, finance has all too often been subordinated to "productive" investment and access to credit has been predicated on the promise of an adequate rate of return or, in Marxian language, the monetary valorization of finance capital. By privileging the accumulation of productive capital and/or the valorization of finance capital in this manner, the economic profitability of an initiative is highlighted, while other economic, cultural, and political effects are shunted to a secondary position, marginalized, or made invisible. As a result, progressive financial policy has often faced the challenge of promoting radical social change and community development while furthering capitalist production and class exploitation.

In examining progressive financing initiatives, it becomes evident that they offer alternative kinds of radical possibilities, depending on which aspect of financing is emphasized and in what manner. This essay contributes to the theorization of these alternative radical possibilities by highlighting the class dimensions of various progressive initiatives involving bank loans.[1] The essay shows that if in some instances the class aspects and effects of bank lending are considered, then communal and associated forms of production may be fostered, thereby furthering community development in a manner that enables nonexploitative class relations. By recognizing the multiple understandings of what may characterize a progressive community, it argues for developing broader notions of "productive investment" and "return," thereby decentering the monetary valorization of industrial capital and bank capital to enable the incorporation of other important gender, racial, class, or environmental considerations. Thus, while highlighting the class dimension of moneylending, this essay does not aim to inscribe class as the fundamental or most important aspect of progressive financing initiatives. The analysis is developed by considering three aspects of bank lending: the manner in which moneylending decisions are made; the kinds of expenditures that are financed; and the manner in which loans are repaid. Each offers distinct possibilities for furthering radical social change.

Democratizing Moneylending

Many progressive initiatives have called for the "socialization" or "democratization" of credit (*Parti socialiste* 1980; Pollin 1995). These strategies attempt to radically transform the way in which moneylending decisions are made by including new constituents or stakeholders in credit allocation decisions, from local government officials and "community" representatives to productive laborers, consumers, environmental activists, or small-scale industrial capitalists and merchants. In these initiatives banks are recognized as providing the arena for establishing some form of collective control over loan allocations. In social formations that have large amounts of income and wealth in a monetized form, banks are a site where "social wealth is condensed and collected" (Gibson-Graham 1996, 175). While bankers do not own most of the money capital they lend out, they do exercise considerable control over who receives this money capital and for what purposes. Bankers, therefore, are an element in the social distribution of monetized wealth. Marx recognized the development of this "social function" along with that of the credit system:

The development of the credit and banking system places all available and even potential capital that is not already actively committed at the disposal of the industrial and commercial capitalists, so that neither the lender nor the user of this capital are its owner or producers. It thereby abolishes the private character of capital and thus inherently bears within it, though only inherently, the abolition of capital itself. Through the banking system, the distribution of capital is removed from the hands of private capitalists and usurers and becomes a special business, a social function. (Marx 1981, vol. 3, 742)

Many progressive initiatives have highlighted the possibility of using banks to influence the allocation of social wealth without directly appropriating it. The moneylending activities of bankers constitute a practice where the link might be broken between the private ownership of monetized wealth and its allocation or distribution. These activities offer opportunities for establishing some sort of community or democratic control over bank capital—a particular form of social wealth. In the early 1980s, for instance, the French Socialists hoped that a "socialization of credit" would allow a "collective will" or "national interest" to shape the logic of financial arrangements and capital accumulation rather than the short-sighted greed of financiers (Biewener 1988, 151).

This abstract notion of establishing some form of social or collective control over moneylending does offer radical possibilities for change. Democratization of credit allocation decisions affects political processes of decision making and control by changing who acts as moneylenders in potentially new and radical ways. The hope is that progressive community-building expenditures will be financed by having credit allocation decisions include people whose identities are consciously constituted as other than financiers. Democratization initiatives attempt to foster a "community consciousness" whereby banks operate in some democratic or representative manner with "community interests" used as a guiding principle in lending decisions. Such initiatives also contribute to a socialization of credit by positing bank capital as a *social* resource and by legitimizing the notion of community control and debate over the use of this form of social wealth.

Compared to enterprises, households, or governments, banks offer a different site for collective deliberation concerning the allocation of social wealth. They can enable a different and particular sense of community. For instance, while collectivization at the enterprise level may enable productive workers to take charge of the labor process and/or to appropriate and distribute their surplus labor in some manner, this level of "community" or "collectivity" is defined in terms of those working in that enterprise. Membership in the community/collectivity and rights to participate in deliberations concerning the production and use of the fruits of the collectivity are, therefore, determined, at least in part, by occupying a position as a productive (and, perhaps, unproductive) laborer in that particular process of production. It is easy to imagine, therefore, that members of such an "enterprise community" might be interested in maximizing the portion of the surplus product retained by the enterprise, whether by using low-cost component parts produced elsewhere under highly exploitative conditions, politicking for lower taxes, polluting the environment without incurring the clean-up costs, or perhaps by discouraging women from joining their "community" because of higher health-care costs and turnover. As Eric Shragge, a Canadian community development activist, has noted, enterprise-level cooperative producers may "mirror the demands of a capitalist economy by looking after their own survival as units in a market place" (1993, iii).

In the case of banks, collective deliberation about the allocation of loans may encompass a broader understanding of who is to be included in the community and of what constitutes a community. While any proposal to establish some form of community or collective control over credit allocation entails ongoing debate about what a bank's community is, it would most likely incorporate a range of sites: industrial workplaces, households, schools, stores, parks, recreational facilities, and roads; and identities: as productive and unproductive capitalist workers, self-employed independent commodity producers, consumers, merchants/retailers, teachers, community activists, urban planners, women's rights advocates, environmentalists, parents, religious leaders, or African Americans. Indeed, the very process of debating and defining what the community is may contribute to legitimizing collective control over the allocation of a social surplus.[2] In such a debate Marxists may argue for incorporating a particular class content along with other progressive concerns and considerations in the democratization of credit allocation decisions; and such a class content may mean that productive and unproductive workers participate in moneylending decisions.[3] For instance, in the Mondragón Cooperative Corporation in the Basque region of Spain, it appears that a worker-based identity is the primary means for defining who may serve on the board of directors for the central savings institution, the *Caja Laboral Popular* (Working Peoples Bank), which serves the worker-controlled cooperatives. Workers in the *Caja Laboral Popular* hold one-third of the seats on the board of directors, with the other two-thirds held by workers from the industrial coopera-tives that it lends to (Gunn and Gunn 1991, 65).[4]

Yet, clearly, a worker-based identity is not the only identity motivat-ing progressive initiatives. For feminists, democratization of credit could have a gender component, with impoverished women, single mothers, self-employed women, women's rights advocates, and/or childcare pro-viders also participating as moneylenders. Some loan circle funds have, indeed, been established with the aim of empowering marginalized women by involving them in lending decisions, as in the case of the Grameen Bank in Bangladesh or CIDEL (*Centre d'innovation en déve-loppement économique local du Grand Plateau*), a community devel-opment organization in Montreal. For antiracist activists, democratiza-tion of credit may mean including people of diverse ethnicities and races in credit allocation decisions to encourage the development of inner-city neighborhoods, "minority-owned businesses," or, more broadly, communities of color. The point here is that progressive initiatives that focus on banks as a means for introducing democratic and community-based practices in the allocation of social wealth broaden what is consti-tuted as "the collectivity" and, thereby, may broaden who participates in moneylending decisions as well as extending the scope of deliberation and debate about what constitutes expenditures to further "community development."

In the United States and Canada, emphasis on local control has proven to be an important and effective means for mobilizing individuals and groups to develop alternative community-based organizations aimed at enhancing community development, including the creation of alterna-tive credit institutions (Gunn and Gunn 1991; Perry 1987; Quarter 1992; Shragge 1993). All too often "outside" ownership of productive and un-productive assets has enabled the transfer of surplus and other revenues out of a community, reducing the amount of financing available locally. As Perry has commented, "research can make it abundantly clear that the so-called low-income area generates considerable savings (that is, available capital), but that these savings are often being deposited in insti-tutions whose decisions do not include local investment. In short, there is available capital, but it is conventionally exported to other localities" (1987, 38).[5]

In response to this some communities have turned to local banks that are democratically owned and operated to ensure that local capital and revenues are lent within a community. Some communities have clearly been marginalized by "outside" banks, receiving small amounts of financing along with limited banking services. The now notorious redlining by U.S. banks in Boston, Chicago, Detroit, Los Angeles, and elsewhere shows how communities of color have been systematically denied access to bank services, mortgage loans, and business financing. In the United States, one response to this has been to use the 1977 Community Reinvestment Act along with community organizing and activism to force large-scale commercial banks to establish loan portfolios targeted for lending in formerly redlined communities.[6] Another response has been to create new credit institutions—community banks, community development credit unions, and community loan funds—that use local monetary resources for local financing, as well as for garnering external, "outside" money-capital for community financing (Squires 1992; Perry 1987).

In and of themselves "local" banks offer no guarantee of engaging in progressive lending practices, nor of financing local, community-based needs. Indeed, local banks often engage in the most conservative lending practices *and* often function to draw money capital and revenues out of communities, rather than bringing new sources of financing in (Gunn and Gunn 1991, 61). With this in mind, the call for "local control" seems to offer more promise if it is coupled with the democratization or socialization of credit, thereby enabling community representatives to foster community development financing and to garner outside resources for local financing, bringing monetary resources into the community rather than channeling them out of it. Indeed, a "socially responsible orientation" may enable community development banks or credit unions to attract deposits from institutional savers, including foundations, public agencies, capitalist corporations, religious organizations, and various mutual funds. As Dymski (1996) notes, the South Shore Bank in Chicago is an oft-touted example of such a successful "greenlining" strategy.

In the United States and Canada, progressives concerned with furthering local democratic control of finance have often turned to credit unions in particular: "The co-ops of the financial world, [credit unions] are run by boards of directors elected by depositors, rather than investor-owners, as in a bank" (Gunn and Gunn 1991, 62). As Gunn and Gunn indicate, "the 1980s brought bank and savings-and-loan failures, but dramatic success for credit unions" (62). Indeed, since 1980, membership in the United States's 11,900 credit unions has grown from 44 million to 70.4 million, while assets have "exploded to $316 billion from $69 billion" (compared to the $4.4 trillion in assets held by the 10,000 commercial banks) (Gilpin 1997, B1). While most credit unions are oriented toward providing financial services such as consumer loans and mortgages for their members, a "special category of community development credit unions has emerged, aimed at serving communities' local development needs, such as housing or minority-owned businesses" (Gunn and Gunn 1991, 62). By the late 1980s, about one hundred community development credit unions were operating in the United States. For instance, Santa Cruz's progressively oriented Community Credit Union has served as a "magnet" to attract outside money capital by participating in the Capitalization Program of the Federation of Community Development Credit Unions, a vehicle for attracting funds from major national philanthropic, religious, and service organizations (64). In Canada, credit unions (*caisses populaires*) are quite widespread and successful, with about $63 billion (Canadian) in deposits by 1989 (Quarter 1992, 155).[7] Thus, despite the imposing financial imperatives of increasingly globalized and deregulated financial markets, it does appear that in some instances credit unions have been able to channel financing toward local uses and, at times, this has involved community development initiatives. Also, while alternative credit institutions account for a relatively small share of lending, where they have been established they do seem to offer important sites for broadening participation in moneylending decisions.

Clearly then, some radical initiatives have furthered progressive community development activities by democratizing credit allocation decisions so that there is more broad-based community representation. In so doing these efforts have fostered social control of bank capital, while at times also augmenting the amount of money available to finance local community development initiatives. This then brings us to the issues of what constitutes "community development investments" and what types of initiatives or expenditures are financed.

What Is to Be Financed?

By considering the question of what types of expenditures are to be financed, we are able to see some of the limitations of efforts that tend to focus primarily on democratizing credit. For without a radical retheorization of the kinds of expenditures to be financed, all too often the focus is that of simply furthering "business development" in general or "productive investment" in particular. From a Marxian perspective this usually means financing capital accumulation to further capitalist exploitation. It also means marginalizing the effects of lending other than accumulation: the gender, environmental, racial, class, or imperialist aspects of credit.

The French Socialist government of the early 1980s provides an important example of this trend, having come to power with an initial emphasis on "socializing credit" to further radical social change. The Socialists had a power-based understanding of class, whereby class exploitation was understood as a political process defined by power and control rather than an economic process defined in terms of surplus production and extraction (Biewener 1987). Rather than developing a Marxian analysis of economic relations, the French Socialists relied on Keynesian economic thinking for their theorization of financial and economic processes (Biewener 1988, 1990). The "collective will" became identified with investments to expand employment, strengthen the industrial fabric, reconquer the domestic market, and render the French nation more "autonomous." Government credit policies became focused on reorienting bank lending toward financing productive investment that economized on energy and raw materials, enhanced production for export, modernized production techniques, automated the production process, or promoted new innovations (Biewener 1989b, 132–152).[8] All too quickly the aim became that of simply fostering capitalist growth to achieve full employment and higher levels of output and income; and the economic class consequences, when articulated, were seen as providing job security and higher real incomes for capitalist waged workers.

By only considering class in political terms of power and force, the French Socialists were unable to offer any radical redefinition in economic class terms of those purposes for which money should be lent.

Their radical Keynesian approach included a concern with new investment spending as a condition for prosperity and growth, but it neglected theorization of the class origins and distributed destinations of such wealth or prosperity. From a Marxian perspective, the French Socialists' "radical" credit policy, with its focus on "productive investment," was rapidly reduced to efforts to promote capitalist growth rather than transform the class character of production and growth.

This tendency to ignore class processes of surplus production, appropriation, and distribution and to define progressive financing primarily in terms of productive investment is also clearly evident in the United States (Squires 1992; Dymski, Epstein, and Pollin 1993). Alternative credit institutions (credit unions, development banks, and community loan funds) have usually been justified in terms of financing housing and small-scale businesses in neighborhoods that are "underserved" by the existing commercial banks, with "business" more or less explicitly referring to small-scale capitalist production, independent commodity production, or some type of retail outlet (Dymski 1995/96; Bond and Townsend 1996; Squires 1992; Minsky 1993).[9]

If the class processes of surplus production, appropriation, and distribution are considered, then the potentially exploitative character of such "business" investments would have to be taken into account when elaborating a vision of community development. Further, theorization of class processes may enable a progressive understanding of investment whereby investments in communal class processes are financed rather than in capitalist or independent commodity production (Biewener 1989a). There are different class consequences associated with productive investment, depending on what kinds of class relations or processes are enabled through the purchase of productive capital. From a Marxian perspective, investment in capitalist production is productive only if the acquired constant capital or means of production is successfully used to produce commodities that embody surplus labor whose value can be realized as surplus value. Productive investment is capitalist, that is, insofar as it enables capitalist exploitation. Money lent to finance such productive investment functions as industrial capital for the capitalist (as well as functioning as loan capital for the bank) insofar as its valorization is accomplished via capitalist exploitation.

Alternatively, if money is lent to finance investment in a *noncapital-*

ist class process, then it ceases to function as capital in the process of production, though it may still function as capital for the bank.[10] Further, when money is lent to finance investment in associated forms of production whereby surplus labor is collectively appropriated by the direct producers, it enables productive investment in a communal or communist sense. Thus, if "socially responsible" moneylenders incorporate such a class-based understanding of "productive investment," they may then strive to foster communal or communist production by lending to finance workers' cooperatives or by using access to investment credit as a "bargaining chip" to enable workers within capitalist enterprises to gain greater collective control over the appropriation and distribution of their surplus labor.[11]

In Canada and, to a lesser extent, in the United States, there are some examples of initiatives that finance cooperative production. Perry (1987) and Quarter (1992) comment on the "Antigonish movement" in Nova Scotia, Canada, with its tradition of supporting the creation of producer and consumer cooperative associations to counteract "the power of economic interests outside each community" (Perry 1987, 13). In Montreal, CIDEL-GP's loan fund initiative, which is oriented toward financing income-generating projects for poor women, is in part motivated by a concern with encouraging cooperative and collectivist types of associations: "While each individual's business is important, the longer-term goal is to provide support to circle participants to aid them in the development of cooperative and community projects that respond to their needs" (McMurtry 1993, 70). Also, the Evangeline group of fifteen cooperatives in southwestern Prince Edward Island includes "a credit union; a fish-processing plant; a supermarket/mall; a health clinic; a seniors' home; a tourist facility including a hotel restaurant, theatre and tour company; a handicraft enterprise; a forestry business; a potato chip producer (Olde Barrel); a cable television service; a funeral service; and a youth cooperative" (Quarter 1992, 104).

In the United States, the Santa Cruz Community Credit Union (SCCCU) was established in 1977 with the publicized goals of "democratic management, recirculation of members' savings within the county, and community development lending." The SCCCU set out to distinguish itself by deemphasizing consumer loans and concentrating "a majority of their lending on community development projects, especially locally owned, cooperatively managed businesses." To this end they "made significant early loans to businesses such as a worker-owned print shop and a Hispanic strawberry production co-op" (Gunn and Gunn 1991, 63).[12] Also, the Cooperative Fund of New England (CFNE) is a nonprofit revolving loan fund that "focuses on systemic reform through equitable sharing of economic power." Established in 1975 with a $25,000 investment base, CFNE has lent over $25 million to more than 175 borrowers who are primarily "low and moderate income cooperatives and nonprofit organizations, including consumer, worker, marketing, housing, land trust and self-help organizations" (Grassroots Economic Organizing [GEO] Newsletter January/February 1997, 6).

In addition to financing communal production and appropriation within a particular enterprise, moneylending institutions could also become a site for involving workers in decisions affecting class processes outside of their own particular enterprises, thereby furthering a socialized allocation of surplus between different cooperative or associated work processes. This would occur to the extent that monetary revenues realized by an enterprise are deposited in a community bank so that loans could be made on the basis of such new deposits. In this manner, not only could socialization be promoted within a capitalist enterprise via bank lending, but also between enterprises and between enterprises and other social sites (governments, communities, households). As discussed above, bank lending could enable socialization on a wider scale, with workers and other community representatives determining allocations of surplus and nonclass revenues across an array of sites and activities. This seems to be what the editorial coordinator of the GEO newsletter, Bob Stone, had in mind when he recently called for the formation of a regional cooperative bank in the manner of Mondragón's *Caja Laboral Popular* to finance a network of producer cooperatives. Referring to "intercooperation" that involves local or regional intermediate support associations for grassroots cooperatives, Stone commented that "the movement lacks 'in-house' credit or technical services like those at Mondragón" (GEO Newsletter April/May 1997, 2).[13]

It seems that while limited in scope, there are some encouraging examples of efforts to finance cooperative and associated forms of production.[14] It is not clear, however, how much attention has been paid to analyzing and understanding the character of such cooperative efforts.[15]

There are many different ways to cooperate—in decision making, in marketing, in financing, in purchasing, in sharing inputs, in the labor process—without also enabling the collective appropriation and distribution of surplus labor. In other words, it is possible to promote cooperatives and collectivities without also promoting what Marxists would call a communal or communist class process (Resnick and Wolff 1988). Further, there are many different communal forms of surplus-labor appropriation and distribution some, perhaps, even "hideous" (Amariglio 1984a; Cullenberg 1992). It is important, therefore, that radicals consider the alternative meanings of cooperation and communal production to understand the different class character and effects of each. By recognizing the multiple meanings of "communal production" and "cooperatives," radicals can no longer simply presume that such production relations are beneficial or even desired. Instead, we must explore the alternative motivations, possibilities, and effects that each meaning enables.[16]

Throughout the community development literature there is an emphasis on promoting small-scale production, "microenterprises," and/or independent commodity production via self-employment. It would seem that, aside from the notable exception of the Mondragón Cooperative Corporation's industrial cooperatives, there is a striking absence of initiatives that promote communal class processes in "large-scale" industry.[17] This may be tied to the community development literature's emphasis on local-level institutions, with "small-scale" explicitly or implicitly attached as a modifier.[18] As a result, when "large-scale" production is considered, it is, seemingly by default, assumed to mean capitalist industry. In this manner, defining community development primarily in terms of local control not only occludes the surplus-labor aspects of production, it also neglects theorization of progressive strategies for transforming large-scale capitalist enterprises in a radical manner.

The tendency to both neglect class relations of surplus appropriation and distribution and to identify "large-scale" as necessarily capitalist is also evident in the United States and Canada when lending to "marginalized" communities is emphasized. Marginalization is usually characterized in terms of powerlessness, low income, lack of control, high unemployment, or "economic disenfranchisement," rather than in class terms of surplus production and appropriation (Shragge 1993; Gunn and Gunn 1991; Perry 1987). Indeed, the harsh circumstances of high unemployment often seem to impose a hierarchy of need in which the provision of waged labor, and thereby income, becomes the overriding imperative, with concern about class relations of production seen as almost a luxury. As one community development activist commented:

BCA [Banking Community Assets in Cape Breton] is in a community that has 25–30% unemployment, and its survival is truly threatened. We as developers in the community are willing to look at virtually anything in order to survive. There is no time for the frills to take issue with the quality of the workplace and improving workplace conditions. In our situation of high unemployment, out migration, buildings being boarded up, in this sort of situation, you will do most anything for the people you serve. (GEO Newsletter, April/May 1997, 9)

Similarly, in the economically depressed community of Eggleston-Jackson in Boston, a long-standing community development corporation, Urban Edge, has begun to broaden its focus from providing affordable housing to that of promoting economic development. Such development is oriented primarily toward bringing much-needed retail outlets and commercial services into the community, as well as providing jobs for the largely unskilled residents. To this end Urban Edge has brokered deals with large-scale corporations that have resulted in the establishment of a Fleet Bank branch office and a McDonald's franchise that is owned by a local resident, while plans are being made for Walgreens and CVS drug stores. When asked about the possibilities of furthering cooperatively owned retail outlets or producer cooperatives, the director of Urban Edge dismissed such possibilities as unpractical and secondary to the more pressing needs of jobs and income.[19]

This focus on marginalization and low income is reflected in the orientation of many alternative credit initiatives in the United States. For instance, the 1977 Community Reinvestment Act placed "affirmative responsibilities on depository institutions beyond the mere obligation to operate safely and soundly" (Dennis 1978, 694). Banks have been charged with "rebuilding and revitalizing communities in decline" (Hayden and Swanson 1980, 359). Also, since the late 1970s, community development loan funds have been established to borrow and lend at moderate interest rates "to benefit communities and individuals denied sufficient access to traditional capital markets," and development banks have been created to "service depressed areas or nontraditional borrowers" (Gunn and Gunn 1991, 67, 69).[20] In 1994 Congress passed the Community Development Finance Institution Act, which created a new independent agency to manage a $125 million fund designed to "invest and assist" local community development financial institutions. One key priority of the new fund is to help develop businesses that "provide jobs for, and are owned by, low income people, or that enhance the availability of products and services for low income people" (GEO Newsletter, December 1994/January 1995, 2).

While mobilizing "marginalized" communities so that new lending may occur in them is certainly important for promoting progressive change, the emphasis on income levels, job availability, and the provision of retail outlets and banking facilities has at least two problematic effects on strategies for radical social change. First, class relations involving the performance, appropriation, and distribution of surplus labor are not captured with reference to income divisions. Exploitative class relations may be promoted in the name of raising income levels when, for instance, loans are made to finance capitalist industry with the hope that they will bring jobs. Progressive initiatives that only focus on promoting productive investment in capitalist production are forever entangled in the contradiction of trying to promote progressive change while ensuring the valorization of money via capitalist exploitation.

Second, a focus on financing community development solely in marginalized areas, however defined, means that explicit strategies for transforming "unmarginalized communities" in a progressive sense are not developed. Either these communities are understood as having already achieved a desirable state of existence by dint of their not being marginalized, or they are ignored. The focus on marginalized communities thus has its own forms of exclusion by not theorizing progressive finance initiatives for middle- and upper-income communities, or even for prosperous working-class communities.

The argument here is *not* that radical finance initiatives should deemphasize productive investment or community development in "marginalized" communities. Rather, the aim is to problematize or destabilize what it means to be productive and marginal so as to enable a range of productive investments and antimarginalization strategies, including those concerned with class exploitation along with income inequalities. This means developing a broader, noncapitalist understanding of productive investment. Such a redefinition of "productive investment" in noncapitalist terms opens up myriad radical possibilities for progressive financial policy. First, as discussed above, it allows us to theorize differences in productive investment in terms of the class relations or class processes these investments may foster, thereby enabling recognition of investment in noncapitalist class processes as *productive*. This understanding is important not only for promoting the financing of investment in communal class processes but also for financing investments in other noncapitalist class processes. Here feminists have long argued that investments are needed to render women's unpaid labor in noncapitalist class processes more "productive." Kabeer considers some of the implications of this in her discussion of the Grameen Bank:

> In its early years, Grameen Bank offered credit for a very narrow range of "productive" activities which related to market-oriented production. However, it became clear that if credit was intended to enhance household survival and security, it needed to be fungible between different uses of women's time, all of which contributed to the well-being of household members. Loans for health-related activities could act simultaneously as a time-saving measure (since women had to take time off from economic activities to take care of the sick) as well as an asset-preserving one (since families often had to sell off productive assets to pay for medical treatment). Recognizing the fungibility of labour and resources within the household, Grameen has expanded its loan-giving activities. Since the mid-eighties, it has sought to develop viable borrower cooperative groups to undertake such activities as primary health care, child nutrition, sanitation, literacy and family planning. It is also planning to add a health programme to its activities in view of the fact that enterprise profits are often wiped out by expensive medical costs. (1994, 234–35)

Clearly, the Grameen Bank is lending to finance "productive activities" beyond those associated with market-oriented capitalist or independent commodity production. In this instance, not only is women's unpaid labor recognized as productive, there is also a broadening of the notion of what it means to be productive.

This raises a second aspect of how broadening our understanding of productive investment may enhance radical initiatives concerned with class exploitation along with gender subordination, racial discrimination and subordination, poverty, imperialism, and/or environmental degradation. If we are able to understand that what is "productive" in a capitalist class sense is a very particular and narrow notion of "productive" (productive of surplus value) then, by considering noncapitalist class processes, we are able to broaden our understanding of "productive" investment, and thereby redefine productivity in non-surplus-value terms and even, perhaps, in nonmonetary terms.

We could, for instance, measure productivity in terms of a vector of use-values (rather than as a sum of exchange-values) that may include adequate housing, education, nonexploitative forms of production, urban renewal, women's empowerment, ecologically sound production, job expansion, income-generation projects for people of color, or the establishment of "green spaces." [21] In this manner not only are capitalist-based notions of productivity decentered but also what is considered "productive" is not defined strictly in class terms. Thus by recognizing these class aspects of productive investment the class project is, ironically, decentered and understood as only one aspect of what constitutes a productive investment. This consideration of what renders an investment or expenditure "productive" brings us to the third aspect of how bank lending may contribute to furthering progressive community development initiatives—how a loan is to be repaid and bank capital valorized.

Repayment and Valorization

Interestingly, some radical traditions that do theorize a "social surplus" have also developed a critique of finance inspired by antiusury sentiments, as evidenced by the broad-based dependency and world systems theorists (Amin 1974, 1977; Frank 1969; Rodney 1974; Wallerstein 1974). These traditions tend to focus on the money–capital circuit and the valorization of finance capital per se, while drawing on moral arguments that criticize the private ownership of monetized wealth as a basis for "extracting" or receiving interest payments.

In Marxian terms, such antiusury initiatives aim to promote progressive change by abolishing money as capital for moneylenders. While this may have radical effects, it leaves open the question of whether or not such initiatives also aim to transform exploitative capitalist class processes, as this depends on what the money is lent for. Generally, radical antiusury initiatives focus on two types of strategies: providing cheap financing by reducing the amount of interest paid, or redefining what is accepted or counted as repayment. Let us examine each in turn.

Private wealth holders often expect to expand their wealth by valorizing it via moneylending. Given such a "normal" expectation that savings should realize market rates of return, private wealth holders frequently must be tempted by tax incentives or appealed to through moral suasion to "invest" in community development–oriented credit institutions that pay low interest. Credit unions in the United States, for instance, are tax-exempt organizations, and this has allowed them to offer depositors attractive returns on their deposits while providing loans at below-market rates.

There are examples, however, of lending institutions obtaining funds at zero or concessionary real rates of interest, which they relend at favorable, below-market rates of interest. Perry discusses the example of community loan funds that offer what he calls "friendly money on concessionary terms." [22] In itself there is nothing radical about reducing or eliminating interest payments. Yet, when tied to financing particular types of expenditures deemed "progressive," initiatives to provide financing at below-market rates may be embraced as radical or progressive. Further, by limiting the amount of interest that accrues to moneylenders, presumably more social wealth is available to be spent in other ways.

Interest payments are often viewed critically as drains on the social surplus;[23] and this interest "drain" is often understood as coming at the expense of domestic or community-level productive investments. The simple opposition between interest payments and productive investment, however, is problematic in at least two respects. First, the payment of interest in and of itself does not mean that such money is eventually spent unproductively.[24] A financier might use accumulated interest payments to finance new loans for productive investment, and in this case the interest would be spent productively. Of more concern, perhaps, should be who controls the allocation of "social surplus" represented by the interest—capitalist financiers, alternative community development credit institutions, or corporate managers and boards of directors. When considered within the context of national and/or community development, this becomes a complicated issue. Interest payments have often been understood as contributing to an "external drain" by transferring a portion of a community's locally produced social surplus to "outside" or "foreign" financial institutions.[25] As discussed above, radicals have argued that locally based financial institutions are more likely to relend any accumulated interest within the communities from which the interest originated, especially if the lending institutions have community representatives who are involved in credit allocation decisions.

Another problematic aspect of criticizing interest payments as "drains" on a social surplus is that all too often the amount drained is measured against its desired use as "productive investment" without any explicit theorization of "productive investment" in terms of its class or gender or racial effects. This leaves the door open for promoting productive investments that further capitalist exploitation, gender subordination (Elson and Pearson 1981), racial discrimination, or environmental degradation. Here again we see that it is not enough to argue that bank capital should finance productive rather than unproductive investments. The notion of what "productive" means also must be theorized and specified so as to enable and legitimize noncapitalist and other alternative understandings of what constitutes productive investments for a community. Otherwise, in societies imbued with capitalist notions of productive investment, capitalist exploitation will be furthered and alternative notions of community will be stymied.

This brings us to consideration of how the second antiusury initiative—redefining what is accepted as repayment for a loan—might contribute to promoting progressive social change. By transforming how a loan is repaid or "valorized," units of account or measures of value other than that of monetary valorization would need to be recognized. For instance, as Susan George suggests, a loan may be repaid and valorized "in kind" (George 1990). George offers a lengthy list of how such "creative reimbursements" might be made in her discussion of Third World debt. Her list includes: conservation of biodiversity; social conservation/antierosion measures; reforestation; development of wells and small-scale irrigation techniques; recording of building techniques, particularly for traditional earthen architecture; development of new biomass sources for energy; collection of traditional knowledge about agriculture, medicine, nutrition, and pharmacy; improvement of local and village-level food- and water-storage facilities; and compilation of dictionaries and grammars of local languages (250–51).

Such forms of "repayment in kind" clearly transform the nature of the "return" on the bank loan and displace valorization in a monetary sense. Instead, a new notion of return or valorization is enabled, one in which the qualitative nature of the use-values generated in "payment" is at least as important as their quantitative worth. In a similar vein, Quarter (1992) emphasizes the importance of fostering credit that is based on social objectives rather than monetary rates of return (156). Feminists have likewise argued for redefining economic development in terms of the well-being and creativity of all members of society rather than in terms of per capita gross domestic product (Kabeer 1994). Such a definition not only enables the inclusion of nonmarketed goods and services in evaluating economic productivity, it also shifts the focus away from the products of labor (whether bearers of use-value and/or exchange-value) to that of understanding human labor as both "a means and an end of development, of instrumental as well as intrinsic value" (83). If our notions of development, growth, and productivity are reshaped in this manner, then "activities which contribute to the health and well-being of people would be recognized as productive, whether or not they are carried out within personalized relations of family production, the commercialized relations of market production, or the bureaucratized relations of state production" (83). This clearly has important consequences for how women's activity is viewed, as women's work to reproduce labor, both biologically and socially, not only would be recognized as productive but would also be valued more highly.[26]

While often it may be necessary to promise valorization to receive a loan, this promise should be understood as deriving from particular cultural, political, and economic contexts, which presume the necessity of valorization in a capitalist sense. If noncapitalist class relations or other alternatives are conceived and socially valued, then noncapitalist and other forms of valorization are also conceivable. Theoretical and political work that helps construct such an alternative discursive space will contribute to enabling progressive financing schemes that validate initiatives other than those promising high monetary rewards.

Conclusion

In conclusion, in this chapter I have outlined a variety of strategies available for using bank financing as a means of furthering radical social change. With banks understood as sites for the condensation and collection of social wealth, progressives can work to socialize credit by establishing some form of democratic community control over credit allocation decisions. Such community control may foster the use of local resources for financing local community development initiatives and it may enhance a bank's ability to garner outside sources of loanable funds. Further, by enabling a sense of community with respect to credit allocation decisions, discussion and debate over what types of expenditures should be financed will be broadened. Community development may then be understood as fostering cooperative relations in industrial enterprises, as well as in and between households, recreational activities, educational institutions, retail outlets, and government agencies. In this manner, new noncapitalist and other alternative standards for assigning social value will be fostered. We can "invest" in our communities with the promise of an adequate "return" in the form of environmentally sound lifestyles, economically secure neighborhoods, nonexploitative forms of production, and nonpatriarchal social relations. We can create other yardsticks by which to measure "returns" and in so doing build the conditions for progressive communities.

Notes

1 There are other progressive financing initiatives that involve nonbank financing via pension funds, mutual funds, and equity holdings. These types of financing are not addressed in this essay.

2 Collective deliberation and a sense of community do not, however, in themselves ensure radical or progressive notions of community and collectivity. There are many conservative and repressive notions of community, as evidenced by movements to restrict social services to recent immigrants, to establish English as the only acceptable community language, and to coerce single mothers to identify and/or live with the fathers of their children.

3 Marxists concerned with analyzing the conditions and effects of how surplus labor is produced, appropriated, and distributed may put forth notions

of "collectivity" that are defined, in part, in terms of these class processes. From the perspective of the anti-essentialist Marxian approach that informs this essay, however, this does not mean that collectivities must *only* be defined in terms of class, but that theorizing the class content or class meaning of a community offers important opportunities for considering the causes and consequences of class exploitation.

4   "Created as a savings institution for the Basque provinces [in 1959, the *Caja Laboral Popular*] also is a lending institution to help finance workers' co-ops. Its assets in 1987 totaled close to $3 billion. . . . The Caja is an amalgam of several kinds of banking institutions. In addition to the typical saving-consumer loan function of a credit union, it is an investment bank for the co-ops of the system, and it has an entrepreneurial division that provides technical assistance and planning services to new co-ops in the process of forming and to co-ops in need of reorganization or rejuvenation. . . . Its activities have expanded into research on Basque, Spanish, and European economies, into elements of urban and industrial planning, and into consulting to its members" (Gunn and Gunn 1991, 65–66). The *Caja Laboral Popular* is itself a cooperative and "is the largest savings bank in the region and the seventeenth largest of seventy-one banking entities in all of Spain" (Kasmir 1996, 30).

   Overall, by 1987 the Mondragón system included "a consumer co-op, Eroski, employing approximately sixteen hundred people regionally, fifteen housing co-ops, forty-six educational co-ops (from elementary schools to a polytechnic institute), eight agricultural co-ops, and nine service and support co-ops, including a healthcare system serving over forty-six thousand people" (Gunn and Gunn 1991, 66). Kasmir notes that "the Mondragón system has grown to employ approximately twenty-one thousand worker-owners in some one hundred fifty cooperatives. . . . The industrial cooperatives emphasize state-of-the-art, high-tech production and are strong in the sectors of machine tools and numerical-control systems as well as refrigerators, washing machines, stoves for homes, restaurants, and hotels. Turnkey plants have been exported to Chile, Argentina, Libya, Egypt, and other countries" (1996, 29).

5   Within the community development literature there is a more or less explicit debate about the extent to which outside financing is needed to finance revitalization of low-income communities. Yet even strong proponents of locally based strategies, such as Perry (1987), recognize the need for outside capital. In his comparison of the Grameen Bank in Bangladesh with the South Shore Bank of Chicago, Dymski (1996) argues that low-income urban communities in the United States must have resources transferred

into them in some manner to accomplish revitalization because of a "higher capital intensity of both consumption and accumulation activities for rich and poor. . . . Substantial financing is required even for 'mom and pop' enterprises in the U.S. So a significant inflow of funds is needed to avoid the depreciation of both residential and commercial assets" (6–7).

6 Squires (1992) indicates that by the early 1990s approximately "$18 billion in urban reinvestment commitments have been negotiated with lenders by over three hundred groups in more than seventy cities throughout the United States" (2).

7 Quarter does note, however, that only a small portion of these funds are devoted to financing investments in "the social economy."

8 Interestingly, it was recognized that the socialist state's elaborate system of subsidized credit programs (*crédits bonifiés*) amounted to "paying bankers to carry out its policy" by providing interest-rate subsidies on loans for such "priority" investments (MEF/Bloch-Laine 1982, 30).

9 Perry (1987) discusses the various pitfalls associated with single focus business development plans including: "beggar-your-neighbor" policies that offer location incentives that are largely ineffective and basically result in income transfers for major corporations "after they have made their location decisions"; "boost-your-city" approaches that ignore the importance of broader quality-of-life concerns for management and their families in business location decisions; "big-bang" theories that may spell disaster for unprepared communities due to the abrupt changes that come with massive development projects; and belief in the miracles of high-tech industries, which are high-risk industries with many low-paying jobs and minimal labor mobility (46–47).

Yet while Perry argues for a broader conceptualization of community and economic development, one that is not simply reduced to business development, he does place "business development" as a cornerstone of community development and his notion of business is clearly that of capitalist production and/or independent commodity production, not communal or cooperative enterprises.

10 Money may act as capital in multiple ways. When considering bank financing of investment, money acts as capital in a double sense: as loan capital for bankers and as productive capital for industrial capitalists. Additionally, money may act as capital for depositors if the money is deposited with the expectation that it will receive a real rate of return. In all of these cases money functions as capital if it is "deployed" (lent or spent) with the expectation that it will be valorized by realizing a positive rate of return.

These differences in how money functions as capital have important implications for progressive financial policies. Some initiatives eliminate one aspect of money as capital, while retaining or even reinforcing other aspects. Many radicals who focus on financing productive investment go after this distinction, lamenting financiers' profit from unproductive investments (in real estate, financial markets, trade credit, or consumer credit). Often the radical character of their proposals is to refocus lending toward productive accumulation rather than merchanting or real estate or the purchase of financial assets. Yet, by privileging the valorization of loan capital via the financing of productive investment, capitalist class exploitation is often furthered.

11 Of course, there is no guarantee that workers will *want* to collectively produce, appropriate, or distribute their surplus labor! In recent interviews among community development organizations in the Boston metropolitan area, I have been struck by the absence of explicit worker-based identities and understandings of community, along with any desire for fostering cooperative forms of production. As one of the founders of an alternative community development bank on Cape Breton Island commented, "When we step in and purchase a failing business, workers are grateful to have their jobs and an ongoing paycheck. But when I start to ask for their involvement and talk about worker co-ops they are not interested. The time I would have to commit to changing their minds is more than I can provide, in terms of staff resources, and there is no guarantee of succeeding. So we operate on the next level of a locally controlled community business development corporation" (GEO Newsletter, April/May 1997, 7). Thus, part of the work of enabling noncapitalist alternatives clearly entails building identities that are in part constituted by the desire for noncapitalist and/or communist relations of production. Quarter notes that in Canada "the most striking examples of community-based systems of co-operatives are in locations where the people are a minority group, united by a common culture, religion and language" (1992, 106). This leads him to ask if a "tightly knit community with people who have a tradition of working together" is a prior condition "to develop an integrated co-operative system" (106–7).

12 By 1988, the SCCCU had made 115 business loans, totaling $2.5 million. No indication is given, however, as to how much of this lending was to finance cooperative production (Gunn and Gunn 1991, 64).

13 Kasmir (1996) desribes the *Caja*'s links to the industrial cooperatives: "Each cooperative is linked to the bank through a contract of association, which limits the autonomy of the individual firm in matters of product line and capital investments but also gives the small firm access to a wide range of business and financial services, including investment counseling and ac-

counting assistance. . . . The close ties between the producer co-ops and the Caja has insured that the banking decisions remain responsive to industrial development. Whereas other banks are tempted by speculative strategies—for example, favoring real estate over industry—the integration of the bank with economic development is one of the signal features of the system, and is considered to be a crucial element in its success. . . . In 1991, the Entrepreneurial Division of the bank became an independent consulting cooperative, with the goal of business creation" (33).

14   An important question remains, however, concerning the extent to which progressive financing has helped *initiate* cooperative forms of production or, instead, whether the expansion of worker cooperatives has been inhibited by a lack of adequate credit. Quarter (1992) notes that worker cooperatives in Canada have "been the most difficult of all cooperative models to develop" (as compared to consumer and marketing cooperatives), "largely because of problems of finance" (46). Quarter characterizes Canadian worker cooperatives as largely small-scale, labor-intensive, and stuck in low-capital economic ghettos. He refers to the Fabian assessment of worker cooperatives in which inadequate financing was one of the key reasons the Fabians concluded that they could not succeed: "Beatrice Potter observed that worker co-operatives took hold in market sectors with low capital needs ('in those trades untransformed by the industrial revolution'), but even so, the workers lacked the resources to capitalize the business properly. To overcome this problem, workers turned to outside investors, with the consequence that they had to pay high rates of interest, thereby reducing the amount the members could pay themselves for their labour. In some cases they had to give outside investors voting rights, which sometimes resulted in a loss of control. One consequence of the financial problems described by Potter is that the members of the co-operative came to exploit hired labour (paying these employees less than worker-members received for the same task) in an effort to keep the business afloat" (29–30).

   Observers in the United States also note that "locating outside money without voting rights is difficult. Venture capitalists are unwilling to forfeit these rights. Traditional banks are wary of the unusual cooperative structure and hesitant to make equity or working capital loans" (Bauen 1995, 60). But, Carol DiMarcello who works with Boston's ICA Group, a nonprofit providing technical assistance to worker-owned firms, disagrees. DiMarcello has commented that "money does exist for groups to start worker-owned cooperatives, through intermediary groups such as ICA, which makes loans nation-wide, as well as regional and local credit unions" (60).

15   There is also the important issue of the context in which cooperative forms

of production are promoted. In some cases, an emphasis on fostering local, community-based cooperatives may be part of a strategy of bypassing existing working-class organizations and institutions, thereby undermining the power and authority of such groups. A community development activist commented to me that in his community the introduction of such "progressive" financing initiatives was an attempt to deal with the massive unemployment problems caused by the shutdown of a large-scale company in his region. Rather than working through the existing radical trade unions, these financing strategies seemed to be aimed, in part, at establishing alternative centers of decision making and control, thereby undermining the trade union's power and potentially inhibiting alternative progressive initiatives.

16 Some of the multiple possibilities for what constitutes "cooperative" production and "collectivist" organizations can be seen in the notion of a "social economy" embraced by many progressive community development activists in Canada. A social economy includes cooperative enterprises, mutualist associations, consumer cooperatives, and marketing cooperatives and the emphasis is on communities controlling their own resources: land via land trusts, labor via worker cooperatives, and capital via financial institutions (Shragge 1993; Quarter 1992). This articulation of community development in terms of cooperative development highlights the principles of direct democracy and community control over property and/or resources rather than class processes of surplus-labor appropriation and distribution. An important project remains for radicals concerned with furthering cooperative and communal class relations to develop our understanding of these different notions of collectivization, showing the potentialities (and the limitations) of each.

Quarter, for instance, challenges progressives to broaden our understanding of who creates value and, therefore, of who should have a stake in cooperative production. He discusses "stakeholder theory," which rejects the premise of cooperatives based on one type of membership. He cites Jordan (1989) who, in providing a rationale for who to include as a stakeholder, writes: "Who creates the value in an enterprise, and should therefore be entitled to it? . . . If one surveys how [this question] has been addressed in various ideologies, one finds a common thread in the positions taken: a single exclusive interest should take all. Thus, for example, the conventional consumer and producer co-operative tradition relies fundamentally on the logic of the primacy of use. . . . Worker co-operative advocates, on the other hand, often justify their claims by reference to a Marxist-derived labour theory of value: Surplus is created exclusively by the efforts of the workers, and they alone are entitled to the surplus generated in the firm.

Capitalists . . . believe it is capital which is the generative force in enterprises and should thus be solely credited with the resulting rewards. In considering these opposed claims, one might well ask why each must be exclusive. . . . The Co-operators [an insurance holding company] concluded that
each of these groups can be creators of value, and should have the right to
participate in the organization" (34–35).

17 Kasmir's important recent ethnographic study (1996) is a sobering critical analysis of the Mondragón system. She problematizes the extent to
which worker ownership and formal structures of participation have enabled worker participation, democracy, and political activism. She argues,
further, that there is significant class conflict within the Mondragón cooperatives. Thus, here too, in the case of large-scale industrial enterprises,
Kasmir reminds us of the importance of questioning what "cooperative"
or "collective" means in formal as well as substantive terms.

18 It may also be due to the fact that, in the United States, financing of large-
scale productive investment is usually accomplished via direct financing on
securities markets rather than via bank lending.

19 Gunn and Gunn provide an extensive analysis of McDonald's in terms of
the generation and disbursement of social surplus (1991, 25–37). They also
offer an innovative suggestion for communities to invest in franchises such
as McDonald's so that the franchise is owned by a community development organization. They give the examples of the "Black People's Unity
Market (BPUM) in Camden, New Jersey, a for-profit corporation that operates Burger King and Chicken George franchises. West Oak Lane Community Development Corporation, in a predominantly African-American
inner-city area of Philadelphia, owned a subsidiary that operated a Dunkin'
Donuts franchise. Despite the concern for the food products provided and
the typical terms of employment, these franchises provide a business service in their neighborhoods, jobs and job training, and channel any profit
they make back into their communities through their parent CDCs" (93).

20 Development banks are "typically not-for-profit corporations that accept
federally insured deposits. . . . They deliver not only money but technical
assistance and management training, acting as a bridge between private-
sector capital and expertise and public-sector development programs"
(Gunn and Gunn 1991, 69).

21 I am indebted to Bruce Roberts for suggesting this type of formulation,
whereby productive investment is measured according to a vector of use-
values.

22 These funds are from "local, independent, nonprofit organizations that lend
money to feasible local community projects which cannot qualify for con-

ventional loans or which cannot pay current interest rates. . . . They are capitalized by private individuals, church organizations, foundations, and others who lend their capital to the CLF at very low rates, sometimes at zero percent interest. These funds are then re-lent. . . . CLFs concentrate on housing projects and short-term loans because housing projects offer more security and because CLF's own funds are usually on relatively short-term deposit from their backers. The typical CLF loan is a sort of a bridge loan" (Perry 1987, 153; see also Gunn and Gunn 1991, 67).

23 The concept of a "social surplus" often is not itself theorized, resulting in the rather vague notion that all interest payments are a payment of surplus. Banks lend money to finance many different types of expenditures in addition to the purchase of productive capital. Thus, from a Marxian class-analytic perspective, some interest payments are paid out of nonclass revenues and incomes, rather than from surplus. Finance capital may thus be valorized in myriad ways other than with a payment of surplus value. This is the case with loans made to finance consumer credit, trade credit, speculative purchases of real estate or financial assets, or even noncapitalist class processes.

24 Here a distinction must be made between a *distribution* of money and its *expenditure*. Interest is a distribution or a payment from a borrower to a lender. It is not an expenditure or a purchase. In this sense interest is analogous to other distributions or payments made from surplus-value revenues (taxes, rent, merchants' profit margins) or from nonclass revenues (gifts, taxes).

25 An extensive literature focusing on "external drain" exists in development studies. Scholars in the dependency school and world systems traditions have carried out important and extensive work theorizing the problematic nature and the negative consequences of these interest payments to foreign-based financiers (Frank 1966, 1969; Wallerstein 1974; Rodney 1974). In this case, even if interest payments have been used to finance new productive investment, they have often been reinvested in the "home" nation, the "First World," rather than in the community in which they were generated. In this sense, then, the labor of the "Third World" has financed productive investments in the "First."

26 Feminist scholarship has been particularly insightful in showing how reliance on market pricing for conferring value renders invisible much of the work carried out by women (Benería 1982; Kabeer 1994; Massiah 1990; Sparr 1994; Hay and Stichter 1984). The conflation of value and prices "generates a hierarchy of production" that devalues the work necessary for the care and reproduction of human beings, work that is largely carried out by women without remuneration (Kabeer 1994, 78).

J.K. GIBSON-GRAHAM

AND DAVID RUCCIO

□

"AFTER" DEVELOPMENT

Re-imagining Economy and Class

The postdevelopment project pioneered by Arturo Escobar and others represents a rich new source for radically transforming concepts and practices of development. Within this "antidevelopment" approach the condition of the "Third World"—its underdevelopment as well as its need for development—is understood to be in part a product of the representations and knowledges deployed by the development profession as it emerged in the post–World War II period.[1] One of the primary goals of postdevelopment theory is to negotiate alternatives to development, to conceive and bring into existence new forms of economy and society within the Third World. To achieve this goal, theorists fix their attention on local cultural practices and models of social organization, especially those associated with new social movements (Escobar and Alvarez 1992).

In this essay we would like to build on the pathbreaking contribution that postdevelopment theory has made to rethinking development. Our collaboration with this project begins, however, with the critical observation that the strategies used thus far to unmake the Third World and negotiate alternatives to development are weakened by the power still granted by postdevelopment theorists to "the economy."

Most postdevelopment theory attributes to the global capitalist system a naturalized role as the preeminent and self-regulating essence of development. Development is seen to have been created and disseminated as the discourse of capitalism, and global capitalism is the system of power against which local communities and new social movements are struggling:

Local communities bring their material and cultural resources to bear in their encounter with development and modernity. The persistence of local and hybrid models of the economy, for instance, reflects cultural contestations that take place as capital attempts to transform the life of communities. (Escobar 1995, 99)

Despite recognition that "a universal model of the economy [has] to be abandoned" (1995, 97) and that "in rethinking development from the perspective of the economy . . . [there is a need] to make explicit the existence of a plurality of models of the economy" (1995, 98), in the work of Escobar and others repeated references to "global capital," "global systems of economic, cultural and political production," and "capitalist megamachines" constitute an economic hegemony that cannot be easily dislodged. Local cultural formations are represented as only ever mediating the effects of external global forms of capital without, in turn, having any impact on capitalism itself (except in the cases where weak instances of noncapitalism serve to feed the voracious appetite of an expansive, powerful capitalism).

The discursive constitution of capitalist hegemony is so common in left approaches to and criticisms of development that its negative implications are often overlooked. What, we might ask, are some of the effects of allowing the "global capitalist economy" to escape the deconstructive techniques that postdevelopment theorists have so effectively turned on development? We would like to suggest that one effect of this ubiquitous capitalist centering is to constrain the possibility of imagining and bringing into existence alternatives to development, including noncapitalist forms of economy. Another effect of this positioning is to understand noncapitalist economic formations (where such forms can already be seen to exist) not only as inherently unviable but as cultural practices or resistances that lack sufficient economic potential for development.

We propose to utilize an antiessentialist form of class analysis to reclaim some of the ground ceded to the capitalist economy and dislodge the central role played by capitalism in conceptions of development. The approach to class analysis outlined here identifies a range of forms in which surplus labor is appropriated and distributed in a multiplicity of class processes that can be seen to constitute social structures and identities within Third World countries. By respecifying the relationship between multiple noncapitalist class processes and instances of capitalist class relations, we hope to contribute to a rethinking of the economy and to strategies for empowering different knowledges and practices "after" development.

Postdevelopment

The work of Escobar (1995, building on 1984 and 1992) is perhaps the best-known example of what has become a wide-ranging critique of Third World development as it has been understood and practiced throughout the postwar period.[2] This critique is a powerful discursive intervention aimed at defamiliarizing the terms within which development has traditionally been construed. Its effect is to create the conditions for a relation to the economic and social practices of development that is radically different from that posited both by existing development practitioners and many left critics. In particular, it calls into question the idea that "development is always the cure, never the cause" (Crush 1995, 10) of the misery and inequality, authoritarian regimes and civil strife, ecological devastation and social deprivation that are visible in much of the Third World today.

The novelty of this critique of development stems from its appropriation of the work of Foucault, its reading of Said's "orientalism," and its use, more generally, of postmodern and poststructuralist modes of analysis to bracket (and thereby denaturalize) the terms in which development and underdevelopment have been conceived. The basic argument is that development, especially as it emerged in the postwar period, can be recognized as a discourse, a historically produced cultural and institutional space, within which both the problem of underdevelopment and its supposed solution—the enacting of Western-style development—were elaborated. Rather than seeing underdevelopment as an original state characterizing the countries of the Third World, to which the panoply of development projects and assistance offered by international agencies were the necessary response, Escobar and others view development as a way of producing a specific kind of knowledge of the Third World—

literally creating (theoretically and socially) the condition of underdevelopment to which it alone offered the answer.

Development discourse arose out of the material conditions of post–World War II reconstruction in Western Europe, Asia, Africa, and Latin America, dominated as they were by the growing economic and political supremacy of the United States and the discursive positioning of economics as the preeminent form of social knowledge in the West (Arndt 1987; Oman and Wignaraja 1991; Escobar 1995). As a response to socialist initiatives in the "old world" and postcolonial or anticolonial movements in the previously colonized areas of the "new world," it constituted the so-called Third World as a Cold War battleground where the future of capitalism and modern society was to be decided.

As a system of representations, development discourse served to universalize and homogenize Third World cultures, creating the possibility of subjecting developing countries to economic, cultural, and political transformations offered in the name of eradicating underdevelopment and ushering them onto the path of development. The professionalization of development and the emergence of an array of development institutions (including universities, national and multilateral granting and lending agencies, specialized think tanks, and nongovernmental organizations) created a veritable army of development specialists (theorists as well as practitioners) who have defined the "symptoms" and "causes" of underdevelopment and devised the means to eradicate them. In this manner, power is exercised among and over the peoples of the Third World not so much through repression (although that, too, as the histories of Latin America, Asia, and Africa clearly show) but through normalizing the condition of underdevelopment and naturalizing the need for development.

Development has produced forms of subjectivity through which people have come to recognize themselves and others as developed or underdeveloped. It has portrayed and brought into being "abnormal" subjects, such as the illiterate, the malnourished, small farmers, and landless peasants, who need to be "reformed" for development to "take off." It has constituted what it means to be a villager, a Third World woman, a member of the informal sector—the various others who populate the landscape of underdevelopment and in whose name development projects have been formulated and carried out. The collective subjectivity and sociospatial domain of the Third World—defined by overpopulation, the threat of famine, widespread illiteracy, to name but a few of the prevalent images—has been fabricated in the name of development.

Development was fashioned and disseminated as the only force capable of destroying the archaic relations, institutions, and superstitions that stood in the way of modernization. Codified most notably in development economics, the project of development was centered on the economy (as a distinct social space) and driven preeminently by capitalist industrialization.

It is perhaps not surprising that the postdevelopment critique has led to a call for alternative regimes of representation and practice, discourses and modes of intervention that both challenge and exceed the terms imposed by the development/underdevelopment dyad. These alternatives can be recognized in the local knowledges and social movements that have been marginalized in the name of development and that are being foregrounded and fostered as it becomes possible to "marginalize the economy" and to imagine the "end of development" (Sachs 1992).

Clearly the strategy of postdevelopment theory stands in opposition to mainstream modernization discourse. It also differs in important ways from inherited left critiques of modernization. The unique focus on discourse and the very different strategic alternatives it offers are telling reminders of the novelty of this approach. But these distinctive features should not blind us to some of the similarities between postdevelopment theory and its others.

Oddly enough, one axis of similarity that links modernization theory, left theories of dependency and underdevelopment, and postdevelopment approaches to questions of development is the positioning of the economy within a realist epistemology. By this we mean the presumption that economic knowledge reflects the true state of a real entity called "the economy" (generally understood as a locus of capitalist dominance). While not surprising in the context of modernist theories of development, whether of the right (modernization) or left (dependency/underdevelopment) variety, this presumption contradicts the general epistemological position of the postdevelopment theorists, who see knowledge as constitutive rather than reflective of reality. Such a positioning of the economy, we argue, places severe limitations on rethinking development, allowing the putative dominance of capitalism in the "real" world of the economy to go unquestioned and to continue to define and constrain the development potentialities of other economic and social practices.

"The Economy" and Discourses of Development

The advocates of modernization, their left critics, and those who argue in favor of moving beyond development put forward quite different ways of understanding development as well as alternative strategies for achieving it. While we want to keep these differences in mind so as to highlight the challenge that postdevelopment thinkers pose to the other two theoretical traditions, we also wish to explore the similar ways in which the economy is constituted in these related literatures.

In modernization theory, capitalist economic growth represents the necessary solution to underdevelopment. The particular strategies advocated for promoting capitalist growth have changed over the course of the postwar period: Where once capitalist development was predicated on state intervention and aid transfers, now it is based on the freeing up of domestic markets and extensive integration into world markets. Capitalist development is seen to be preceded by backward, primitive, and—during the transition to development—dual forms of economy and society. Definitions of the dual economy have, however, changed over time with "backwardness" originally conceived in terms of the predominance of agriculture and rural life, and associated today with protected markets and urban corruption. The role of the "informal" sector in the development process has similarly changed; once the target of active elimination, it is now seen as the seedbed of microenterprises that will be the building blocks of a fully developed capitalist economy (Lubell 1991). Despite slight changes in orientation and strategy, the modernization school positions the capitalist economy as the only viable and ultimately developmental form of economy.

In contrast, for much of the left, the capitalist economy is the problem rather than the solution. The international spread of capitalism inaugurated the "development of underdevelopment." Until they were drawn into and subjected to the maelstrom of the capitalist world economy, a variety of precapitalist modes of production represented autonomous forms of development (Frank 1966; Ruccio and Simon 1986a). It was the process of capitalist development itself that blocked or distorted this autonomous development trajectory. Thus, for development to occur, it is necessary to break from capitalism and to construct socialism.

The economy, as mapped by dependency and underdevelopment theories, is represented as either structured by duality or by an articulation of different modes of production. The international capitalist sector is seen as unevenly linked to remnant fragments of a feudal sector and a sector of independent commodity producers in the rural economy, and a comprador capitalist sector and petty bourgeois sector in the urban economy. In the light of this representation of a diversified economy, left theorists, certain of the heightened power of the capitalist economy, have highlighted the impossibility of even development and have turned their attention to the unequal distributional consequences of the articulation of different sectors with a hegemonic capitalism.

Like left development theory, postdevelopment theory is critical of capitalism in the sense that development, which has served to colonize reality, to circumscribe local cultural constructions, to break down local communities and expose them to the vicissitudes of the global economy, has done so in the name of capitalism. The postdevelopment theorists call for a "semiotic resistance" to all discourses within which (under)development and the economy have become privileged terms of reference. Their project requires the creation or recognition of a world of difference, populated with a diversity of local economic practices and cultural constructions, a space whose identity is not fixed and singular but open and heterogeneous. This is a major contribution to the task of deconstructing the identity and fullness of existing development models, challenging their definitional closure, apprehending—and intervening to promote—alternatives to development.

But the critique of economic monism and the proliferation of antidevelopment possibilities that we recognize in the work of Escobar and other postdevelopment thinkers is constrained by the terms in which the concept of capitalism is invoked. Semiotic resistance eventually comes up against the hard realities of global capital and in this confrontation the cultural and social identities of local organizations may be seen to be insufficient to the task of true resistance:

Global capital . . . relies today not so much on homogenization of an ex-
terior Third World as on its ability to consolidate diverse, heterogeneous social forms. . . . The global economy must . . . be understood as a decentered
system with manifold apparatuses of capture—symbolic, economic, political.
(Escobar 1995, 99)

Some of these (new social) movements in structure and character strike me as
populist . . . and hence as part of a long lineage within modernity itself, which
raises the question . . . of their relation to class and forces of co-optation. . . .
At the very least there is a need for careful analyses of the relations between
new social movements and the hegemonic class forces of capitalism. (Watts
1993, 268)

A powerful notion of capitalist hegemony situates capitalism at the center
of development, thus limiting or closing off economic and social alternatives.

For traditional modernization and left approaches to development the
capitalist economy is an extra-discursive reality—something that can be
cultivated wherever underdevelopment is found, or something that dominates and actively restricts the autonomy of other economic forms. For
postdevelopment theory the global capitalist economy is similarly positioned as somehow extra-discursive—something that contains and cap-
tures heterogeneous local practices and operates outside and beyond the
forces of deconstruction. Since capitalism exists as the "real," it is not
subject to destabilization in the play of intertextuality like other terms in
the development discourse. It appears in postdevelopment theory as an
ontological given, disproportionately powerful by virtue of its indisput-
able reality in a world of multivalent concepts, shifting discursive practices and unstable meanings.[3]

While the theorists of postdevelopment successfully shift our attention
to local differences, movements, and forms of resistance, these turn out
to be the weaker "other" to the dominant structure and larger force of
capitalist development. The effect is to maintain capitalism as the central referent of development and indeed of what comes "after" development. This narrows the gap that separates the postdevelopment approach
from the other two. Rather than representing the economy as a radically
heterogeneous social space, postdevelopment critics reinforce the dis-

cursive hegemony of capitalism and thereby tend to marginalize the very alternative economic practices they seek to promote.

Capitalocentrism and Its Effects

It is not too far-fetched to say that development, in all three approaches, is governed by capitalism in the same way that writing is dominated by logos, gender and sex by the phallus, and exchange by money in their respective discursive domains. In each case, difference and incommensurability are ultimately defined by and subsumed within the sphere of an apparently self-sufficient master term. Development discourse, including traditional, left, and postdevelopment approaches, is unified by *capitalocentrism,* in the sense that each of these three otherwise different approaches to development operates with a similarly centered and centering notion of capitalism.

Building on a feminist definition of phallocentrism (Grosz 1990), we identify capitalocentrism wherever noncapitalism is seen as either: (a) the same as; (b) the opposite of; (c) the complement to; or (d) located inside capitalism itself (Gibson-Graham 1996).[4] We would like to ask how a capitalocentric vision of the economy weakens or limits a radical rethinking of development. In what follows we explore each type of capital-centering and the effects it has had on our conception of Third World economies.

Noncapitalist forms of economy and social life are frequently considered to be the *same* as or indistinguishable from capitalism.[5] Thus independent commodity producers who have effective possession of (by owning or renting) the means of production, who appropriate and distribute their own surplus, and buy and sell commodities on markets are often considered to be either the same as capitalists, or the same as proletarians. It is mainly the market that is seen to homogenize different economic practices, binding them within the dense and expanding web of capitalism. Neoclassical economists, for example, are likely to view small coffee growers in Central America or independent rice growers in the Gambia as profit-maximizing economic agents, responding like capitalist enterprises to price (Schultz 1964; Bliss and Stern 1982). Critics of orthodox development theory and policy might understand their behavior as obeying the same logic, albeit under different constraints (Bardhan 1984; Basu

1990). At other times left analysts see the force of the "capitalist" market as reducing such producers to the status of de facto proletarians, forced to intensify their labor on their plots to meet quotas imposed by marketing authorities (Pred and Watts 1992, 82).

The role of the market in rendering these producers the "same" as capitalists/workers is seen again in the case of the petty commodity producers of the urban informal sector. Because they operate in markets that, in the end, are seen to be tied into and governed by global capitalism, they become subsumed to the laws and identities of the capitalist sector. Most recently this sector has been the subject of development initiatives to promote existing microenterprises under the assumption that entrepreneurship and capitalism are synonymous (Lubell 1991). The result in all these cases is that the specificities and differences of capitalism and noncapitalism are elided in favor of capitalism.

Noncapitalist practices are also often portrayed as being the *opposite* of capitalism as, for example, when they are seen to be primitive or traditional, stagnant, marginal, residual, about to be extinguished, weak. Communal or tribal practices of hunting and gathering, craft activities, or indigenous agricultural production involving the production of use-values that are not commodified and/or of commodities that are not designed to garner profits in the market are viewed as incapable of growth and development in their own right (de Janvry 1981; Sender and Smith 1986). Despite their resilience and viability over centuries of practice, these noncapitalist activities become the negative image of capitalism, which is characterized as dynamic, powerful, and endowed with the capacity for infinite expansion. Modernizers attribute to traditional activities the condition of backwardness—they must be eliminated or transformed so that development can take place—while left critics and the advocates of postdevelopment may see them as signs of underdevelopment or of ineffectual resistance to development (since the development of global capitalism more or less inevitably constrains, undermines, and, eventually, eliminates them). Here, a hierarchy is established between a vigorous, effective capitalism and its passive and insubstantial noncapitalist other.

When noncapitalism is analyzed in terms of its articulation with capitalism, it is often understood to play a *complementary* role. This is the case, for example, when rural activities are seen as providing the conditions of existence of capitalist activity elsewhere. In the "articulation of modes of production" approach, the relationship between capitalism and noncapitalism is conceived to be governed by the laws and needs of the capitalist mode of production (see Wolpe 1980; Ruccio and Simon 1986b). Rural noncapitalism is cast in the role of providing underutilized savings and labor for promoting capitalist industrialization, cheap means of production and wage goods, a reserve army of labor that serves to keep the value of labor power lower than it otherwise might be, thereby creating the conditions for an unequal exchange to take place between center and periphery. In the literature on unequal exchange (e.g., Emmanuel 1972; Amin 1977), noncapitalism is relegated to the margins of the world of capitalist exchanges: Either noncapitalist forms of production disappear from view or they serve merely to satisfy the conditions of existence of peripheral capitalism, such that the set of international commodity exchanges leads to a net transfer of value from the hybrid (capitalist and noncapitalist) periphery to what is considered to be the fully capitalist center. Noncapitalism only persists, therefore, in the local, heterogeneous sites in and through which global capitalism is continually invigorated and reinvented.[6] Here, noncapitalism derives both its trajectory and its raison d'être from serving the needs of capitalist development.

Finally, noncapitalism occupies a position *inside* capitalism to the extent that it exists within a container called the capitalist world economy. While there may be islands of noncapitalism—say, in grassroots producer cooperatives, local development efforts, alternative "intentional" economies, and community initiatives—they have no independent, self-governing, unfettered existence. They often are seen as remnants of another era (prior to the rise of capitalism), unable to expand their reproduction, destined to fill the small spaces that capitalism has not yet saturated with its own economic practices and structures of meaning. Although not the same as capitalism, the fragments of noncapitalism that persist are isolated, perhaps experimental elements of a landscape that is otherwise governed by the laws of capitalist development.

It seems that capitalism has become such a powerful and centering presence that it would take a superhuman effort to imagine, let alone fashion and sustain, viable noncapitalist practices and institutions with their own identities, energies, and trajectories. It is here that our more modest intervention may have some value. We would like to suggest an alternative conception of class that could help render instances of capitalism smaller, more fragmented, and dispersed, and thereby liberate an economy of difference and divergence. Our aim is to produce a new economic knowledge of development that reshapes the discursive relationship between noncapitalist and capitalist economic practices. This project of using class to negotiate the paths beyond development is not unlike that of the postdevelopment critics. We, too, are interested in modifying political economies through semiotic resistance for the purpose of making other models visible. By producing the discursive conditions for a different relation to economic practices, we hope to foster new relations to the economy and to development more generally. A reinvented language of class can be an important part of this project.

Class Processes and Development Stories

We define class, quite simply and minimally, in terms of the processes of producing, appropriating, and distributing surplus labor (Resnick and Wolff 1987). The distinctiveness of different class processes emerges as they are particularized or concretized in a variety of social and discursive settings.[7] Some of the most familiar are the feudal, independent or ancient, communal, slave, and of course capitalist class processes. In each process surplus labor is appropriated in a particular form (for example, as surplus value or as feudal rents) and the distribution of appropriated surplus labor is conducted in particular ways (via contracted payments, gifts, intergenerational allocations, and so on).

   To define class as a process is to shift the focus away from subjects and social groups— "class" as a noun—and toward certain practices and flows of labor in which subjects variously and multiply participate—class as an adjective. This approach unyokes property relations, power relations, and organizational capacities from the definition of class, allowing these determinants to interdependently interact with the processes by which the production, appropriation, and distribution of surplus labor takes place. So, for example, a communal class process in which surplus labor is communally produced may also be one in which the distinction between necessary and surplus labor is communally agreed on and the destination of distributions of appropriated surplus labor communally determined. But such "communism" might take place in very different contexts—of private or communally owned property, of equalized or uneven power relations, within highly politicized or distinctly apolitical organizations. In each situation the practice of a communal class process will be uniquely overdetermined as will the constitution of communal class subjects. What this antiessentialist perspective on class enables is the envisioning of a diverse economic landscape in which noncapitalist class processes are liberated from the law of the capitalist "father" and economic subjects are always in the process of becoming.

A conception of class as a process differs markedly from the notion of class as a social grouping defined in terms of an amalgam of income-generating capacity, property, power, or organizational capacities. This latter categorical conception of class locates its members in terms of mutually exclusive positions in a stable structure, or in terms of a process of class formation whereby groups with common interests are seen to emerge in tandem with structural transitions. It is this conception of class that has largely been employed within discourses of development.

In that class is, in this view, primarily bestowed by location in an economic structure, and this structure is in turn dominated by capitalism (or a capitalist mode of production), it is not surprising that, as a conceptual tool, the categorical notion of class has not been able to break away from capitalocentric visions. Thus Third World societies undergoing transition are seen as producing a new proletariat, or a new capitalist class, or most recently, a new "middle" class,[8] and these social mappings serve to reinforce the hegemony of an existing or emerging capitalist economic order.

We would like to deploy our language of class in a project of undermining capitalocentrism and unmaking the global capitalist economy as a discursively hegemonic entity. In the remainder of this essay we pursue a number of different strategies toward this end. One is to recognize class diversity and the specificity of economic practices that coexist in the Third World and to show how modernization interventions have themselves created a variety of noncapitalist (as well as capitalist) class processes, thereby adding to the diversity of the economic landscape rather than reducing it to homogeneity. This is a discursive strategy aimed at re-reading the economy outside the hold of capitalocentrism.

The second strategy opens up the economy to new possibilities by theorizing a range of different and potential connections between class processes. It sketches an imagined political project that could perhaps articulate with the actions of the new social movements identified by post-development theory that are creating new subjectivities and forging new economic and social futures.

Strategy 1: Reading against Capitalocentrism

The process of modernization and the development of global capitalism — including, to use Escobar's language, the "making of the Third World" — is represented as involving the creation of a hierarchically structured and predominantly capitalist landscape of developed and developing countries, with some nations designated more and others less developed. Our new mapping seeks to disrupt and reconfigure this ordered landscape by representing a terrain of latent diversity and disorder that can be described in class terms.

We start with all the premodern forms of economic and social organization that the project of modernization was supposed to have eliminated or transformed into capitalism — for example, feudal (e.g., plantation), independent, and communal forms of agricultural production. For many left critics of modernization, the demise of these forms of production is assumed to have occurred through the more or less inexorable "original accumulation of capital" or, for the postdevelopment theorists, the rise to dominance of global capital.[9] But if we shift our focus from these teleological narratives, we might observe that the so-called destruction of these forms has often created the conditions for the emergence and reproduction of new noncapitalist forms of surplus-labor appropriation, perhaps alongside but never subsumed to both local and global instances of capitalism.

Michael Watts's fascinating study of contract agricultural labor in the Gambia focuses on changes in production relations prompted by the introduction of a state-sponsored rice irrigation project (Pred and Watts 1992). His study provides an excellent illustration of how a project of modernization destroyed one set of differentiated class processes, only to replace them with another. Household production in the local Mandinka society was traditionally based on the cultivation of both individual fields and collectively owned familial property and, under customary law, the rights of ownership and distribution of the crop produced on each type of property were different. The product of labor performed on collectively owned land was communally appropriated but controlled and distributed by the senior male in the household, while the product of labor performed on individual land was appropriated individually. In the terms of our class analysis we have here two different class processes with different conditions of existence: a communal class process in which the distributive moment is controlled by the patriarch (we could call it a patriarchal communal class process), and a self-appropriating class process in which each producer appropriates and distributes his or her own surplus.

Prior to the introduction of the irrigation project, rice production was women's work and was concentrated on swampland owned by women by individual right. With the introduction of the rice irrigation project and the movement of men into contract rice production for the global market, this property complex and mix of household class processes was altered.[10] The sequestering of land to the project and associated re-arrangement of property rights meant that women's access to their traditional land and to a self-appropriating class process was largely destroyed.

One response made by women who had been rendered landless was to join together with other similarly dispossessed women to sell their labor power. Drawing on traditional organizational practices and "customary social relations as a basis of recruitment" (Pred and Watts 1992, 96), women formed groups of similar age to work in gangs in the rice paddies. The labor teams (*kafo*) utilized reciprocal labor practices and negotiated a collective wage that was distributed equally among the members. In effect the women swapped a self-appropriating class process for a capitalist class process in which they sold their labor power to the growers. As members of a team of "proletarian gang labor" (p. 96), the women are exploited but powerful in the sense that the growers are entirely dependent on them. We could see here one of the contradictory effects of state intervention into rice production as enabling the establishment of a women's capitalist class process in which their produced surplus was partially distributed back to them (in the form of a wage premium) because of their bargaining power.

The men, on the other hand, were operating in two class processes: as independent self-appropriating rice producers, and as capitalists extracting surplus value from the women's *kafo*. Despite their independent and capitalist class positions, the men retained little surplus once the women's wage premium and state costs were met. This new articulation of class processes was overdetermined by a multiplicity of determinants and conditions of existence and had as one of its effects the exacerbation of struggles between men and women in Mandinka society.[11]

Reading for class outside of a capitalocentric discourse releases us from the imperative to homogenize the experience of men and women and see them as members of an emerging global proletariat (Pred and Watts 1992, 96).[12] The representation of class diversity in any one place or individual becomes possible only if we distinguish relations of power (whether exercised directly over the labor process or indirectly via financing and exchange) from relations of property, exploitation, and organizational capacity and, in so doing, open up the linkages between these different sets of relations to examination. Then we can recognize the range of labor practices and class processes (communal, self-appropriating, capitalist), the various class and nonclass identities, the different kinds of power struggles and their loci—between men and women in households and in their different class practices within communities; between producers and the state in commodity and finance markets—that make up the economic landscape.

Even if we focus on the emergence of capitalist class processes associated with successful projects of modernization, this need not mean that the class landscape becomes uniformly capitalist. When we broaden our view to consider social sites other than farms, factories, streets, and offices—the formal sites of modernization or the public economy—we find evidence, in households and community structures, of class changes that are not simply governed by or reducible to capitalism. Rather than reading households and communities simply as sites of capitalist reproduction, our anticapitalocentric reading makes visible the variety of noncapitalist class processes in the households of workers employed in capitalist industry (Gibson-Graham 1996).

Much attention has been given to the participation of Third World women in capitalist wage employment and their *proletarianization* in export-processing zones or *maquiladora* border industries. Commentators point to the patriarchal nature of this kind of capitalist development, emphasizing the ways in which new spatial and gendered divisions of labor are dominated by the twin and codependent logics of capitalist exploitation and patriarchal oppression (e.g., Nash and Fernandez-Kelly 1983). There are, however, a growing number of studies that highlight how these changes are precipitating what we would read as new class relations in the household sector (Cravey 1997; Phongpaichit 1988; Strauch 1984).

Women who, in the global factories, participate in capitalist forms of surplus-labor appropriation engage in many practices of resistance and transformation not only in the sites of their formal sector employment (Ong 1987; Porpora and Prommas 1989) but also in their households and communities. Thus we find that these wage laborers are often able to disrupt the existing exploitation practices of their parents, husbands, in-laws, or community elders, in some cases enacting the formation of independent or communal class processes at home or in the communities in which they live. Altha Cravey (1997) describes the reshaping of Mexican households and the increased contribution of men to domestic labor associated with the factories established most recently along the United States–Mexico border. In class terms these households may be experiencing a transition from a class process in which a man appropriates surplus labor from his female partner (in what we could call a domestic feudal class process) to a more communal class process in which surplus labor is jointly produced and appropriated. In the process gender relations are being renegotiated in ways that have interesting effects on class politics at the factory. In this sense, the development of capitalism in some social sites — successful modernization, by most accounts — is accompanied by the development of new forms of noncapitalism in other social locations.

Reading the economic landscape outside of a capitalocentric discourse allows us to see sites of economic invention woven into the very fabric of a so-called newly emerging capitalist society. This reading also enables us to situate subjects in a variety of class subject positions. No longer are we tempted to position a young woman worker in an export processing zone factory only as a proletarian (with all the expectations of a workerist subjectivity that accompany this designation). She can now be seen to occupy a class position within a domestic class process, and perhaps another class position within a more extended or distant family-based class process. Her political subjectivity will be overdetermined by these multiple class positions as well as a range of other social, cultural, and physical relations. The complex picture of economy and subjectivity that emerges from an anticapitalocentric reading opens the way even further for imagining different forms of noncapitalist politics.

Strategy 2: Economic Politics "After" Capitalocentrism

A new class mapping of the economic and social landscape of modernization both disrupts and poses an alternative to existing capitalocentric discourses of development. The economy is seen to be different from itself—made up of multiple class processes and decentered economic subjects who negotiate markets, commodification, investment flows, and enterprises in a variety of indeterminate ways. Outside of a colonizing capitalocentric discourse, the economic realm can be represented as a site not only of limits and constraints but also of freedoms and openings, where transformations and capture are not always into and by capitalism. This vision of a new economic terrain suggests a range of imaginative possibilities for enacting noncapitalist class politics and bringing into being an even more diversified economy.

In our class reading against capitalocentrism we identified *noncapitalist* class processes and illustrated instances of their continual creation in and alongside projects of modernization in the Third World. An anticapitalocentric reading can also be turned on *capitalist* class processes to illustrate their decentered and overdetermined nature. Destabilizing the capitalist identity and breaking apart the association of *markets, commodities, money,* and the *enterprise* with capitalism creates openings for noncapitalism to emerge. To conclude this essay we explore one actual and one imaginary intervention that are enabled when commodities, markets, money, and the enterprise are liberated from capitalocentric discourse.

Many of the projects of the Singapore-based NGO ENGENDER are aimed at preserving and revaluing the traditional craft skills and indigenous knowledges (especially those of women) of endangered communities in Asia and the Pacific.[13] These communities are still largely sustained by noncapitalist class processes in which surplus labor is produced, appropriated, and distributed either individually or collectively. One of ENGENDER's projects involves establishing a Gender and Development

Resources Bank, a "multinational corporation of the poor" in which a wealth of survival skills and environmental knowledges are deposited and translated into market values that can generate earnings for women in rural and indigenous communities. Working with community-based researchers in Bangladesh, Kathmandu, Thailand, Malaysia, Singapore, and Indonesia, ENGENDER and associated NGOs are helping document knowledges and practices that are fast being destroyed, replaced, or stolen. This documentation process represents an intervention to protect a crucial condition for the continued existence of noncapitalist livelihoods. It articulates with another important project that involves building economic relationships between women's craft collectives and TNCs by "capturing space in existing markets for products and services derived from [women's] indigenous skills and knowledges" (ENGENDER 1996, 19). With the help of ENGENDER, GAIA Crafts, for example, has established a market niche by tapping into the internal markets of a large tourist industry and computer corporations in the vicinity of producer communities and supplying locally made products such as soaps, printed cloth, and woven carry bags as substitutes for imported goods. The aim is to develop links between rural craft producers and global commercial markets that incorporate the poor "as partners in production" (ENGENDER 1995, 10) and that foster a different form of "socio-cultural interfacing" between capitalist business operations and traditional communities.

By engaging with the global economy in new and innovative ways, ENGENDER has developed an active politics of protection and development of noncapitalist class processes and indigenous lifestyles. This intervention has introduced commodification and money flows into noncapitalist and previously noncommodified class processes. It has engineered an engagement with the global market and contact between TNCs and local indigenous communities. But it has turned its own apparatus of capture onto the capitalist TNC. The result has been an income flow into the local community that sustains noncapitalist class processes, protects traditional knowledge, and maintains indigenous technologies. The market is the conduit through which flows of money ensure the sustainability of local life styles and a viable noncapitalist economy alongside capitalist industrialization.[14]

The last intervention we would like to review is one focused on the internal operations of the capitalist enterprise as a site of generative possibilities for noncapitalist class practices. Our antiessentialist class analysis highlights the importance of the distributive as well as the exploitative class process. The distributive class process involves the allocation of appropriated surplus labor (in whatever form) to a range of claimants who in turn provide the conditions of existence for continued class appropriation. Within the capitalist enterprise surplus value is distributed, for example, to a wide variety of destinations both inside and outside the enterprise, including investment in capital expansion (accumulation), the payment of supervisory labor, accounting, merchanting, the servicing of debt, state taxes, bribes, and so on. Each constellation of such distributions is the result of competitive tensions and struggles, negotiations and agreements, that take place in and around the firm. Diverse economic and social practices are currently enabled by flows of surplus value that percolate around and through capitalist enterprises. We are interested in exploring the possibilities of changing the quantitative and qualitative dimensions of those flows and exploring their potential for creating new class practices.

The recognition of stakeholders in capitalist enterprise has recently extended the range of subjects (beyond the traditional grouping of workers, management, and shareholders) ostensibly connected to and interested in corporate practice. Local communities, retrenched workers, traditional landowners, and even residents at some distance from capitalist industrial activities whose environment has been degraded have all asserted claims on corporate funds for compensation or environmental or cultural restitution. In different governmental and legal contexts these claims have been recognized and distributions of surplus value redirected accordingly. There is growing international pressure for accepted ethical and environmental standards that will ensure that what were once viewed as irregular or occasional distributive payments become part of the regular enterprise calculus. This suggests that distributions of surplus could potentially be tapped by those interested in establishing noncapitalist economic alternatives.

New alliances—among, for example, indigenous peoples, national and international human rights and green activists, labor organizers, and independent or collective producers using "appropriate" technologies—could emerge to put pressure on and bargain with the directors of the enterprise to divert some of the appropriated surplus value into a fund to improve the local conditions under which capitalism operates or to support the development of noncapitalist class practices. In a number of sites such strategies have been pursued. Local communities in the vicinity of large multinationals have made claims, based on arguments from natural right, on the surplus value circulating within the enterprise and have exacted flows from capitalist firms into their own noncapitalist enterprises. Aborigines in Northern Australia, for example, initiated a project to create a cooperative, sustainable, and renewable resource extraction industry (fish-farming) by diverting funds from a transnational mining company undertaking nonrenewable resource extraction on aboriginal land (Howitt 1994, 1995). Projects such as this illustrate the way that diverse alliances (including with capitalist appropriators themselves) might change existing distributions and create new ones, thereby altering the capitalist environment. In such cases, the conditions traditionally associated with capitalism are disrupted and transformed; while relying on (and perhaps even strengthening) the capitalist appropriation of surplus labor, the surplus extracted in that process is directed to noncapitalist activities or their conditions of existence (Gibson-Graham and O'Neill, in this volume).

What these examples suggest is not only the range of possibilities of developing new class practices and new forms of surplus appropriation and distribution but also the role of class discourse in making such innovations possible. The ability to describe and envision class processes other than capitalist ones is a crucial condition of existence of alternative class possibilities.[15]

Conclusion

Postdevelopment theory fundamentally questions the need for development, arguing in favor of greater autonomy for local social and cultural models. It recognizes that predevelopment models of economy persist, albeit in hybrid form, through their "transformative engagement with modernity" (Escobar 1995, 219) and advocates creating conditions conducive to local and regional experiments that do not necessarily conform to a single, overarching development scheme. We have argued that an antiessentialist class analysis can aid in the project of building new economic futures after development.

A language of class can be used to constitute a landscape of economic difference within which an anticapitalist imaginary can flourish. Outside the (discursively constituted) "hegemonic class forces of capitalism" (Watts 1993, 268) projects of noncapitalist construction might articulate with the political energies of new social movements. Our task has been simply to make noncapitalist class processes and projects more visible and less "unrealistic" as one step toward invigorating an inventive anticapitalocentric economic politics. In this way we may perhaps contribute to the emergence of a new panorama of community, in which communal relations of surplus appropriation and distribution are centrally involved in projects of economic and social transformation after development.

Notes

The authors would like to acknowledge the helpful comments and suggestions made by the participants in the workshop on class analysis that took place at the University of Massachusetts, Amherst, in June 1996. We would also like to thank Serap Kayatekin for her contributions to the conversations that preceded the writing of this chapter and Steve Resnick and Rick Wolff for their thoughtful comments on earlier drafts. Finally, we would like to acknowledge our debt to Arturo Escobar, for his work and for the generous way in which he has entered into dialogue with us around the topic of this essay.

1 In his excellent review of the discursive turn in development studies, Michael Watts (1993) identifies a coherent antidevelopment discourse associated with the work of Escobar (1992), Shiva (1991), Pieterse (1991), Manzo (1991), and Norgaard (1992).

2 Other contributions include Alvares (1994), Banuri (1990a, b), Beverley and Oviedo (1993), Crush (1995), Dallmayr (1992), Manzo (1991), Marchand and Parpart (1995), Nandy (1987), Rahneema (1997), Sachs (1992), and Slater (1992).

3 This positioning effects an interesting complication of what Althusser identified as economic essentialism:

   According to the economistic or mechanistic hypothesis, the role of the essence/ phenomena opposition is to explain the non-economic as a phenomenon of the economic, which is its essence. In this operation, the theoretical (and the "abstract") is surreptitiously substituted for the economy (since we have its theory in *Capital*) and the empirical or "concrete" for the non-economic, i.e., for politics, ideology, etc. The essence/phenomena opposition performs this role well enough so long as we regard the "phenomena" as the empirical, and the essence as the non-empirical, as the abstract, as the truth of the phenomena. The result is to set up an absurd relationship between the theoretical (the economic) and the empirical (the non-economic) by a change in partners which compares the knowledge of one object with the existence of another—which is to commit us to a fallacy. (Althusser and Balibar 1970, 111)

When a realist epistemology is added to the essentialist thinking outlined by Althusser, we see the representation of the economy as both the abstract essence of all things noneconomic and as the true "real."

4 "Whenever women or femininity are conceived in terms of either an identity or sameness with men; or of their opposition or inversion of the masculine; or of a complementarity with men, their representation is phallocentric" (Grosz 1990, 150).

5 Bagchi (1992), for example, tends to see sharecropping and other nominally noncapitalist forms of agricultural production not as forms of precapitalism (itself another capitalocentric formulation) but rather of "retarded capitalism."

6 According to this vision, the nature of capitalism is "not to create an homogeneous economic system but rather to dominate and draw profit from the diversity and inequality that remain in permanence" (Berger 1980).

7 For more complete elaborations of the category of class and certain of its forms, see Resnick and Wolff (1987) and Gibson-Graham (1996).

8 Meanwhile traditional class positions—such as feudal landlord or rural peasant—are seen as declining.

9 See de Janvry (1981) and Harvey (1982) for traditional and teleological interpretations of Marx's discussion of the primitive accumulation of capital.

10 Land for the project was sequestered from collective household property as well as from individual women, and in addition was newly cleared by men who argued, drawing on customary law, that this labor conferred ownership on the clearer of land, and that they were now the traditional owners.

11 Women not only withdrew from working on their individual land—this had been taken—but also withdrew their labor from collective household production in order to work in the *kafo*. This resulted in domestic violence and divorce (Pred and Watts 1992, 96).

12 Watts's interest in empirically illustrating the ways in which "capitalism

may contribute to the reproduction of nonwage labor" (p. 105), that is, produce a de facto working class, leads him to produce a capitalocentric analysis that fails, in our eyes, to highlight the political potentialities of an intensely varied terrain of production relations, property relations, oppositional struggles, and symbolic conflicts.

13 The work of ENGENDER is aimed at disrupting many of the dichotomies that structure traditional development discourse, both in its overarching philosophy and in projects carried out in its name. As their report notes,

Our aim is to contribute to a paradigmatic shift in development thinking, planning and practice, through the formation of new modes of sustainability and equity that would be viable and relevant in a modern world-system. In this context, ENGENDER is examining the experiences of different development choices, ideologies and practices, with the aim of evaluating their consequences for human development and environmental sustainability. This includes different combinations of (1) labour intensive and capital intensive production, (2) public and private sector participation, and (3) the degree of consistency between state ideologies on the one hand and on the other hand government and private sector practices. (1995, 6)

14 ENGENDER's relations with TNCs can be seen as aimed at constituting a corporate philanthropic subjectivity in its attempts to capture corporate internal markets not only in the name of a better product but also a local product whose sale will support an endangered livelihood.

15 This does not mean that we advocate all the class processes we foreground, or even the political projects that we envision as possible.

ANJAN CHAKRABARTI

AND STEPHEN CULLENBERG

□

DEVELOPMENT AND CLASS TRANSITION IN INDIA

A New Perspective

I am always reminded of one thing which the well-known British economist
Adam Smith has said in his famous treatise *The Wealth of Nations.* In it he
has described some economic laws as universal and absolute. Then he has
described certain situations which may be an obstacle to the operation of
these laws. These disturbing factors are the human nature, the human tem-
perament or altruism inherent in it. Now the economics of Khadi is just the
opposite of it. Benevolence which is inherent in human nature is the very
foundation of the economics of Khadi. What Adam Smith has described as
pure economic activity based merely on the calculations of profit and loss is
a selfish attitude and it is an obstacle to the development of Khadi; and it is
the function of a champion of Khadi to counteract this tendency.—Gandhi
1958, vol. 59, 205–6[1]

We are trying to catch up, as far as we can, with the Industrial Revolution
that occurred long ago in Western countries.—Nehru 1954, vol. 2, 93

These quotations by the two stalwarts of India's independence struggle
are striking for their different, almost contradictory views of the goal of
development in postindependence Indian society. Both were no doubt
motivated by the desire to build a fair and just future. But from within
the Congress party, the dominant anti-British party at the time of independence in 1947, each espoused a different "model of development"

and vision of social progress. Gandhi's championing of an indigenous cottage-based economic system was no match for the capitalist catch-up plan that became known as "Nehruvian socialism."

The debate over transition that began with Gandhi's and Nehru's different conceptions of development paths continued in the 1990s as India joined the seemingly worldwide rush to embrace capitalism. While the liberalization policies first introduced in 1991 by Prime Minister Narasimha Rao did not challenge the fundamental Nehruvian belief in growth-through-industrialization, they certainly questioned the wisdom of the state's involvement in output and pricing decisions and contested the import substitution approach to development that has been the hallmark of India's industrialization process since independence. These "new economic policies" have been directed at significantly reducing the state's involvement in the Indian economy and supporting an export-oriented growth and industrialization strategy of development.

Whether explicit or not, any development model is predicated on a particular theory of economic transition and a particular vision of economic justice. It must specify how a new set of economic relations emerges from or is built on the old. And its practice effects a distinctive distribution of national income, producing a different landscape of production in which certain ways of creating surplus labor or product are promoted over others. We agree with Marx (1977) who pointed out in his critique of the Gotha Program—a program drawn up by German socialists for the creation of a future German communist society—that every society has a dominant concept of "fairness" and just distribution and it follows that any model of development draws on its own particular version of this discourse of fairness for legitimation.

Gandhi was clearly interested in promoting an economic system that was built on benevolence and collectivity at the point of production. Moreover he assumed that traditional rural and peasant ways and institutions could be accommodated within modernization. Nehru, by contrast, along with subsequent national leaders supported the development of a completely new industrial system in which markets and the state would work together to produce efficient growth for the benefit of all.

Alongside and against the ideas of Gandhi, Nehru, and the latter's followers, Indian Marxist theorists have also debated transition and development pathways. Most notable have been the debate over Indian modes of production and the intervention of the subaltern studies school. Currently, however, in the face of the government's liberalization policies, Marxist and leftist debates about development have been somewhat muted. While this can be seen in part as a result of recent attempts by neoclassicists to exorcise Marxism from academic and social discourse in India, it is also, we suggest, related to the historicist conceptual framework that underpins traditional Marxist theories of transition. As the liberalization program has, perhaps unwittingly, opened a new space for debate and reconsideration of various aspects of development, we offer this essay as a Marxist intervention that keeps alive the (Gandhian) possibility of alternative (noncapitalist) development paths.

In this chapter we provide a critique of orthodox Marxian theories of transition and the development models to which they give rise. We offer a new class perspective on transition that adopts a decentered conception of society and a multidirectional vision of transition. Through the lens of this new perspective, we examine the changing class structure of India since the enactment of economic liberalization in the early 1990s.

Concepts of Transition

In the Indian modes of production debate, transition is attributed to a once-and-for-all macro-shift in the mode of production (or the economy) that effects subsequent change in the social totality.[2] Though the desired outcome is a transition or revolution that ushers in a socialist or communist mode of production, in the Indian case capitalism has been seen to be triumphant. Given the logic of unidirectional systemic change embraced by participants in the modes of production debate, a central concern of this debate has been to explain why the capitalist mode of production failed to become dominant in Indian agriculture. In line with the historicist[3] and essentialist logic of historical materialism, this formulation was thoroughly anti-Gandhian as it was based on the assumption that capitalism cannot accommodate traditional rural and peasant institutions that were considered to be backward and outmoded.

The Marxian subaltern studies school challenges the fundamental premise that transition must be a complete process and that capitalism cannot accommodate precapitalist elements of society.[4] An alternative model of transition for Third World countries is posited whereby aspects of precapitalism are appropriated by and accommodated within capitalism in what is called capital's "passive revolution." [5] In the subaltern literature, the desired development model involves a transition from the form capitalism takes in underdeveloped societies (produced by the passive revolution of capital) to a socialism of communities.

A number of elements are present in both theories of transition: The movement of society is grounded in a pregiven totality understood to develop progressively in a prescribed manner until it reaches its telos; complex social formations or totalities are reduced to a more basic totality or essence—the mode of production; commonality is foregrounded against the chaos of the uncommon, the unpredictable, and the unknown; order, certainty, and continuity are the principles for arranging events and time; historical changes are no more than the reflections of the journey of the essence; and revolutionary transitions are ultimately driven by an underlying historical consciousness emanating from that essence (Chakrabarti 1996). Foucault (1972) refers to such a constellation of elements as *total history*—the arrangement of time and events by a unified totality driven by a manifest motive or philosophy.

In both approaches, the economy is visualized as a homogeneous space where, at every site of production, relations of production behave uniformly. By this logic, a new stage in the process of economic transition is understood as a synchronic and "progressive" change in all the production sites in the economy. This applies whether the posited developmental logic involves the progression of modes of production as in the Indian modes of production debate, or takes the modified form associated with the subaltern studies school, where the passive revolution of capital intercedes as a new phase between feudalism and capitalism. No allowance is made for variety in the types of fundamental class transitions nor for changes in the form of a particular class process (from, say, one type of capitalist class process to another capitalist class process).

Indian theories of transition reinscribe three problems associated with orthodox Marxian theories of transition: first, transition is conceived as a macro-, "big bang" change—society is understood as a unified totality and transition involves the complete replacement of an outmoded social totality with a new one; second, in line with historical materialism, transition is understood as a diachronic and teleological process of succession; and, third, transition is linked with a concept of progress, understood as an ever-expanding and irreversible set of economic opportunities.

These three features mark out our differences from the concept of transition deployed in the Indian mode of production debate and the subaltern studies debates. In contrast, we prefer to adopt a decentered conception of transition that is predicated on an open and heterogeneous social totality. We are concerned with synchronic shifts in the multiplicity and mixture of class processes within a society. In our vision of *decentered transition,* history has no inner logic and follows no necessary arrangement into a series of periods driven by a Hegelian teleology of reason or the preordained succession of Marxian modes of production. History is not the progressive unfolding of a universal truth that can be deciphered by theory (such as historical materialism). Rather, it is always and everywhere contingently produced.

In order to flesh out our understanding, it is necessary to introduce a disaggregated class approach to the social totality and its transitions. We can then explain the nonhistoricist developmental structure of our theory of transition and the alternative idea of progress it entails.

Decentering Society and Transition with a Disaggregated Class Analysis

A framework that defines specific types of class processes and "class sets" (Cullenberg 1992) presents a useful way to see the complex coexistence of classes in society and the complexity involved in the process of transition. Building on Resnick and Wolff's class analytics, we identify class sets in terms of a fundamental class process—the manner of appropriation of surplus labor;[6] and two nonclass conditions—the type of remuneration received by workers and the form of the distribution of the outputs of production. We consider three forms of appropriation of surplus labor: (1) the form of appropriation whereby the performer of surplus labor can exclude all others from appropriation and therefore appropriates the surplus labor completely and individually (as in the ancient or independent class process); (2) the form of appropriation whereby the performers of surplus labor are excluded from any appropriation of their surplus labor (as in the slave, feudal, and capitalist class

Table 2

Class Set	Class Process	Worker's Access to Appropriated Surplus Labor	Worker Remuneration	Output Distribution
1	independent	all	wage	commodity
2	independent	all	wage	noncommodity
3	independent	all	nonwage	commodity
4	independent	all	nonwage	noncommodity
5	private capitalist state capitalist	none	wage	commodity
6	private capitalist state capitalist	none	wage	noncommodity
7	feudal slave	none	nonwage	commodity
8	feudal slave	none	nonwage	noncommodity
9	communal	shared	wage	commodity
10	communal	shared	wage	noncommodity
11	communal	shared	nonwage	commodity
12	communal	shared	nonwage	noncommodity

processes); and (3) the form of appropriation whereby all performers of surplus labor share in its appropriation and no one is either completely excluded from appropriation or can exclude others (as in the communal or collective class process). So as not to complicate our class taxonomy unduly we utilize a binary disaggregration of wage and nonwage forms of remuneration for workers, and commodity and noncommodity forms of distributing output. The combination of the different possibilities among these three forms of appropriation and the manner of labor remuneration and output distribution give us the twelve "class sets" seen in Table 2.[7]

At any point in time, all these distinct class sets could potentially co-exist together within a society. The existence of each of these class sets in turn depends on other economic (including other class sets) and non-economic conditions of existence. Their articulated existence is what we refer to as the class structure of society. Transition, now, can be reconceived as the change of one configuration of class sets (a society's class structure) to another distinctive configuration brought about by micro-changes within a landscape of unevenly distributed and disaggregated class relations.

This representation of a social formation made up of multiple class sets provides a direct contrast to the orthodox Marxian conception of a social totality structured by a dominant mode of production. Moreover, this disaggregated micro-class representation precludes any notion of a pre-conceived and necessary order, certainty, or continuity in the transition between and within class structures. Unlike orthodox Marxism where the progressive evolutionary order of society must be maintained, in the micro-approach to transition, capitalist class structures can, for example, be transformed into feudal or independent class structures. From this perspective, such cases of transition would not be understood as historical aberrations, but rather as always possible outcomes of society's multi-faceted and uneven developmental processes. The current transitions in the former Soviet Union and other East European countries suggest the importance of such unexpected and undertheorized transitions.

The conception of transition implied by our analysis allows for the discontinuity of social orders and the inability of a social totality to close itself via any particular class structure. It enables us to see the unpredictable movement of class structures and associated social processes and the possibility for mutations and transformations in other areas of society as a result of a change in class structure. What is lost in this approach to transition is the eschatological, diachronic, and systematic ordering of societies according to a dominant notion of "progress." This loss leaves us not with a chaotic theory of history where "anything goes," as is often mistakenly claimed, but rather with a discursively ordered and systematic understanding of history (the order and system being given by the discursive focal point of class) that is potentially able to describe the multifaceted and shifting dimensions of societal reproduction.

Class Structures and Transition in India

When disaggregated in terms of class sets, Indian society can be seen as having a heterogeneous class structure.[8] But rather than lay out a class taxonomy in abstract terms, we are interested in using our framework to interpret the contemporary transition that is resulting from the liberalization policies recently introduced by the Indian government.

The transition spurred by the liberalization program is designed to produce a uniform and progressive change to capitalism within Indian society:

Decades of development experience in dozens of countries show that a good economic environment combines the discipline of competitive markets with efficient provision of key public utilities. . . . Fostering an economic environment which promotes rapid, broad-based development will not be easy. Old habits of thinking and working must be shed. . . . Within a generation, the countries of East Asia have transformed themselves. China, Indonesia, Korea, Thailand, and Malaysia today have living standards much above ours. What they have achieved, we must strive for. (Government of India, Ministry of Finance 1993, 1–2)

The new liberalization policies are justified as a necessary reaction to a combination of economic "crises." Macroeconomic crisis is seen as having arisen from the significant fiscal deficit and the balance of payments problem. Microeconomic crisis is seen to have arisen from serious efficiency and incentive failures. In response to these pressures, the government has taken the road to reduce the fiscal deficit by cutting down its expenditures (especially its transfer payments) by dramatically reducing subsidies; selling sections of state industries to private interests and disinvesting in and restructuring many services such as banking; shifting toward a market-determined exchange rate and open-door trade policies; and adopting a set of industrial, agricultural, and banking policies that pays more attention to profitability, efficiency, and outward- (export-) oriented growth. In addition, the Indian government has supported the reduction of state involvement in economic decisions, especially those related to output and pricing.

This set of government policies has directly and indirectly affected class structures in all sectors of the economy, setting in motion a class transition that is still in process. Changes in specific sectors are, through a social chain reaction, producing a dramatically different social totality — today's India.[9] The once torpid economic, cultural, and political aspects of society are now undergoing rapid transformation and hitherto accepted ideas regarding development, progress, the proper role for central and state governments, the meaning of democracy, and embedded cultural values are in a state of profound turmoil. Where transition in the Indian economy is taking us and what its effects might be on class politics are crucial questions that we discuss in the conclusion of this chapter. But first we focus on the transitions in class sets taking place in the important sectors of agriculture, state-owned enterprise, and Indian households.

Transition and the Class Structure in Agriculture

The largest proportion of the agricultural population in India comprises agricultural laborers and small farmers who produce and buy agricultural products in order to reproduce their families. The agriculture sector as a whole is made up of a number of different class sets. Many farms are operated by single workers involved in an independent class process who produce and appropriate their own surplus labor. Depending on whether their surplus is exchanged for money or consumed in its product form, these workers occupy class sets 3 and 4. As it is unlikely that farmers pay themselves in money form, class sets 1 and 2 are assumed to be rare in India. Many family farms in which family members communally produce surplus labor and appropriate it together resemble class sets 11 and 12. Other family farms operate with a feudal class process, resembling class sets 7 and 8, where the surplus produced by the family is appropriated by the head of the household, remuneration for family members involved in production is paid in kind, and the surplus product could be either sold as commodities, exchanged for goods, or simply consumed.

Much farming in India also takes place within a sharecropping system in which the farmer uses the land of a landowner to produce a crop. The sharecropping system has a complex class structure with independent, feudal, and capitalist class processes involved.[10] Depending on the tenurial arrangements, the sharecropping system could take the form of class set 5, where the sharecropper employs wage labor, sells the produce as a commodity, and appropriates the surplus value in a capitalist class process, paying off a certain ground rent for the land leased from the landlord. Where the landlord leases out land to the sharecropper to work as a direct producer, directly appropriates the surplus product, and distributes part of it in kind to the sharecroppers, this involves a feudal class structure resembling class set 7 or 8. Interestingly, under the sharecropping system, there can even be independent class structures resembling class sets 3 or 4 where the direct producer, who is also the only producer, appropriates his own surplus labor, part of which is then distributed as ground rent to the landlord. All of these forms of sharecropping can be found in India, along with capitalist forms of agricultural production.

The current government's agricultural policy is directed toward raising the ratio of agricultural gross capital formation to current government expenditure on agriculture, decreasing the state's involvement, and increasing the role of private investment in the agricultural sector (*Economic Survey* 1994–95, 130–32). To carry out this policy, the government has cut back its current expenditures on fertilizer and both input and interest subsidies, and increased investment in irrigation and rural communication in the hope that this will lead to an increase in capital formation. To encourage private investment, it is opening up previously closed sectors (like the power industry) to private investors and pursuing open-door trade policies designed to encourage the private sector to invest in agriculture to garner gains from trade through exports. It has also sharply increased the state procurement price for certain agricultural products, thereby increasing the trend toward favorable terms of trade for agriculture.

Fertilizer subsidies, input subsidies (especially for water and electricity), interest subsidies, administrative price support, easy loan guarantees, and many other services provided by the government support the conditions of existence for the diverse class structure of the contemporary Indian agricultural production sector. The reduction in these subsidies and the redirection elsewhere of government payments constitutes a threat to certain of the existing class sets within the sector. Attempts by the government to overcome the crisis in the state sector and to increase private capital formation in the agricultural sector may end up producing a crisis for many farms, resulting in the following inequality expressed in class analytic terms:

$$SL + \sum SCR + \sum NCR < \sum SC + \sum X + \sum Y$$

where SL = various forms of surplus labor produced and appropriated on the farm;

$\sum SCR$ = subsumed class revenue (e.g., dividends, ground rents, and merchant fees obtained by wealthier farmers);

$\sum NCR$ = nonclass revenue (e.g., government subsidies for fertilizer, water, electricity, and loan support);

$\sum SC$ = sum of subsumed class payments (e.g., taxes, merchant fees, ground rent, and interest payments to secure the conditions of the fundamental class process);

$\sum X$ = sum of payments made to secure SCR;

$\sum Y$ = sum of payments made to secure NCR.

The severity of the crisis will vary depending on the amount of difference between the revenue side and the expenditure side of the equation. Since the revenue and the expenditure components reflect the different class and nonclass processes involved in a farm enterprise, a crisis would imply that the prevailing form of class structure of the farm might change. If the extent of the crisis is mild, there will probably be a few minor changes in the class structure of the farm while, if the extent of the crisis is severe, there could be a major change in class structure or even its closure.

For all farmers, whether involved in independent, communal, feudal, or capitalist class processes, the reduction of state subsidies will increase production costs and other payments, thereby reducing the surplus that can be appropriated. For the more marginal farms run by the most vulnerable sector of the population, this policy of detachment by the government can create severe problems. The increase in payments for processes that provide the conditions of existence for the reproduction of a small independent or communal producer could lead to a situation whereby the small farmer would be compelled to transfer the right of appropriating surplus product from the farm land to a moneylender or to a richer farmer who buys the land. The independent or communal producer might be forced to become a sharecropper, and a transition from class sets 3, 4, 11, and 12 to class sets 7 and 8 might take place. More dramatically, the independent or communal producers could be forced off their land altogether to become agricultural laborers or unemployed. This surrender of rights of appropriation may lead to a concentration of capital in agriculture, to the intensification of exploitation, and the increased incidence of inequality, unemployment, and poverty.

The government defends its policies on the basis that they will lead to the greater efficiency and competitiveness of Indian farms and to general prosperity across the board. It fails to recognize that its policies will have different effects for distinct types of farms. Not all farms will survive in their present form and the changes will not always be to the benefit of the existing set of appropriators. As a result of government policies, some farms will benefit, with increased production of surplus value and income, and some farms will be put at a great disadvantage.

Government spokesmen argue that the removal of agricultural subsidies in developed countries, as required by the World Trade Organization, will drive up the international prices for agricultural products, thereby benefiting India's farmers and agro-industry, who enjoy a comparative advantage in these products. It must be noted, however, that higher agricultural prices will benefit only those farms whose output takes the commodity form and is covered by the state's procurement prices. Moreover, higher prices will be advantageous to only those farmers whose marketable return outweighs the loss from an increase in subsumed class payments (to agents such as moneylenders and merchants) and nonclass expenditures (for example, on inputs).

While it is true that the terms of trade may turn in favor of agriculture, this will disproportionately benefit the rich farmers, who are usually but not exclusively capitalist (class sets 5 and 6). The largest number of agricultural producers in India are small farmers (belonging to class sets 3, 4, 8, 11, and 12) who either do not produce for the market or have little access to markets. Whatever little marketable surplus these farmers have is normally taken by the traders who would in this case gain most from any increase in prices.

With higher prices of food-grains, the expenditure side of the farming family budget increases, leading to a crisis in the reproduction of such families. This will create a crisis situation for the class structures of these farms as well, especially those in which labor is remunerated in wage form and subsistence goods purchased. The high inflation rate (averaging 10 percent in the years associated with the liberalization policies) has contributed disproportionately to the misery of families living around the poverty level since, unlike the inflations of previous periods, this inflationary pressure has been driven by a sharp rise in the prices of food-grains that constitute the means of subsistence of such families in India. Furthermore, higher food-grain prices are also bound to intensify urban poverty.[11]

It would seem that attempts by the government to overcome the fiscal crisis in the state sector may end up producing a crisis in the agricultural sector, and, while the transition initiated in its class structure may lead ultimately to a growing concentration of capital in the sector, this will occur alongside growing rural unemployment and rural and urban poverty.

Transition and the State Capitalist Sector

The state sector in India, comprising 240 central public sector enterprises and many more public sector establishments, employs 19.2 million people. By contrast, the private, nonagricultural sector employs 7.8 million people (*Economic Survey* 1994–95, S-54). In a predominantly agricultural country like India, the state sector occupies an important place in the industrial economy. Until quite recently Indian government planning deemed that state enterprises were to have sole control over the capital goods sector, raw materials, and the important services sector, consisting of the organized banking system, telecommunications, airlines, railways, and insurance.[12]

Contrary to the claim made by many that this represents an indicator of India's socialist nature—because state enterprises are supposed to be fundamentally differentiated by their property relations from capitalist enterprises, and therefore socialist—we find evidence that India's state sector exhibits a complex capitalist class structure.[13] Most state enterprises belong to class set 5, where a state-appointed board of directors appropriates the surplus value produced by state workers. Some of the output produced by state enterprises is sold on the market as commodities, while other output is distributed in various noncommodity forms. State firms in the defense sector, for example, where outputs are simply handed over to the army without any monetary exchange, are in class set 6.[14]

State enterprises have been the targets of the most far-reaching of the economic reforms introduced in the 1990s. Liberalization policies have been focused not only on the deregulation of entry and exit into particular industries but also on changing the class structures of state capitalist enterprises. Most of the production and service establishments that have been previously closed to the private sector have now been opened to different degrees. For example, private enterprises are now being encouraged to invest in infrastructure industries like energy, mineral extraction, telecommunications, banking, and heavy industries like iron and steel. New private capitalist class structures are emerging in these spheres of the economy. The more interesting parts of the liberalization policy, however, are the government's two responses to what it perceived as a crisis situation in the state capitalist enterprises.

First, state capitalist enterprises have been either phased out or transformed into private capitalist enterprises through the actions of the Bureau of Industrial and Financial Reconstruction (BIFR). One of the tasks of the BIFR is to check the viability of loss-making state enterprises and pass judgment on whether restructuring would or would not revive the enterprise. If the answer is negative, the government calls an auction to sell the enterprise. If there are no bidders, then the enterprise is shut down. When state capitalist enterprises are transformed into private capitalist enterprises, the right to appropriation and distribution of surplus labor passes from government hands to private hands. While in terms of our class sets in this case there is no transition out of class set 5, in some other cases there may be a transition from class set 6 to 5. In the Indian defense industry, for example, takeover by private capital has seen the increased sale of military products in the market. Sell-offs such as this have been an extremely contentious political issue. There are significant concerns about the way a private, as opposed to a state capitalist, enterprise might engage in appropriative and distributive class practices.[15]

Second, BIFR recommendations for a restructuring of state enterprises are driven by demands to make them more competitive in domestic and global markets. Even when they are not sold off to private interests, the enterprises are forced to undergo major restructuring. The new industrial policies have abolished the monopoly power of state enterprises, thereby opening previously closed product markets to domestic competition and, in light of the open-door trade policies, to foreign enterprises, as well. The concern over efficiency and profits has produced a host of significant changes in the ways in which state capitalist class structures are reproduced. In those enterprises deemed unviable, the government has closed off the option of those "soft budget constraints" that automatically ensured a state sector enterprise against closure, whatever its state of profitability. They have initiated changes in management structures, the labor process, and in the goals of the enterprises, making them run on what is being called a "commercial" (that is, profitable) basis. In many state enterprises, including some profit-making ones, the state's equity is being reduced by up to 49 percent, principally to finance government deficit reduction.[16] By keeping 51 percent of the equity share, the government retains the power to appoint the board of directors and is still in control of the appropriation of the surplus value produced in these enterprises.

In other words, in this case, while the ownership and therefore the subsumed class relations and payments are drastically changed, control over the fundamental class process of surplus-value production and appropriation remains with the government. Financial changes, such as new relationships between the increasingly privatized banking sector and the state enterprises, are drastically changing the subsumed class structure of these enterprises. New conditions for the capitalist appropriation and distribution of surplus value are being engineered and the constituencies who control these class processes are being reconfigured such that "public" claims are being subordinated to "private."

Transition and Indian Households

As the household is not considered a site of production in the *Economic Survey,* the official government statistics of India, we do not have precise information or specific quantitative data on this sector of the economy. Nevertheless, a few observations can be made. Indian families largely participate in what might be called a feudal household class structure (class set 8), where the surplus labor of the housewife is appropriated by the husband or the husband's family (usually represented by the mother-in-law). In rural areas where many families are involved in agriculture or small-scale enterprises, such as handloom, leather, coir, and pottery works, women and children are seen as "economically active." [17] Here women might participate in a number of different class processes—one associated with the family enterprise (typically feudal or family communal) and another with domestic production (typically feudal). Some sole-person or single-parent households, which are rare in India and more likely to be found in urban areas, might involve an independent household class structure (class set 4). The communal household class structure (where surplus labor is produced inside the household and appropriated jointly) is becoming increasingly common in India and would be a form of class set 12. While the Indian household class structure is complex, we would suggest that the feudal (and typically patriarchal) class structure is dominant. Class transitions are, however, taking place as feudal class structures undergo internal change and give way to independent and communal class structures.

One of the effects of the new economic policies, especially on urban households, has been the increased introduction of time-saving technologies like dishwashers, refrigerators, washing machines, and cooking utensils into the domestic production process. Along with the adoption of these means of production has come changed cultural perceptions of what the socially necessary basket of commodities for a household unit might be. New commodities like televisions or fashionable clothing are increasingly being seen as necessary consumer goods for a typical household. Figures on gross domestic savings indicate that there has been a sharp decline from a peak of 20 percent of gross domestic product in 1990–91 to 15.9 percent in 1993–94. One explanation for this may be the increased household expenditure on productive and personal consumption commodities. Certainly there is concern for the effects of this shift in domestic economies.[18] In the absence of any detailed studies, we can but speculate on the potential class effects of such increased expenditure.

With the increased purchases of consumer durables, the feudal household may become more entrenched, as the new means of production contribute to higher feudal productivity in the home and free up women's time to work outside the house. In this case, the newly emerging private capitalist sector in manufacturing could be seen as providing capitalist commodities that help reproduce feudal households, while those same feudal households help secure private capitalism by extending the market for its produced durables and providing it with a new, and perhaps cheaper, source of labor power.

On the other hand, the entry of women into paid work outside the home, especially in urban areas, may lead to a crisis of the feudal household, especially given the increasingly prevalent cultural attack on the traditional naturalistic role of the woman as housewife and mother. The entry of new commodities into the household and changes in domestic labor processes, household labor supervision, credit structures, and incomes, as well as new cultural perceptions, might indeed be hastening a transition to a communal household class structure in which all adult household members perform and collectively appropriate surplus labor.

Perhaps just as likely is the movement toward an independent class structure. For many Indian families, letting a woman work outside the home would be tantamount to a social scandal, and this perception may lead to irreconcilable differences between the husband (or husband's family) and wife, culminating in divorce. An increase in divorces would probably lead to the creation of independent household class structures, in which women alone or as single parents produce, appropriate, and distribute their own surplus domestic labor.

The household sector is a significant site of production, appropriation, and distribution of surplus labor. It is, moreover, an arena where many of the social and cultural transformations taking place in Indian society are being discussed and struggled over. Liberalization policies directly affect this sector and, in turn, new household activities and practices will produce class transitions in Indian society. As more women enter the capitalist work place, traditional domestic class processes will be modified and transformed.

In summary, it would appear that the Indian government's liberalization policies have been based on a vision of uniform economic spaces and the assumption that change in one site would be replicated in all other sites. The government defends its actions by arguing that the benefits of reforms will be universally effective across various economic sites—for example, raising productivity across the board. The opposition similarly emphasizes that the problems of these policies are problems for all sites. As we explained above, this assumption follows from a macro-concept of totality, where transition means a movement from one homogeneous configuration to another, requiring in the process that constituent parts replicate themselves in a more or less identical manner.

Given the decentered concept of the social totality and the disaggregated class-based analysis of transition elaborated here, it is clear that government policies will have a range of different effects on existing class structures. Policies designed to have uniform effects will produce instead an uneven and multifaceted process of change.

The above discussion suggests that in the quest for efficiency and growth, recent economic policies are initiating private capitalist class structures in the agricultural sector at the expense of independent, feudal, and communal class structures; the reduction of state capitalist class structures in what were once the "state sectors," in favor of growth in private domestic and foreign capitalist class structures; and the possible entrenchment of feudal class structures in Indian households, along with emergence of new independent and communal household class structures. A profound reshaping of the ways in which surplus labor is produced, appropriated, and distributed within the complex social totality known as Indian society is taking place. It remains for us to discuss how this transition can be seen in terms of the different conceptions of "just" development paths and "progress" with which this chapter began.

Transition, Marxism, and the Meaning of Progress

Our aim in this chapter is not only to contribute to a reinvigorated Marxist debate about transition, but also to raise the question of what might constitute a "progressive" intervention in the struggles being waged around the new economic policies of the Indian government. It is time, we feel, to revisit Gandhi's championing of *Khadi* against the universalist claims of the prophets of industrialization in postindependence India, and in the same spirit to look for ways to promote economic development paths that differ from both the orthodoxies of the past and the empty promises of liberalization.

Our decentered Marxian approach to transition is not agnostic or indifferent to the direction of societal change, as some might mistakenly infer. We do not abandon the terms "progress" and "development," but rather redefine them to encompass the transformation of the class structures of a social formation toward nonexploitative forms and toward a more "fair" distribution of produced wealth. We advocate a change in Indian society so that those who produce surplus labor also appropriate it. But we also hold that such a change in a society's fundamental (or appropriative) class processes must be intimately linked to changes in subsumed (or distributive) class processes and the distribution of national income more generally.

Unless we can formulate radically new and different ideas of progress and development, the discursive space of debate will be colonized by neoclassical economic visions that celebrate the "virtue" of efficiency, competition, and markets and the "progressive" dynamic of capitalist growth.[19] Among advocates of the mainstream development path, it is often assumed that capitalist growth is also productive of fair distributions, though how this outcome is to be achieved is only ever vaguely specified with gestures toward "market mechanisms." Implicit in this discourse is a valuing of capitalist growth over the growth of any other class structure and belief in the superior "fairness" of capitalist distributive mechanisms over alternatives.

In order for Marxists to intervene distinctively in debates such as that taking place about development pathways in India today, there is a need to articulate concepts of distributive "fairness" that go along with the advocacy of nonexploitative class processes.[20] Mainstream measures of progress and development are conceived in terms of the growth of gross domestic product, per capita GDP, or even the Human Development Index. The latter two measures take into account the distribution of resources in a society but ignore the articulation of production and growth with class appropriations and distributions.

Our view of fairness, by contrast, involves the promotion of redistribution toward those who produce under nonexploitative conditions and whose distributive class payments are skewed toward supporting a wide section of the community. In the case of a society dominated by exploitative class structures, our conception of fairness would promote an initial redistribution toward the "doers" of surplus labor (in whatever class structure) and away from the "non-doers." But it would also involve an equitable ultimate distribution of income, encompassing those who are excluded from labor for reasons of age, infirmity, or other bases of exclusion.

Since the decentered, micro-focused concept of class transition implies a continuous process of incremental change within and between class structures where the direction of change is not pregiven, there is ample political space to work for changing class and nonclass processes in the direction of such a vision of progress and development. That is, since capitalist class structures cannot close society on their own, there remain possibilities for other class structures to make their presence felt. As Marxists, we would situate the politics of class struggle within that range of possibilities.[21] This vision displaces the concept of progress and development and that of the associated politics of class to a micro-level; but given the political failure of attempts at macro-transitions to socialism, perhaps this should be seen as a desirable displacement.[22]

In India today, the "rush toward globalization" and the dominant project of economic reform need not blind us to the diversity of the economic and social fabric. A disaggregated micro-class analysis may potentially contribute to a Marxian micro-politics of class transition that promotes progressive and fair appropriative and distributive class processes. With a new vision of progress and development — encompassing the dual aims of nonexploitative class structures and "fair" distribution — we may produce new conceptions of society that are decentered and yet radically progressive. Gandhi's work might still provide an inspiration and guide to bringing such a society into existence.

Notes

1 *Khadi* literally means "indigenous cloth." It is also a symbol for an economic system characterized by labor intensive, village- (and family-) based production and marketing processes.

2 The Indian modes of production debate can be divided roughly into three areas of concern. The first involves the question of whether, in addition to commodity production, the creation of potential "free" wage labor was a necessary and sufficient condition for defining capitalism, or whether the additional condition of productive investment was required (Patnaik 1978 versus Chattopadhyay 1990a,b). The second debate was between the semi-feudal school (Bhaduri 1973, 1977, 1981, 1983; Prasad 1973, 1979, 1990) and the capitalist school (Bardhan and Rudra 1978, 1980, 1981), where the major

question was whether some social institutions (usury, sharecropping, and the like) necessarily constituted precapitalist relations of production, which thereby inhibited the development of the forces of production (indexed by technological development). The final major issue involved a shift from a focus on modes of production per se to the process of class formation and class differentiation in Indian agriculture (Patnaik 1976, 1987; Bhaduri 1981, 1983; Rudra 1984, 1988).

3 By historicism we mean a linear view of historical development guided by a teleological logic, where successive historical epochs or modes of production replace each other. Historicism in this sense posits the developmental logic of history as a rational progression where subsequent modes of production are superior to previous ones (see Bottomore 1997, 239).

4 In opposition to the shared traditional Marxist terrain of the Indian modes of production debate, the subaltern studies school, which became influential during the 1980s (Guha 1982–1990; Chatterjee and Pandey 1992), has recently challenged the fundamental premise that capitalism cannot accommodate precapitalist elements of society. Subaltern studies theorists have created an alternative general model of transition for Third World countries where one moment of the transition process is "the passive revolution of capital" that roughly signifies the incorporation and accommodation of precapitalism by capitalism. Abandoning the base-superstructure correspondence model of historical materialism, these theorists focus instead on the agency of the subaltern in explaining the failure of a Western European type of full-fledged capitalism or a new democracy to take hold in India. Specifically, they examine the means by which the elite establishes capitalism's hegemony over the working class and various precapitalist elements (Chatterjee 1986, 1993; Chaudhury 1988, 1991–92, 1994; Sanyal 1988, 1991–92).

5 More precisely, "passive revolution" of capital, which was first popularized by Gramsci (1971), can be understood as the process of creating a hegemonic rule of capital over precapital such that capital accumulation can proceed relatively freely without any substantive opposition from elements of precapitalism. (See also Chaudhuri 1988, 1991–92; Chatterjee 1988, 1993; Sanyal 1988; and Chakrabarti 1996.)

6 In this analysis, we focus on fundamental class processes and will not attempt to delineate different forms of the distribution of appropriated surplus labor, i.e., subsumed class payments.

7 It should be noted that these class sets do not involve the specification of property ownership, power relationships, or income distribution. Inclusion of these nonclass processes would create a further differentiation of class

structures. The exact number and way of delineating class sets depends on the purpose and context of a particular analysis. In this preliminary application we have pragmatically adopted a rather limited scope.

8 While we have not undertaken a detailed study of different production sites in Indian society to determine their class nature, we have been able to re-interpret a good number of existing reports and studies of these sites in terms of our class set taxonomy. We draw on this secondary literature in our discussion.

9 Liberalization policies have specifically affected class relationships in state capitalist enterprises, private agriculture, private capitalist industries, the household sector, and service sectors, such as banking and insurance, which provide critical conditions of existence for these enterprises and farms.

10 See Kayatekin (1996–97) for an analysis of the various class processes that may be referred to by the term "sharecropping."

11 One hope was that a reduction of the budget deficit would lead to a decline in the rate of inflation. The rate of inflation, however, has in fact risen to over 10 percent and has remained resilient during the years of reform. It is to be noted that inflation has various ramifications. First, it affects different sections of the population disparately, depending on their consumption patterns, since it involves differential increases in the prices of commodities. Second, the change in the relative price structure changes the distribution of money income since increases or decreases of prices increase or decrease factor income as well. Because of the present trend, which shows that increase in food-grain prices far exceeds the overall rate of inflation (showing itself in a higher increase in the consumer price index for agricultural workers than the increase in the consumer price index for industrial workers and nonmanual employees), there are studies that claim that the present bout of inflation has adversely affected the agricultural laborers, small farmers, and urban poor, leading to a transfer of income from these sections of the population to those categories of the population who spend a smaller proportion of their income on primary food articles (Mehta 1994; Sen 1994; Ghosh 1995). These studies also show that increases in agricultural wages are unable to compensate for the price increases and, consequently, real income has gone down. The situation is worst for the urban poor, whose nominal wage has stagnated. Using the additional source of a study on consumption of food-grains conducted by the Indoor Gandhi Institute for Development Study, Ghosh points out that, "per capita availability of total foodgrains available for consumption (defined as net output adjusted for net imports and net changes in stock) declined from 510 Grammies per day in 1991 to 465 Grammies per day in 1993" (1995, 1073). He also

points out that the present bout of inflation has directly increased poverty in India to 40.5 percent. These studies indicate a growing intensification of inequality and poverty, partly brought about by the increasing inflation rate. Ironically, all of this happened when the critical stochastic factor of inclement weather was not present, leading to a steady growth of Indian agriculture.

12 In the postindependence period, government planners made a distinction between those sectors in which private capitalist enterprises would be allowed and those in which state capitalist enterprises permitted to dominate. Private enterprises were given the sector of consumer goods.

13 According to Resnick and Wolff:

State capitalism means that persons within a state apparatus exploit labor in state institutions. State capitalism also has its varieties. . . . State capitalist enterprises may sell their products as commodities, thereby realizing surplus value and then distributing it so as to secure their continued existence; or their products may be administratively distributed with administered prices attached to them. State capitalist enterprises may exist within a predominantly private capitalist system. A small minority of state capitalist enterprises may then have to compete with private enterprises in all markets. Alternatively, private capitalist enterprises may be marginalized or delegitimated altogether, leaving most or all production to occur through state capitalist enterprises. (1995, 212–13)

14 Similarly Resnick and Wolff (1994 and in this volume) argue that state enterprises in the former Soviet Union were capitalist even though their output was not sold as commodities. They argue that the output was consistently valued by state administrators and therefore, given the form of surplus labor appropriation, surplus value was created by state capitalist enterprises.

15 One interesting case concerns an exchange of enterprise from the central government to a state government. In 1995, the Bengal Pottery, a central government undertaking, was auctioned and bought by the state government of West Bengal. Along with the ownership change, the right to appropriation and distribution of surplus labor was transferred not into private hands but from one level of the state to another. This can be seen as an intervention to maintain some form of public control over the production, appropriation, and distribution of surplus value in this industry.

16 From July 1991 to December 1994, thirty-five central public sector enterprises have been approved for such disinvestments by the government (*Economic Survey* 1994–95, 109).

17 The female labor force (including female children) in rural areas makes up roughly 84 percent of all economically active females in India.

18 Patel makes the comment, for example: "At a time when India is being rapidly transformed by imported technologies, it might have been useful to study the social implications of these technologies, particularly the manner in which these affect the family budget" (1994, 122).

19 As expressed, for instance, in the work of Bhagwati and Srinivasan (1993) and Bhagwati (1993).

20 Interestingly, Marx rejected the idea of an absolute, universally applicable notion of "fairness" or "equality" and questioned the idea that the "undiminished proceeds of labor" belong to all members of society. He argued that socialists needed to develop their own ideas of fairness. Here Marx was responding critically to the ideas of Lasalle and other German socialists about the creation of a future German socialist society, as expressed in the Gotha Program (1977, 564–68).

21 While this may involve taking part in macro- or state-level politics, we want to emphasize that political attention should not ignore micro-level class changes as a site for politics. Since orthodox Marxists have for so long tended to consider class struggles explicitly in macro terms, we invoke the term "micro" to differentiate our postmodern approach. Here we partially draw on Foucault's notion of the micro-politics of resistance.

22 The concept of a class-based micro-politics is focused on changing the exploitative class structures of society to nonexploitative ones, with the belief that such a change will, via its overdetermined and contradictory effects, produce substantial changes in other class and nonclass processes, thereby having a profound effect on society or the social totality. In this context, Gibson-Graham (1993) argue that the apparent monolithic macro-existence of "capitalism" can be decentered in terms of a micro-level politics of subversion and resistance.

SATYANANDA J. GABRIEL

A CLASS ANALYSIS OF THE IRANIAN

REVOLUTION OF 1979

The Iranian Revolution of 1979 (henceforth referred to as the 1979 Revolution) has been described as one of the epochal events of the twentieth century, inaugurating a period of Islamic revivalism and struggle against "modernization" in many nations where Islam is the predominant religion. In discussions of the 1979 Revolution, the significance of Islamic fundamentalism, the use of political repression by the regime of Mohammed Reza Shah (hereafter referred to as the monarchist regime), particularly the violence perpetrated by the Information and Security Organization of the Nation, a.k.a. SAVAK (the secret police), widespread corruption and official favoritism, rising income and property ownership inequality, and the impact of "Western" imperialism and global capitalism have all played causal roles.[1] Jahangir Amuzegar (1991) provides a relatively comprehensive review of the standard explanations for the 1979 Revolution.

Amuzegar rejects linking the 1979 Revolution to any fixed set of causes and implies that it was sui generis, indicating that the processes that shaped the revolution were both serendipitous and unlikely to have corollaries in other social formations, whether of the past or future. While this chapter is in agreement with Amuzegar's antireductionism, it is more sanguine about the prospects for finding characteristics of the 1979 Revolution that are common to other social formations of both the past and the future. This optimism about the possibility of learning something from the 1979 Revolution comes, in part, from a recognition that analyses of the revolution have tended to ignore or downplay important internal struggles over class processes, defined as the particular forms in which surplus labor was produced and distributed, that may have been catalysts in the revolution.[2] In particular, discussions of the 1979 Revolution have failed to recognize: (1) the role of internecine conflict within the ranks of capitalist appropriators; and (2) the importance of ancient (or self-exploiting) direct producers and their allied agents in the collapse of the monarchist regime.[3] In general terms, it is the argument of this chapter that struggles over class processes were a significant factor in shaping the crises that culminated in the 1979 Revolution.[4] In particular, it is argued that the wide-scale presence of self-exploitation, and the dependence of a vast range of social agents on self-exploitation, coupled with the internecine disputes among capitalist appropriators, created conditions ripe for a revolutionary change in the political processes constituting the Iranian state.

The primary thesis of this essay is that the efforts of the monarchist regime to create a particular form of capitalism dominated by large-scale capitalist firms under the control of a small elite of families, herein described as *oligarchic capitalism,* created a range of social crises that threatened the survival of ancientism (or self-exploitation) and non-oligarchic capitalism.[5] The policies of the monarchist regime, sometimes referred to as the "Modernization Program," had a definite impact on class processes in Iran, and created some of the conditions for its own demise. These policies, while *explicitly* directed toward fostering economic growth, created and then deepened the social crises that threatened preexisting forms and configurations of surplus appropriation and distribution, particularly the prevalence of self-exploitation in the rural villages and urban bazaars, but also capitalist appropriation of the non-oligarchic type. The dual threats to both small-scale capitalism and to self-exploitation, and the ways of life related to these distinct class processes, resulted in complex forms of resistance. Among those with a stake in opposing the modernization program were a wide range of social agents who perceived the crises as a direct threat to their survival, including nonoligarchic capitalist appropriators, ancient direct producers, and social agents allied to one or the other or both of these groups of appropriators, including the Shi'a Islamic *ulama* (theologians and clergy).

Self-exploitation was arguably the most widespread form of surplus appropriation in terms of numbers of direct producers.[6] Insofar as the monarchist regime's Modernization Program threatened to displace self-exploitation with oligarchic capitalist exploitation, the 1979 Revolution that stopped, or, at least, slowed this process, might better be described as a *counterrevolution.* In this scenario—the 1979 Revolution as counter-revolution—one of the objectives was to initiate a *political revolution* in order to avert a gradually progressing *economic revolution.* Viewed thus, the movement against the monarchist regime was fundamentally reactionary in nature. The use of conservative religious discourse as a tool in this struggle reinforces the notion of 1979 as a moment of counter-revolution, rather than of broad-based social (political, cultural, and economic) revolution.

If, on the other hand, the selection of the adjective used to define a social formation in class terms is based on the fundamental class process wherein the largest *market value* is created, then Iran was capitalist both prior to and after the 1979 Revolution. Capitalist exploitation was clearly dominant in terms of the total market value of produced commodities in Iran during both periods, primarily because capitalism dominated the markets for industrial and extractive output. Insofar as monarchist Iran was, in aggregate market value terms, a capitalist social formation, with a significant presence of self-exploitation, it remained such a social formation after the 1979 Revolution, although the trajectory of change may have been altered.

Nevertheless, in agriculture and handicraft production, self-exploitation prevailed in both market value and in numbers of direct producers involved. The same can be said of the numbers of allied agents involved in the Iranian economy. Merchants, moneylenders, landlords, and clergy who depended on received shares of ancient surplus were far more numerous than those who depended on received shares of capitalist surplus. In the villages and urban bazaars it was self-exploitation, not capitalism, that dominated economic and social life. Thus, an argument can be made that Iran was not really a capitalist social formation but an ancient one, with the presence of a significant and powerful capitalist sector.

In the next section, the role of self-exploitation within Iranian villages, including the relationship between ancient direct producers and a subset of their allied social agents, is examined as one of the preconditions for the 1979 Revolution.

Ancient Villages, Ancient Democracy, and the Foundations of Revolution

To the extent that the monarchist regime created positive conditions for the development of oligarchic capitalism, it simultaneously created negative conditions (crises) threatening the survival of noncapitalist appropriators and their allied agents, particularly ancient producers, landlords, merchants, and moneylenders. Although it is difficult to gauge whether and to what extent feudalism might have persisted in rural Iran beyond the 1920s, when the dominance of the countryside by rural warlords, the so-called *khans,* was ended by a military-dominated monarchist regime, it is possible that some landlords may have maintained the position of feudal appropriators and that the sharecroppers on their land occupied the position of feudal direct producers well after feudalism had ceased to be prevalent in the country.[7]

Based on the best available evidence, it is assumed in this chapter that feudal appropriation did not prevail in the Iranian countryside during the monarchist regime of Mohammed Reza Shah. Nevertheless, to the extent it existed at all, it would have been threatened by the same dynamic that threatened other noncapitalist forms of appropriation. This would add an additional element to justify the landlords' opposition to the monarchist regime, which will be discussed later.

The argument here proceeds under the assumption that the prerevolutionary Iranian countryside was not feudal. Indeed, it is assumed that the vast majority of rural direct producers, called *nasaq-holders,* were neither feudal nor capitalist. Each of these nasaq-holders distributed his surplus to a wide range of social agents, including, but not limited to, landlords. Since the nasaq-holder was the first distributor of the surplus he created, then it is assumed that he was also the first receiver of that surplus. This defines self-exploitation. Given that nasaq-holders comprised approximately 65 percent of the direct producers in agriculture, it can be further assumed that the rural villages were, in class terms, ancient.

To reinforce this argument, it is noted that ancient farmers were not the only ancient producers in the villages. Self-exploitation also prevailed among barbers, blacksmiths, carpenters, cobblers, health practi-

tioners, printers, tailors, and a variety of other nonfarming direct producers. These ancient producers participated in numerous and complex
social relationships—often described in the literature as "backward" and
"semifeudal." [8] These relationships reproduced some of the conditions
necessary to continued self-exploitation. A subset of these relationships
resulted in ancient producers being subject to claims on their self-
appropriated surplus, including claims by ancient landlords, moneylenders, merchants, water distribution coordinators, teachers, and the clergy.
No village resident could avoid some form of relationship with ancient
producers and/or the social agents allied to ancient producers.

In other words, self-exploitation infused every aspect of life in the
Iranian villages. It provided the basis for a wide range of social interactions and alliances. These interactions might be properly described
as relatively nonhierarchical. For the most part, individuals negotiated
the terms of their economic relationships with each other as individuals, rather than as the representatives of larger social institutions. In
this ancient social environment, even the individual Shi'ite clergy enjoyed a certain "relative autonomy" from each other. These decentralized, "grassroots" relationships of the Iranian village, like those of
the bazaars in the cities, placed constraints on the exercise of state
or corporate power, impeded the encroachment of capitalism into the
countryside, and created conditions conducive to the reproduction of
self-exploitation. As it turns out, these conditions may also have been
conducive to a political revolution against a regime that threatened to displace the ancient way of life with an alternative set of social relationships.

Thus, those commentators, such as Amuzegar (1991), who assume that
landlords were dominant over rural life in twentieth-century Iran are
ignoring the way day-to-day decision making occurred in the villages and
dismissing the possibility that self-exploitation could provide the basis
for an economic "system" on a par with feudalism or capitalism. Unlike
the period when the khans (tribal warlords) dominated rural life, individual self-exploiting direct producers in the twentieth-century Iranian
villages were stubbornly insistent on having a voice in most of the major
decisions of village life. It was rare that these producers would acquiesce
to the dictates of external institutions, whether they came from the state
or from absentee landlords.

Self-exploiting direct producers typically came to agreements among themselves about key aspects of village life. For example, ancient producers in the Iranian villages had a long tradition of cooperation in the use of village resources, including the supply and distribution of water.[9] The producers agreed among themselves about how these resources would be used and maintained.

This should not be surprising, given the conclusion that the vast majority of direct producers in the villages were self-exploiting. The very act of self-exploitation requires a strong sense of the *self* and of one's individual power to control one's destiny. How else can the ancient producer have the will to act "alone" to secure his own surplus labor? Ancient cultural programming—the belief in the power of the "independent" individual—might be expected to create an environment within which direct producers feel free to make relatively autonomous decisions about a wide range of issues.

The relationships formed in a world shaped by this ancient cultural programming and by a shared economic dependence on self-exploitation had as much significance in shaping the "rules of the game" in rural Iran as any political process occurring in Teheran. Iran's ancient villages remained belligerently independent of the authority of the monarchist regime of Mohammed Reza Shah.

The above argument implies that Iranian villages of the twentieth century were governed by a form of *ancient democracy,* that is, the collective political will of the ancient producers and their allied agents. This political will was typically exercised through informal social relationships, rather than through formal political institutions. Again, the role of landlords in the political functioning of these villages is often exaggerated. As indicated, many of these landlords were not even present in the villages and most of the other unproductive (of surplus labor) social agents had direct, albeit often informal, relationships with the ancient direct producers, not with the landlords. Thus, political processes in the Iranian villages were far more open and democratic than is often recognized. Ancient producers met informally to discuss issues related to shared resources, common economic problems, and social concerns. Although much has been made of the illiteracy of rural direct producers, these ancient producers had a keen understanding of the history of their village, of production techniques, of the impact of climatic changes on agricultural production, and a variety of other issues that informed their arguments and subsequent decisions regarding appropriate solutions to economic and noneconomic problems. Thus, village life depended on a sense of ancient equality akin to notions of equality and democracy associated with ancient Greece. A side effect of this ancient democracy within the village was that it facilitated grassroots organizing. Grassroots organizing was important on numerous occasions when Iranian villages opposed state policies, including the prelude to the 1979 Revolution.

Land Reforms and Ancient Crisis

While it is clear that ancient landlords did not perceive the land reforms as beneficial to them, why did not the ancient producers who received land not become staunch supporters of the monarchist regime? It is, indeed, possible that the initial effect of the land reforms was to increase support for the monarchist regime among some segment of the rural population. To understand the dynamic by which a large consensus against the regime was formed, however, one needs to look more closely at the way the reforms evolved over the period from 1962 to 1978 and at the side effects of the reforms.

The land reforms were designed to: (1) free up "underemployed" labor in agriculture to expand the capitalist wage labor markets;[10] (2) "modernize" agricultural technology such that agricultural productivity would increase and the unit cost of agricultural commodities fall; (3) transfer surplus from the agricultural sector to the industrial sector through higher land taxes, higher prices for manufactured inputs, lower agricultural output prices, and direct control by the state of a greater share of agricultural surplus via state farms; (4) encourage the development of capitalist agricultural enterprises, particularly large-scale agribusiness firms; and (5) gain the support of the rural population for the monarchist regime or, at least, make it more difficult for the rural direct producers to organize into a cohesive opposition. The Shah and his ministers were committed to land reform, partly because the 1949 Chinese Revolution had become a potent symbol of the explosive potential of a disaffected peasantry. Indeed, in a precursor to the 1960s land reforms, Mohammed Reza Shah had attempted, in 1950, to win support from among the rural population by distributing some of the royal lands to ancient farmers. Nevertheless, the various objectives of the land reform were not always compatible.

This becomes clear when we examine the three stages of the land reform. The first stage was the land distribution to the nasaq-holding ancient producers. The Land Reform Act of 1962, embodying the rules of the first stage of the land reform, was adopted by executive fiat after the regime dissolved the landlord-dominated national legislature. This bold political act began the process by which some ancient farmers were gifted with a land redistribution. The state exerted eminent domain over a significant share of the property held by largely absentee landlords in exchange for providing these landlords with financial compensation. A subset of the lands confiscated by the government was sold directly to farmers, primarily ancient direct producers who had a traditional right to cultivation. These nasaq-holders signed contracts with the state to pay for the acquired land in fifteen cash installments that would equal the amount of compensation to the landlords plus a 10 percent tax.

This stage primarily antagonized the ancient landowners, who agitated against the monarchist regime from their urban bases. Nevertheless, the monarchist regime hoped that the reforms would win over the vast majority of the rural direct producers. One of the lessons of the 1949 Chinese Revolution was that it was sometimes in the interest of the national government to act against the interests of the landlords if, by doing so, the peasantry could be pacified. Certainly the land redistribution had its strong supporters among the nasaq-holding, ancient producers. But even this group would eventually be lost by the monarchist regime's attempts to achieve its other objectives, particularly those related to the development of oligarchic capitalism.

During the transition to the second stage, some unsuccessful ancient farmers lost their land and were forced into capitalist labor-power markets, primarily in the cities, although a few stayed home to work for their more successful neighbors. Former ancients who migrated to the cities were among the more zealous street organizers during the anti-Shah demonstrations leading up to the 1979 Revolution.

In the second stage of the land reform, the monarchist regime, still conscious of a need to counteract any Chinese-style "peasant" movement, pushed the successful farmers, mostly ancients but some now also involved in capitalist agriculture, to join state-controlled cooperatives. These cooperatives were epitomized by constant meddling by state-appointed bureaucrats into the production-level decisions of the farmers

—a clear deviation from traditional political processes in the ancient villages. Matters would become worse, however.

The third stage of the reform brought an unambiguous effort to destroy the ancient villages. The monarchist regime moved to eliminate self-exploitation by encouraging ancient farmers to exchange their land for equity shares in newly formed capitalist agribusiness corporations. The new scheme was highly unpopular, but the regime systematically removed conditions for the reproduction of self-exploitation in order to push ancient farmers to comply. The regime raised input prices for electricity, fertilizers, and farm equipment, "dumped" subsidized capitalist agricultural goods onto rural markets, and drastically cut the budgets for rural services, including schools, irrigation, and road maintenance.[11] This squeeze on ancient producers guaranteed that any success at gaining broad-based, rural support for the monarchist regime and its "White Revolution" would be negated. The deliberately manufactured *ancient crisis* stimulated increased opposition to the regime among some of the most organized producers in the countryside.

In hindsight, it is clear that the land reforms were never intended to provide all rural direct producers with the land and other means of production necessary for them to engage in self-exploitation. For the monarchist regime, capitalism and modernity were integrally intertwined. Granting land to some ancient producers could be used for the purpose of weakening the political power of the landlords, who are said to have controlled approximately 60 percent of the seats in the national legislature, but the monarchist regime never accepted self-exploitation as a component in its Modernization Program.

Indeed, even the nasaq-holders who received land found themselves struggling to obtain the other means of production necessary to self-exploitation. The state banks that were established in rural Iran showed a clear preference for capitalist farmers. The extension service agents provided by the monarchist regime encouraged successful ancient farmers to expand their production by acquiring more land and hiring wage laborers to work that land. Large capitalist agricultural domains, such as tractor farms, orchards, and tea plantations, were never included in the land reform. Overall, it was clear that farmers who hired wage laborers and produced cash crops were favored by the regime and more likely to receive state benefits. This could occur both through the competitive process described by Lenin in *The Development of Capitalism in Russia* — whereby successful ancient farmers were transformed into capitalists and the unsuccessful ancient farmers were transformed into wage laborers — and by the ancient producer/landlords hiring traditionally landless rural direct producers who had not benefited from the land redistribution. Either way, capitalism would grow and the ancient way of life in the villages would be undermined.

We may now look at this process in more detail, in order to see precisely how land reform might contribute to an erosion in the ancient rural economy, by fostering divisions among ancient producers, and the development of the capitalist rural economy. First, the land reforms were designed to increase the cash needs of ancient direct producers, forcing them to increase their production of cash commodities. For example, it was necessary for those ancient producers who acquired confiscated land to generate sufficient revenues to make their installment cash payments to the state. Second, those ancient producers who had become their own landlords gained social status vis-à-vis those ancient producers who continued to rent their land, and this created the basis for a new social division within the ranks of the self-exploiting. Third, the state sale of confiscated lands helped establish the principle of alienating rural lands from *traditional* owners by the process of buying and selling; thus, the means by which the more well-to-do direct producers might acquire the land of the less well-to-do was established. This would prove important, as some of the ancient producers who purchased land would fail to generate sufficient revenues to keep their land. More successful producers might expand their holdings by acquiring the land and, perhaps, equipment and other materials of these unsuccessful producers. Ancient producers with more land and other means of production, given the encouragement of institutions, such as state banks, would likely evolve, if they had not already done so, into full-time or, at least, part-time capitalists. To further divide the ranks of the ancients and former ancients, these new capitalists would often hire some of the less fortunate direct producers who had lost their land. The monarchist regime considered the development of new capitalists from among the ranks of ancient producers to serve a positive social purpose. However, this drift toward capitalism in agriculture was a direct threat to the ancient way of life in rural Iran and to all those who depended on the reproduction of this way of life.

Ancient Crisis in the Urban Bazaars

The monarchist regime's assault on ancientism was not restricted to the countryside. Urban areas in Iran were epitomized by the presence of special zones, spatially demarcated from the rest of the town or city, where scores of small storefront enterprises operated. These storefront enterprises, collectively referred to as the *bazaar,* were comprised of a wide range of ancient artisans, merchants, moneylenders, and restaurateurs. Most of the entrepreneurs operating within the bazaars, referred to as *bazaaries,* were either directly engaged in self-exploitation (primarily the so-called *pishivaran*) or dependent on the receipt of shares of ancient surplus.

The bazaaries had their own political organizations and relations of power, vocabularies, and discourses, and maintained close ties to the Shi'a Islamic ulama. The bazaaries had a long history of active participation in shaping the cultural, political, and economic life of the country. Indeed, the bazaaries were important catalysts for the so-called Constitutional Movement of 1905–1911, a movement that was culturally nationalist, politically democratic, and economically pro-ancient.[12] As Afshari (1983) has pointed out, the pishivaran and allied agents, particularly the merchants, had suffered during the feudal period in Iran, as warlords from the countryside and Qajar monarchs frequently extorted goods or money from the pishivaran and other bazaaries.[13] The bazaaries had developed a strong political consciousness and organized to resist arbitrary expropriations and other such interferences.[14] Thus the bazaar represented not simply a production and commercial space but a realm shaped by particular notions of acceptable social relationships, strongly influenced by strongly delineated conceptions of identity and democracy, by specific interpretations of divine Islamic law, and by well-organized collective efforts to reproduce the existing political, economic, and cultural relationships on which the bazaar's survival depended.

These collective efforts were fostered by the fact that the bazaaries were organized into well-financed and politically powerful guilds (*as-*

naf). These ancient guilds united the bazaaries—pishivaran and their allied agents—and served as social sites for promoting the philosophy of self-exploitation and respect for those direct producers who had attained senior artisan status, teaching associated ideas of ancient political organization, such as the resolution of internecine disputes by consensus, mobilization of financial resources to satisfy common objectives, and election of executive officers of the guild from among pishavaran elders. The primary coordinating body of the guild organizations was the High Council of the Asnaf, which, in cooperation with the Shi'a Islamic ulama, wielded considerable influence over the social and political life of Iran's towns and cities. As one of the oldest political machines in Iran, the guilds posed a problem for a monarchist regime bent on revolutionary changes in the configuration of class processes in the nation.

Just as the monarchist regime attempted to neutralize the political power of the ancient landlords, it pursued a similar policy with regard to the guilds. The regime simultaneously pursued policies that undermined the viability of the bazaars, while using SAVAK to infiltrate the High Council of the Asnaf. It is believed that the monarchist regime bribed some members of the High Council to gain their political acquiescence. Thus, the monarchist regime hoped to bring about a revolutionary change in economic relationships—the White Revolution—with a minimum of political opposition.

The so-called White Revolution provided the framework for the expansion of oligarchic enterprises into areas that directly threatened the survival of the bazaaries. The regime adopted regulations and macroeconomic policies that promoted the growth of both large-scale capitalist enterprises that competed directly with ancient artisans and large-scale merchanting enterprises, such as department stores, shopping centers, and supermarkets, that competed with ancient merchants in the bazaars. The expansion of state banks eroded the share of loanable funds markets controlled by the ancient moneylenders in the bazaars, while the creation of public health clinics and pharmacies cut into the market for ancient herbalists, midwives, and other self-exploiting health care providers.

In 1975, the monarchist regime adopted a rigid stance toward price increases by the bazaaries, who were already at a competitive disadvantage vis-à-vis the larger-scale capitalist enterprises that had the full support of the regime. Thousands of bazaaries were fined and hundreds jailed for violating the so-called anti-inflationary laws. Bazaaries, faced with a frontal assault on their market share, rising input prices, and higher taxes, were not allowed to compensate for these problems by sufficiently raising the prices of finished commodities. In other words, the monarchist regime was deliberately making it difficult for the pishivaran and their allied agents to take measures necessary to their survival. Thus, while the regime continually attempted to gain control over (corrupt) the political leadership of the bazaaries, it pursued a policy aimed at destroying self-exploitation and related social relationships.

This strategy was, in hindsight, clearly unsuccessful. The bazaaries, particularly the pishivaran, were both more democratic and more "class-conscious" than the monarchist regime had anticipated. Efforts by the regime to "buy off" the top leadership of the High Council of the Asnaf did not lead to blind obedience by pishivaran to the monarchist regime's policies. If anything, the pishivaran became more militant in their opposition to the monarchist regime and recognized the regime's efforts to corrupt their guild leadership and undermine the conditions for their economic survival.

Consequently, the pishivaran were among the most vocal opponents of the monarchist regime and provided many of the foot soldiers in the revolutionary organizations that were instrumental in the 1979 Revolution.

Ancient Crisis and the Shi'a Islamic Ulama

Some elements of the Shi'a Islamic ulama compared the attempts by the regime to corrupt the leadership of popular organizations, such as the guilds and leading figures within Shi'a Islam, to the way in which the national leadership of Iran had been corrupted by the "West." The growing influence of transnational corporations, particularly those from the United States, on Iranian life was viewed as symptomatic of a displacement of traditional moral values with "Western" moral values. If the ancient way of life of the villages and bazaars was an important condition of existence of traditional moral values, and there is every reason to believe that the clergy thought so, then the capitalist way of life epitomized by the United States and carried into Iran by transnational corporations represented the antithesis to those traditional moral values. Anti-Americanism in Iran became a way of protesting the local oligarchy (which was viewed as Americanized), transnational corporations, and the cultural mores associated with American-style capitalism.

Shi'ism, as a particular set of assumptions about appropriate ("good") human behavior and relationships, provided the conceptual tools and logic for this opposition to oligarchic capitalism and the way of life associated with oligarchic capitalism. It simultaneously provided a cultural condition for the reproduction of ancient social relationships and the underlying prevalence of self-exploitation in Iranian villages. The ulama defended the traditional way of life in the village with a specific *discourse* that was accepted by a large part of the population as transcendent, that is, the embodiment of *truth*. This transcendental discourse simultaneously attacked the social changes that would have promoted oligarchic capitalism and promoted values that were supportive of self-exploitation: reinforcing beliefs in the right of the ancient producer to be the first appropriator of the fruit of his labor, the right of the ancient landlord to claim a share of that self-appropriated ancient surplus, and the obligation of the ancient producer to support the spiritual mission of the clergy by sharing yet another portion of that self-appropriated surplus. Any attempt by the monarchist regime to alter traditional village relationships could be interpreted as an incarnation of "evil."

Thus the Shi'a Islamic ulama played an important role in providing ideological justification, by their interpretation of divine Islamic law, for the social relationships of the ancient villages, including the rights of ancients to engage in self-exploitation, the role of the absentee landlords, and the social relationships of the bazaars. The ulama were often among the staunchest defenders of the ancient way of life in Iranian villages, towns, and cities.

Why did the Shi'a Islamic ulama support self-exploitation? Was this simply a manifestation of conservatism, a desire to maintain traditional ways of life, or is it possible to identify a concrete class aspect to the actions of the clergy? Were the ulama linked to self-exploitation in such a way that they were directly impacted by the monarchist regime's assault on ancientism?

The ulama had a close relationship with ancient producers in the villages and the bazaars. The mosque was the center of social life in the villages and bazaars. The ulama were the educators of the children of the bazaaries, who were among the better educated citizens of Iran. At times, the ulama provided the spiritual and tactical leadership in organizing direct actions to oppose anti-ancient policies of the state. Indeed, the decentralized political organization that facilitated grassroots opposition to the state and made it so difficult for the monarchist regime(s) to coopt the ulama can be interpreted as a by-product of ancient democracy.

This close connection between the ancients and the ulama was also economic. The ulama received a share, a tithe, if you will, often in-kind, of the surplus each ancient producer self-appropriated. The ulama also received nonclass payments from the ancient merchants and landlords, who were, in turn, dependent on the self-appropriated surplus of ancient producers. Ancient producers and their allied agents, particularly the merchants, paid tuition to the ulama for educating their male children and this tuition revenue constituted a significant portion of the ulama's income. The modernization campaign began to sever the economic lifeline between the ulama and the ancient producers and other allied agents. Secular schools were established. Supermarkets and department stores displaced ancient merchants. Landlords lost large portions of their rent-generating land. Additionally, the encroachment by capitalist enterprises on the territory of ancient enterprises threatened the surplus-appropriating ability of ancient producers, going directly to the economic heart of ancient society. Thus the generosity of ancient farmers, craftspersons, landlords, and merchants was compromised by the growth in capitalism.

It seems safe to say that, for the most part, the land reform and urban modernization campaign negatively affected the incomes of the clergy. Although some members of the ulama might have benefited from the reforms, most did not. Given the decentralization of the ulama, even if the monarchist regime provided favors to a select few members of the group, this would not, in and of itself, have likely won much allegiance by the group as a whole.

But this is not the only economic connection between the ulama and the ancient producers. As it turns out, the ulama were the direct beneficiaries of subsumed class payments from ancient producers (nasaq-holders) in the form of rent on charitable land endowments. Thus among the various social roles played by members of the ulama was the role of ancient landlord. The land reforms represented interventions by the state into the traditional relationship between these religious landlords and their ancient tenants; likewise they would come to intervene in a wide range of other ancient landlord-ancient producer relationships. In particular, the land reforms compelled the ulama to enter into long-term (ninety-nine-year-) contracts with those ancient producers who had traditionally worked the ulama-controlled lands and, like the nonclerical landlords, to accept rents below the historical norm. This imposition of the state between the ulama qua ancient landlords and their tenants qua ancient producers could not have been passively received by the ulama.

Indeed the potential erosion in the economic conditions of existence of the Shi'a Islamic ulama to which this interposition contributed might constitute one of the motivating factors for the ulama's opposition to the land reforms, in particular. Thus the ideological support provided by the ulama for the social organization of the ancient villages and bazaars was not only directed to justifying self-exploitation, the role of the absentee landlords, the status of the bazaaries and their guilds, but may also have been directed to justifying their own role as landlords and, more generally, as beneficial participants in ancient social relationships.

As has already been indicated, the changes in social relationships initiated by the land reforms and urban modernization undermined the traditional relationships of the villages, towns, and cities. Even if the capitalists had made up for the revenue effects on the ulama of these changes, there could be no guarantee that the overall status of the ulama could be reproduced in such an environment. The very process by which ancient Iran was threatened called into question the traditional social status and role of the ulama. It was in this context that many members of the ulama proclaimed the changes inconsistent with divine Islamic law. And this defiance of the monarchist regime by the ulama, often considered among the most conservative elements of Iranian society, was certainly an important step in the direction of the 1979 Revolution.

Conflict within Capitalist Iran

The monarchist regime further weakened its position by not only neglecting but acting against the interests of small-scale capitalists. This "petty" capitalist segment of the population might have been more supportive of the monarchist regime if the White Revolution had simply been designed to encourage the growth of capitalism, rather than the advance of oligarchic capitalism. As it was, the monarchist regime benefited a relatively small elite of oligarchic capitalists and transnational corporations. These favored firms received a wide range of public supports for their development and domination of labor markets, markets for loanable funds, access to infrastructure, and markets for the sale of finished commodities. The oligarchic elite, including members of the Shah's family, benefited directly from these policies. To some extent, the favorable treatment of oligarchic families has been linked to corruption—specifically, illegal subsumed class payments from the oligarchy to public officials in exchange for such treatment. It is also clear, however, that the monarchist regime viewed large-scale firms as more "modern" and "Western" and, given the elite's privileged access to finance capital, it was easier for them to construct large-scale capitalist firms.

Furthermore the elite families that came to dominate large-scale manufacturing and agriculture were part of a larger—although still relatively small in absolute size—oligarchy that included directors of big banks, insurance companies, and new mega-merchanting enterprises. This capitalist oligarchy cooperated to dominate the Iranian economy and to share in the surplus extracted by the oligarchic capitalists and industrial transnationals. They were often involved in export-oriented businesses and consistently received special treatment by the regime. The economic success of this oligarchy often came at the expense of the traditional capitalists, small-scale moneylenders, and the traditional merchants.

The monarchist regime, under the rubric of modernization, instituted industrial and agricultural policies designed to promote higher profits within enterprises controlled by the oligarchy. Smaller-scale domestic capitalist and noncapitalist enterprises were put at a competitive disadvantage. This was done by the adoption of discriminatory taxing policies, state control over the licensing of economic activities and the use of public spaces, and discrimination in the allocation of public resources, including sanitary water, roads, electrical lines, and credit. It was widely understood that the Shah's family and associates within the oligarchy and certain transnational corporations were given preferential treatment at all levels of the government.

It was precisely this bias in favor of oligarchic capitalism that made it impossible for capitalists to develop a united front in favor of the monarchist regime and against the ancient sector of Iranian society. It is even possible that a united front of capitalists might have been successful at "buying off" a larger segment of the ulama and neutralizing the religious opposition to the monarchist regime. To the extent petty capitalists were contributing to the religious authorities, however, there was no clear message of support for the monarchist regime. To a significant extent, the message that came from the petty capitalists was in opposition to that regime, further bolstering the antimonarchist consensus among the ulama.

Conclusion

Iran was a social formation with a sharply dualistic character. There was a *capitalist Iran,* with its internecine conflict between oligarchic capitalism and petty capitalism, and an *ancient Iran.* Most of the Iranian people lived in ancient Iran, including most of the ulama. So long as the boundaries of these two Irans did not intersect, there was probably not sufficient tension in the society to generate a revolutionary crisis. Despite the struggle of nonoligarchic capitalists to resist the encroachments of oligarchic capitalism, it seems unlikely that these small-scale capitalists were either numerous enough or collectively powerful enough to have successfully fought the oligarchy. The monarchist regime, however, not only created internecine strife within capitalist Iran by encouraging the growth of oligarchic capitalism but it continually pushed the boundaries of capitalist Iran into ancient Iran, threatening the survival of ancientism. This was a critical catalyst in the 1979 Revolution.

The underlying realities—that self-exploitation was a significant catalyst in the 1979 Revolution and that ancient direct producers and their allied agents constituted a majority of those participating in the Iranian economy—has eluded social analysts, even those who acknowledge the presence of this "precapitalist" element in Iranian society. This chapter has sought to open minds to the importance of self-exploitation and related processes in the 1979 Revolution, as well as to the importance of self-exploitation more generally. It is clear that direct producers engaging in self-exploitation constitute a unique body of economic agents, capable of securing the conditions for their continued existence as self-exploiting direct producers and of organizing against their opponents. In the case of Iran, they were joined by a potent coalition of social agents, many of whom had direct interests in the preservation of ancientism, and the end result was a political revolution of such dramatic force as to capture the attention of the rest of the world.

Notes

1 Polemical arguments from the Iranian left tended to favor the argument that so-called Western imperialism and global capitalism were the driving forces behind the monarchist regime and, therefore, the cause of the 1979 Revolution. The most prominent organized left groups were the National Front, the Tudeh Party, the Mujahedin Khalq, and the Fedai'iyan Khalq. Both the Fedai'iyan Khalq, a Marxist-Leninist political organization with links to guerrilla groups that had fought against the monarchist regime, and the Tudeh Party supported the establishment of an Islamic republic because of their reductionist belief that imperialism was the condition of existence of capitalism in Iran and the further conclusion that the Islamic government would eliminate imperialist influences on Iran. The Mujahedin Khalq is best described as a left Islamic organization grounded in a philosophy akin to the philosophical foundations of the Socialist People's Libyan Arab Jamahiriya. This group was subjected to the most violent suppression under the new Islamic government.

2 A number of social analysts, such as Jazani (1980), Afshari (1983), Bayat (1987), and Milani (1988), have analyzed Iranian revolutions as the consequence of class struggles, where class is defined in terms of ownership of means of production or, alternatively, in terms of power relationships. Afshari, for instance, in examining the foundations of the 1905–1911 Constitutional Revolution, draws a clear one-to-one correspondence between ownership of the means of production and political power. He therefore recognizes the economic independence of urban artisans (*pishivaran*) because most of them own their means of production, but views the rural direct producers (*peasants*) as a homogeneously exploited (by others) group because, for the most part, they do not own the means of production. Class struggle is analyzed primarily as the struggle between owners and nonowners of the means of production over control of the state.

3 For a discussion of the ancient fundamental and subsumed class processes and self-exploitation, see Gabriel (1990, 85–106).

4 There is a rather large and varied literature on the 1979 Iranian Revolution. In addition to Jazani (1980), Bayat (1987), and Milani (1988), see Zabih

(1979), Jabbari (1981), Katouzian (1981), Ricks (1981), Abrahamian (1982), Moghadam (1988), Pesaran (1982), Amuzegar (1991), and Moaddel (1991).

5 The Shah's family was part of this elite, as were many of his close friends and allies.

6 The number of self-exploiting farmers can be roughly estimated based on the number of such direct producers who were nasaq-holders. Nasaq-holding farmers distributed their own surplus among various claimants, retained a "traditional right of cultivation," and were not subject to arbitrary changes in the rent payments required by landlords. The existence of a long-term tenancy with rents unrelated to the absolute size of the surplus produced on the land mitigates against the landlord gaining control over the entire surplus and transforming the relationship into one that might properly be described as feudal. These conditions indicate that most nasaq-holders were self-exploiting, and therefore ancients, but all non-nasaq-holding farmers cannot be assumed to be nonancient. Given that many craftspersons were also self-exploiting, any attempt to estimate the total number of rural ancient producers based solely on the number who were nasaq-holders can be considered conservative. Milani (1994, 47) quotes an estimate of 2.1 million nasaq-holding direct producers in 1961. Moaddel (1991, 318) quotes an estimate of "nearly a million families" dependent on self-exploitation in the urban bazaars.

7 The regime of Reza Shah had come to power in a military coup that ended the Qajar dynasty. Reza Shah was able to come to power, in part, because of the success of a pro-ancient movement, the Constitutional Movement, in the cities. This movement was funded and organized by merchants and the self-exploiting artisans with whom they were allied. The regime, free from the old feudal ties of the Qajars, moved decisively to destroy the economic and political power of the khans, who were at the top of a feudal hierarchy that had been loyal to the Qajars. This action was, in class terms, revolutionary and helped set the stage for the events leading to the 1979 Revolution.

8 See, for example, Amuzegar (1991, 184). Rural economies within which self-exploitation prevails are often described as semifeudal because the social analysts refuse to accept the possibility that a nonfeudal, noncapitalist, nonbipolar fundamental class process might prevail in such an economy.

9 Katouzian (1981) describes these relationships among ancient producers as "communal" and specifically discusses the importance of cooperation among producers over the use and distribution of water.

10 As Katouzian (1981) points out, officials of the monarchist regime estimated that 35 percent of the Iranian rural sector was "underemployed." It is inter-

esting that this is precisely equal to that portion of the rural population that did not meet the definition of "self-exploiting."

11 The regime provided the corporate capitalist farms and state capitalist farms with cheap inputs, easy credit, and other advantages that allowed these firms to underprice both ancient farmers and smaller-scale capitalist farmers.

12 The Constitutional Movement pressured the monarchist regime of Mozaffar ad-Din Shah to create a national legislature, the *Majles,* and an ecclesiastical committee of ulama, as mechanisms for, among other things, restricting the authority of the state to impose taxes on land and sales, and imposing onerous rules on the bazaaries. There are strong similarities between the configuration of social forces behind the Constitutional Movement, ancient craftspersons, merchants, landlords, and the ulama, and the movement that culminated in the 1979 Revolution. There is however, one component of the 1970s antimonarchist movement that was missing from the turn of the century Constitutional Movement—the ancient farmers. While it is clear that self-exploitation was prevalent in the bazaars throughout the nineteenth century, and that ancient artisans and their guilds played an important role in the Constitutional Movement, it appears that rural Iran remained feudal during this period of Iranian history. It is possible that changes set in motion by the Constitutional Movement, including the military coup that put Reza Khan, later to become Reza Shah, into chief executive authority, ended the dominance of feudal exploitation in the Iranian countryside and created the prevalence of self-exploitation in the countryside.

13 See Afshari (1983, 140–43).

14 See Afshari (1983, 143–53) for an extensive discussion of bazaari resistance, including various alliances with other social agents, such as the clergy.

SERAP AYSE KAYATEKIN

SHARECROPPING AND FEUDAL CLASS PROCESSES

IN THE POSTBELLUM MISSISSIPPI DELTA

Sharecropper forced to flee after producing 30 acre cotton crop
—*Jackson Advocate,* September 24, 1949

*Negro preacher-farmer leaves family of twelve in flight from state cotton
plantation. . . . Tells story of slave-like treatment of sharecropper family*
—*Jackson Advocate,* June 20, 1953

State farmers freed on charges of forcing negro to work off debt
—*Jackson Advocate,* October 23, 1954

*Young sharecropper charges planter beat wife who would not leave sick
baby to pick cotton*—*Jackson Advocate,* November 20, 1954

This chapter presents a class analysis of the sharecropping system that
came to prominence in the aftermath of the Civil War in the Mississippi
Delta region of the United States and continued to exist until the rise of
the civil rights movement in the 1950s. Although most of the material
discussed pertains to the Delta region, the analysis could probably be applied to the sharecropping system in the Southern regions of the United
States in general.

   The main thesis I would like to advance is that sharecropping in the
Delta region had a feudal character in which surplus labor produced by
the tenant was extracted by the landlord in the form of rent.[1] In order to
substantiate this claim, I look at the broader context of Southern sharecropping and conceptualize the ways that certain legal, political, cultural,
and economic processes shaped this form of surplus labor extraction.

What I analyze in particular are: first, the distinctive legal conditions in the form of state laws that regulated the relation of sharecroppers to the means of production and to the product of their labor; second, the specificity of an American culture of racism that helped shape the ways the sharecropping laborer and the landowner perceived and behaved toward one another; and third, the economic conditions of a credit system that helped bond the sharecropper to the landowner who provided the credit. Taken together, these three social processes form the basis of my argument that the typical sharecropping relation in this region was feudal in nature.[2]

I should mention at the outset that my conceptualization of a feudal class process diverges from that proposed by Marx and other prominent participants in the famous debate over the transition from feudalism to capitalism.[3] In contrast to these theorists, I argue for a feudal class process where the direct producers—in this case the sharecroppers—are *separated* from the means of production. As many will recognize, the condition of separation from the means of production is often identified as a defining attribute of the capitalist class process, and indeed Southern sharecropping has often been represented as one form of capitalist economic practice. My argument is that when one looks into the overall picture of rural life in the postbellum South, the representation of sharecropping as feudal becomes less fantastic than it might originally seem.

A crucial factor here is the particular culture of racism that emerged as slavery was dismantled. Though certain humans could no longer be seen as chattels, they could be placed into a social hierarchy that legitimized the call for those at the bottom to provide the manual labor for those at the top. In return for their labor those who were positioned by racist discourse as "childish" and therefore incapable of taking care of themselves were "cared for" by their superiors. In the postbellum South this "care" took the form of a type of employment and credit relation controlled by the landowner, in which exploitation and racism were cloaked in a social relationship based on a notion of "reciprocity." Just as in the feudal cultures of Europe, a rigid ideology of social hierarchy underpinned an exploitative class process that was commonly perceived as reciprocal.

The ensuing analysis offers several theoretical insights, one of which bears directly on the debate around sharecropping per se. Elsewhere I have argued that, contrary to much of the literature on sharecropping, there is no inherent necessity for sharecropping to be *either* capitalist *or* feudal.[4] The class nature of sharecropping needs to be understood in reference to the particular forms of surplus-labor appropriation and distribution that are practiced and the specificity of the social context in which it is situated.

The representation here developed of feudal surplus-labor appropriation involved in sharecropping in postbellum Mississippi bears striking similarities to forms of surplus-labor appropriation that characterized the *metayage* in France and the *mezzadria* in Italy, both forms of share tenancy that flourished in the thirteenth century during the decline of the demesne and continued to survive into the twentieth century (Andrews 1996a,b). Similarities also exist with contemporary sharecropping arrangements, such as those in Bengal (Cooper 1983) and Madagascar (Jarosz 1990). But elsewhere and at other times sharecropping has emerged in capitalist forms, as in strawberry production in contemporary California (Wells 1984a,b) or in the Ecuadorian highlands (Lehmann 1985), or in forms that remind us of self-exploitation, as in colonial Java (Alexander and Alexander 1982).

"Discovering" a feudal element in the recent past of the United States —a country whose modern social formation postdated the demise of what is commonly understood as feudalism in Western Europe—helps shed light on the class complexity of any social formation. More significantly, by tracing this particular class relation in the sharecropping arrangements that pervaded the South, we are helped to comprehend the present we have inherited in the United States. I suggest that this feudal economic practice played a crucial role in transmitting racist ideologies suited to the slave system of the eighteenth and nineteenth centuries into modern U.S. capitalist society. The distinct patterns of development that capitalist class processes assumed in the North and the South of the United States can be attributed, in part, to a Southern past that contained and perhaps still contains elements of a feudal class process. I will return to this point in some detail in the conclusion.

Forms of Land Tenure in Southern Agriculture

There have been a large variety of forms of land tenure in the history of the U.S. South and any general typology of tenure in the region must abstract from local variations. The broadest typology for the South includes the categories of cash-tenant, share-tenant, and sharecropper. The distinctions between these forms depend on the form (and proportion) of payment of rent, the proportion of the contribution of the different parties to the costs of production, the amount and the conditions of credit, and the amount of supervision provided by the landowner.

"Cash-tenants" pay a fixed amount of cash for the land they operate. Production expenses are paid and the marketing of the crop is undertaken by the tenant. Usually there is no supervision of the tenant's activities. A variation of this form is the "cash-and share-tenancy" where the tenant pays a fixed sum of cash and a fixed share of the farm products.

In a second category known as "share-tenancy," probably the dominant tenurial form after sharecropping, the tenant furnishes his own teams and equipment, pays for part or all of the seed, for part of the fertilizer, pesticide, and ginning. There is considerable variation in the share of costs borne by the landlord and the tenant, and in the proportion of the product paid as rent paid by the latter to the former.

In what is known as "sharecropping," or sometimes the half-and-half system, the landlord "furnishes" the cropper with the land, work stock, feed, equipment, seed, and part of the costs of fertilizer. The cropper provides family labor and the crop is split, theoretically, in half.[5] An integral part of the system of sharecropping is the credit advanced by the landlord to the tenant in the form of food, clothing, and cash.

One often finds a confusion in the literature on the status of sharecropping: In the agricultural census reports, it is classified as a form of tenancy. It is similarly treated in most studies of agricultural labor, but in many analyses the sharecropper is referred to as a "wage-hand" rather than a tenant (Raper and Taylor 1949). In any case a tenant, unlike a sharecropper, is supposed to provide his or her own work stock, equipment, and feed for the work stock; to have legal "possession" of the land for the duration of the contract; and to have complete ownership of the crops produced. This legal distinction of sharecropping from other forms of tenancy is important, and I will return to it in the section that follows. My intent is to draw attention to the issues of possession and ownership of the means of production in the context of Southern sharecropping and point to their importance in overdetermining the class process involved in this agricultural practice.

Ownership, Legality, and the Feudal Class Process

Distinctive politicolegal processes defined the relation of sharecroppers to the means of production and to the crops they produced, shaping the extraction of what could be seen as feudal rent. These processes in effect were the same as those that defined the legal status of the Southern share-cropper. As indicated in the typology above, in sharecropping arrangements all the means of production were provided by the landowner, and, in contrast to share-tenancy, land was not considered to be under the possession of the laborer. Whereas in a contract of share-tenancy the tenant had control over the land for the duration of the agreement, in a share-cropping agreement the landowner could enter the property on will and terminate the contract. Frequently linked to this legal provision was the determination that the crops produced by sharecroppers did not belong to them but to the owner of the land.

Given the classical Marxist definition of feudalism it might appear that this separation of the sharecropper (the direct producer) from the land (the means of production) and from the crop (the product of his labor) might eliminate the possibility of a feudal class process. In most Marxist definitions of feudalism the direct producer has property in, or possession of, the means of production and surplus labor is extracted via extra-economic means—relations of political dependence and fealty, for example. Takahashi (1980) offers the following intervention in the well-known "transition debate":

In feudalism, since the immediate producers appear in combination with the means of production, and hence labor power cannot take the form of a commodity, the appropriation of surplus-labor by the feudal lords takes place directly, by extra-economic coercion without the mediation of the economic laws of commodity exchange. (1980, 71)

Takahashi's main inspiration for this argument is Karl Marx:

In all previous [i.e., pre-capitalist] forms the landowner, not the capitalist, appears as the immediate appropriator of others' surplus labor. . . . Rent appears as the general form of surplus labor, unpaid labor. Here the appropriation of this surplus labor is not mediated by exchange, as with the capitalist, but its basis is the coercive rule of one part of the society over the other part, hence direct slavery, serfdom, or a relation of political dependence. (Marx as quoted in Takahashi [1980, 69, footnote 5])

According to Takahashi's reading, the basis of the feudal appropriation of surplus labor is the union of the direct producers with the means of production, and since laborers can reproduce themselves and their families without resort to commodity exchange, there are no "economic" reasons for the laborer to perform surplus labor for the landlord. The forces that underlie the appropriation of surplus labor have, therefore, to be looked for in the so-called extra-economic realm.

This conceptualization can be criticized from a number of angles. First, it assumes a clear conceptual prioritization of one of the conditions of existence of a class process over others. Second, it narrowly represents the "economic" as constituted by commodity-exchange relations and therefore absent from the determination of feudal class relations. Third, it reduces class relations to property relations in that the particularity of the feudal appropriation of surplus labor is seen to lie in the nonseparation of the laborer from the means of production, not in the politically, socially, and economically overdetermined transactions by which surplus labor is appropriated and distributed.[6]

In postbellum Southern sharecropping, the landowner provided the land, work stock, equipment, and part of the costs of fertilizer, pesticide, and ginning, and the cropper provided the labor and the additional costs of fertilizer, pesticide, and ginning. The crop that was harvested was split, the sharecroppers receiving half (or some designated proportion) as payment for their labor and the landowner receiving the rest. This union of land, landowner's resources, and cropper was necessary for the performance of labor in the first instance, but it was also the context in which surplus labor was produced and appropriated and a feudal class process enacted.

In light of the discussion above it is legitimate to ask how I am conceptualizing the feudal appropriation of surplus labor without relying on the nonseparation of the direct producer from the means of production. Here I draw encouragement from the work of Hindess and Hirst (1977) who have also problematized this issue of separation and nonseparation.

In defining a sharecropper, the state laws in the U.S. South used the term "dominion" to denote the landowner's relationship to the land the sharecroppers worked. The laborers had no legal "possession" of the land for the duration of their contracts, but possessed the right to enter, cultivate, and harvest the crops of that land. The landlord did not surrender the land to the cropper but agreed to pay the occupants a share of the crops that they cultivated and harvested.

The sharecropper's occupancy could be terminated at any time. If croppers could not perform the labor required, the landowner could evict them from the premises. The state laws were also clear that the cropper did not have the right to complain about the landowner trespassing on what was, after all, legally their own land. The potential for legal exclusion of the sharecropper from the occupancy and right to use land and the legal protection of the landowner's right to monitor the cropper's labor functioned as a coercive force that ensured the performance of surplus labor.

It was not long after the Civil War that courts in most of the Southern states came to the decision that sharecroppers were paid *wages* by the landowner as a portion of the crop they produced on his land, but that tenants, whose crops were deemed to be in their possession, paid *rent* to the landowner whose land they used (Woodman 1995, 68). Although state laws were clear about the distinction between a sharecropper and a tenant, the legal interpretation of whether a particular relation was one of landowner–sharecropper or of landowner–tenant was riddled with ambiguities.[7] Given the significance of the consequences of this distinction, it is not difficult to understand why postbellum Southern history is replete with court cases over precisely the matter of such definitions. It was declared that sharecroppers could be made to move at any time, but that they might be able to sue their "employers" for damages in certain instances. For example, they had some right to challenge a decision to evict, if they were made to move "without cause." Given the legal vagueness of this term, in historical practice sharecroppers were rarely successful in challenging such decisions.[8]

The legal ownership of the crop by the landowner was seen to be derived from the possession of the land by the landowner. Woodman (1979) writes that when the relation was deemed to be that of a cropper and landlord, the landlord had possession of the crop until the division was made. According to the laws of most Southern states and in Mississippi, at the point of division the landowner had a lien on the crop that had priority over any other lien. This meant that the landowner's lien had priority over not only that of the sharecropper but those of merchants. Struggles over the legal status of the laborer (whether tenant or sharecropper), therefore, had implications for the historic relation between landowners and merchants.

Marked ambiguities concerning the legal conditions that obtained in a sharecropping relation arose out of the confused process of institutionalizing "new" relations between the landowning classes, merchants, and laborers in the aftermath of the Civil War. Battles in the courts were one arena where the gradual domination by the former plantation owners of a once enslaved but now formally "free" labor force was witnessed. Soldberg (1950) notes that, in Arkansas, Mississippi, Texas, Oklahoma, and Louisiana, *under a cropping relation* the title and possession of the crop was in the hands of the landowner and the sharecropper had a lien for his labor (285). In the first three of these states *under tenancy,* the title and possession of the crop was in the hands of the tenant prior to its division (284). In some states the postbellum legislature took the radical stand of providing support for workers' claims. Woodman shows how in Mississippi in 1872 the state legislature gave priority to workers' liens over those of "all landlords, sub-lessors, and all other persons interested in such agricultural products" (1995, 78). Similarly, in Arkansas and South Carolina, the progressive legislature gave superiority to laborers' liens, a move that was later reversed in favor of all other lien holders.

The legal conditions of dominion over land and possession of the crop by the landowner legitimized the coercive power of the landlord over the laborer, and all of these forces conspired to replace slavery with a form of sharecropping that was feudal in nature. The very absence of any rights of the sharecroppers over the land they cultivated and the crop they produced perpetuated a situation of dependence of the sharecropper on the landowner for survival.[9] It is this aspect of dependence that is crucial in discerning the feudal nature of the class relation.

In his seminal analysis of feudalism, Bloch argues that the dependence of one individual on another is *the* distinguishing element of feudal society (1961). Comprehension of the precise nature of this dependence in the postbellum South requires consideration of the culture of racism that pervaded this time. As a legacy of slavery, racism has not only been important in the persistence of sharecropping over a very long stretch of history but has been a central factor in its adaptation. To understand the feudal character of sharecropping, the legal setting, which constantly sought to place landlords' rights over and above sharecroppers' rights, has to be related to a culture that bred a hardened perception of the world in which human beings were defined in terms of their place in a naturalized social hierarchy.

The Culture of Racism and the Appropriation of Surplus Labor

Racism is a cultural process of meaning construction that defines "self" and "other" in terms of a hierarchical structure. As a cultural process it contributes an all-encompassing world-view and presents certain essentialized conceptualizations of "a people" and "the other." In the United States a racist ideology of white supremacy and black inferiority has been one of the cultural legacies of slavery.[10]

In the aftermath of the Civil War a significant number of the sharecroppers were "freedmen" or former slaves. In my view it is impossible to understand the functioning of the system of sharecropping in which the sharecroppers were engaged without understanding the form that racism took as slavery was dismantled in the South. I would like to argue that racist ideology played a significant role in constituting Southern sharecropping as a feudal class process.

There are striking similarities between the notion of white supremacy in the postbellum South and the dominant ideology of feudal Western Europe. In pioneering studies of texts of the period from the ninth to the sixteenth century, Duby (1978) and Le Goff (1988) have explored feudal society as it was imagined by the people. In what is called the "tripartite" society, there are three orders: those who pray to secure the kingdom of God on earth, those who fight, and those who do what the "inferior" ought to do—till the land.

The members of the highest order turn their attention heavenwards, while those of the two others look to the earth, all being occupied with the task of upholding the state. . . . The intermediate order provides security, the inferior feeds the other two. (Duby 1978, 1)

What is notable in this representation is the hierarchical order of things. In the way feudal society imagined itself, the prevailing notion is not that of social equality but that of natural hierarchy and inequality.[11]

Postbellum Southern thinking was akin to Western European medieval ideology. In the hierarchical division of labor, performance of manual labor was carried out by those who were at the bottom. Blacks, the predominant labor force of the Southern share-system in the plantation areas, were seen as being naturally suited to manual labor because they were inferior. They were perceived as childish, incapable of being on their own, and needing to be protected and cared for. Sharecroppers occupied a servile status — while not legally slaves, they were nonetheless seen to be unfree, bonded, and completely dependent on the care, nurturing, and economic aid of the white landowner. As one of the legacies of slavery, this paternalistic perception of direct laborers nurtured the Southern feudal sharecropping system for a long stretch of time.

Such paternalism extended to the landlord's control over the behavior of the sharecropper and the sharecropper's family. The landlords, for example, could make demands on sharecroppers' attitudes and frustration of their expectations could have dire consequences:

They (the tenants) shall obey all lawful orders from me or my Agent and shall be honest-truthful-sober-civil-diligent in their business and for all wilful Disobedience of any lawful orders from me or my Agent, drunkenness, moral or legal misconduct, want of respects or civility to me or my Agent or to my Family or any one else, I am permitted to discharge them forfeiting any claims upon me for any part of the crop. (quoted in Taylor 1943, 123)[12]

Like the state laws in the South, racism was a powerful social force that helped create and perpetuate the feudal class position of a cropper. The relation between racism and class was, however, a complex one. Just as the perception of blacks conditioned the process of class, the latter, too, shaped racism. For example, any individual, irrespective of his or her color, became black once he or she became a cropper, a feudal laborer. Brandfon offers an interesting perspective on this conflation in his discussion of racism against the Italian immigrants in the Yazoo-Mississippi Delta region in the late nineteenth century:

The identification with nonwhite labor, especially the Negro, robbed the Italian of his status as a white man. This status decline was reinforced by the servility associated with working on the plantation. In the Delta, no self-respecting white man labored on the huge cotton plantations. This was Negro's work. It was the badge of his inferiority. By replacing the Negro in the same type of work and under the same conditions, the Italians assumed the status of the Negroes. (1967, 163)

It was such an identification of manual labor with being black, and hence inferior, that explains why often the most virulent form of racism was that expressed by poor whites, the "fallen" yeoman farmers who gradually became sharecroppers and by extension "blacks."

It is important, however, to understand that for the perpetuation of this relation between class and racism, the participation of the direct producers in the cultural process of racism was also necessary. The idea of the inferiority of the performers of surplus labor did not only belong to the appropriators of the surplus labor—to a degree it also belonged to the performers of it. The institution of slavery, stretched over centuries, colonized the minds of the very laborers themselves, manifesting itself in attitudes and behaviors that differed from those of whites:

Though whites and Negroes are found on the same plantations, the white tenants and croppers, who are imbued with the idea of their racial superiority, can assert themselves more freely than Negroes. It is probably for this reason that the landlords generally prefer Negro tenants to white tenants. (Frazier 1949, 222)

Racism as a cultural process should not be viewed only as coercion.[13] Following the work of Gramsci and Foucault, racism can be seen as creating consent. As Thompson, the eminent scholar of Southern plantation history, notes,

Under the influence of daily and intimate association among its members the plantation was transformed into a cultural group. The authority and power of the planter were not required for daily use; time generated new customs, and everyone within the plantation community came to know what was expected of him and to feel some sense of obligation to meet these expectations. Alongside the personal leadership and control of the planter a form of control grew up which was not imposed from the outside by a master, a form of control which the group imposed upon itself by common consensus. The forces that controlled Negroes as slaves and later as share tenants were to a large extent within the laborers themselves. (1975, 99)

Clearly we cannot see control as coming "largely" from the black labor force; but seeing the hierarchical relation between landowners and share-croppers only in terms of coercion and repression is to miss out on the other, equally important, aspects of power—those of consent and legiti-mation.

Just like the power of the state vis-à-vis civil society, power in the con-text of class relations needs to be legitimized, and what lent legitimacy to the feudal class relation between sharecroppers and landowners was not only the naturalized vision of a social hierarchy and the consent of the direct laborers but the notion of "reciprocity."

At the core of reciprocity was the institution of credit—a system of advances, or "furnishing," as it was locally known in the South. The particular credit system through which the landlord advanced food and clothing to the tenant gave the former direct control over the reproduc-tion of the tenant, all wrapped in the perception of taking care of those in the "family." [14]

Credit and the Feudal Sharecropping System

Many factors operate to lodge power over tenants in the hands of the planter, but the essential mechanism of control is to be found in his relation to the nutrition process. Food and other supplies are made available to the tenant directly or indirectly through the medium of the planter. The best use of the commissary is to get the tenant in debt. Its chief function is to furnish food during [the] crop production period. For this "furnishing," as the practice is called in the South, the planter is paid out of the tenant's performing work ex-pected of him. . . . This dependence upon the planter for food, although it has been present in all forms of plantation control which the South has known, has moved to a position of central importance in the system of share-tenancy. (Thompson 1975, 254–55)

As Thompson seems to suggest, while fortifying the notion of reci-procity that was so important to legitimizing the landowner's authority, the system of advances also tied the sharecropper to the former through an inextricable web of dependency. In their seminal analysis of the South, Davis et al. (1941) describe in detail how the system worked itself into a cycle of indebtedness. What the laborers earned from a year's work was merely enough to get them through half the year. As a result, in the fall they were forced to sell not only the cotton (which was the most significant crop in the Southern states long after the Civil War) but also most of their food crops so as to repay those loans that had allowed them to last from March to September, while they were "making" cotton. The money left was only enough to get them through to the end of winter or early spring, at which time they had to borrow again (1941, 344).[15]

In class-analytic terminology, the credit extended by the landowner is a nonclass payment.[16] Such revenues allowed the sharecropper to live over the entire crop year. The credit extended by the landlords to the sharecroppers, when added to the annual fall payment for feudal necessary labor, enabled the latter to reproduce themselves.[17] The continual need for these loans, however, coupled with high interest rates, eventually bound the cropper to the landlord and rendered imperative the performance of surplus labor, to be appropriated in the form of feudal rent. Because the sharecropper's fall receipt for necessary labor was insufficient to meet both consumption needs and debt payments, the cropper was forced into still more debt. Thus was created a cycle that, often enough, entrapped the sharecropper in debt peonage. We can render more concrete the burden of furnishing by mentioning that tenants were furnished at "time prices" which meant prices higher by 10–70 percent than cash prices. When the accounts were settled after the harvest, the tenants were charged an additional 10–25 percent (McMillen 1990, 132).

Debt peonage continued well into the 1960s (Daniel 1972). Sharecroppers in debt peonage lost freedom of mobility and in many cases the debts of a parent, often the father, became the responsibility of one of the children in the case of flight or death. In these ways, the credit system had the built-in ability to produce forms of bondage very close to slavery.

Historically the credit system has been one of the most direct and effective mechanisms of control by the Southern landowning classes. By controlling the supply of food and clothing—the essentials of reproduction—the landowners not only made claims on the necessary labor of the sharecroppers but also shaped the specific use-value form that sharecropper subsistence took. By controlling the kind and quantity of food the laborers consumed, the landowner controlled the very sources of their nutrition. This kind of dependency among black sharecroppers was one factor compelling DuBois to refer to the system as the "modern serfdom" (1989, 124).

Such direct control of the sharecropper via the credit system gave Southern sharecropping a particularly feudal character, reinforcing the dependence of the sharecropper on the landowner. It is possible to compare the institution of furnishing via the plantation commissary to that of the medieval institution of the *banalité*. These monopolies held by the lord at the expense of the serfs comprised a range of exactions, such as the right of the lord to sell beer and wine at certain times of the year, the forcing of peasants to grind their corn at the lord's mill, to make their wine at his wine press, and to bake their bread in his oven. Bloch notes that the tradition of the *banalité* was carried to extremes where central power was at its weakest, as in France (1961, 251). Perhaps, then, it was also the strong tradition of the local power of the plantation owners that could account for the prevalence of the furnishing system in the U.S. South. It has been noted that, in some cases, the landlords would actively discourage or forbid tenant gardens as a way of increasing tenants' dependency on the commissary supplies (McMillen 1990, 133).

The same system of advances, however, later contributed to the decline of sharecropping in the mid-1960s. Given the dramatic reduction in the size of plots assigned to landowners during the New Deal and later, the effects of large-scale mechanization, and the civil rights movement, the constant indebtedness of the sharecroppers became more of a problem for the landowners than a mechanism for ensuring and controlling a labor force.

Conclusion

There is a substantial literature on the nature of the sharecropping system that emerged in the aftermath of the Civil War. In those works by neoclassical economists, sharecropping is understood as an arrangement responding to the new circumstances of the postbellum South—the exigencies of capitalist markets.[18] In the last two decades there has emerged a tradition of social history that explains the continuation of sharecropping in terms of the dynamics of social forces within the region and elsewhere (see, for example, Wiener 1978; Davis 1982; Wayne 1983; and Mandle 1978). The analysis here is within that tradition, but has as its focus the process of class.

The share system was institutionalized amidst the ruin and confusion of the aftermath of the Civil War. By all accounts it was a compromise between the plantation owners or landlords, who desperately needed a labor force to resume production, and a predominantly African American labor force of former slaves who refused to work as wage laborers under conditions of gang labor and whose dreams of becoming "independent peasants" had been shattered. Sharecropping appeared to be a preferable option, due to the fact that it made family-based production units feasible, indeed necessary. Yet this system, which was to continue for a considerable stretch of time, was crucially dependent on several conditions that rendered it hardly an improvement over slavery.

The culture of racism, although no longer allowing for the sale of human beings, was based on a strict social hierarchy that identified the manual tasks of the sharecropper with being black and inferior (so that whoever performed these "lowly" manual tasks became "black" by association). The vengeance of poor whites against blacks needs to be understood in the context of a feudal world-view that denigrated manual labor and identified it with inferiority. The credit system peculiar to Southern sharecropping and the institution of furnishing that so often resulted in peonage was similarly rooted in this world-view and shaped by landlord paternalism. The extension of essentials such as food and clothing not only confirmed the "superior" position of the landlord in the human hierarchy but also legitimized the provision of labor by the sharecropper. It was only just, after all, that the landlord would demand labor in return for such "care." The longlasting battles in the South over the definition of sharecroppers' legal status should also be seen in this light. Such struggles were manifestations of the will of the landowning classes to redefine their "hegemony" albeit under the new conditions of the South.

Just as the sharecropping system was marked by vestiges of slavery, the system of capitalist agricultural production that replaced Southern sharecropping can be seen to have been shaped by a feudal inheritance. Mechanization, for example, was not the only reason behind the waves of African American migrations to the northern cities after World War II as capitalist agriculture began to consolidate itself in the Southern plantations. As important for blacks was the desire to escape from a culture that insisted on a hierarchical vision of the world that placed them at the bottom.[19] For white landowners reluctantly adjusting to the political climate created by the civil rights movement and the collapse of the sharecropping system (Anderson 1973; Dunbar 1968), mechanization and the displacement of labor could be seen as a way of avoiding the liberal-capitalist ethos of equality.

In addition, sharecropping had doomed laborers to subsistence and, at times, to below-subsistence levels of existence. It is worth reflecting on how this system may have prepared the way for contemporary societal tolerance of lower wages for African American workers, particularly in the South, and for current cases of "unfree" labor.

Some readers may react against the general claim of this essay—that postbellum sharecropping in the U.S. South was constituted by a feudal class process. Questions may be raised as to how this is possible when the Civil War, according to prevalent interpretation, represented the military, political, and economic victory of Northern capitalism over Southern slavery. How is it possible to make claims about the existence of feudal relations in the late-nineteenth-century United States? These questions are informed by the classical Marxist idea that capitalism eventually destroys its others or renders them subservient to its own logic. The argument here implicitly challenges this particular conceptualization of capitalist dynamics.[20] I am not denying that the development of capitalism had an impact on the development of sharecropping as a feudal institution, but this is a different statement to one that sees the rise of Southern sharecropping as an aspect or imperative of the rise of industrial capital in the North. A representation of the historical and contemporary variety of class processes in advanced capitalist social formations undermines the classical notion of a unidirectional and homogeneous pathway toward capitalist development. It also invites new ways of theorizing social formations, challenging along the way received notions of core and periphery. The way we interpret the past bears on the way we understand the present, and our particular comprehension of the present bears on the future we hope to create.

Notes

1 Rent, here, corresponds to the appropriated surplus labor. Under different conditions rent can also be a cut from the appropriated surplus labor. For an extensive discussion of different forms of rent, see Kayatekin (1996–1997).

2 The choice of these particular conditions of existence of a feudal class relation should not in any way convey the idea that these were the only ones that mattered. Other conditions emanating from the local power structure were also important. For instance, a major aspect of this economic practice was the coercion of sharecroppers by their landlords, frequently in collusion with a legal authority, such as the sheriff. A common form of coercion was the resort to organized forms of violence, perpetuated by institutions such as the Ku Klux Klan (KKK). As Bloch (1961) has shown, the use of violence was also a key aspect of the lord–serf relation in medieval Europe.

3 The Marxist debate on the transition from feudalism to capitalism originally took place in the pages of the journal *Science and Society* between 1950 and 1953. The contributors to this debate include M. Dobb, R. Hill, P. Sweezy, and K. Takahashi. See Sweezy et al. (1980) for a collection of key essays.

4 For a class analysis of sharecropping see Kayatekin (1990, 1996–1997).

5 The variations in sharecropping are usually in the proportion of the costs of fertilizers, pesticide, and ginning paid by each party. Sometimes the proportions are equal, at other times the landlord furnishes one quarter or one third.

6 One could also say that this definition fails to take into account those laborers of the feudal era in Western Europe who had possession neither of land nor any other means of production. On this point see the works of Kosminskii (1956) and Duby (1968).

7 Woodman (1995, 74–75) writes that only in the states of Alabama and North Carolina was this distinction abolished. In Alabama in 1877, during the more liberal aftermath of the Civil War, the courts made both croppers and tenants into tenants, whereas in North Carolina in 1923 both tenants and croppers were considered to be croppers.

8 For example, in a legal case in Georgia a lower court had ordered that a cropper who had been evicted from his land after taking ill was entitled to be paid for the portion of work he had completed before getting sick. This decision was subsequently reversed by the Supreme Court, which held that it was due to the cropper's own misfortune of being unable to work on account of falling ill, and not to any action of the landlord, that was depriving him of his laborer's lien rights to payment (Woodman 1995, 80–81)

9 The absence of any rights of the sharecropper also characterized the *mezzadri* in the Tuscan countryside in Italy from the time of its inception in the thirteenth century to its eventual decline in the 1960s. Here, the contract of the sharecropper could be terminated at the end of the agricultural year and this could be done for essentially any reason (Andrews 1996a, 3).

10 Clearly U.S. history has involved varying forms of racism and versions of white supremacy. It seems possible to posit, for example, that the Civil War and later the civil rights movement were followed by shifts and modifications in racist ideology. A specific ideology of white supremacy could perhaps be seen as arising as a cultural creation of the postbellum period. Under slavery, slaves were viewed not as human but as chattels. The Civil War dealt a severe blow to this world-view. When former slaves became understood as human beings, one cultural adjustment made in the South was to consider them human within the limits of a hierarchical natural order in which whites were superior to nonwhites.

11 According to Giovanni Cherubini's study of the medieval peasant:

Satire often emphasized not only the peasant's filth, poor clothing, and minimal diet, but also a sort of bestiality that at times placed him almost at an intermediate level between beasts and humans. (1930, 312)

12 Similar demands on the behavior of the peasant were part of sharecropping contracts in the *mezzadri* system of Tuscany:

Should the tenant give himself over to a disreputable or scandalous mode of life, whether or not offending against the law, then the landlords shall have the right to demand the termination of the contract of tenancy. (Quoted in Andrews 1996a, 1)

13 This is not to say that coercion was not a crucial aspect of landlord control, but only to indicate that it is inadequate as the sole explanation of the particular human psychology formed under conditions of racism. As the following news headlines from the *Jackson Advocate* indicate, coercion and outright violence was clearly an integral aspect of racism right up until the mid-twentieth century:

"Mississippi sharecropper slain after dispute over crop settlement" (December 10, 1949)
"Negro farm family all but wiped out by guns of convicts" (January 14, 1950)
"Father says son wounded and his wife killed by plantation boss" (June 30, 1951)
"Share cropper flees 20 bale cotton crop . . . Cabin riddled with bullets as cotton

picking starts . . . Unable to get help of law enforcement following incident"
(November 1, 1947)

"Highly regarded and trusted young plantation worker father of three killed
in ambush by white tenant . . . Brother makes vain attempt to lay case before
Governor White" (August 30, 1952)

"Negro tenant farmer whose son-in-law is accused of theft shot to death . . .
Shooting officer cleared on charge resisting arrest" (April 3, 1954).

14 For an elaboration of the coercion and consent in the context of the Southern
sharecropping system, see S. A. Kayatekin and S. Charusheela, "Reconstituting the Feudal Subject: Toward a Non-Modernist Approach." Paper
presented at the Marxism 2000 Conference, University of Massachusetts
Amherst, September 21–24, 2000.

15 In most sharecropping arrangements the sharecropper was allowed to grow
food crops in a small allotment. The size of these plots was always a matter of contention between the sharecropper and the landowner, and during
times of commercial growth the sharecroppers were ordered to grow cotton
on these plots as well.

16 The question of who extends the credit to the sharecropper is of crucial importance in defining this payment in class terms (Resnick and Wolff 1987).
Whether it is the landlord or the merchant who extends the credit changes
the analysis. It is almost impossible to substantiate the sources of credit
from the agricultural census data. What we do know is derived from individual case studies, rather than systematic studies of plantations. One of
the few studies that offer us any insight on this matter is Soldberg's (1950).
In a sample of Mississippi and Arkansas farms, he found that the croppers
and the blacks were the chief recipients of landlord credit. The degree of
control noted over the tenant through the credit mechanism is interesting:

> Landlords, particularly in Arkansas, Mississippi, and Texas can influence
> sources of credit available to tenants and croppers refusing to waive their statu-
> tory liens on the crop for rents and advances, the inclusiveness of which varies
> from state to state, depending on the nature of the leasing agreements. (299)

Despite all of the problems involved, I will assume in this section that the
tenant receives the credit from the landlord.

17 As the loans were mostly for consumption purposes, few productivity gains
resulted from them.

18 Some of these works employ competitive markets as their underlying model
(for example see Higgs 1971, 1977; Reid 1973, 1975; DeCanio 1974), while
others use the model of monopoly (Ransom and Sutch 1977).

19 Thompson believes that the decline of the plantation system in the U.S. South followed the undermining of the ideology of racism:

> The unsavory reputation of the plantation in the modern world derives from the fact that race and caste are no longer accepted as bases of worker subordination and exploitation. We no longer are disposed to recognize any explicit racial "right" to command nor any explicit racial "obligation" to obey. The decline of the plantation in the South and around the world has followed the rejection of such alleged rights and obligations and their replacement by milder forms of social deference. (From the Foreword to Mandle 1978, xiii)

> See Rio (2000), however, for an interesting analysis of the perpetuation of racist ideologies in the work relations of African American women domestic workers who gained employment in the early part of this century in households in the North.

20 For a recent critique of "the logic of capital" approaches, see Gibson-Graham (1996).

DEAN J. SAITTA

□

COMMUNAL CLASS PROCESSES AND

PRE-COLUMBIAN SOCIAL DYNAMICS

A major goal of archaeology is to explain past cases of social change. To the extent that archaeology is the only social science capable of study- ing variation in social form and causality over the entirety of human- kind's existence on this planet, its results should be of interest to Marxists (Saitta 1995). Archaeological studies can illuminate the organizational novelty or radical "otherness" (Hodder 1991) of past social forms, their long-term viability relative to historically known forms, and variation in the causal processes that transform them. This information can not only enhance our understanding of the past but also provide a guide for imag- ining alternative ways that humans might live; that is, it has both scientific and political import.

Within archaeology, in recent years, thinking about causality has in- creasingly turned from environmental explanations of change (i.e., those invoking climate change or population-resource imbalance as the key causal factor) to ones focused more on social factors and the role of conscious human agency. In human agency models the actions of indi- viduals and/or groups of individuals around different aspects of social life (e.g., resource distributions, the exercise of power, control of ideol- ogy) create the dynamic of social change. While the trend toward agency modeling is occurring throughout the discipline, it is especially pro- nounced in the study of so-called middle-range societies. Middle-range societies—otherwise known as tribes and chiefdoms—are societies that on anthropology's continuum of organizational variation fall between hunter-gatherer bands and complex states. These village-based, agricultural societies are important to archaeologists (as well as to Marxist anthropologists) because they are presumed to contain, at least in embryonic form, the kinds of social inequalities that would eventually come to characterize states and civilizations.

The purpose of this paper is to draw out some of the social dynamics of change in middle-range societies of pre-Columbian North America, using class as a theoretical point of entry. My focus is on Cahokian society of the American Southeast, and Chacoan society of the American Southwest. These societies—both dating to between A.D. 900–1150—are widely taken to be two of the most complex to have developed in pre-Columbian North America. Their precise organizational form and the processes creating change in form over time are, however, still poorly understood.

In other places (Saitta 1994a,b, 1997) I have reconstructed the fundamentally *communal* nature of these social formations; that is, archaeological evidence from each area concerning settlement structure, patterns and levels of labor investment in civic architecture, and distributions of both subsistence and luxury goods suggest that most surplus labor was appropriated and distributed via communal class processes. In these communal societies means of production are held in common, and access to strategic factors of production is guaranteed. Surplus labor—required for care of the sick and infirm, replacement of strategic factors of production, and maintenance of socioceremonial life, among other activities—is collectively appropriated. Primary producers participate in decision making about the amounts of surplus produced, its form (products or labor service), and its conditions of production. Such conditions of production can be quite variable, involving different ways of dividing labor, organizing work, producing goods, redistributing products, exercising authority, and regularizing access to positions of authority.

In this paper I take the communal organization of Cahokian and Chacoan society for granted, and limit myself to a discussion of processes of change within these societies. In both cases, mainstream archaeological theory has stressed the causal role of external exchange dynamics in creating long-term social change. I want to show that the picture of change in each case is more complex by considering exchange in the context of "internal" class processes of labor flow. By inserting a concern for class processes into models of middle-range society, we can draw out a wider variety of social struggles, establish more dynamic contexts of change, and better explore the conceivably radical "otherness" of the ancient past. And, with regard to the cases at hand, we can also show the elasticity and durability of communal forms—a significant issue for Marxist theorists and political activists.

In the first part of the essay I will briefly review the dominant model of exchange dynamics that has been used to account for change in the Cahokian and Chacoan areas, and discuss some theoretical and empirical critiques of the model that alert us to the need for new theory. This model is known as the prestige good model, and versions have been widely used, not only across North America but in many other places to account for social development (Earle 1994). In the second part I will outline a class-theoretical framework for understanding the social dynamics of middle-range societies. In the final part I will illustrate how the archaeological application of this approach enhances our understanding of social change in pre-Columbian North America.

The Prestige Good Model in Archaeological Theory

Social trade and exchange have long figured prominently in theories of change for middle-range societies. This is because middle-range societies depend on exchange relations not only to offset the productive short-falls that can plague small-scale agricultural economies but also to meet the needs of social reproduction. A wealth of ethnographic research has revealed how, in village societies characterized by close social contact, foreign objects made from materials exotic to a region are used to help meet political obligations, make the peace, and lubricate ritual cycles (e.g., Helms 1992). These objects also fund status displays and competitions, and it is often through the manipulation of exchange that individuals and groups gain social power. With social power comes the ability to regulate the production and distribution of resources for one's own benefit.

Archaeological prestige good models incorporate these observations into an account of how social elites in middle-range societies come to be established and their power maintained via the tactical manipulation of regional and interregional exchange (for summaries, see McGuire 1989; Schortman and Urban 1992; Baugh and Ericson 1992; Blanton et al. 1996). The model is an offshoot of the importation, beginning in the 1970s, of world systems theory (Wallerstein 1974) into archaeology (Schneider 1977; Kohl 1979). World systems theory had the useful effect of alerting archaeologists to the importance of long-distance relationships — and especially inequalities in those relationships — in shaping social interaction and change.

Specifically, the prestige good model assumes that social power stems from the control of "exotic" valuables necessary for important life transitions (initiations, marriages, etc.). Lineage elders (senior men) exercise such control, and juniors subordinate themselves to elders in order to obtain socially necessary items. These elites extract surplus (objects and food) from subordinates, which they then use to compete with other elites, build political alliances, and obtain more valuables. In this model valuables are "instruments of power": they are a means to appropriate the labor of subordinates. Over time, successful elite strategies can generate institutionalized social hierarchy and inequality. Prestige good systems are considered inherently unstable, however, because of the fact that many valuables come from distant sources where elites are unable to exercise direct control over their production and exchange.

Several useful critiques of prestige good models have been presented in the archaeological literature. Charles Cobb (1993) presents one in his survey of archaeological approaches to the political economy of non-stratified societies. For Cobb, prestige good models pay insufficient attention to conceivable diversity in the roles/meanings of exotic goods; that is, they do not clearly distinguish between when valuables are serving as indicators of genuine economic power (i.e., the ability of some to coerce labor out of others), and when valuables are simply serving as markers of social status.

Ronna Bradley makes another criticism in her study of shell exchange at Casas Grandes, a complex fourteenth-century polity in northwestern Chihuahua, Mexico (1992). Bradley argues that there is no attention in many prestige good models to how goods, once procured, are distributed to the general population. I take her to be asking about the social context within which transactions are made. Are goods redistributed in a social context of group feasting? In a context of individualized exchanges, where valuables are exchanged for perhaps more utilitarian goods? Or, does the distribution occur only with the completion of some labor service performed by subordinates for elites? In most prestige good models the relationship between interacting parties is not very well specified.

I have also critiqued prestige good models (Saitta 1994a,b). A central ontological problem with these models is the implicit assumption that within any social formation there are always a few people motivated by ambition and natural acquisitiveness. It is assumed that, whenever environmental conditions permit, these ambitious individuals will seize the opportunity to manipulate social relations for their own benefit. Methodological individualism governs such models: The biological individual is privileged as the subject of inquiry, often at the expense of the wider social structures and institutions that create individual subjectivities and shape a wide variety of self- and social consciousnesses (Patterson 1990). In practice this has resulted in essentialist, teleological accounts of change that ascribe to pre- and noncapitalist social formations the same kinds of dynamics that characterize capitalist formations. In this approach past and present are conflated, behavior is homogenized, and nothing new is learned.

A more specific criticism has to do with the way in which the nature of labor-flows from subordinates to elites is theorized in prestige good models. Most models assert, or strongly imply, that the elite–subordinate relationship is exploitative. Elites are said to "extract," "usurp," or "preempt" the surplus labor of subordinates (Upham 1982; Tilley 1984; McGuire 1989). Such labor, in the societies of interest here, takes the form of subsistence goods and/or labor service in agricultural or other activities. The implication, perhaps unintended, is that the class relationship linking elites and producers is tributary or even feudal in nature. However, this is not the only way to understand the relationship. Alternatively, it could be understood as a distinctly nonexploitative and fundamentally *communal* relationship *if* we see the goods and/or services that move against valuables as payments, allocated by subordinates to elites as compensation for their work in procuring socially important valuables — what can be termed a *communal subsumed class* payment (Amariglio 1984a,b). On this view the status of the valuables also changes — they become *communal social entitlements* rather than instruments of power. As a third possibility, the goods and labor transfers can be understood as reciprocal exchanges of equivalents — subordinates perform labor in return for the valuables provided by elites.

In short, prestige good models tend to conflate several different kinds of material transfers and relationships. This conflation is reinforced by their failure to sufficiently distinguish class relations—that is, social relations of surplus-labor appropriation and distribution—from the nonclass relations (power relations, exchange relations) that organize human social life. Elites in middle-range societies can have a measure of power that derives from their roles in brokering long-distance exchange, but such authority does not necessarily translate into direct or coercive control over surplus labor/product. The conflation needs to be addressed, because how we understand material transfers and other relationships in middle-range societies influences the way in which we think about the internal dynamics of change.

In addition to these theoretical criticisms, there are empirical warrants for rethinking prestige good models; that is, the models have trouble accounting for exchange patterns in several areas of North America where exotics are an important part of the archaeological record. One such area is the Mississippian area of the American Southeast. In archaeology, the term "Mississippian" refers to social formations—including the Cahokian—that developed in the main river valleys of this region between A.D. 700–1700. The societies described as Mississippian show varying degrees of emphasis on maize agriculture; interregional trade in exotic goods, including certain cherts (high-quality, fine-grained stone used for manufacturing tools), shell, copper, mica, and other materials; as well as the construction of monumental public architecture in the form of large, flat-topped earthen temple mounds and other structures. Mississippian societies are usually described as chiefdoms whose political economy is based on the extraction of tribute from rural farmers by political elites residing at major mound centers.

Patterns at several key Mississippian moundbuilder sites, however, do not easily square with the assumption that valuables served as elite instruments of power within class-divided, tributary political economies. John Blitz's work on the Lubbub Creek polity in Alabama is a particularly instructive example (1993). Blitz's distributional study of exchange goods reveals the widespread availability of exotics (fine ceramics, shell beads, and micro-drills used for bead manufacture) to *both* rural farmstead and mound-center households. Blitz thus infers that there was little or no centralization of prestige goods exchange, nor greatly restricted access to exotic goods, at Lubbub Creek. He also documents a wider dispersion of production loci for finished goods than would be expected if control of the prestige goods economy was being monopolized by a few individuals. Blitz is especially provocative in his inference that the Lubbub Creek farmer and mound-top actor were the *same* person, rather than members of different social classes. He sees activities occurring at major mound centers — for example, ceremonial feasting and ritual observances — as public and maximally inclusive in nature. Blitz thus alerts us to some conceivably novel organizational relationships in this polity, including the possibility of *communal* class relationships. At the very least, Blitz's work suggests that classic prestige good/tribute models are not applicable to all Mississippian polities.

Some recent work in the American Southwest produces similar results. James Bayman's work on twelfth- and thirteenth-century Hohokam communities is one example (1995). The term "Hohokam" refers to the great southern tradition of ancestral Southwestern pueblo society, centered in the Gila and Salt River valleys of southern Arizona. The Hohokam constructed large, platform mound settlements and complex irrigation systems, trafficked widely in exotics, such as marine shell and macaw feathers, and built large, public structures such as earthen ballcourts. In his study of the multisettlement Marana community near Phoenix, Bayman finds, like Blitz, that the production and distribution of valued objects (specifically, obsidian tools) across the community was a bit more widespread than expected. One does not find that evidence for obsidian production and consumption is concentrated in the presumably elite household areas immediately surrounding the central platform mound in the largest settlement of the community. Instead, such evidence is found at households *throughout* the platform mound settlement. While settlements away from the platform mound have less dense concentrations, the observable patterns are nonetheless consistent with communal activities of the sort implicated by Blitz for Lubbub Creek (i.e., collective feasting and ceremony). Minimally, Bayman's observations about exchange behavior at the Marana community suggest the limitations of classic prestige good models as applied to the Hohokam.

This empirical work suggests that the organization of pre-Columbian North American exchange, and its linkage to power and class relations, was variable and complex. Earle (1994) recently argued that the question of whether emergent, exchange-brokering elites in North America were "first among equals" or, alternatively, incipient exploitative classes has been settled in favor of the latter. However, empirical evidence such as that just described indicates that this is still an open question.

Theorizing Class Contexts for Pre-Columbian Exchange

We still lack theories of society that allow us to engage this open question in productive ways. However, Marxian thought offers one way to clarify the sort of organizational variability and complexity discussed above. The nonessentialist, class-theoretical Marxism pioneered by Resnick and Wolff is especially useful in this regard. A class-theoretical approach recognizes that people participate, often simultaneously, in a number of different class and nonclass processes. They differentially participate in class processes as producers, extractors, recipients, and/or distributors of surplus labor. They differentially participate in nonclass processes having to do with the way labor is divided, work organized, exchange regulated, ceremonies conducted, and so forth. As part of their differential participation, people can engage in class struggles over the form, amounts, and distribution of surplus labor produced in society, and, in nonclass struggles, over the form and terms of the social conditions that sustain relations of surplus appropriation and distribution. The conflicts created by people's occupancy of multiple class and nonclass positions in turn create complex, nonteleological dynamics of change. In this approach there can be no "essential" cause of social struggle and change.

Several scholars have explored the nature of these class and nonclass relationships and struggles for communal social formations in history and prehistory (Amariglio 1984a,b; Jensen 1982; Resnick and Wolff 1988; Saitta 1988, 1994a,b). These models are very useful for drawing out variation in the political economies of middle-range societies. They make a clean break with normative and typological approaches by insisting that the communal formation is not a single organizational type characterized by an invariant set of features. Instead, communal formations can combine communal class processes with well-developed political hierarchies, complex divisions of labor, long-distance exchange relations, and various forms of productive specialization. Communal formations can accommodate a variety of subsumed, "managerial" positions and activities that are supported (via flows of surplus labor) by the wider commune. Exchange agents, political functionaries, ritual specialists, and craft specialists can all be part of the subsumed class mix, and can articulate in different ways with the production and distribution of communal surpluses. Political functionaries (e.g., "chiefs" or "big men") may receive cuts of communally extracted surpluses to secure their activities of organizing and scheduling religious ceremonies, coordinating communal hunts and agricultural tasks, supervising communal labor projects, and negotiating alliances with external groups. Such subsumed classes can operate relatively benignly as "first among equals," but can do so in some interesting and unpredictable ways that preserve the capacity for tension and struggle. The tensions and struggles between different social groups over communal labor flows and other conditions of communal life in turn create the overdetermined, teleonomic dynamic of the communal formation. The analytical challenge is to clarify the social positions and activities of these agents/groups and how they are complicated by changing environmental and historical circumstances.

Accomplishing this requires the input of specific empirical case material. In the remainder of the essay, I will briefly turn to the Cahokia and Chaco cases as a way to show how a class-theoretical perspective on middle-range, communal social formations opens up new possibilities for understanding pre-Columbian social change.

Exchange, Class, and the Dynamics of Pre-Columbian Social Formations

The Cahokian and Chacoan social formations both date to the time period A.D. 900–1150. As noted, prestige goods exchange has been viewed as central to the dynamics of social change in both cases. However, ambiguities in the meaning of the exchange data in each area alert us to the presence of other kinds of causal dynamics. The precise nature of communalism in both of these cases remains to be more firmly established, including the variety of forms that surplus labor took in each society, the ways in which agricultural land was distributed and producer work groups organized, how surplus labor and products were distributed, how collective decisions about production and distribution were made, and so on. What we currently have as evidence for communalism in both cases consists of broad patterns in available data, enough to allow an innovative framing of interpretive possibilities.

Social Change at Cahokia

Located in the American Bottom area east of St. Louis, the Mississippian site of Cahokia is widely thought to be the center of the most complex and regionally influential political entity ever to have evolved in pre-Columbian North America. The site has elaborate temple mound architecture, a high density of exotic material from, for example, the Gulf Coast and Great Lakes, and distinctive ceramic styles restricted in their distribution. All are observations that indicate the presence of an elite class. Indeed, most scholars view Cahokia as a complex, tributary chiefdom. Cahokian complexity is generally recognized as peaking during the Stirling Phase, dated at A.D. 1050–1150.

What is curious about Stirling Phase developments, however, is that increased political complexity appears to be associated, contrary to the expectations of classic prestige goods and tributary models, with a *decrease* in the intensity of long-distance exchange. Some scholars (e.g., Pauketat 1992) have interpreted this as reflecting increasing sacralization of political authority associated with the rise of a single, dominant paramount elite, and the replacement of prestige exchange as a form of control with other mechanisms of control (e.g., the use of coercive force, as one might find in feudal or tributary societies). These scholars still allow, however, that Cahokian power remained tenuous because of factionalist struggles and competition among subordinate but upwardly mobile elites. This competitive dynamic eventually led to an organizational collapse at Cahokia around A.D. 1150.

An alternative, class-theoretical model broadens and deepens this social dynamic, replacing the teleology of exchange models with a more complex set of causes (for a full account, see Saitta 1994b). In this view, the Stirling Phase at Cahokia represents just one of a series of crises in, and struggles over, the social appropriation of basically *communal* surplus labor, rather than a relatively narrow struggle among self-aggrandizing political elites in a well-established tributary economy based on prestige goods.

In this model elites receive communal subsumed class revenues from the collective appropriators for providing them with exotics gained from long-distance trade. These exotics help sustain communal conditions of existence enabling collective appropriation to occur at Cahokia. As Blitz documented for Lubbub Creek, we have evidence at Cahokia for the widespread distribution of exotic goods across both elite and nonelite contexts. This extensive type of distribution suggests their function as communal social entitlements to the tribal producers and appropriators of surplus labor to help reproduce communalism's nonclass conditions of existence. The latter collectivity distributed to these elites shares of the appropriated surplus in the form of other economic goods and labor. In this model, elites participating in the acquisition and distribution of exotics occupy a communal subsumed class position, serving as communal political functionaries who draw support for brokering exchange from allocations of communal surplus labor (communal subsumed class processes), rather than from tribute extraction or some other exploitative relationship. Such communal support could have been realized by subsumed classes in any number of forms, including the receipt of extra shares of harvested food or game, labor service to their households for tending and harvesting gardens, preparing food, or generally maintaining the house. Material patterns in mound architecture, ceramics, and landscape design buttress this inferential vision (Saitta 1994b).

If this vision is correct, then the Stirling Phase decrease in exotics — perhaps stimulated by changing fortunes of exchange in outlying frontier areas that limited the number of exotics coming into the American Bottom — would have thrown the communal social order into crisis. The loss of such exotics could have compromised the subsumed class incomes (in goods and/or services) sustaining those Cahokian elites responsible for organizing long-distance exchange and distributing its products. As a response to a real decline in subsumed class incomes, these communal functionaries may have used their positions (in ways that are still unclear) to build exploitative, tributary relations of production. Such efforts would have brought elites into conflict with rural producers — themselves conflicted by the loss of entitlements — as well as with other subsumed elites, resulting in myriad social struggles over surplus flow and its conditions of existence. This alternative model illustrates how a (subsumed) class struggle in a communal society could produce the conditions of transition from that communal to a noncommunal, that is, exploitative, society.

The form and timing of developments in the Stirling Phase material record at Cahokia bear witness to new elite strategies to institutionalize and legitimize tributary class relations (Saitta 1994b). For example, there is evidence from mound excavations that more frequent attempts were made by elites to command labor for civic constructions. There is also ceramic evidence that efforts were made to stylistically link (via new designs on specialist-produced containers) elites with "godlike" forms of control over nature and the cosmos. Along with evidence for these elite domination strategies, however, we find evidence for producer resistance. Precision is difficult to achieve at this point, but *some* sort of struggle-based social dynamic between elites and nonelites is suggested by evidence for the massive and multifaceted reworking of Cahokia's central architectural core during the Stirling Phase. This reworking included three rebuildings of a palisade separating elite-ceremonial from public-residential space, and several transformations of ceremonial space into residential space and back again. The most interesting indicator of popular resistance, however, is evidence for a Stirling Phase shift, in rural areas, in the storage of corn and other products from *outside* storage pits to pits located *inside* houses. This may reflect efforts by communal producers to conceal household surpluses from would-be tribute takers. Such popular resistance would have compromised the ability of Cahokian elites to consistently extract tribute from the hinterlands.

In the end, Stirling Phase efforts by communal elites to institutionalize tributary class processes did not succeed. Beginning late in the Stirling Phase, we see the outflowing of population from the Cahokia area to rural locales—another indicator of producer resistance to the formation of tributary class relations. By the end of the subsequent Moorehead Phase (i.e., by A.D. 1250) settlements throughout the American Bottom show increased local autonomy and a much deeper emphasis on communal activities. These developments suggest that social tensions and struggles at Cahokia were resolved in favor of communality, although in reorganized forms.

This class-theoretical model of Cahokian social change overlaps with mainstream, non-Marxist models in some important ways (e.g., in its identification of the Stirling Phase as a crisis-ridden prelude to social change). However, it departs in problematizing the status of surplus flows (recognizing communal flows as prevalent over tribute and corvee) and in its different understanding of prestige goods exchange as the socially regulated distribution of communal social entitlements. It also differs in casting the Stirling Phase crisis as a complex struggle over the terms and conditions of communal labor appropriation rather than a relatively narrow struggle among status-seeking elites in an already well-established tributary formation. These struggles culminated not in organizational collapse and transition to an exploitative society but in a reorganization of communal political economies in the American Bottom.

Social Change at Chaco Canyon

The Chaco Canyon case parallels the Cahokian case in many ways. As already noted, Chaco society dates to the same time period as Cahokia, and, like Cahokia, Chaco was the center of an expansive network of interacting communities. The Chaco network covered at least 60,000 square miles of the Four Corners area of the American Southwest, where the states of Arizona, Colorado, New Mexico, and Utah converge. A group of large, multistoried pueblo settlements located in Chaco Canyon in northwestern New Mexico anchored the Chacoan exchange and interaction network. Known as "great houses," these settlements average about 200 rooms in size with the largest great house—a structure known as Pueblo Bonito—numbering 800 rooms. Distributed well beyond Chaco Canyon are other great houses, built in the distinctive Chaco architectural style, known as "outliers." That Chaco Canyon was the center of an expansive interaction network is further indicated by an extensive network of formally constructed and labor-intensive avenues or roads that connect great houses, outliers, and small, more traditional pueblo settlements over the Four Corners area. For some scholars the unprecedented scale and labor-intensive nature of the Chacoan system implies the existence of a complex social entity structured by prestige good exchange (Kohler 1993). Others suggest the existence of a tributary chiefdom or even state (Wilcox 1993). In these models, accumulationist elites reside at the Chaco Canyon great houses, their clients occupy outliers, and both work together to either entice or coerce flows of labor and goods out of small village populations and into the Chaco core. Empirically, both arguments turn on the greater variety and higher density of Chacoan exotics (turquoise, shell, copper, rare pottery) at great house sites.

Other scholars, however, have questioned the empirical reality of this observation. Toll (1991, 86), for example, points out that exotics occur at very small pueblo villages as well as at the great houses, and that they exist in small, even minuscule quantities relative to more mundane, everyday materials at *both* kinds of settlements. Toll suggests that this pattern may even hold for Pueblo Bonito, where exotics are especially densely concentrated. Windes (1992) also questions the concentration of turquoise (arguably the most ritually important Chacoan exotic) at great houses, and suggests that participation in turquoise jewelry manufacture was "nearly universal" across both great houses and villages during the peak of Chacoan development. If Toll and Windes are right, then the distribution of Chacoan exotics is consistent with their function as communal social entitlements and with a notion of guaranteed access to strategic social resources. As at Cahokia, Chacoan elites may have been responsible for brokering exchange in exotic goods as part of their subsumed class functions. The distribution of Chacoan exotics would also be consistent with recent evidence suggesting the *nonresidential* nature of Chaco Canyon great houses; that is, that they were occupied only seasonally by "pilgrims" from hinterland areas coming into the canyon for communal feasting events and other ritual observances (Lekson et al. 1988; Saitta 1995). In this regard Chacoan great houses may have differed little from Mississippian temple mounds in their basic nature; that is, as fundamentally *communal* civic architecture.

Even if it turns out that great houses and villages *do* differ significantly in varieties and densities of exotic goods, this does not necessarily mean that great houses were home to ambitious, prestige-accumulating, exploitative elites. Evidence for differential control of resources and political hierarchy is not necessarily evidence for the kinds of incipient class divisions stipulated by prestige good models. The case for such divisions (and the validity of the prestige good model itself) requires *other* contextual evidence establishing nonguaranteed access to life-sustaining resources, as well as direct claims by elites on the surplus labor of producers that would have affected the ability of those producers to perform the *necessary* labor requisite for reproducing themselves as individuals.

Such a case has not yet been made for Chaco. In the absence of such a case, a model of Chacoan communality remains plausible.

Recognizing Chacoan communality in turn provides a fertile context for understanding twelfth-century social change in new ways. Conventional prestige good and tributary models view Chaco as collapsing from the weight of elite accumulation and competition in a context of environmental deterioration and fragmenting long-distance exchange activity. An alternative, class-theoretical model views Chacoan social change through the lens of class and nonclass struggles over diminishing communal surpluses and a threatened communal ideology (Saitta 1997). In this view, well-documented late eleventh- and early twelfth-century environmental deterioration in the Chaco area would have compromised the social positions of Chacoan political and, especially, subsumed ritual specialists responsible for making rain, ensuring agricultural productivity, and keeping the community in good standing with the spirits. As a response to declining subsumed class incomes and eroding cultural legitimacy created by environmental deterioration and agricultural failures, Chacoan ritual specialists (like Cahokian exchange specialists) could have used their subsumed class positions—again, in ways that are still unclear—to build the noncommunal tribute and/or cliental relations stipulated by prestige good and tributary models. Struggles over the terms and conditions of surplus appropriation and distribution would have been activated between different subsumed classes, and between subsumed classes and primary producers.

As with Cahokia, there is evidence in the Chacoan material record from the late eleventh and early twelfth centuries that bears witness to such strategies and struggles. This includes evidence for massive labor investments in existing great house architecture at precisely that time when we would expect elites to explore new forms of labor control, as well as evidence for the construction of *brand-new* great houses that clearly served as places for food storage and residence as opposed to seasonal pilgrimage sites. Both developments may reflect the emergence of noncommunal (tributary) relations of production in the canyon. At the same time as these changes are occurring, there is architectural and settlement-pattern evidence for countervailing strategies of producer resistance. This includes a decrease in the number of small village sites in the Chaco area, suggesting the flight of people (i.e., primary producers) to other areas (Sebastian 1992). Moreover, as we saw with the Moore-head Phase at Cahokia, by 1250 we see less elaborate material land-scapes across the Chaco region, suggesting the reorganization of com-munal political economies.

Conclusion

This chapter has examined exchange processes in relation to class pro-cesses of surplus appropriation in noncapitalist, middle-range societies. Class processes have not been sufficiently considered by nor integrated into archaeological accounts of social change. The warrant for inserting a concern for class processes in middle-range societies is provided by theoretical and empirical critiques of classic prestige good models. These models, and the assumptions about human behavior that inform them, obscure some interesting social dynamics in past social formations. If we are to illuminate these dynamics, and explain the often puzzling evi-dence for North American exchange, we need new perspectives on the relationships between material objects, labor flow, and social power in middle-range societies.

A class-theoretical Marxism provides such a new perspective. It rec-ognizes a variety of struggles among a diversity of agents over sur-plus appropriation and its conditions of existence. It eschews essen-tialist, "human nature" assumptions about the causes of human action. Use of the theory in the Cahokia and Chaco cases draws out structural variation in specifically communal political economies, and a greater variety of causal dynamics. In both cases communal class processes were threatened by changing historical circumstances, although the proximate causes were different. Changing fortunes of exchange threatened com-munalism in the Cahokian case, while environmental deterioration did so in the Chacoan case. In both areas these changing historical circum-stances activated struggles between and among different groups of social agents, ultimately leading to the reorganization, rather than transforma-tion or collapse, of the communal political economy.

More closely specifying the nature of these communal formations and their respective social dynamics is the challenge for future theoretical and empirical work. By expanding and deepening this analysis we can hope to generate more complex, nonessentialist models of change for pre-

Columbian North American societies. At same time, we can also hope to expand and deepen thought about the "staying power" of communal forms. The Cahokian and Chacoan cases demonstrate that communal relations of production are not easily transformed, and that the most significant challenges to communal lifeways in ancient North America were resolved in favor of reorganized communality rather than in favor of new, class-divided social orders. Given recurring debates about the long-term sustainability of communal formations, this observation is rife with not only scientific but also political significance.

In a recent article about the origins of social inequality, Richard Lee, one of cultural anthropology's most dedicated and influential students of communal societies, had this to say about the status of "primitive communism" in human history:

Primitive communism has existed within a narrow range at the bottom of a scale; future society would operate in a broader range at the top. But whatever the future may hold, it is the long experience of egalitarian sharing that has molded our past. Despite our seeming adaptation to life in hierarchical societies, there are signs that humankind retains a deep-rooted egalitarianism, a deep rooted commitment to the norm of reciprocity, a deep-rooted desire for what Victor Turner has called *communitas,* the sense of community. All theories of justice revolve around these principles, and our sense of outrage at the violation of these norms indicates the depth of its gut-level appeal. (1990, 245)[1]

In this chapter I have acknowledged and begun to explore the possibility of "primitive communism" in two pre-Columbian societies. By tracing communalism's variable social forms and historical trajectories, I hope not only to add to our understanding of the human past but to contribute something to the shaping of its future.

Notes

1 Lest one think Lee guilty of romanticizing communal forms, in the same article he writes that communal forms are, at times, "neither utopian nor pretty. The members of these societies are real people with all the human frailties of people everywhere" (1990, 243).

STEPHEN RESNICK

AND RICHARD D. WOLFF

□

STRUGGLES IN THE USSR

Communisms Attempted and Undone[1]

Introduction: Communism

"Communist" was the adjective eventually applied to almost everything approved by official circles in the USSR. In sheer positivity, it ranked above "socialist." It attached to the goals, policies, and acts of political leaderships, to the qualities of cultural programs, to moral virtues, and to many economic aspects of Soviet life (planning, labor efforts, actual or proposed income distributions, and so on). Yet only rarely, and in very limited domains, were the actual class structures of pre-1917 production systematically reorganized into communist forms. There was never a communist class structure in industry after 1917. The irony of "communism" in the USSR was that, in actuality, most of its diverse, noncommunist class structures were not transformed into communist class structures. Thus, whatever "failed" in the demise of the USSR in 1990, it was not a "social experiment" in communist class structures.

Before explaining why communism never was sustained in the USSR on a society-wide basis, despite some limited attempts to establish it at particular locations, we need to define precisely and clearly what we mean by this kind of class structure. This is required in part because of the daunting presence of multiple, often confusing, and not infrequently incompatible usages of the term *class* in the vast literature on the USSR. We also, however, intend our definition and analysis here to contribute to a better understanding of what conditions would be needed for future attempts to construct communist class structures to be more successful.

A communist fundamental class process denotes the absence either of individual or collective exploitation. No individual appropriates his or her own surplus labor, the surplus produced by some other individual, or the surplus produced by a collectivity of individuals.[2] No collective appropriates the surplus produced by some other individual or some other collectivity of individuals. Instead, the label "communist" signals the presence of a collective appropriation of surplus labor by the same workers that produced that surplus. From the latter condition, it follows that the producers of the surplus must also be its first distributors: Surplus-producing workers occupy, as a collective, both the appropriating (fundamental) and distributing (subsumed) class positions. A communist class *structure* goes beyond this particular boundary, for it also includes others in society who receive a distributed share of the surplus for securing conditions of communist appropriation. Such a receiver of a distributed share—a communist subsumed class position—is one remove from (although thereby linked to) those engaged in the communist production and appropriation of surplus.

The label "communism" signals, then, the presence of two distinct conditions: (1) the appropriators and distributors of the surplus are the *same* individuals as those who produced it; and (2) the appropriation and distribution is *collective* and not individual. The first condition supports, in our view, a morality of fairness and equity: No individual or collectivity is able to gain more (surplus) for itself than it gives in return. The second condition supports a morality of relatedness and community: The production and appropriation of surplus is to be made an explicitly communal affair.

For evidence (in the USSR or elsewhere) of the existence of communist surplus appropriation, we search for signs of cultural, political, and economic processes that combine to enable and persuade a group of workers to appropriate and distribute their own surplus labor collectively. The ensemble of these social processes we refer to as a society's nonclass structure in order to distinguish them from the processes of producing, appropriating, and distributing surplus labor, which we call that society's "class structure." In examining any concrete society, we presume that its nonclass structure will support different class structures at the same time. We also presume that the particular class structures within a society at any time and their interrelationships will significantly influence its history.

In the USSR we have found evidence that its nonclass structure did enable and persuade a few households and a few collective farms after the revolution to establish and operate communist class structures. Communist households, as we shall show, were few in number and did not long survive. Communist collective farms, likewise few in number in the 1920s, became widespread in the immediate aftermath of agricultural collectivization in the early 1930s. But they, too, began to shrink soon after in favor of noncommunist class structures in Soviet agriculture. The USSR's nonclass structure across its entire history chiefly supported a variety of noncommunist, that is, exploitative, class structures in industry, households, and agriculture. Thus, exploitative class structures prevailed over communist ones at most sites of production through the majority of the USSR's history.

The specific communist class structures that did arise in households and collective farms were associated with a set of nonclass social processes that displayed a remarkable degree of equality, democracy, and interpersonal solidarity. The attractiveness to us of communist class structures includes their associations to such nonclass processes, although we recognize that it is possible for communist class processes also to occur within social contexts where democracy, equality, and solidarity are absent. Among the lessons to be learned by close examinations of the very limited communist experiments in the USSR are the conditions under which they will or will not be associated with political and cultural processes favoring solidarity, equality, and democracy.

Industrial Enterprises

Communist class structures were hardly even tried in Soviet industrial enterprises after 1917. In a remarkable turn of events, the groups and committees of revolutionary industrial workers who early took control of "their" enterprises, did not utilize that control to establish communist class structures. That is, they did not organize the collective production of surplus labor, its collective appropriation by the workers themselves, and the collective distribution of that surplus by these same workers to others across Soviet society. They did not take such steps because their concepts of socialism and communism did not require them; the acute pressures of the historical moment made them seem impractical, and for many other reasons as well (Sirianni 1982). Here, however, we will focus on the concepts of socialism and communism, as on the immediate historical context, in offering our partial explanation for the absence of communist class structures in Soviet industrial enterprises.

The concepts of class — and hence of socialist or communist class structures — prevalent in the minds of Soviet industrial workers derived from popular images of class and from the common terminology of Bolshevik, Menshevik, and other left organizations (Diskin 1990). These concepts focused on property and on power. With reference to industrial enterprises, the property concepts defined capitalists as those who owned the means of production (factory buildings, machines, money capital, and so forth). The power concepts defined capitalists as those who wielded the dominant political power in industry (made all of the determining decisions) and also socially via their dominance over the state apparatus. Often these concepts merged in a definition of capitalists as those with the dominant wealth and power.

With such concepts in mind, revolutionary industrial workers understood themselves to be overthrowing capitalism by two simultaneous acts. First, they transferred ownership of industrial property from private citizens to the state. Second, they transferred control over the state (and hence the now state-owned industrial property) from capitalists to the political party of these same industrial workers, the Communist Party. Property and power had shifted from one group, the capitalists, to another group, the workers. Capitalism had been transformed into socialism, understood as a transitional stage on the way to communism.[3]

With the transition out of capitalism understood and accomplished in this way, the details of the organization of industrial production inside enterprises seemed of minimal relevance or importance. Revolutionary workers presented the factories they had seized to their workers' state. The surpluses they continued to produce they also delivered to their state's representatives — now delegated to manage their productive enterprises, as well. The workers themselves collectively produced, but did not collectively receive, their own surplus labor's fruits. Nor did they collectively distribute those fruits. The fact that surplus labor in socialized industries was not collectively appropriated or distributed by the same workers who produced that surplus did not trouble the overwhelming majority of those workers, Soviet state functionaries, or Communist Party spokespersons.

Moreover, when questions were sometimes raised about the more authoritarian measures of state managers vis-à-vis industrial workers, the response was often to cite the pressures of the immediate historical situation. These included the foreign invasions (British, French, U.S., and Japanese) against the Bolsheviks, the civil war, and the continuing external political and military threats even after the invasions were defeated and the civil war won. Survival of the nation and the revolution were blended into an imperative to maintain or increase productive output. "Utopian" experiments in radical new internal organizations of production were "impractical": They risked the inefficiencies associated with putting workers in managerial positions, and so on. The momentous historic achievements of overthrowing private property in industrial means of production and of transferring state power from the czarist and bourgeois parties to the Communist Party sufficed to prove that capitalism had been vanquished. To risk jeopardizing those achievements by further turmoil inside industrial enterprises seemed absurd or counterrevolutionary.

The few leftist efforts to keep alive the possibility and necessity of transforming the internal organization of production in the directions of workers' "control" did not succeed (Sirianni 1982; Chase 1990). Indeed, their concept of control was vague with regard to whether it would extend beyond workers managing their own labor activity to the collective production, appropriation, and distribution of their surplus labor. Most workers' control advocates, too, rarely focused on the organization of surplus labor. In the end, then, despite these radical changes in who owned the means of production and controlled state power, Soviet industrial enterprises retained their pre-1917, internal noncommunist class structures. Workers' surplus labor was appropriated by state functionaries, namely, the newly organized Vesenkha, later reorganized as the Council of Ministers. State functionaries within state-owned enterprises replaced private boards of directors within privately owned enterprises as appropriators of the workers' surplus labor.[4] As we have argued in detail elsewhere, state industrial capitalism replaced private industrial capitalism (Resnick and Wolff 1994). Soviet "communism" thus comprised a state capitalism in its industrial class structure.

Households: Some Communisms Attempted[5]

Households are sites of production that, like their enterprise counterparts, display class structures (Fraad, Resnick, and Wolff 1994). That is, households typically contain laborers who sustain themselves there (do necessary labor) and also produce a surplus. Traditional Russian households assigned the roles of laborer to the wife and appropriator of her surplus labor to her husband. The particular household class structure prevalent across Russia before 1917 was a kind of feudalism, although the single adult household—Marx's notion of the ancient class structure— was also widespread.[6] The questions for us to answer here are: Did post-1917 Soviet society witness a change in household class structures, and were communist class structures part of that change? Other class analysts have not asked such questions because they usually presume that class categories apply only to production outside the household (Bettelheim 1976, 1978).

The class history of household class structures after 1917 differs from the class history of industrial enterprise class structures during the same time. Whereas industrial enterprises saw a change from private to state capitalism, feudal and ancient class structures remained the norm for most households. This situation poses a key question—yet unanswered —for all those attempting to understand the history of the USSR: How did the survival of exploitative class structures inside Soviet households influence both the attempts to move toward socialism and communism as well as attempts to preserve the USSR's existing class structures?

A significant, if relatively small, number of households did experiment with communist class structures, and these received government support through the 1920s (Stites 1989; Goldman 1993). The communist class structures that appeared nowhere else in Soviet society in the decade after the revolution did arise in some households. Their forms and their interrelationships with the rest of Soviet society may provide important lessons about the relationship of communism to Soviet history.

It was chiefly a subset of revolutionary militants who established communist household class structures, performing household labor collectively and likewise appropriating and distributing the fruits of their household surplus labor. Perhaps frustrated by being unable to establish communist class structures in industrial enterprises, some militants tried to prefigure them inside their own households. Radical ideals of democracy, community, sexual freedom, and gender equality, coupled with hostility to the prerevolutionary forms of family and household relationships legitimized the new communist households. The practical pressures on the personal lives of revolutionary militants—frequently shifting assignments, travel, danger—contributed to explorations with new household systems as well. Finally, the social pressure to maintain industrial and agricultural production did not apply equally to household activities, since centuries-old traditions relegated household production to a marginal, subordinated importance in social life.

The Leningrad Commune of 133, one of the few to be systematically described by a Soviet contemporary (M. Yankovsky), reached all decisions about its internal life collectively by means of a "continuous democratic talkfest" (Stites 1989, 214). Housework (including cooking, shopping, housecleaning, and laundry) was equally distributed and rotated among the 133 members. Property was held in common. All incoming packages to individuals were opened so that their contents could be equally distributed to all. Individual rooms were torn down in favor of large, open, "communal" living spaces. Issues surrounding personal privacy, sexual connections, coupling, and children were intensely and openly discussed, and conclusions rarely lasted very long before being reopened for debate and change. Other communes organized themselves in variations on these themes; their freedom to decide most of these issues for themselves was nearly complete (Stites 1989, 214–22). Such communes created a kind of "free zone" where ideals of communism could be reasonably and legally pursued. While some communes did not include the production, appropriation, and distribution of household surplus labor among the social processes handled collectively, others clearly did so. In ways rarely seen elsewhere in Soviet society, the communist class structured households of the 1920s combined the values of solidarity, democracy, equality, and collectivism in concentrated examples of how the revolution's stated goals might be realized.

The changed circumstances of the later 1920s changed the Soviet state's attitude toward the family and household, however. We show below why the state ceased subsidies to communes, including those with communist household class structures, and why it mounted a sustained campaign to celebrate instead the traditional family and its exploitative household class structures (although not, of course, in such a language of class).

Agricultural Enterprises

The Bolshevik alliance with the left Social Revolutionaries reflected their strategic acceptance of the indispensability of distributing land to the masses immediately after the 1917 revolution. This meant providing government sanction and support chiefly to one particular noncommunist class structure, what Marx labeled as the "ancient": Individual farmers produced, appropriated, and distributed their own surplus labor on their now privately owned land parcels. The tactical retreat of the New Economic Policy (NEP) further confirmed the freedoms of individual peasants to produce within the ancient class structure (Male 1971).

The NEP experience with ancient class structures in agriculture during the 1920s also displays a differentiation among these self-employed peasants. Some were indeed able to produce and distribute sufficient surplus labor to secure the conditions of their existence; some even secured the conditions for their own growth (buying or leasing more land, farm animals, equipment, and so on). Others succumbed to inclement weather, market difficulties of all sorts, illness or departures of family members, and the like. Out of the differentiation among ancient peasants emerged a different nonancient class structure that grew in the Soviet countryside.

Increasingly, the successful ancient peasants entered into a capitalist class relation with the unsuccessful ancients. The former bought or leased the land, farm animals, and equipment from the distressed or failing ancients. The latter then often sold their labor power to the former for a wage. In this way, the differentiation among ancient peasants matured—in some places and at some times—into the juxtaposition of agricultural capitalists and agricultural proletarians. The farms of the USSR in the 1920s thus demonstrated a multiple class structure composed mostly of a mass of ancients punctuated by a growing population of small and then medium capitalist farms.

The available evidence suggests that Soviet agriculture in the decade after the revolution also contained some collectivized farms with communist class structures (Wesson 1963, 54–63, 92–94, 109–37). The three types of collective farms—communes, artels, and *toz*—comprised at most 5 percent of all farms in these years. They varied chiefly in their degrees of collective and private property in land, animals, and equipment: from the communes that collectivized the most to the toz that did so least. Among a few of the communes and artels, their collectivization of property, labor, and consumption was accompanied by the collectivization as well of the appropriation and distribution of surplus. Hence in these few collective farms a communist class structure existed.[7] Wesson (1963) has carefully charted the erratic shifts among official support (including subsidies), neglect, and discouragement of the collectivized farms before 1929.

Relations between Industry and Agriculture

By the later 1920s, Soviet economic and political conditions prompted an intense debate over whether to maintain this multiple class structure, although not in the class terms used here. Stalin's rhetoric depicted Soviet agriculture in a very different class typology: as a vast terrain of class struggle between the rich ("capitalist kulaks") and the poor. The kulaks were denounced for price-gouging, generally abusing the rural poor, and keeping back grain and other products from the urban, industrial areas, thereby thwarting urgent economic development there. The latter, Stalin claimed, threatened Soviet survival; the former demanded the extension of the 1917 revolution to the countryside.

In the Bolshevik view, establishing large-scale state (i.e., socialist) industry as quickly as possible would limit and control this emerging capitalist (kulak) structure in agriculture associated with the NEP. Slow industrialization, especially one that provided agricultural inputs and consumer goods to farmers, was deemed dangerous, for it would give space and time for "capitalist agriculture" to grow stronger politically. At the same time, a strategy of fostering chiefly large-scale industry fit precisely into what the Soviets understood socialism to be all about. Because their revolution had displaced capitalist in favor of socialist relations of production (by socializing productive property and establishing a workers' state), economic development, now freed from its capitalist fetters, could be unleashed. The essential problem thus became one of developing the unconstrained forces of production. Large-scale industry embodying advanced technology offered the solution to this remaining singular and technical problem. Other considerations played a role as well. For example, many Soviet leaders feared that without the weapons and increased consumer goods that would eventually flow from large-scale industrial development, socialism would be vulnerable to dangerous external and internal pressures. For all such reasons, Soviet policy in the 1920s moved increasingly toward fostering state capitalist industrialization—not agriculture—as rapidly as possible.

This was to be accomplished by two kinds of industrial strategies: expanding capital accumulation in already existing state capitalist enterprises and creating additional state capitalist industrial complexes. The mechanism to accomplish these strategies was the first of several five-year plans. Their goal, the most rapid industrialization possible, required the mobilization of a growing food surplus from agriculture to feed what would become a growing industrial and urban proletariat. They also stressed drawing ever more agricultural raw materials to supply the input needs of expanding state capitalist industry.

In the later 1920s, the dominant position within the Bolshevik party—advocated by Stalin (although he initially opposed it)—urged, in the terms used here, state capitalist industrialization at the expense of the ancient and emerging private capitalist farmers in agriculture. State officials would plan to maximize the surplus value they appropriated from workers in state capitalist enterprises. Then they would distribute as much of that surplus as possible to expand capital in existing state capitalist industries and to establish still new ones. Moreover, whatever increased labor productivity that resulted from such a strategy would not be reflected in any cheapening of the state-administered prices of industrial goods available for farmers to buy.

On the contrary, over the entire NEP the terms of trade—the ratio between state-administered prices of agricultural goods and state-administered prices of industrial goods—favored state capitalist industry. The Bolshevik theoretician Preobrazhensky articulated the best-known formulation of this state-administered price strategy (1965). The point was to squeeze the maximum resources out of agriculture at the minimum cost to state capitalist industry, thereby leaving the state able to plow the maximum back into state capitalist industrial expansion. In addition, by so constraining the prevailing ancient and capitalist class structures in agriculture, the strategy would sap their political strength.

In our class-analytical terms, the problem faced by the Bolsheviks was that the surplus value (*sv*) produced by workers in state industrial enterprises and appropriated by state officials was less than the state's primary demand on that surplus: rapid capital accumulation in state industry. In simplest terms,

$$SV < SSCP_{(\Delta c + \Delta v)} + \sum SSCP_{\text{others}}.$$

Here, $SSCP_{(\Delta c + \Delta v)}$ is the portion of the appropriated surplus destined for capital accumulation in existing and newly established state industries. $\sum SSCP_{\text{others}}$ are the portions to pay for the planned growth in state bureaucracy to manage, politically control, and legitimate the regime of rapid state capitalist industrialization. In other words, the USSR's growth plan produced a major crisis for state capitalism as signaled in the above equation's inequality between the available surplus and the demands put upon it. If not resolved, that crisis would undermine the growth plan that the Bolsheviks thought crucial to realize socialism and preserve the USSR.

The pool of productive laborers in state capitalist industries could not generate sufficient surpluses, even as the industrial workday and the intensity of labor were repeatedly raised and even as wages were kept low. Preobrazhensky concluded that "primitive socialist accumulation" must get the necessary additional resources from *outside* of the state capitalist sector. Industry was to colonize agriculture by turning the internal terms of trade against it.

In our class terms, "where" the additional resources to finance industry were to be found can be shown by adding a new revenue term (NCR) to the left-hand side of the above equation. This was not an additional surplus appropriated from industrial workers; rather it was a *nonclass revenue,* NCR. It was a revenue gleaned for industry by administratively enforcing price ratios between industrial and agricultural products that favored the former. State capitalist industries could charge more for their products than their costs of production while farmers had to settle for less than theirs. In this way, such unequal exchanges between state capitalist industry and all the class structures in Soviet agriculture would siphon resources out of the latter and make them available for industrial accumulation.[8] The more the state tilted the terms of trade against farmers, the higher would be the nonclass revenues obtained to add to surpluses appropriated from industrial workers to finance state capitalist industrial growth.

This strategy, however, immediately provoked contradictions. The mass of ancient farmers, and especially the emerging capitalist farmers who supplied most of the grain and raw material surpluses for industry reacted to the enforced unequal exchange by holding back grain and raw material deliveries. The NCR destined to finance a quickened industrialization therefore tended to diminish in size. It threatened to disappear altogether in reaction to a continued decline in the terms of trade. If unchecked, this would thwart the goal of expanding accumulation in existing and newly established state capitalist industries. The more state capitalist industry relied on ancient and private capitalist (kulak) class structures in agriculture for its external resources, the more risky became its own continued development.

A Communism Attempted

Stalin's response to this contradiction was to take the revolution that had "succeeded" in the urban, industrial areas in 1917 and bring it to the countryside. He would extend "communism" from industry to agriculture, from town to country. In 1929 and 1930 he would collectivize agriculture and thereby "complete" the Bolshevik revolution begun in 1917. The hitherto marginal forms of commune, artel, and toz would be generalized throughout Soviet agriculture. Such collectivization would, the regime hoped, give the state a much more secure claim on the agricultural surpluses needed for rapid industrialization.

The slogans and contexts of the collectivization campaign, politicized as a drive to establish communism over against rural capitalism, contributed to the only widespread experiment in communist class structures attempted in Soviet history. So, too, did the actual conditions in the countryside. The mass of poorer ancient farmers and landless peasants, however hostile to richer ancient and capitalist farmers, also feared and opposed top-down, large, state-owned and -operated landholding units as likely reincarnations of centuries of feudal exploitation and oppression. They would thus not have welcomed massive state farms in which their positions would have been those of agricultural proletarians.

One key part of Stalin's solution thus lay in establishing pointedly non-state collective farms incorporating poor and landless peasants. These "private" collective farms were either mergers of individual peasants or obtained the land, animals, and equipment taken from the "class enemies": the kulaks and their ancient peasant allies.[9] In this "private" quality, the collective farms differed markedly from state industrial enterprises. Most of the latter had remained largely inside the state after 1917. As NEP gave way to the five-year plans, almost no industrial enterprises remained outside of the state apparatus. The new collective farms also differed from the simultaneously established state farms, which did function along industrial lines as large agricultural enterprises incorporated into the state. Stalin's policies in 1929 and 1930 repeatedly affirmed that the nonstate collective farms would be the overwhelmingly prevalent new form in agriculture; the state farms would be strictly limited.

In class terms, the collective farms differed from both state industrial and state farm enterprises. The latter were state-capitalist in their class structures. Large agglomerations of workers received wages for performing labor in them. State-appointed functionaries—first the members of Vesenkha and later of the Council of Ministers—appropriated and distributed the workers' surplus labor. The workers did not collectively appropriate and distribute their own surplus labor. In contrast, collective farm workers often did. At the sixteenth Party Congress in July 1930, the People's Commissar of Agriculture Yakovlev stressed the need to make sure

that questions about the distribution of the harvest are decided not behind the backs of the collective farmers in some office but, as is laid down by the directives of the party central committee, by the collective farmers themselves, by the general meeting of the collective farmers, with the approval of the general meeting of collective farmers.[10]

To the extent that such commitments at the top were actualized below, the class structure of the collective farms was communist.[11] The considerable degree of such actualization followed in part from the utopian impulses of the major organizers of the collectives, the famous "25,000ers," and in part from the complex of communal traditions and current conditions of the Soviet peasantry (Viola 1987).[12]

After they were formed in the crisis and chaos of the collectivization drives, many collective farms (*kolkhozy*) functioned roughly within the framework of communist class processes. Labor was performed collectively, the means of production were owned collectively, and the grains produced belonged first to that collective labor: "In the kolkhozy, peasant families had no personal connections with a particular piece of land, plough or horse, but the means of production and farm output belonged to them collectively as a group of private persons" (Davies 1980, 86). Endless meetings of the assembly of collective farm members effectively appropriated the surplus labor and distributed it. For example, the *Borietz* ("Fighter") kolkhoz 45 miles south of Moscow included 2,000 people working 6,300 acres in the mid-1950s (Dumont 1957, 510–13). Its top management comprised an elected council of nine persons, of whom eight participated in the regular agricultural work. Only the president was exempted from such labor. The council met twice per month and called a general meeting of the whole collective every three months (a periodicity reminiscent of the meetings of capitalist boards of directors). Laborers were organized into six brigades doing the different kinds of work included on this particular collective farm. The norms of labor (and hence remunerations) for each brigade were debated and decided by the general meeting; so, too, were the dispositions of surplus other than the mandated distributions to the state.

Of course, the sizes of the communist labor surpluses as well as the sizes of the shares of the surplus distributed to its various recipients/claimants were subject to (overdetermined by) all sorts of pressures from outside, as well as inside, of the collective farms' communist class structures.[13] These included the predictable Communist Party pressures, state demands for deliveries of major portions of the surplus for rapid industrialization, and a host of influences from the spectrum of political and cultural processes occurring within and around the collective farms.

There was also the pressure exercised, often quite subtly, by the competing demands of the collective farm members' interests in their own private plots of land. Members of the collective were given the right under statute to possess limited private plots and a specified number of different kinds of livestock. It is estimated that 40 percent of total agricultural labor was expended on these private plots; they were a major factor of Soviet rural life (Durgin 1994, 213–14). The production on such plots operated within an ancient class structure; individual collective farmers produced and appropriated their own surplus on those plots. Thus, members of collective farms participated in both communist and ancient class structures on a regular basis.[14] On the one hand, labor done within one class structure often substituted for labor done in the other; resources applied to one were therefore unavailable for the other; the culture of one class structure conflicted with and undermined that of the other; and so forth. On the other hand, complementarities also were present: Livestock used on ancient farms could be grazed on, and sometimes also used on, the collective land; horses and equipment used in the communist class structure were made available to the ancient class structure; and the income from ancient farming could supplement communist returns. In short, the collective farm members' participations within both ancient and communist class structures influenced the quantitative dimensions of both. Generally, however, "the tension between household plot and collective work remained a permanent feature of the kolkhoz, usually resolved by the collective farmer in favor of his own plot" (Davies 1980, 110).

To this complexity we must add the further pressures exercised on the collective farms' communist class structures by other class structures operating in the countryside. For example, throughout the 1930s and beyond, some peasants remained outside the collective and state farms as independent farm households.[15] Inside the collective farm's households, feudal class structures of household labor imposed particular burdens on the wives, whose functioning as household serfs often precluded their full participation in, and hence influence on, the communist class processes within the collective farms. To mention yet another example, the evidence of some collective farms hiring wage laborers raises the issue of how such noncommunist class structures influenced the communist class structures of the collectives (Fitzpatrick 1994, 148). In any case, the thoughts and behaviors of collective farm members reflected their participation in multiple, interactive, and often contradictory class structures there. Moreover, that participation was further conditioned by the context of all the nonclass processes (cultural, political, and economic) that combined to overdetermine the collective farm's set of interacting class structures.

Communisms Abandoned

The establishment of communist class structures in the collective farms had economic, political, and cultural consequences other than providing agricultural surpluses for industrialization. The communist collectives also challenged Soviet state policies in several ways. In their new and heady positions as collective appropriators and distributors, the farmers could and did clash with state officials on a host of issues (Viola 1987; Davies 1980). Their attitudes toward fulfilling production plans for food and raw materials (to be delivered to the state for rapid heavy industrialization) were different from those of state planners, as were their assessments of the resources they needed as agricultural inputs. The political and cultural conditions they viewed as crucial for collective farm success were not identical to the political and cultural conditions favored by the central state, focused as it was on its industrial priorities.

Perhaps the most striking example of these differences concerned how the state would acquire the food and raw materials needed for state capitalist industrial expansion. The state wanted not only to continue Preobrazhensky's squeeze on agriculture—now largely comprised of collective farms—by keeping the terms of trade against them but also charged high rents on (or inflated prices for) the machine tractors that collectives increasingly had to use. The collective farms had to distribute huge shares of their communist surpluses to the state as either rents or purchase prices for the tractors. While this strategy might boost the state's revenues available for industrial growth, it also tended to erode the viability of the collectives' communist class structures. With so large a portion of their communist surpluses distributed to the state (via unequal exchanges and tractor costs), too little surplus remained to secure the other conditions of existence of the collective farms.[16]

Consider communist collectives in which grain was produced for sale to the state. The price the state set for the collectives was below the labor cost for that same commodity. Under these circumstances, the value equation for the communist production of grain became:

$$(COM\ C + COM\ NL + COM\ SL) - NCR = P \times UV.[17]$$

Here *COM C* stands for constant capital (the cost of the tools, equipment, and raw materials) used up in grain production. *COM NL* represents the cost of the collective workers (what they require as their income). *COM SL* is the value of the surplus labor produced and also appropriated by that same collective of workers. Before explaining the term *NCR*, we need to consider the right-hand side of this equation. The term *UV* represents the total units of grain output, while *P* represents the price of grain set by the central state-planning authorities. Insofar as that price was set *below* the cost of producing grain (*COM C + COM NL + COM SL*), the equation has to contain a term representing how much of the communist collective farm's cost of producing grain was *not* recovered in the price paid by the state for that grain: This difference is the *NCR* and thus appears as a subtraction on the left side of the equation.

The economic well-being of communist collectives eroded so long as this *NCR* was subtracted from the communist surplus available to support the collectives' class structure. Yet even this price-coercion was not the only constraining force hindering communist class structures in the collectives. The Soviet state ordered communist appropriators within the collectives to pay for still other state services (tractor rentals and sales, education, protection, and so on) with other distributed portions of their appropriated surpluses.[18] The latter formed a communist subsumed class revenue (COMSSCR) added to the other kinds of value flows received by the state. Thus, total revenues available to expand state capitalist industry were the surpluses appropriated inside state capitalist industries supplemented by "external sources": (1) the state-mandated unequal exchanges between industry and agriculture; and (2) the state-mandated distributions to itself of portions of communist surpluses produced and appropriated by communist collective farmers. Whereas before collectivization the source of revenue had been ancient and capitalist farms, after collectivization it became the communist farms.

The existence and size of this so-called external source shows how in the history of the USSR—under Stalin's collectivization drive and five-year plans—communist class structures in agriculture were able to secure one of the key conditions of existence for the expansion of state capitalism in industry. In that sense, there was no inevitable conflict between the existence of communism and capitalism. On account of the state's continued attempts to increase both NCR and COMSSCR, however, pressure on the collectives mounted. Indeed, the standard of living of communist workers declined. They were caught in the double bind presented by the state's moves to simultaneously reduce its purchase price of grain and increase its subsumed class revenues from the collectives. If collectives could not reduce their other subsumed class payments (many of which were mandated by the same state officials) or reduce its costs of constant capital, its communist, necessary labor would be reduced. This incessant pressure on the standard of living within communist class structures helped push their workers to seek out new kinds of revenues.

The collective farm workers found those revenues partly in their individual private plots, which became progressively more important to them and thereby created problems in securing both collective farm members' labor contributions and loyalty to the collective farm. This in turn worked to undermine the success of the collective farms in meeting the state plans for agricultural surpluses needed for industrialization. One reaction of the Soviet state to these contradictions was to substitute state capitalist for communist class structures in Soviet agriculture, hoping thereby to facilitate the transfer of agricultural surpluses to industry and the cities. Of course, this was not done with an explicit discussion of the class aspects and implications of such a strategy, since no such class analysis was available or tolerable. Instead, debates and policies appeared exclusively concerned with product flows.

Thus, even though the collective farms persisted until the end of the USSR, communist class structures continually gave way to noncommunist class structures in Soviet agriculture from the 1930s until the USSR's demise. One way this happened was through the steady shift of agricultural labor from collective to state farms (*sovkhoz*). The state farms were organized explicitly along the lines of industrial enterprise, that is, as state capitalist enterprises with workers receiving wage payments for their labor power. In 1940, there were 29 million active workers on collective farms but less than 3 million on state farms.[19] By 1970, state farm employment had risen to 9.8 million, while collective farm labor had fallen to 17 million. By 1990, state farm employment nearly equaled collective farm employment: 11 million to 11.3 million workers. In this sense, the history of the USSR displays the substitution of capitalist for communist class structures in agriculture.

That substitution took place not only by the shift from collective to state farms; it occurred as well within the collective farms themselves. The shift to wage-labor conditions inside collective farms partly followed from their expansion: from 81 households per collective farm in 1940 to over 400 (on average) after 1970. The large size of the collectives made them resemble the state farms, which may have stimulated their imitation of the latter's internal class structures, as well. Similarly, the development of rural industrial enterprises, based on wage labor and jointly owned and operated by the state and collective farms (for the purposes of constructing farm buildings, canning, machine repair, operating feed lots, and the like), brought collective farm members closer to the state farm's kind of class structure. Kerblay summarized the situation: "Since 1967, kolkhoz workers have been paid regular monthly wages based on sovkhoz pay scales . . . the kolkhoz worker is now paid as an employee and no longer out of . . . profits" (1983, 98). Similarly, a Soviet study of rural migrants to cities in the early 1960s ascertained:

The young people feel that they are not so much the masters (*khoziaevy*) as hired laborers in agricultural production; as a rule, they have no share in managing the collective farm, the section, or the brigade; they do not participate in the making of important decisions.[20]

This and much other evidence supports the notion that the mix of communist and noncommunist class structures inside collective farms was shifting toward the latter.

The state's nearly total prioritization of heavy industry also led the it to rethink its attitudes toward family and household class structures (Goldman 1993). The revolutionary commitments to women's equality grew in the 1920s to a sustained assault on women's traditional positions as a form of enslavement. Divorce, abortion, alimony entitlements, job opportunities, and political inclusion for women were dramatically liberalized. A consensus emerged that insofar as the traditional individual household had been a prison for women, the state should abolish it in favor of transforming cooking, cleaning, childcare, and so on into industries.

The individual household would totally cease to be a site of production of any of these services. Instead the state would establish them as industries delivering their products for collective consumption (for example, in mass dining, laundry, and childcare centers) rather than individual household consumption. In this way, the state would realize its revolutionary promises in a double sense: Women would be free from traditional household imprisonment and free for labor and politics on an equal footing with men.

While many aspects of this plan did reach fruition in the 1920s, contradictions and problems arose, as well. Long pent-up familial tensions split millions of families. Abandoned wives and children, without support from impoverished husbands unable or unwilling to pay alimony, turned to the state for costly support. When it did not materialize, vast populations of vagrants brought crime and intense social tensions to both the city and countryside; it also brought demands for the state to solve this problem. Establishing a massive industry to deliver collective consumption in place of individual household production and consumption likewise placed massive demands on a state with far too few resources to meet them, especially given its focus on industrialization.

By the later 1920s, the decision was clear: The state would abandon its efforts to eliminate the individual household in favor of mass collective consumption industries, and would instead return to the old-style individual households as producers and consumers of household services. The leading Soviet sociologist of the family used the term "compromise" to describe this shift of strategy; the individual family and household were the necessary "social cell . . . an auxiliary social formation" to manage the transition to socialism and communism in the USSR.[21]

In practice, this meant legislative action, such as recriminalizing abortion and making divorce increasingly difficult, as well as cultural actions, including intense campaigns to celebrate and reaffirm the importance of sustained nuclear families in single household units. From them, women and men should go forth to wage labor; in them, the labor needed to raise children and for household consumption should be performed. Because class analysis of the household was never broached, little attention was paid to how the surplus labor involved in such household labor would be organized, nor what effects such organization might have outside the households on Soviet development generally.

As a relatively minor adjunct to this strategic shift, the state abandoned subsidies to, indeed denounced, communal households as contrary to the re-idealized norm of "family life." The brief experiment in communist class structures ended. Their achievements and costs never received the examination and discussion needed to assess whether and how they might have been extended to Soviet society at large. Nor was there ever a subsequent debate over how Soviet history might have been different had such an extension been attempted or achieved. To date, most assessments of the USSR's history neither recognize nor examine the contributions made both by the early experiments in communist household class structures and by their abandonment in favor of feudal and ancient class structures as the Soviet norm after the 1920s. This is doubly remarkable in view of the combination of communist class structures in Soviet households with real, daily lives there characterized by extraordinary experiments in democracy, equality, and collectivism across genders, age differences, and kinship differences.

Communism and Soviet Development

Despite their constriction throughout the history of the USSR, the communist class structures of the early collective farms remain important as the country's only mass experiment of the kind. What never happened on a mass basis in industry or in households did happen in agriculture after 1929. Stalinism did preside, for a while, over a genuine class transition to communism. Nor should this remarkable fact remain obscured by the historical irony that Stalinism also later substituted state capitalist class structures for the few collective farms' communist class structures (and also undermined those class structures in the collective farms that remained). Stalinism, too, had its contradictions overdetermined by the contexts within which it arose, changed, and eventually died.

Protracted discussions, debates, and negotiations might have achieved workable compromises between collective farms and the state. These might have enabled the mutually productive coexistence of communist class structures in collective farms and the various noncommunist class structures elsewhere throughout Soviet society, but the Stalinist Soviet state had neither the theoretical framework nor the political will to engage such discussions, debates, and negotiations. Moreover, the deeply held mutual suspicions between urban and rural, industrial and agricultural, party and nonparty, educated and uneducated no doubt played important roles in overdetermining the breakdown of any negotiations that might have begun.

In different ways, but for many of the same reasons, the Soviet state both erected and eventually destroyed communist class structures in households and on collective farms. While these steps had positive results for the strategy of heavy industrialization, they also provoked costs and suggested the haunting possibility of successful strategies never fully glimpsed, much less pursued. Squeezing communist class structures in collective farms and households and forcing their return to exploitative class structures fostered a deep-seated individualism. In rural areas, this found expression in the focus on private plots at the expense of collective work and in the atrophy of agricultural development, which plague the USSR to its end. Across the society, another such expression lay in the many forms of popular disinterest in collective life, including the tendency to leave politics to an increasingly isolated and alienated Communist Party apparatus. The negative impacts on worker productivity and job-site responsibility flowed in part from household class struggles — class struggles over the feudal wives' household surplus labor and over the surplus ancient households could muster to sustain themselves. How the USSR's class structures contributed to the social costs of divorces, separations, alcoholism, and mental illness in class-conflicted households is unknown. Such issues could never be raised, let alone explored, discussed, estimated, or addressed by public policy.

Conclusion

We may conclude our analysis of communism in the USSR by saying that communist class structures were in fact established there, in its agriculture and in some households, but not in its industry. The relationship between industry and agriculture was such that a state capitalism in industry produced a communism in agriculture, not as its economic antithesis but rather as its complement, as one of its conditions of existence. That relationship helped provide the resources that allowed state capitalism in the USSR to grow rapidly. However, that same relationship also constrained the growth and viability of communism. Eventually, the communist class structure in agriculture gave way to state capitalist farming there, as well as to a reemergence of the ancients as an important part of the agrarian population. Over the same period, the demands of state capitalist industrial growth also undermined the continuation of experiments in communist household class structures that the revolution had originally provoked.

Major class transitions did occur in the USSR in and after the 1917 revolution, but they were not the ones most observers have presumed or claimed. What happened was a transition from experiments in communism (both in households and especially in farming enterprises) to the strengthening of feudal households, the hegemony of state capitalist farm and industrial enterprises, and the reemergence of ancients as a sizable and significant segment of the population. In part, the failure to establish communist class structures in all three sites—industry, households, and agriculture—resulted from the historical context of Soviet history and from the contradictions within and among the class structures at all three sites.

Another part of the explanation lies in the particular sort of culture that was established. Forming part of its nonclass structure, the kinds of Marxian theory developed there lacked an understanding of class structure in terms of the production, appropriation, and distribution of surplus. Lacking such an understanding of class structures and how they interact with one another and with their nonclass context, it is hard to imagine how the Soviet people and their leaders would have resolved their problems otherwise, even if and when historical circumstances provided the possibility of doing so. Thus, class theory mattered, too, in shaping the peculiar history of "communism" in the USSR. That lesson about the Soviet Union, as we argued in our introduction to this essay, can prove useful in new attempts to construct viable communist class and nonclass structures.

Notes

1 We gratefully acknowledge three readers who provided insightful and useful comments on an earlier draft of this essay. Kathie Gibson pressed us to further elaborate why communism might be an attractive class structure and what Soviet communist households and farm enterprises were like.

Julie Graham provided us with what we always hope to receive: an extensive, interesting, and useful set of comments on almost every aspect of this essay. Joseph Medley emphasized the contradictory relationship between what we call here "ancient" and "communist" farming, clarified the role of collectives in Soviet agricultural history, and provided valuable quantitative data sources.

2 For an extended definition and discussion of surplus labor—roughly, the workers' labor (or product) that exceeds what they take for their own consumption—see Resnick and Wolff (1987, especially chap. 3). The notions of exploitation and of fundamental and subsumed class process and positions used here are presented there as well.

3 Communism thus became a later stage of socialism's development when the total defeat of capitalism, coupled with socialism's presumed acceleration of technical progress, enabled the state apparatus to wither away to a minimum administrative functions and output, such that distribution could become based on need rather than productive effort.

4 We have explained elsewhere why we identify these particular state functionaries as the first appropriators and distributors of surpluses produced by Soviet workers (Resnick and Wolff 1994).

5 We would like to thank Sheila Rowbotham, who responded to an early presentation of the ideas in this essay by urging us to explore and include a systematic consideration of household relationships within the core of our argument.

6 The wife functioned as a household feudal serf bound by custom, law, and religion to the husband/lord whom she served by, among other things, performing household surplus labor and delivering its fruits to him (see Fraad, Resnick, and Wolff 1994, on the specificity of feudal household class structures). The pre-1917 households also displayed nonfeudal class structures. For example, adults often lived alone (with or without children). Their household labor—cooking, cleaning, clothing manufacture and repair—entailed not only the performance of both necessary and surplus labor but also individually appropriating and distributing their own surplus. This amounted to the kind of distinct nonfeudal class structure that Marx sometimes referred to as the "ancient" class structure (Gabriel 1990). Cameron (1996–97) and Gibson-Graham (1996) have argued persuasively that households (like enterprises or states) may well be sites that include the interaction of multiple class structures—feudal, ancient, and communist. While we agree, we have not yet incorporated their insight into our discussion of households here.

7 Wesson (1963) and also Male (1971, 56ff) indicate that most of the 1920s collective farms—including the communes—were not communist class organizations of production.

8 Suppose Gosplan estimates that eight hours of abstract labor are socially
   necessary to produce a unit of grain in ancient farms, and four hours of abstract labor are necessary to produce a unit of cloth in state capitalist industry. Suppose Gosplan also establishes an exchange ratio of one unit of grain
   equal to two units of cloth. Hence ancient farmers acquire two units of cloth
   for every unit of grain sold to the state. The state-set exchange ratio—like
   any market price—abstracts from the different class structures producing
   the two commodities.

   Suppose that the state sets a different exchange ratio; for example, that
   one unit of grain equals one unit of cloth. Then state capitalists need give up
   less cloth (four hours' worth) to gain the same amount of grain (eight hours'
   worth). This gain in resources of four hours defines our term NCR in the text;
   NCR is completely different from Marx's notion of class exploitation. The
   latter concerns the surplus labor appropriated in the ancient production of
   grain and the state capitalist production of cloth. The NCR represents rather
   an unequal exchange in which the state capitalist gains at the expense of the
   ancient farmer.

9 As Wesson shows, this was the same procedure as had been used right after
   the revolution to provide most collective farms with their initial endowments of land, animals, and equipment (1963, 92–94).

10 Quoted in Davies (1980, 13), whose research shows that the Soviet leadership generally recognized that the collective farm would function internally
   in ways different from what they viewed as the "well-organized Soviet
   factory" (Davies 1980, 12). Thus, a major reason why the early drive to
   organize huge collective farms (often referred to as "gigantomania") was
   quickly aborted in favor of much smaller units was precisely the difficulty of
   making the former conform to the commitment to have collective farmers
   themselves appropriate and distribute the fruits of their own surplus labor
   (Davies 1980, 57, 65).

11 Most analysts have used different terms to conclude that these collective
   farms were communist or socialist. For them, farm workers' collective
   ownership of the means of production seems to be the sole or most important sign of communism. Parallel, however, to our analysis of the class
   nature of industrial enterprises, we looked in the Soviet context to the presence of several other kinds of social processes (in addition to ownership) to
   conclude that, at least in many instances, collective farm workers appropri-

ated and distributed their own produced surplus labor. We found Davies's (1980) work especially useful in this regard.

12 There is more than a little irony here. The "25,000ers" sent to organize the collective farms were militants drawn largely from the ranks of urban, state capitalist industries. For them to transplant into the Soviet countryside the class structures they knew in industry suggests that they would have favored state capitalist class structures (called "socialist" in Soviet discourse then), not communist class structures. Yet the resistance of peasants to including their farms within the state, as well as their resistance to huge agglomerations of peasant families taken together with their long-standing communal traditions, proved to be issues on which the "25,000ers" and the Soviet leadership had to compromise. That compromise, as reflected in Yakovlev's speech quoted in the text above, emerged as a kind of communist class structure coexisting with an ancient class structure (on the individual family "private plots") in the nonstate collective farms.

13 To say that the collective farmers were the sole appropriator and distributor of their surplus is not the same as saying that they alone determined the sizes of the surplus and each of its distributions. That is, "communist" here refers to a kind of *class* process, not to the different *power* processes that influenced the size of the communist surpluses and its subsumed class distributions.

14 While posed in terms different than the class concepts used here, most analysts have recognized that members of collective farms participated in different kinds of economic structures. See, for example, the discussions on the contradictory relationship between collective (communist) and noncollective (ancient) farming activities in Davies (1980, chap. 4, 5), Nove (1989, 233–34), and Lewin (1985, chap. 7).

15 Fitzpatrick (1994, 106) notes that in 1933 such independent peasant households comprised 35 percent of rural households. While this fell quickly to only 7 percent in 1937, the existence of such presumably ancient class structures exerted its influence on collective farmers.

16 On the other hand, Dobb (1966, 252–53) argues that the state's mass investment in tractors likely helped raise the productivity of labor on the collective farms. In our class-analytical terminology, increased productivity released the labor time of some communist farm workers to engage either in ancient farming on their private plots or to leave the farms for state capitalist industry.

17 The terms of this equation utilize notations derived from our reading of Marx's discussion of capitalist enterprises and are adjusted instead to ac-

count for communist enterprises such as the Soviet collective farms. Thus *COM C* is the communist analog to Marx's constant capital; *COM NL* is the communist analog to Marx's necessary labor or wages; and *COM SL* is the communist analog to Marx's surplus labor or surplus value. As in Marx's original exposition, all of the terms in our formulation here are counted in hours of "socially necessary abstract labor time."

18 These communist subsumed class distributions can be seen as: *COM SL* = $COMSSCP_{culture} + COMSSCP_{(\Delta c + \Delta v)} + COMSSCP_{mts} + COMSSCP_{party\ officials}$ + . . . where the respective subscripts on the various communist subsumed class payments (*COMSSCP*) indicate the several different social processes secured. The $COMSSCP_{mts}$ indicates the rents or monopoly premium paid on the machines made available to the commune by the state's machine tractor stations. Such rents, an important part of the state's revenue flows, are denoted as a communist subsumed class revenue.

19 Data in this section are taken from the useful summaries of Soviet statistical studies in Kerblay (1983, 74–109) and Durgin (1994).

20 The study, performed by T. I. Zaslavskaia and her colleagues in Novosibirsk Province, is extensively discussed in Powell (1974).

21 These were the words of S. Vol'fson in 1929, as quoted in Goldman (1993, 310).

REFERENCES

□

Abrahamian, E. 1982. *Iran between Two Revolutions.* Princeton: Princeton University Press.

Afshari, M. 1983. "The Pishivaran and Merchants in Precapitalist Iranian Society: An Essay on the Background and Causes of the Constitutional Revolution." *International Journal of Middle East Studies* 15: 133–55.

Aglietta, M. 1979. *A Theory of Capitalist Regulation: The U.S. Experience.* Trans. D. Fernbach. London: New Left Books.

Alcaly, R. E. 1978. "An Introduction to Marxian Crisis Theory." In *U.S. Capitalism in Crisis,* ed. Crisis Reader Editorial Collective, 15–22. New York: Union for Radical Political Economics.

Alexander, J., and P. Alexander. 1982. "Shared Poverty as Ideology: Agrarian Relationships in Colonial Java." *Man* 17(4): 597–619.

Althusser, L. 1969. *For Marx.* Harmondsworth: Penguin.

———. 1970. *For Marx.* New York: Vintage Books.

———. 1971. *Lenin and Philosophy.* New York: Monthly Review Press.

Althusser, L., and E. Balibar. 1970. *Reading Capital.* Trans. B. Brewster. London: Verso.

Alvares, C. 1994. *Science, Development and Violence.* Delhi: Oxford University Press.

Amariglio, J. 1984a. "Economic History and the Theory of Primitive Socioeconomic Development." Ph.D. diss., Department of Economics, University of Massachusetts Amherst.

———. 1984b. *Forms of the Commune and Primitive Communal Class Processes.* Association for Economic and Social Analysis Discussion Paper 19. Department of Economics, University of Massachusetts Amherst.

———. 1998. "Poststructuralism." In *Handbook of Economic Methodology,* eds. J. Davis, D. Hands, and U. Maki. Cheltenham: Edward Elgar.

Amariglio, J., and D. Ruccio. 1994. "Postmodernism, Marxism, and the Critique of Modern Economic Thought." *Rethinking Marxism* 17 (3) (fall): 7–35.

Amin, S. 1974. *Accumulation on a World Scale: A Critique of the Theory of Underdevelopment.* New York: Monthly Review Press.

————. 1977. *Imperialism and Unequal Development.* New York: Monthly
Review Press.

Amuzegar, J. 1991. *The Dynamics of the Iranian Revolution.* Albany, N.Y.:
State University of New York Press.

Anderson, J. R. 1973. *A Geography of Agriculture in the United States
Southeast.* Budapest: Akademiai Ridao.

Andrews, R. 1996a. "Mezzadria (Sharecropping): The Conditions of Life of
Tuscan Peasants until around 1960." Department of Italian, University of
Leeds.

————. 1996b. "The End of Sharecropping in the Province of Siena: 1943–
1960." Department of Italian, University of Leeds.

Aoki, M. 1992. "Rethinking the Education Crisis." Paper presented at the
conference Marxism in the New World Order, University of Massachusetts
Amherst.

Arndt, H. W. 1987. *Economic Development: The History of an Idea.* Chicago:
University of Chicago Press.

Bagchi, A. K. 1992. *The Political Economy of Underdevelopment.*
Cambridge: Cambridge University Press.

Bales, K. 1999. *Disposable People: New Slavery in the Global Economy.*
Berkeley and Los Angeles: University of California Press.

Banuri, T. 1990a. "Development and the Politics of Knowledge: A Critical
Interpretation of the Social Role of Modernization." In *Dominating
Knowledge: Development, Culture, and Resistance,* eds. F. Appfel-Marglin
and S. Marglin. Oxford: Clarendon Press.

————. 1990b. "Modernization and Its Discontents: A Cultural Perspective
on the Theories of Development." In *Dominating Knowledge:
Development, Culture, and Resistance,* eds. F. Appfel-Marglin and
S. Marglin. Oxford: Clarendon Press.

Baran, P., and P. Sweezy. 1966. *Monopoly Capital: An Essay on the American
Social and Economic Order.* New York: Monthly Review Press.

Bardhan, P., and A. Rudra. 1978. "Interlinkage of Land, Labour and Credit
Relations: An Analysis of Village Survey Data in East India." *Economic
and Political Weekly* 13 (February).

————. 1980. "Terms and Conditions of Sharecropping Contracts: An
Analysis of Village Survey Data in India." *Journal of Development Studies*
16 (April): 287–302.

————. 1981. "Terms and Conditions of Labour Contracts in Agriculture:
Results of a Survey in West Bengal 1979." *Oxford Bulletin of Economics
and Statistics* 43 (February): 89–111.

Bardhan, P. K. 1984. *Land, Labor and Rural Poverty: Essays in Development Economics.* New York: Columbia University Press.

Barrow, C. 1990. *Universities and the Capitalist State.* Madison: University of Wisconsin Press.

Basu, K. 1990. *Agrarian Structure and Economic Underdevelopment.* New York: Harwood Publishers.

Bauen, R. 1995. "Co-ops, ESOPs, and Worker Participation." *Dollars and Sense* July/August: 58–61.

Baugh, T., and J. Ericson. 1992. "Trade and Exchange in Historical Perspective." In *The American Southwest and Mesoamerica: Systems of Prehistoric Exchange,* eds. J. Ericson and T. Baugh, 3–20. New York: Plenum Press.

Baumol, W. J., and W. E. Oates. 1979. *Economics, Environmental Policy and the Quality of Life.* Englewood Cliffs, N.J.: Prentice Hall.

———. 1988. *The Theory of Environmental Policy.* Cambridge: Cambridge University Press.

Bayat, A. 1987. *Workers and Revolution in Iran: A Third World Experience of Workers' Control.* London: Zed Books.

Bayman, J. 1995. "Rethinking 'Redistribution' in the Archaeological Record: Obsidian Exchange at the Marana Platform Mound." *Journal of Anthropological Research* 51: 37–63.

Behdad, S. 1989. "Winners and Losers of the Iranian Revolution: A Study in Income Distribution." *International Journal of Middle East Studies* 21: 327–58.

Benería, L. 1982. "Accounting for Women's Work." In *Women and Development: The Sexual Division of Labor in Rural Societies,* ed. L. Benería, 119–47. New York: Praeger.

———. 1996. "Thou Shalt Not Live by Statistics Alone, But It Might Help." *Feminist Economics* 2(3): 139–42.

Berger, S. 1980. "Discontinuity in the Politics of Industrial Society." In *Dualism and Discontinuity in Industrial Societies,* eds. S. Berger and M. Piore, 129–41. Cambridge: Cambridge University Press.

Bernstein, E. 1961. *Evolutionary Socialism: A Criticism and Affirmation.* Trans. E. C. Harvey. New York: Schocken Books.

Bettelheim, C. 1976. *Class Struggles in the USSR: First Period: 1917–1923.* Trans. B. Pearce. New York: Monthly Review Press.

———. 1978. *Class Struggles in the USSR: Second Period: 1923–1930.* Trans. B. Pearce. New York: Monthly Review Press.

Beverley, J., and J. Oviedo, eds. 1993. "The Postmodernism Debate in Latin America." *Boundary 2* 20 (fall).

Bhaduri, A. 1973. "A Study of Agricultural Backwardness under Conditions of Semi Feudalism." *Economic Journal* 83 (329): 120–37.

———. 1977. "On the Formation of Usurious Interest Rates in Backward Agriculture." *Cambridge Journal of Economics* 1 (March): 341–52.

———. 1981. "Class Relations and the Pattern of Accumulation in an Agrarian Economy." *Cambridge Journal of Economics* 11 (March): 36–46.

———. 1983. *The Economic Structure of Backward Agriculture.* London: Academic Press.

Bhagwati, J. 1993. *India in Transition: Freeing the Economy.* Oxford: Clarendon Press.

Bhagwati, J., and T. N. Srinivasan. 1993. *India's Economic Reforms.* New Delhi: Ministry of Finance, Economic Division.

Bhaskar, V., and A. Glyn. 1995. "Investment and Profitability: The Evidence from the Advanced Capitalist Countries." In *Macroeconomic Policy after the Conservative Era,* eds. G. A. Epstein and H. M. Gintis, 175–96. Cambridge: Cambridge University Press.

Biewener, C. 1987. "Class and Socialist Politics in France." *Review of Radical Political Economics* 19 (2): 61–76.

———. 1988. "Keynesian Economics and Socialist Politics in France: a Marxist Critique." *Review of Radical Political Economics* 20 (2–3): 149–55.

———. 1989a. "Socialist Politics and Theories of Money and Credit." *Review of Radical Political Economics* 21 (3): 58–63.

———. 1989b. "Credit Policy and Industrial Development: Strategies of the Socialist Government in France, 1981–1985." Ph.D. diss., Department of Economics, University of Massachusetts Amherst.

———. 1990. "Loss of a Socialist Vision in France." *Rethinking Marxism* 3 (3–4): 12–26.

Blanton, R., G. Feinman, S. Kowalewski, and P. Peregrine. 1996. "A Dual-Processual Theory for the Evolution of Mesoamerican Civilization." *Current Anthropology* 37: 1–14.

Bliss, C. J., and N. H. Stern. 1982. *Palanpur: The Economy of an Indian Village.* Oxford: Oxford University Press.

Blitz, J. 1993. *Ancient Chiefdoms of the Tombigbee.* Tuscaloosa: University of Alabama Press.

Bloch, M. 1961. *Feudal Society.* Chicago: University of Chicago Press.

Boden, D. 1994. *The Business of Talk: Organizations in Action.* Cambridge, Mass.: Polity Press.

Bond, P., and R. Townsend. 1996. "Formal and Informal Financing in a

Chicago Ethnic Neighborhood." *Economic Perspectives* July/August: 3–27.

Bottomore, T., ed. 1997. *A Dictionary of Marxist Thought.* London: Blackwell Publishers.

Bowles, S., and H. Gintis. 1976. *Schooling in Capitalist America.* New York: Basic Books.

Bowles, S., D. Gordon, and T. Weisskopf. 1986. "Power and Profits: The Social Structure of Accumulation and the Profitability of the U.S. Economy." *Review of Radical Political Economics* 18 (1/2): 132–67.

Bradley, R. 1992. "Marine Shell Exchange in Northwest Mexico and the Southwest." In *The American Southwest and Mesoamerica: Systems of Prehistoric Exchange,* eds. J. Ericson and T. Baugh, 285–92. New York: Plenum Press.

Brandfon, R. L. 1967. *Cotton Kingdom of the South: A History of the Yazoo Mississippi Delta from Reconstruction to the Twentieth Century.* Cambridge, Mass.: Harvard University Press.

Breneman, D. W. 1994. *Liberal Arts Colleges—Thriving, Surviving or Endangered?* Washington, D.C.: The Brookings Institution.

Callari, A., and D. Ruccio. 1996. "Introduction: Postmodern Materialism and the Future of Marxist Theory." In *Postmodern Materialism and the Future of Marxist Theory: Essays in the Althusserian Tradition,* eds. A. Callari and D. Ruccio, 1–48. Hanover, N.H.: Wesleyan University Press.

Callon, M., ed. 1998. *The Laws of the Markets.* Oxford: Blackwell Publishers.

Cameron, J. 1996–97. "Throwing a Dishcloth into the Works: Troubling Theories of Domestic Labor." *Rethinking Marxism* 9(2) (summer): 24–44.

Chakrabarti, A. 1996. "Indian Debates on Transition and Development: A Critique and Reformulation." Ph.D. diss., Department of Economics, University of California, Riverside.

Chase, W. J. 1990. *Workers, Society, and the Soviet State: Labor and Life in Moscow, 1918–1929.* Urbana: University of Illinois Press.

Chatterjee, P. 1986. *Nationalist Thought and Colonial World: A Derivative Discourse.* Delhi: Oxford University Press.

———. 1988. "On Gramsci's 'Fundamental Mistake.' " *Economic and Political Weekly: Review of Political Economy* 23 (3).

———. 1993. *Nation and its Fragments: Colonial and Post Colonial Histories.* Princeton: Princeton University Press.

Chatterjee, P., and G. Pandey, eds. 1992. *Subaltern Studies* vol. 7. Delhi: Oxford University Press.

Chattopadhyay, P. 1990a. "On the Question of the Mode of Production in Indian Agriculture: A Preliminary Note." In *Agrarian Relations and Accumulation: The 'Mode of Production' Debate in India,* ed. U. Patnaik, 72–83. Bombay: Oxford University Press and Sameeksha Trust.

———. 1990b. "An 'Anti-Kritik.' " In *Agrarian Relations and Accumulation: The 'Mode of Production' Debate in India,* ed. U. Patnaik, 98–106. Bombay: Oxford University Press and Sameeksha Trust.

Chaudhury, A. 1988. "From Hegemony to Counter Hegemony." *Economic and Political Hegemony: Review of Political Economy* 23 (3).

———. 1991-2. "From Hegel to Gramsci: Capital's Passive Revolution." *Society and Change* 8 (3/4).

———. 1994. "On Colonial Hegemony: Toward a Critique of Brown Orientalism." *Rethinking Marxism* 7 (4): 44–58.

Cherubini, G. 1990. "The Peasant and Agriculture." In *Medieval Callings,* ed. J. Le Goff, 113–37. Chicago: University of Chicago Press.

Cobb, C. 1993. "Archaeological Approaches to the Political Economy of Nonstratified Societies." In *Archaeological Method and Theory,* vol. 5, ed. M. Schiffer, 43–99. Tucson: University of Arizona Press.

Colton, J. 1988. "The Role of the Department in the Groves of Academe." In *The Academic Handbook,* eds. A. L. Deneef et al., 261–81. Durham, N.C.: Duke University Press.

Connolly, W. 1997. "Suffering, Justice and the Politics of Becoming." Paper presented at the Borderlands Conference, The Australian National University, Canberra, July.

Cooper, A. 1983. "Sharecroppers and Landlords in Bengal, 1930–50: The Dependency Web and Its Implications." *Journal of Peasant Studies* 10 (2/3): 227–55.

Cravey, A. 1997. "The Politics of Reproduction: Households in the Mexican Industrial Transition." *Economic Geography* 73 (2): 166–86.

Cropper, M., and W. E. Oates. 1992. "Environmental Economics: A Survey." *Journal of Economic Literature* 30 (June): 675–740.

Crush, J., ed. 1995. *Power of Development.* New York: Routledge.

Cullenberg, S. 1992. "Socialism's Burden: Toward a 'Thin' Definition of Socialism." *Rethinking Marxism* 5 (2): 64–83.

———. 1994. *The Falling Rate of Profit: Recasting the Marxian Debate.* London: Pluto Press.

Dallmayr, F. 1992. "Modernization and Postmodernization: Whither India?" *Alternatives* 17: 421–52.

Daly, H. E., and J. B. Cobb. 1994. *For the Common Good.* Boston: Beacon Press.

Daniel, P. 1972. *The Shadow of Slavery: Peonage in the South, 1901–1969.*
Urbana: University of Illinois Press.

Darity, W., and B. L. Horn. 1988. *The Loan Pushers: The Role of Commercial
Banks in the International Debt Crisis.* Cambridge, Mass.: Ballinger.

Davies, R. W. 1980. *The Soviet Collective Farm, 1929–1930.* Cambridge,
Mass.: Harvard University Press.

Davis, A., B. Gardner, and M. R. Gardner. 1941. *Deep South: A Social
Anthropological Study of Caste and Class.* Chicago: University of Chicago
Press.

Davis, R. L. F. 1982. *Good and Faithful Labour: From Slavery to
Sharecropping in the Natchez District, 1860–1890.* Contributions in
American History, no. 100. Westport, Conn.: Greenwood Press.

de Janvry, A. 1981. *The Agrarian Question and Reformism in Latin America.*
Baltimore: The Johns Hopkins University Press.

DeCanio, S. 1974. *Agriculture in the Postbellum South: The Economics of
Production and Supply.* Cambridge, Mass.: MIT Press.

DeMartino, G. 1993. "The Necessity/Contingency Dualism in Marxian Crisis
Theory: The Case of Long-Wave Theory." *Review of Radical Political
Economics* 25 (3): 68–74.

Dennis, W. L. 1978. "The Community Reinvestment Act of 1977." *Banking
Law Journal* 95 (September): 694–96.

Dimock, W. C., and M. T. Gilmore, eds. 1994. *Rethinking Class: Literary
Studies and Social Formations.* New York: Columbia University Press.

Diskin, J. 1990. "Classical Marxian Economic Theory and the Concept of
Socialism." Ph.D. diss., Department of Economics, University of
Massachusetts Amherst.

———. 1996. "Rethinking Socialism: What's in a Name?" In *Postmodern
Materialism and the Future of Marxist Theory; Essays in the Althusserian
Tradition,* eds. A. Callari and D. Ruccio, 278–99. Hanover, N.H.:
Wesleyan University Press.

Dobb, M. 1966. *Soviet Economic Development since 1917.* New York:
International Publishers.

Donaldson, M. 1981. "Steel into the Eighties: The Rise and Rise of BHP."
Journal of Australian Political Economy 10: 37–45.

Donaldson, M., and T. Donaldson. 1983. "The Crisis in the Steel Industry."
Journal of Australian Political Economy 14: 33–43.

Dryzek, J. S. 1992. "Ecology and Discursive Democracy: Beyond Liberal
Capitalism and the Administrative State." *Capitalism, Nature, Socialism*
2 (June): 18–42.

Du Bois, W. E. B. 1989. *The Souls of Black Folk.* London: Penguin Books.

Duby, G. 1968. *Rural Economy and Country Life in the Medieval West.* Trans.
C. Postan. London: Edward Arnold.

———. 1978. *The Three Orders: Feudal Society Imagined.* Chicago:
University of Chicago Press.

Dumont, R. 1957. *Types of Rural Economy: Studies in World Agriculture.*
New York: Frederick A. Praeger.

Dunbar, A. 1968. "The Will to Survive: A Study of a Mississippi Plantation
County Based on the Words of its Citizens." Southern Regional Council
and the Mississippi Council on Human Rights.

Durgin, F. A. 1994. "Russia's Private Farm Movement: Background and
Perspectives." *Soviet and Post-Soviet Review* 21 (2/3): 211–52.

Dymski, G. 1995/6. "Business Strategy and Access to Capital in Inner-City
Revitalization." *Review of Black Political Economy* 24 (2/3) (fall/winter):
51–65.

———. 1996. "Financing Strategies and Structures of Impoverishment: The
Grameen and South Shore Models." Working Paper in Economics 96–09,
Department of Economics, University of California, Riverside.

Dymski, G., G. Epstein, and R. Pollin, eds. 1993. *Transforming the U.S.
Financial System: Equity and Efficiency for the 21st Century.* Armonk,
N.Y.: M. E. Sharpe.

Earle, T. 1994. "Positioning Exchange in the Evolution of Human Society."
In *Prehistoric Exchange Systems in North America,* eds. T. Baugh and
J. Ericson, 419–37. New York: Plenum Press.

Ellerman, D. 1984. "Entrepreneurship in the Mondragón Cooperatives."
Review of Social Economy 42: 272–94.

Elson, D., and R. Pearson. 1981. "The Subordination of Women and the
Internationalization of Factory Production." In *Of Marriage and the
Market: Women's Subordination in International Perspective,* eds.
K. Young, C. Wolkowitz, and R. McCullagh, 144–66. London: CSE.

Emmanuel, A. 1972. *Unequal Exchange: A Study of the Imperialism of
Trade.* New York: Monthly Review Press.

ENGENDER. 1995. "Report on Work Activities, 8 December 1992–31 March
1995." Manuscript, ENGENDER, Centre for Environment, Gender, and
Development, 14C Trenggany Street, Singapore 0105.

———. 1996. "The Gender and Development Resource Bank: A Concept
Paper for an Innovative Approach to Poverty Alleviation." Manuscript,
ENGENDER, Centre for Environment, Gender, and Development, 14C
Trenggany Street, Singapore 0105.

Ericson, J., and T. Baugh, eds. 1992. *The American Southwest and
Mesoamerica: Systems of Prehistoric Exchange.* New York: Plenum Press.

Escobar, A. 1984. "Discourse and Power in Development: Michel Foucault and the Relevance of His Work to the Third World." *Alternatives* 10 (3): 377–400.

———. 1992. "Reflections on 'Development': Grassroots Approaches and Alternative Politics in the Third World." *Futures* 24 (5): 411–36.

———. 1995. *Encountering Development: The Making and Unmaking of the Third World.* Princeton, N.J.: Princeton University Press.

Escobar, A., and S. E. Alvarez, eds. 1992. *The Making of Social Movements in Latin America.* Boulder, Colo.: Westview Press.

Fagan, R. H. 1984. "Corporate Strategy and Regional Uneven Development in Australia: The Case of BHP Ltd." In *The Geography of Australian Corporate Power,* ed. M. Taylor, 91–124. Sydney: Croom Helm.

———. 1986. "Australia's BHP Ltd—An Emerging Transnational Resources Corporation." *Raw Materials Report* 4: 46–55.

Fine, B. 1983. "Accumulation." In *Dictionary of Marxist Thought,* ed. T. Bottomore, 3–4. Cambridge, Mass.: Harvard University Press.

Fine, B., and L. Harris. 1979. *Rereading Capital.* New York: Columbia University Press.

Finkin, M. W. 1988. "The Tenure System." In *The Academic Handbook,* eds. A. L. Deneef et al., 86–100. Durham, N.C.: Duke University Press.

Fitzpatrick, S. 1994. *Stalin's Peasants: Resistance and Survival in the Russian Village after Collectivization.* New York: Oxford University Press.

Fligstein, N. 1997. *Markets, Politics and Globalization.* Uppsala, Sweden: Uppsala University Press.

Foran, J., ed. 1994. *A Century of Revolution: Social Movements in Iran.* Minneapolis: University of Minnesota Press.

Foster, J. B. 1993. "The Limits of Environmentalism without Class: Lessons from the Ancient Forest Struggle of the Pacific Northwest." *Capitalism, Nature, Socialism* 4 (March): 11–41.

Foucault, M. 1972. *The Archaeology of Knowledge.* Trans. A. M. Sheridan Smith. New York: Harper and Row.

Fraad, H., S. Resnick, and R. Wolff. 1994. *Bringing It All Back Home: Class, Gender and Power in the Modern Household.* London: Pluto Press.

Frank, A. G. 1966. "The Development of Underdevelopment." *Monthly Review* 18 (Sept): 17–31.

———. 1969. *Capitalism and Underdevelopment in Latin America: Historical Studies of Chile and Brazil.* New York: Monthly Review Press

Frazier, E. F. 1949. *The Negro in the United States.* New York: Macmillan.

Gabriel, S. 1990. "Ancients: A Marxian Theory of Self-Exploitation." *Rethinking Marxism* 3 (1): 85–106.

Gandhi, M. K. 1958. *The Collected Works of Mahatma Gandhi.* 90 vols. New Delhi: Publications Division.

Garwood, G. L., and D. S. Smith. 1993. "The Community Reinvestment Act: Evolution and Current Issues." *Federal Reserve Bulletin* April: 251–67.

George, S. 1990. *A Fate Worse than Debt.* New York: Grove Weidenfeld.

Ghaffari, R. 1995. "The Economic Consequences of Islamic Fundamentalism in Iran." *Capital and Class* 56: 91–115.

Ghasimi, M. R. 1992. "The Iranian Economy after the Revolution: An Economic Appraisal of the Five-Year Plan." *International Journal of Middle East Studies* 24: 599–614.

Ghosh, A. 1995. "Economy and the Budget." *Economic and Political Weekly* 30: 18–19.

Gibson-Graham, J. K. 1993. "Waiting for the Revolution, or How to Smash Capitalism while Working at Home in Your Spare Time." *Rethinking Marxism* 6 (2) (summer): 10–24.

———. 1996. *The End of Capitalism (As We Knew It): A Feminist Critique of Political Economy.* Oxford and Cambridge, Mass.: Blackwell.

Gibson-Graham, J. K., S. Resnick, and R. Wolff, eds. 2000. *Class and Its 'Others.'* Minneapolis: University of Minnesota Press.

Gilpin, K. 1997. "Piggy Banks with Muscles. As Credit Unions Boom, Financial Rivals Cry Foul." *New York Times,* February 26, B1, B21.

Gismondi, M., and M. Richardson. 1994. "Discourse and Power in Environmental Politics: Public Hearings on a Bleached Kraft Pulp Mill in Alberta, Canada." In *Is Capitalism Sustainable: Political Economy and the Politics of Ecology,* ed. M. O'Connor, 232–52. New York: Guilford Press.

Goldman, W. 1993. *Women, the State, and Revolution: Soviet Family Policy and Social Life, 1917–1936.* Cambridge: Cambridge University Press.

Goodwin, C. D. 1988. "Some Tips on Getting Tenure." In *The Academic Handbook,* eds. A. L. Deneef et al., 101–9. Durham, N.C.: Duke University Press.

Gordon, D. 1978. "Up and Down the Long Roller Coaster." In *U.S. Capitalism in Crisis,* ed. Crisis Reader Editorial Collective, 22–35. New York: Union for Radical Political Economics.

Gordon, D., R. Edwards, and M. Reich. 1982. *Segmented Work, Divided Workers.* Cambridge: Cambridge University Press.

Gordon, J. 1995. "Ok Tedi: The Law Sickens from a Poisoned Environment." *Australian Law Society Journal* 33 (9): 58–62.

Government of India, Ministry of Finance Discussion Paper. 1993. *Economic Reforms: Two Years after and the Task Ahead.* New Delhi: Ministry of Finance, Economic Division.

————. 1995. *Economic Survey 1994-95.* New Delhi: Ministry of Finance, Economic Division.

Graham, J. 1992. "Post-Fordism as Politics: The Political Consequences of Narratives on the Left." *Environment and Planning D: Society and Space* 19 (4): 393-410.

Gramsci, A. 1971. *Selections from the Prison Notebooks.* Trans. Q. Hoare and G. N. Smith. New York: International Publishers.

Granovetter, M. 1973. "The Strength of Weak Ties." *Sociology* 78: 1360-80.

Grassroots Economic Organizing Newsletter (GEO). Various issues. The Ecological Democracy Institute of North America, Stillwater, Pa.

Grossman, H. 1992. *The Law of Accumulation and Breakdown of the Capitalist System: Being Also a Theory of Crises.* Trans. J. Banaji. London: Pluto Press.

Grosz, E. 1990. "Philosophy." In *Feminist Knowledge: Critique and Construct,* ed. S. Gunew, 147-74. New York: Routledge.

Gudeman, S., and A. Rivera. 1990. *Conversations in Colombia: The Domestic Economy in Life and Text.* Cambridge: Cambridge University Press.

Guha, R. 1982-1990. *Subaltern Studies,* 6 vols., ed. R. Guha. Delhi: Oxford University Press.

Gunn, C., and H. D. Gunn. 1991. *Reclaiming Capital: Democratic Initiatives and Community Development.* Ithaca, N.Y.: Cornell University Press.

Guskin, A. E. 1994. "Reducing Students Costs and Enhancing Student Learning—The University Challenge of the 1990s: Part I: Restructuring the Administration." *Change* (July/Aug): 23-29.

————. 1994. "Reducing Students Costs and Enhancing Student Learning: Part II: Restructuring the Role of the Faculty." *Change* (Sept/Oct): 16-25.

Hall, J. R., ed. 1997. *Reworking Class.* Ithaca, N.Y.: Cornell University Press.

Hamermesh, D. S. 1996. "Not So Bad: The Annual Report on the Economic Status of the Profession." *Academe* (March–April): 14-39.

Harvey, D. 1982. *The Limits to Capital.* Chicago: University of Chicago Press.

————. 1993. "The Nature of Environment: The Dialectics of Social and Environmental Change." In *Socialist Register 1993,* eds. R. Miliband and L. Panitch, 1-51. London: Merlin Press.

Hay, M. J., and S. Stichter. 1984. *African Women South of the Sahara.* New York: Longman.

Hayden, F. G., and L. D. Swanson. 1980. "Planning through the Socialization of Property Rights: The Community Reinvestment Act." *Journal of Economic Issues* 15 (2): 351-69.

Helms, M. 1992. "Long Distance Contacts, Elite Aspirations, and the Age of Discovery in Cosmological Context." In *Resources, Power, and Interregional Interaction,* eds. E. Schortman and P. Urban, 157–74. New York: Plenum Press.

Higgs, R. 1971. *The Transformation of the American Economy, 1865–1914: An Essay in Interpretation.* New York: Wiley.

———. 1977. *Competition and Coercion: Blacks in the American Economy, 1865–1914.* Cambridge: Cambridge University Press.

Hilferding, R. 1981. *Finance Capital: A Study of the Latest Phase of Capitalist Development.* Trans. M. Watnick and S. Gordon. Boston: Routledge and Kegan Paul.

Hindess, B., and P. Hirst. 1977. *Pre-Capitalist Modes of Production.* London: Routledge and Kegan Paul.

Hodder, I. 1991. "Interpretive Archaeology and Its Role." *American Antiquity* 56: 7–18

hooks, b. 1994. *Teaching to Transgress: Education as the Practice of Freedom.* New York: Routledge.

Hopwood, A. G., and P. Miller, eds. 1994. *Accounting as Social and Institutional Practice.* Cambridge: Cambridge University Press.

Horstman, M. 1996. "BHP Strikes in Dominica . . ." *Multinational Monitor* 17 (9): 6–7.

Howard, M. C., and J. E. King. 1989. *A History of Marxian Economics;* Volume 1, *1883–1929.* Princeton: Princeton University Press.

Howitt, R. 1994. "Aborigines, Bauxite and Gold." *Raw Materials Report* 10 (2): 18–24.

———. 1995. "Developmentalism, Impact Assessment and Aborigines: Rethinking Regional Narratives at Weipa." NARU Discussion Paper 24, North Australian Research Unit, Darwin.

Ironmonger, D. 1996. "Counting Outputs, Capital Inputs and Caring Labor: Estimating Gross Household Product." *Feminist Economics* 2 (3): 37–64.

Jabbari, A. 1981. "Economic Factors in Iran's Revolution: Poverty, Inequality, and Inflation." In *Iran: Essays on a Revolution in the Making,* eds. A. Jabbari and R. Olson, 163–214. Lexington, Ky.: Mazda Publishers.

Jackson Advocate. Various issues.

Jarosz, L. A. 1990. "Rice on Shares: Agrarian Change and the Development of Sharecropping in Alaotra, Madagascar." Ph.D. diss., University of California, Berkeley.

Jazani, B. 1980. *Capitalism and Revolution in Iran.* London: Zed Press.

Jensen, M., and W. Meckling. 1976. "Theory of the Firm: Managerial

Behavior, Agency Costs and Ownership Structure." *Journal of Financial Economics* 3 (4): 305–60.

Jensen, R. 1982. "The Transition from Primitive Communism: The Wolof Social Formation." *Journal of Economic History* 42: 69–78.

Jordan, J. 1989. "The Multi-stakeholder Approach to Worker Ownership." In *Partners in Enterprise,* eds. J. Quarter and G. Melnyk, 118–35. Montreal: Black Rose.

Joyce, P., ed. 1995. *Class.* Oxford: Oxford University Press.

Kabeer, N. 1994. *Reversed Realities: Gender Hierarchies in Development Thought.* London: Verso.

Kallia-Antoniou, A., N. Paleologou, and S. Portoliou-Mihail. 1989. *The Greek and the European Community Law for the Protection of the Environment (1987–1988).* Athens: A. Sakkoula Editions.

Kasmir, S. 1996. *The Myth of Mondragon: Cooperatives, Politics, and Working-Class Life in a Basque Town.* Albany: State University of New York Press.

Katouzian, H. 1981. *The Political Economy of Modern Iran: 1929–1979.* New York and London: New York University Press.

Kautsky, K. 1971. *The Class Struggle.* New York: W. W. Norton.

Kayatekin, S. A. 1990. "A Class Analysis of Sharecropping." Ph.D. diss., Department of Economics, University of Massachusetts Amherst.

———. 1996–97. "Sharecropping and Class: A Preliminary Analysis." *Rethinking Marxism* 9 (1): 28–57.

Kayatekin, S. A., and S. Charusheela. 2000. "Reconstituting the Feudal Subject: Toward a Non-Modernist Approach." Paper presented at the Marxism 2000 Conference, University of Massachusetts Amherst, September 21–24.

Keddie, N. R., and E. Hooglund, eds. 1986. *The Iranian Revolution and the Islamic Republic.* Syracuse, N.Y.: Syracuse University Press.

Kerblay, B. 1983. *Modern Soviet Society.* Trans. R. Swyer. New York: Pantheon.

Kohl, P. 1979. "The 'World Economy' in West Asia in the Third Millenium B.C." In *South Asian Archaeology 1977,* ed. M. Taddei, 55–85. Naples: Instituto Universitario Orientale.

Kohler, T. 1993. "News from the Northern American Southwest: Prehistory on the Edge of Chaos." *Journal of Archaeological Research* 1: 267–321.

Kosminskii, E. A. 1956. *Studies in the Agrarian History of England in the Thirteenth Century.* Oxford: Blackwell.

Kumar, A., ed. 1997. *Class Issues.* New York: New York University Press.

Laclau, E. 1984. "The Controversy over Materialism." In *Rethinking Marx,* eds. S. Hanninen and L. Paldan, 39–43. New York: International General/IMMRC.

Laclau, E., and C. Mouffe. 1985. *Hegemony and Socialist Strategy.* London: Verso.

Larcombe, G. 1983. "Corporate Strategies or Economic Planning? The Future of Australia's Industrial Regions." In *Policy Priorities for Australian Steel Regions,* eds. M. T. Gordon and B. L. T. Gordon, 47–63. Institute of Industrial Economics, Newcastle: University of Newcastle.

Le Goff, J., ed. 1988. *The Medieval Imagination.* Chicago: University of Chicago Press.

Lee, R. 1990. "Primitive Communism and the Origin of Social Inequality." In *The Evolution of Political Systems,* ed. S. Upham, 225–46. Cambridge: Cambridge University Press.

Lee, S. 1997. "The Ok Tedi River: Papua New Guinea or the Parish of St Mary Le Bow in the Ward of Cheap?" *Australian Law Journal* 8: 602–18.

Leff, E. 1992. "A Second Contradiction of Capitalism? Notes for the Environmental Transformation of Historical Materialism." *Capitalism, Nature, and Socialism* 3 (December): 109–16.

———. 1993. "Marxism and the Environmental Question: From the Critical Theory of Production to an Environmental Rationality for Sustainable Development." *Capitalism, Nature, Socialism* 4 (March): 44–66.

———. 1995. *Green Production: Toward an Environmental Rationality.* New York: Guilford.

Lehmann, D. 1985. "Sharecropping and the Capitalist Transition in Agriculture: Some Evidence from the Highlands of Ecuador." *Journal of Development Economics* 23.

Lekson, S., T. Windes, J. Stein, and W. J. Judge. 1988. "The Chaco Canyon Community." *Scientific American* 259: 100–109.

Levy, H. M. 1987. "The Yeshiva Case Revisited." *Academe* (Nov–Dec): 34–37.

Lewin, M. 1985. *The Making of the Soviet System.* New York: Pantheon Books.

Lipietz, A. 1987. *Mirages and Miracles: The Crises of Global Fordism.* London: Verso.

Low, N., and B. Gleeson. 1998. "Situating Justice in the Environment: The Case of BHP at the Ok Tedi Copper Mine." *Antipode* 30 (3): 201–26.

Lubell, H. 1991. *The Informal Sector in the 1980s and 1990s.* Paris: OECD.

Luxemburg, R. 1972. *The Accumulation of Capital: An Anti-Critique.* Ed. K. J. Tarbuck; trans. R. Wichmann. New York: Monthly Review Press.

Magner, D. K. 1996. "A Parlous Time for Tenure." *Chronicle of Higher Education* (May 17): A21–A23.

Malam, L. 1998. "What Does the Creation of BHP's 'Guide to Business Conduct' Tell Us about Corporate Culture in the Late 20th Century?" Unpublished BSc (Hons) thesis, Department of Geography and Environmental Science, University of Newcastle, NSW, Australia.

Male, D. J. 1971. *Russian Peasant Organization before Collectivization.* Cambridge: Cambridge University Press.

Mandel, E. 1990. "Karl Marx." In *The New Palgrave, Marxian Economics,* eds. J. Eatwell, M. Milgate, and P. Newman, 1–38. New York: W. W. Norton.

Mandle, J. R. 1978. *The Roots of Black Poverty: The Southern Plantation Economy after the Civil War.* Durham, N.C.: Duke University Press.

Manzo, K. 1991. "Modernist Discourse and the Crisis of Development Theory." *Studies in Comparative International Development* 26 (summer): 3–36.

Marchand, M. H., and J. L. Parpart, eds. 1995. *Feminism/Postmodernism/Development.* New York: Routledge.

Marin, A. 1990. "Environmental Policy." In *Economics of the European Community,* ed. A. M. El-Agraa, 373–92. New York: Philip Alan.

Marx, K. 1967. *Capital: A Critique of Political Economy.* New York: International Publishers.

———. 1973. *Grundrisse: Foundations of the Critique of Political Economy.* Trans. M. Nicolaus. New York: Vintage Books.

———. 1977. *Capital; A Critique of Political Economy,* vol. 1. Intro by Earnest Mandel; trans. B. Fowkes. New York: Vintage Books.

———. 1977. "Critique of the Gotha Programme." In *Marx: Selected Writings,* ed. D. McLellan. New York: Oxford University Press.

———. 1981. *Capital.* Vols. 2 and 3. Intro by Earnest Mandel; trans. D. Fernbach. New York: Vintage Books.

Massarrat, M. 1980. "The Energy Crisis: The Struggle for the Redistribution of Surplus Profit from Oil." In *Oil and Class Struggle,* eds. P. Nore and T. Turner, 26–68. London: Zed Press.

Massiah, J. 1990. "Defining Women's Work in the Commonwealth Caribbean." In *Persistent Inequalities: Women and World Development,* ed. I. Tinker, 223–38. Oxford: Oxford University Press.

Massy, W. F., and A. K. Wilger. 1995. "Improving Productivity: What Faculty Think About It—and Its Effect on Quality." *Change* (July/Aug): 10–20.

Mathien, F. 1992. "Exchange Systems and Social Stratification among the Chaco Anasazi." In *The American Southwest and Mesoamerica: Systems of Prehistoric Exchange,* eds. J. Ericson and T. Baugh, 27–63. New York: Plenum Press.

Mattick, P. 1969. *Marx and Keynes: The Limits of the Mixed Economy.* Boston: Porter Sargent.

McGuire, R. 1989. "The Greater Southwest as a Periphery of Mesoamerica." In *Centre and Periphery: Comparative Studies in Archaeology,* ed. T. Champion, 40–66. London: Unwin Hyman.

McMillen, N. R. 1990. *Dark Journey: Black Mississippians in the Age of Jim Crow.* Urbana: University of Illinois Press.

McMurtry, T. 1993. "The Loan Circle Programme as a Model of Alternative Community Economics." In *Community Economic Development: In Search of Empowerment and Alternatives,* ed. E. Shragge, 60–75. Montreal: Black Rose Books.

Mehta, J. 1994. "Price and Distribution." In *Alternative Economic Survey 1993–94.* Delhi: Public Interest Research Group.

Milani, M. 1988. *The Making of Iran's Islamic Revolution: From Monarchy to Islamic Republic.* Boulder, Colo.: Westview Press.

———. 1994. *The Making of Iran's Islamic Revolution: From Monarchy to Islamic Republic,* 2d ed. Boulder, Colo. and London: Westview Press.

Miller, P. 1998. "The Margins of Accounting." In *The Laws of the Markets,* ed. M. Callon, 174–93. Oxford: Blackwell Publishers.

Ministère de l'Economie et des Finances, and J. M. Bloch-Lainé (MEF/ Bloch-Lainé). 1982. "Propositions pour l'Évolution du système bancaire" (March).

Ministry for the Environment, Physical Planning, and Public Works. 1995. *Greece: Ecological and Cultural Endowment. Data, Activities and Projects for the Protection of the Environment.* Athens: Ministry for the Environment, Physical Planning and Public Works.

Minsky, H. 1993. "Community Development Banks: An Idea in Search of Substance." *Challenge* March–April: 33–41.

Moaddel, M. 1991. "Class Struggle in Post-Revolutionary Iran." *International Journal of Middle East Studies* 23: 317–43.

Moghadam, F. 1988. "An Historical Interpretation of the Iranian Revolution." *Cambridge Journal of Economics* 12: 401–18.

Mouffe, C. 1995. "Post-Marxism: Democracy and Identity." *Society and Space* 13 (3): 259–66.

Nandy, A. 1987. "Cultural Frames for Social Transformation: A Credo." *Alternatives* 12: 113–17.

Nash, J., and M. P. Fernandez-Kelly, eds. 1983. *Women, Men, and the*

International Division of Labor. Albany: State University of New York Press.

Nehru, J. 1954. *Jawaharlal Nehru's Speeches,* vol. 2. New Delhi: Publications Division.

Nielsen, K. and R. Ware, eds. 1997. *Exploitation.* Atlantic Highlands, N.J.: Humanities Press.

Nisinoff, L., et al. 1992. "Stories out of School: Poor and Working Class Students at a Small Liberal Arts College." Paper presented at the conference Marxism in the New World Order, University of Massachusetts Amherst.

Norgaard, R. 1992. *Development Reportrayed.* London: Routledge.

Norton, B. 1992. "Radical Theories of Accumulation and Crisis: Developments and Directions." In *Radical Economics,* eds. B. Roberts and S. Feiner, 155–93. Boston: Kluwer Academic.

———. 1994. "Moses and the Prophets! Radical Economics and the Search for a Foundation (In Marx's Analysis of Accumulation in Volume One of *Capital*)." *Review of Radical Political Economics* 26 (3): 111–18.

———. 1995. "The Theory of Monopoly Capitalism and Classical Economics." *History of Political Economy* 27 (4): 737–53.

Nove, A. 1989. *An Economic History of the U.S.S.R.* London: Penguin Books.

O'Connor, J. 1988. "Capitalism, Nature, Socialism." *Capitalism, Nature, Socialism* 1: 11–38.

O'Connor, M. 1993. "On the Misadventures of Capitalist Nature." *Capitalism, Nature, Socialism* 4: 7–40.

Oman, C. P., and G. Wignaraja. 1991. *The Postwar Evolution of Development Thinking.* New York: St. Martin's Press.

O'Neill, P. M. 1994. "Capital, Regulation and Region: Restructuring and Internationalisation in the Hunter Valley, NSW." Ph.D. diss., School of Earth Sciences, Macquarie University, Sydney, NSW, Australia.

———. 1997. "So What Is Internationalisation? Lessons from Restructuring at Australia's 'Mother Plant.' " In *Interdependent and Uneven Development: Global-Local Perspectives,* eds. S. Conti and M. Taylor, 263–308. Aldershot: Ashgate.

O'Neill, P. M., and J. K. Gibson-Graham. 1999. "Enterprise Discourse and Executive Talk: Stories that Destabilize the Company." *Transactions of the Institute of British Geographers* 24 (1): 11–22.

O'Neill, P. M., and R. Green. 2000. "Global Economy, Local Jobs." In *Journeys: The Making of the Hunter Region,* eds. P. McManus, P. M. O'Neill, and R. Loughran. Sydney: Allen and Unwin.

Ong, A. 1987. "Disassembling Gender in the Electronics Age." *Feminist Studies* 13: 609–26.

Organization for Economic Cooperation and Development (OECD). 1989. *Economic Instruments for Environmental Protection.* Paris: OECD.

Parti socialiste. 1980. *Projet socialiste: Pour la France des années 80.* Paris: Club Socialiste du Livre.

Patel, A. 1994. In *Alternative Economic Survey 1993–94.* Delhi: Public Interest Research Group.

Patnaik, U. 1976. "Class Differentiation within the Peasantry: An Approach to the Analysis of Indian Agriculture." *Economic and Political Weekly* 11 (39).

———. 1978. "Development of Capitalism in Agriculture: I and II." In *Studies in the Development of Capitalism in India,* ed. A. Rudra. Lahore: Vanguard Books Limited.

———. 1987. *Peasant Class Differentiation: A Study in Method with Reference to Haryana.* Delhi: Oxford University Press.

Patterson, T. 1990. "Some Theoretical Tensions within and between the Processual and Postprocessual Archaeologies." *Journal of Anthropological Archaeology* 9: 189–200.

Pauketat, T. 1992. "The Reign and Ruin of the Lords of Cahokia: A Dialectic of Dominance." In *Lords of the Southeast: Social Inequality and the Native Elites of Southeastern North America,* eds. A. Barker and T. Pauketat, 31–43. Washington, D.C.: American Anthropological Association.

Pelekassi, K., and M. Skourtos. 1992. *Air Pollution in Greece.* Athens: Papazisi Editions.

Penrose, E. T. 1976. "The Development of Crisis." In *The Oil Crisis,* ed. R. Vernon, 39–57. New York: W. W. Norton.

Perry, S. 1987. *Communities on the Way. Rebuilding Local Economies in the United States and Canada.* Albany: State University of New York Press.

Pesaran, M. H. 1982. "The System of Dependent Capitalism in Pre- and Post-Revolutionary Iran." *International Journal of Middle East Studies* 14: 501–22.

Phongpaichit, P. 1988. "Two Roads to the Factory: Industrialisation Strategies and Women's Employment." In *Structures of Patriarchy: the State, the Community and the Household,* ed. B. Agarwal, 150–63. London: Zed Press.

Pieterse, J. N. 1991. "Dilemmas of Development Discourse: The Crisis of Developmentalism and Comparative Method." *Development and Change* 22: 5–29.

Polanyi, K. [1957] 1971. "The Economy as Instituted Process." In *Trade and Market in the Early Empires,* eds. K. Polanyi, C. Arensberg, and H. Pearson. Chicago: Henry Regnery Co.

Pollin, R. 1995. "Financial Structures and Egalitarian Economic Policy." *New Left Review* 214: 26–61.

Poovey, M. 1998. *A History of the Modern Fact: Problems of Knowledge in the Sciences of Wealth and Society.* Chicago: University of Chicago Press.

Porpora, D., M. Lim, and U. Prommas. 1989. "The Role of Women in the International Division of Labour: The Case of Thailand." *Development and Change* 20: 269–94.

Porter, M. E., and C. van der Linde. 1995. "Green and Competitive: Ending the Stalemate." *Harvard Business Review* 73 (5) (Sept/Oct): 120–34.

Powell, D. A. 1974. "The Rural Exodus." In *Problems of Communism,* vol. 23, no. 6 (Nov/Dec), 1–13; reprinted in *The Soviet Economy: Continuity and Change,* ed. M. Bernstein, 149–63. Boulder, Colo.: Westview Press, 1981.

Prasad, P. H. 1973. " 'Production Relations' Achilles Heel of Indian Planning." *Economic and Political Weekly,* May 12.

———. 1979. "Semi-Feudalism: The Basic Constraint of Indian Agriculture." In *Agrarian Relations in India,* eds. A. N. Das and V. Nilakant. Delhi: Manohar Publications.

———. 1990. "Reactionary Role of Usurer's Capital in Rural India." In *Agrarian Relations and Accumulation: The 'Mode of Production' Debate in India,* ed. U. Patnaik, 227–33. Bombay: Oxford University Press and Sameeksha Trust.

Pred, A., and M. Watts. 1992. *Reworking Modernity: Capitalisms and Symbolic Discontent.* New Brunswick, N.J.: Rutgers University Press.

Preobrazhensky, E. 1965. *The New Economics.* Trans. B. Pearce. Oxford: Oxford University Press.

Quarter, J. 1992. *Canada's Social Economy: Co-operatives, Non-profits, and Other Community Enterprises.* Toronto: James Lorimer and Company.

Rahnema, M., with V. Bawtree. 1997. *The Postdevelopment Reader.* London: Zed Press.

Ransom, R. L., and R. Sutch. 1977. *One Kind of Freedom: The Economic Consequences of Emancipation.* Cambridge: Cambridge University Press.

Raper, A., and C. C. Taylor. 1949. "Landowners and Tenants." In *Rural Life in the United States,* ed. C. C. Taylor, 264–80. New York: Knopf.

Reid, J. D., Jr. 1973. "Sharecropping as an Understandable Market Response: The Postbellum South." *Journal of Economic History* 33 (March): 106–30.

————. 1975. "Sharecropping in History and Theory." *Agricultural History* 49 (April): 426–40.

Resnick, S., and R. Wolff. 1982. "Classes in Marxian Theory." *Review of Radical Political Economics* 13 (winter): 1–18.

————. 1987. *Knowledge and Class: A Marxian Critique of Political Economy.* Chicago: University of Chicago Press.

————. 1988. "Communism: Between Class and Classless." *Rethinking Marxism* 1 (1) (spring): 5–42.

————. 1994. "Between State and Private Capitalism: What Was Soviet 'Socialism'?" *Rethinking Marxism* 7 (1) (spring): 9–30.

————. 1995. "Lessons from the USSR: Taking Marxist Theory the Next Step." In *Whither Marxism? Global Crisis in International Perspective,* eds. B. Magnus and S. Cullenberg, 207–34. New York: Routledge.

Ricks, T. 1981. "Background to the Iranian Revolution: Imperialism, Dictatorship, and Nationalism, 1872 to 1979." In *Iran: Essays on a Revolution in the Making,* eds. A. Jabbari and R. Olsen, 15–54. Lexington, Ky.: Mazda Publishers.

Riggs, H. E. 1996. "The Limits of Fund Raising." *Chronicle of Higher Education* (May 3): B1–B2.

Rio, C. 2000. " 'This Job Has No End': African American Domestic Workers and Class Becoming." In *Class and Its Others,* eds. J. K. Gibson-Graham, S. Resnick, and R. Wolff. Minneapolis: University of Minnesota Press.

Rodney, W. 1974. *How Europe Underdeveloped Africa.* Washington, D.C.: Howard University Press.

Roemer, J. 1982. *A General Theory of Exploitation and Class.* Cambridge, Mass.: Harvard University Press.

————. 1994. *Future for Socialism.* London: Verso.

Rosdolsky, R. 1977. *The Making of Marx's "Capital."* Trans. P. Burgess. London: Pluto Press.

Rosovsky, H. 1990. *The University: An Owner's Manual.* New York: W. W. Norton.

Ruccio, D. 1989. "Fordism on a World Scale: International Dimensions of Regulation." *Review of Radical Political Economics* 21 (fall): 33–53.

————. 1992. "Failure of Socialism, Future of Socialists?" *Rethinking Marxism* 5 (summer): 7–22.

Ruccio, D., and L. H. Simon. 1986a. "A Methodological Analysis of Dependency Theory: Explanation in Andre Gunder Frank." *World Development* 14 (February): 195–210.

————. 1986b. "Methodological Aspects of Marxian Approaches to

Development: An Analysis of the Modes of Production School." *World Development* 14 (February): 211–22.

Rudra, A. 1984. "Local Power and Farm-Level Decision-Making." In *Agrarian Power and Agricultural productivity in South Asia,* eds. M. Desai, S. H. Rudolph, and A. Rudra, 250–80. Berkeley and Los Angeles: University of California Press.

———. 1988. "Emerging Class Structure in Rural India." In *Rural Poverty in South Asia,* eds. T. N. Srinivasan and P. K. Bardhan. New York: Columbia University Press.

Ryan, J., and C. Sackrey. 1984. *Strangers in Paradise: Academics from the Working Class.* Boston: South End Press.

Sachs, W., ed. 1992. *The Development Dictionary: A Guide to Knowledge as Power.* London: Zed Books.

Saitta, D. 1988. "Marxism, Prehistory, and Primitive Communism." *Rethinking Marxism* 1: 146–69.

———. 1994a. "Class and Community in the Prehistoric Southwest." In *The Ancient Southwestern Community,* eds. W. Wills and R. Leonard, 25–43. Albuquerque: University of New Mexico Press.

———. 1994b. "Agency, Class, and Archaeological Interpretation." *Journal of Anthropological Archaeology* 13: 1–27.

———. 1995. "Marxism and Archaeology." In *Marxism in the Postmodern Age,* eds. A. Callari, S. Cullenburg, and C. Biewener, 385–93. New York: Guilford.

———. 1997. "Power, Labor, and the Dynamics of Change in Chacoan Political Economy." *American Antiquity* 62: 7–26.

Saltzman, A., and F. Curtis. 1994. "Social Distress Theory and Teaching about Homelessness: A Retrospective Analysis." *Journal of Social Distress and Homelessness* 2 (2): 99–133.

Sandler, B. 1994. "Grow or Die: Marxist Theories of Capitalism and the Environment." *Rethinking Marxism* 7: 38–57.

Sanyal, K. K. 1988. "Accumulation, Poverty and State in Third World Capital/Pre-Capital Complex." *Economic and Political Weekly: Review of Political Economy* 23 (5).

———. 1991–1992. "Of Revolutions, Classic and Passive." *Society and Change* 8 (3/4).

Schneider, J. 1977. "Was There a Pre-Capitalist World System?" *Peasant Studies* 6: 20–29.

Schoenberger, E. 1997. *The Cultural Crisis of the Firm.* Oxford and Cambridge, Mass.: Blackwell.

Schortman, E., and P. Urban. 1992. "The Political Value of Imports." In *Resources, Power, and Interregional Interaction,* eds. E. Schortman and P. Urban, 153–56. New York: Plenum Press.

Shragge, E., ed. 1993. *Community Economic Development: In Search of Empowerment and Alternatives.* Montreal: Black Rose Books.

Schultz, T. W. 1964. *Transforming Traditional Agriculture.* New Haven: Yale University Press.

Sebastian, L. 1992. *The Chaco Anasazi: Sociopolitical Evolution in the American Southwest.* Cambridge: Cambridge University Press.

Sen, A. 1994. "Agriculture." In *Alternative Economic Survey 1993–94.* Delhi: Public Interest Research Group.

Sender, J., and S. Smith. 1986. *The Development of Capitalism in Africa.* New York: Methuen.

Shaikh, A. 1978. "Political Economy and Capitalism: Notes on Dobb's Theory of Crisis." *Cambridge Journal of Economics* 2: 233–51.

———. 1983. "Economic Crisis." In *Dictionary of Marxist Thought,* ed. T. Bottomore, 138–43. Cambridge, Mass.: Harvard University Press.

Shiva, V. 1991. *The Violence of the Green Revolution.* London: Zed Press.

Sirianni, C. 1982. *Workers Control and Socialist Democracy: The Soviet Experience.* London: Verso.

Slater, D. 1992. "Theories of Development and Politics of the Post-modern—Exploring a Border Zone." *Development and Change* 23 (3): 283–319.

Smith, A. 1937. *An Inquiry into the Nature and Causes of the Wealth of Nations,* ed. E. Cannan. New York: Random House.

Soldberg, E. D. 1950. "Legal Aspects of Land Tenure and Farm Credit." In *Land Tenure in the Southwestern States: A Report on the Regional Land Tenure Project,* ed. H. Hoffsommer, 225–306. Chapel Hill: University of North Carolina Press.

Sparr, P., ed. 1994. *Mortgaging Women's Lives: Feminist Critiques of Structural Adjustment.* London: Zed Press.

Squires, G. D. 1992. *From Redlining to Reinvestment: Community Responses to Urban Disinvestment.* Philadelphia: Temple University Press.

St. Martin, K. 1998. "From Models to Maps: The Discourse of Fisheries and the Potential for Community Management in New England." Ph.D. diss., Department of Geography, Clark University.

Stecklow, S. 1996. "Expensive Lesson: Colleges Manipulate Financial-Aid Offers, Shortchanging Many." *Wall Street Journal* (April 1): A1, A6.

Steindl, J. [1952] 1976. *Maturity and Stagnation in American Capitalism,* 2d ed. New York: Monthly Review Press.

Stites, R. 1989. *Revolutionary Dreams: Utopian Vision and Experimental Life in the Russian Revolution.* New York: Oxford University Press.

Strauch, J. 1984. "Women in Rural-Urban Circulation Networks: Implications for Social Structural Change." In *Women in the Cities of Asia: Migration and Urban Adaptation,* ed. J. Fawcett, S. Khoo, and P. Smith, 60–77. Boulder, Colo.: Westview Press.

Swedberg, R., and M. Granovetter. 1992. *The Sociology of Economic Life.* Boulder, Colo.: Westview Press.

Sweezy, P. 1942. *The Theory of Capitalist Development.* New York: Monthly Review Press.

Sweezy, P. et al. 1980. *The Transition from Feudalism to Capitalism.* London: Verso.

Szasz, A. 1991. "In Praise of Policy Luddism: Strategic Lessons From Hazardous Waste Wars." *Capitalism, Nature, Socialism* 1 (February): 17–43.

Takahashi, K. 1980. "A Contribution to the Discussion." In *The Transition from Feudalism to Capitalism,* eds. P. Sweezy et al., 68–97. London: Verso.

Taylor, R. H. 1943. "Postbellum Southern Rental Contracts." *Agricultural History* 17 (2): 121–28.

Thompson, E. T. 1975. *Plantation Societies, Race Relations, and the South: The Regimentation of Populations.* Durham, N.C.: Duke University Press.

Thompson, G. 1986. *Economic Calculation and Policy Formation.* London: Routledge.

Tietenberg, T. 1985. *Emission Trading: An Exercise in Reforming Pollution Policy.* Washington, D.C.: Resources for the Future.

———. 1992. *Environmental and Natural Resource Economics,* 3d ed. New York: Harper Collins Publishers.

Tilley, C. 1984. "Ideology and the Legitimation of Power in the Middle Neolithic of Southern Sweden." In *Ideology and Power in Prehistory,* eds. D. Miller and C. Tilley, 111–46. Cambridge: Cambridge University Press

Toll, H. 1991. "Material Distributions and Exchange in the Chaco System." In *Chaco and Hohokam: Prehistoric Regional Systems in the American Southwest,* eds. P. Crown and W. Judge, 77–107. Santa Fe, N.M.: School of American Research.

Upham, S. 1982. *Polities and Power.* New York: Academic Press.

Vernon, R. 1976. "An Interpretation." In *The Oil Crisis,* ed. R. Vernon, 1–14. New York: W. W. Norton.

Viola, L. 1987. *The Best Sons of the Fatherland: Workers in the Vanguard of Collectivization.* New York: Oxford University Press.

Vlachou, A. 1983. "A Dynamic Analysis of Energy Demand in U.S. Manufacturing during the 1970s." Ph.D. diss., Department of Resource Economics, University of Massachusetts Amherst.

———. 1993a. "The Contradictory Interaction of Capitalism and Nature." *Capitalism, Nature, Socialism* 4 (March): 102–8.

———. 1993b. "The Socialist Transformation of China: Debates over Class and Social Development." *Rethinking Marxism* 6 (winter): 8–39.

———. 1994. "Reflections on the Ecological Critiques and Reconstructions of Marxism." *Rethinking Marxism* 7 (fall): 112–28.

Wallerstein, I. 1974. *The Modern World-System,* vol. 1. New York: Academic Press.

———. 1983. *Historical Capitalism.* London: Verso.

Watts, M. J. 1993. "Development 1: Power, Knowledge, Discursive Practice." *Progress in Human Geography* 17 (2): 257–72.

Wayne, M. 1983. *The Reshaping of the Plantation Society: The Natchez District, 1860–1880.* Baton Rouge: Louisiana State University Press.

Weisbrod, B. A. 1988. *The Nonprofit Economy.* Cambridge, Mass.: Harvard University Press.

Wells, M. J. 1984a. "The Resurgence of Sharecropping: Historical Anomaly or Political Strategy?" *American Journal of Sociology* 90 (1): 1–29.

———. 1984b. "What Is a Worker? The Role of Sharecroppers in Contemporary Class Structure." *Politics and Society* 13 (3): 295–320.

Wesson, R. G. 1963. *Soviet Communes.* New Brunswick, N.J.: Rutgers University Press.

Wiener, J. M. 1978. *Social Origins of the New South: Alabama, 1860–1885.* Baton Rouge: Louisiana State University Press.

Wilcox, D. 1993. "The Evolution of the Chacoan Polity." In *The Chimney Rock Archaeological Symposium,* eds. J. Malville and G. Matlock, 76–90. Fort Collins, Colo.: USDA Forest Service.

Wilkins, M. 1976. "The Oil Companies in Perspective." In *The Oil Crisis,* ed. R. Vernon, 159–78. New York: W. W. Norton.

Windes, T. 1992. "Blue Notes: The Chacoan Turquoise Industry in the San Juan Basin." In *Anasazi Regional Organization and the Chaco System,* ed. D. Doyel, 159–68. Albuquerque, N.M.: Maxwell Museum of Anthropology.

Winston, G. C. 1994. "The Decline in Undergraduate Teaching: Moral Failure or Market Pressure?" *Change* (Sept/Oct): 8–15.

Wolff, R., and S. Resnick. 1986. "Power, Property, and Class." *Socialist Review* 86: 97–124.

———. 1987. *Economics: Marxian versus Neoclassical.* Baltimore: Johns Hopkins University Press.

Wolff, R. P. 1992. *The Ideal of the University.* New Brunswick, N.J.: Transaction Publishers.

Wolpe, H., ed. 1980. *The Articulation of Modes of Production: Essays from Economy and Society.* London: Routledge and Kegan Paul.

Woodman, H. 1979. "Post–Civil War Southern Agriculture and Law." *Agricultural History* 53 (1): 319–37.

———. 1995. *New South, New Law: The Legal Foundations of Credit and Labor Relations in the Postbellum Agricultural South.* Baton Rouge: Louisiana State University Press.

Wray, M., and A. Newitz. 1997. *White Trash: Race and Class in America.* New York: Routledge.

Wright, E. O. 1978. *Class, Crisis and the State.* London: New Left Books.

———. 1985. *Classes.* London: Verso.

———. 1997. *Class Counts.* Cambridge: Cambridge University Press.

Yaffe, D. 1973. "The Marxian Theory of Crisis, Capital and the State." *Economy and Society* 2 (2): 186–232.

Zabih, S. 1979. *Iran's Revolutionary Upheaval.* San Francisco: Alchemy Books.

CONTRIBUTORS

☐

Carole Biewener is professor of Economics and Women's Studies at Simmons College, where she is chair of the Women's Studies department. Her current work is focused on banks' progressive community development initiatives. She is coeditor of *Marxism in the Postmodern Age: Confronting the New World Order* (1995).

Stephen Cullenberg is professor and chair of the Department of Economics at the University of California, Riverside. He is the author of *The Falling Rate of Profit* (1994), coauthor of *Economics and the Historian* (1995), and coeditor of *Marxism in the Postmodern Age* (1994), *Whither Marxism?* (1994), and the forthcoming *Postmodernism, Economics and Knowledge* (2001).

Anjan Chakrabarti teaches economics at the University of Calcutta. He has published articles on political economy and development in both Indian and foreign journals. He is coauthor, with Ajit Chaudhury and Dipanker Das, of *Margin of Margin: Profile of an Unrepentant Postcolonial Collaborator* (2000).

Fred Curtis is professor of Economics and director of Environmental Studies in the College of Liberal Arts at Drew University.

Satya J. Gabriel is associate professor of Economics at Mount Holyoke College and academic director of the Rural Development Leadership Network.

J.K. Gibson-Graham is the pen name of Katherine Gibson and Julie Graham. Julie Graham is professor of Geography at the University of Massachusetts Amherst. Katherine Gibson is associate professor of Geography at Monash University and a senior fellow in the Department of Human Geography, Research School of Pacific and Asian Studies at the Australian National University. They are coauthors of *The End of Capitalism (As We Knew It): A Feminist Critique of Political Economy* (1996); their current work uses concepts of class to rethink economy and economic possibility.

Serap Ayse Kayatekin is a lecturer in Economics at the University of Leeds. Her recent publications address topics including sharecropping, feudalism, globalization, and economic discourse.

Bruce Norton is Associate Professor of Economics at San Antonio College. He is a former member of the *Rethinking Marxism* editorial board and the author of numerous articles about radical theories of accumulation.

Phillip O'Neill is Director of the Centre for Urban and Regional Studies and Head of the Department of Geography and Environmental Science at the University of Newcastle, NSW, Australia. His major research interest is in the investment behavior of large corporations.

David Ruccio is Professor of Economics at the University of Notre Dame. He is coeditor of *Postmodern Materialism and the Future of Marxist Theory* (1996) and the forthcoming *Postmodernism, Knowledge, and Economics,* and the editor of the journal *Rethinking Marxism.*

Stephen Resnick is Professor of Economics at the University of Massachusetts Amherst. He is author and coauthor of numerous articles and books on Marxian theory, including *Knowledge and Class* (1987) and *Bringing it All Back Home: Class, Gender and Power in the Modern Household* (1994). With his longtime collaborator, Richard Wolff, he has recently completed a book on state capitalism in the former USSR.

Dean J. Saitta is Associate Professor of Anthropology and University Professor of Social Science at the University of Denver.

Andriana Vlachou is Associate Professor of Economics at the Athens University of Economics and Business in Greece. She is the editor of *Contemporary Economic Theory: Radical Critiques of Neoliberalism* (1999) and *Nature and Society: A Debate over Ecology, Marxism and Knowledge* (1995), and is a contributing editor-at-large for the journal *Capitalism, Nature, Socialism.*

Richard D. Wolff is Professor of Economics at the University of Massachusetts Amherst and serves on the editorial board of *Rethinking Marxism.* He has published widely on class and Marxian economic theory, often in collaboration with Stephen Resnick. Among other books, they coauthored *Knowledge and Class* (1987) and a forthcoming book on the history of class transitions in the USSR.

Foucault, Michel, 185
Fundamental class process, 7, 11, 22
    n.8, 86, 108, 186, 196, 265

Gabriel, S., 19
Gibson-Graham, J. K., 12, 13, 15, 16,
    22 n.8, 132, 166
Gismondi, M., and M. Richardson,
    114
Grossman, Henryk, 27, 50 n.5, 52
    n.15
Grundrisse (Marx), 40
Gunn, Christopher, and Hazel Dayton
    Gunn, 136, 137, 144, 156 n.19, 156
    n.20

Historicism, 184, 202 n.3
Households: in India, 197–99, Soviet,
    269–71

Identity: and BHP and Ok Tedi, 72–
    73; and class, 10, 18–19, 74; and
    gender, 68; and political struggle,
    72; and "politics of becoming," 57,
    72
Independent class process, 9, 187;
    in agriculture in India, 190; in
    households in India, 197; and
    investments and community devel-
    opment, 139, 145
Indigenous rights: and the corpora-
    tion, 70–73
Inflation: in India, 194, 203 n.11
Investment, productive: and class
    processes, 145–46, 148; and inter-
    est payments, 147–48; and use-
    values, 146
Iranian Revolution, 206, 224 n.1;
    conditions prior to, 206–09, 225
    n.7, 211, 223; and the Constitu-

tional Movement, 226 n.12; land
    reforms before, 212–16; and the
    Modernization Program, 207; and
    the monarchist regime, 207, 209,
    223–24; self-exploitation in vil-
    lages before, 209–12; and Shi'ism,
    219; and urban bazaars, 216–19; and
    the ulama, 219–20; and the White
    Revolution, 217, 222

Kabeer, Naila, 145, 149
Kasmir, S., 156 n.17
Kautsky, Karl, 30, 31, 50 n.8
Kayatekin, S., 15
Khadi, 182, 201 n.1
Knowledge and Class (Resnick and
    Wolff), 23

Labor, 66. *See also* Necessary labor;
    Productive labor; Surplus labor;
    Unproductive labor
Labor productivity: and environmen-
    tal degradation, 112; and nature,
    107–09, 111, 126; and pollution, 112
Laclau, Ernesto, 9, 21 n.3
Landlords: in Iran, 210, 220, 221; and
    natural resources, 109–10, 119; and
    sharecropping, 230, 235
Lee, R., 263
Leff, Enrique, 107, 128 n.1
Liberal arts college: as a capitalist
    enterprise, 83–94; and class pro-
    cesses, 81, 82, 83–91; as a complex
    social site, 81, 84; and contradic-
    tions between class and education,
    91–99; and distribution of surplus
    value, 87–91; and effect of nonclass
    labor on, 96–99; flow formulas
    for, 86–87, 90; and possibilities for
    class struggle, 99–101; and tenure,
    92

Transition, in India: and agriculture, 190–94; and class structure, 189–94; a decentered Marxian approach to, 199–201; and households, 196–99; modes of production debate, 184–86, 201 n.2; and state capitalist sector, 194–96; and traditional Marxian theories, 184–85, 202 n.4

Underconsumption theory, 30–33, 35
Underdevelopment. *See* Development
Unionism, 61, 70
Unproductive labor, 8, 22 n.9

Unproductive workers. *See* Workers

Value theory, 112–14
Vlachou, Andriana, 11, 19

Wage bargaining, 68
Woodman, Harold D., 233, 243 n.8
Workers, 30, 33; changing conceptions of, 37, 53 n.20; meaning of, 35, 53 n.20; productive and unproductive, 37, 134; and unionism, 70

Library of Congress Cataloging-in-Publication Data

Re/presenting class : essays in postmodern Marxism / edited by J.K. Gibson-Graham, Stephen Resnick, and Richard Wolff.

p. cm.

Includes bibliographical references and index.

ISBN 0-8223-2709-0 (cloth : alk. paper) —

ISBN 0-8223-2720-1 (pbk. : alk. paper)

1. Marxian economics.   2. Capitalism.   3. Communist state.   4. Social classes.   I. Title: Re/presenting class.   II. Gibson-Graham, J. K.   III. Resnick, Stephen.   IV. Wolff, Richard D.

HB97.5 .R46   2001

305.5—dc21   00-067729